Family Spirits

Family Spirits
The Bacardi Saga

Peter Foster

MACFARLANE WALTER & ROSS
TORONTO

First edition

Macfarlane Walter & Ross
37A Hazelton Avenue
Toronto, Canada M5R 2E3

Canadian Cataloguing in Publication Data
Foster, Peter, 1947-
Family Spirits: the bacardi saga

Includes bibliographical references.
ISBN 0-921912-02-1

1. Bacardi family. 2. Bacardi Corporation - History.
3. Rum industry - Caribbean Area - History.
4. Distilling industries - Caribbean Area - History. I. Title.

HD9394.C34B32 1990   338.4'766359'009729
C90-094878-7

Printed and bound in the United States of America

To the memory of Dermot Murray

Contents

ACKNOWLEDGMENTS   *xi*

ABOUT SPANISH NAMES   *xiii*

PROLOGUE   *1*

ONE   Rum and Revolution   *5*

TWO   Answered Prayers   *14*

THREE   Success at Last   *21*

FOUR   Bathing in Bacardi   *34*

FIVE   The Barons of Booze   *48*

SIX   From Pimpernel to Politician   *61*

SEVEN   Taking to the Hills   *77*

EIGHT   From Dream to Nightmare   *94*

NINE   Expropriation: Atlas Shrugs   *108*

TEN   La Lucha and Betrayal   *123*

ELEVEN   Survival and Success   *136*

TWELVE   Dropping the Pilot   *154*

THIRTEEN   Eddy Nielsen's Brief Honeymoon   *172*

FOURTEEN   Diversifying into Trouble   *181*

FIFTEEN   Bacardi Meets Bonfire of the Vanities   *195*

SIXTEEN   Heading for the Legal Hills   *209*

SEVENTEEN   Enough Is Enough   *217*

EIGHTEEN   Family Portraits   *231*

NINETEEN   The Other Bacardi Family   *239*

TWENTY   Cuba Libre?   *252*

EPILOGUE   *267*

BACARDI FAMILY TREES   *270*

APPENDICES   *274*

NOTES   *277*

SOURCES   *285*

INDEX   *291*

Acknowledgments

How a British writer living in Toronto comes to write a book about a Cuban exile family living mostly in and around the Caribbean requires some explanation. Research for my previous book, *The Master Builders*, first brought me in contact with the international liquor business, about which I decided to write a book. However, once I had traveled to Cuba, and met several members of the Bacardi family, I became intrigued and decided to write about them alone. They did, after all, produce the world's largest-selling brand of liquor. But the book developed in unexpected directions: at one level, it became the story of one man, Pepín Bosch; but at a broader level it became an examination of one arena in capitalism's twentieth-century struggle with Communism, a struggle that now appears to be in the process of dramatic resolution.

The man who first introduced me to the Bacardis — for which I hope they forgive him — is Bud Downing, the former chief executive of Hiram Walker Resources. He also helped my understanding of the industry and introduced me to other experts. I owe him a great debt.

Cubans are by nature a warm and hospitable people; they can rarely bring themselves to say no. I admit to exploiting that fact in my research. Although Bacardi family members were engaged in an increasingly complex internal dispute, and have traditionally been publicity-shy, they were surprisingly cooperative. So too, for the most part, was the "non-family family" of Bacardi management and workers. I want to give special thanks to Guillermo Mármol, who devoted countless hours to helping me understand not merely the Bacardi family but Cubans in general. Since he is associated with the "management" side in the present Bacardi dispute, I should stress that the conclusions I draw about that dispute — after spending considerable time with the protagonists from both sides — are my own.

At Macfarlane Walter & Ross, I must first thank Gary Ross for his support in helping me to switch horses in midstream, and also for his exceptional editing skills. Jan Walter provided encouragement and unfailing kindness. Barbara Czarnecki helped in more ways than I can express. Suzan Wookey remained undaunted by unenviable tasks that included tracing the Bacardi family tree, and Robin Brass rendered the final version of that tree with care and sensitivity. Outside MW&R, I want to thank Gini Zaorski for her valuable legwork.

I regard it as a victory for naïveté (my own, that is) that I was allowed into Cuba to undertake research. For the assistance provided by the Cuban government — elusive in Havana, but almost enthusiastic in Santiago — I express my thanks. I was lucky to find help from unanticipated sources. Because of the continuing political condition in Cuba, and the conclusions of this book, I must refrain from naming them. Nevertheless, I thank them and hope that one day soon they will be able to read this book in a free Cuba.

Here, in alphabetical order, is a list of those who gave me interviews — in some cases many times — or who helped in other ways: Professor Luis Aguilar, Gavin Anderson, Amaro Argamasilla Bacardi, León Argamasilla Bacardi, José (Tito) Argamasilla Bacardi, Pepín Argamasilla Giró, José Argamasilla Grimany, Alberto Bacardi Bolívar, María Hortensia Bacardi Bravo, Amalia Bacardi Cape, Daniel Bacardi Rosell, David Beattie, Glyn Berry, Geoffrey Bichard, Alina Blanco, Carlos (Lindy) Bosch, Ermina Eguilior de Bosch, José M. (Pepín) Bosch, Tony Burgess, Sam Butler, Frank Calzón, Luis Casero, Isaac Chertorivski, Adolfo Comas Bacardi, Guillermo Cordera Perdomo, Dr. Graciella Cruz-Taura, Eduardo Cutillas, Manuel Jorge Cutillas, Eduardo del Buey, Roberto del Rosal, Manuel Luis del Valle, Andrew and Enid Duany, Gloria Echarte, Luis Echarte, Enrique Galindo Alonso, Tom Gerth, Gerry Gianni, Mario Gómez, Juan Grau, Warren Hanna, Cliff Hatch, Sr., Emilio Hechevarría Fernández, Ray Hermann, Andrew Jackson, Christian Lapointe, Luis Lasa, Geoff Livesey, Lourdes Pérez, Gisela Mármol, Dr. José Mármol, Dr. Felipe Martínez Arango, Román Martínez IV, Archie McCallum, Mike McCormick, Joel Miller, Eddy Nielsen, Robert O'Brien, Alfred (Pete) O'Hara, Pom Pomeroy, Juan Prado, Mario Portuondo Bacardi, Roberto Pujals, Eric Reguly, Brewster Righter, Dagoberto Rodríguez, Herminia Santos Buch, Jerry Scott, Juan Seralles, Adelina Silver, Carlos Sorrano, David Smith, Indira Somwaru, Dr. Jaime Suchlicki, Rosa Elena Torres, Alberto Torruella, Ignacio and Iliana Triana, Tom Valdez, Augusto Valdez Miranda, Santiago Wanton, Chuck Watt, Bob White, Bill Walker, Cindy Young, and Silvia Zimmerman.

I wish also to thank the staff of the libraries at the University of Miami, the Metropolitan Toronto Reference Library, and the Government Development Bank for Puerto Rico.

About Spanish Names

Spaniards and those of Spanish descent traditionally take the surnames of both their father's and mother's families. (In archaic usage, these were linked by *y*, "and.") Emilio Bacardi Moreau thus had a father whose first surname was Bacardi and a mother whose first surname was Moreau. His marriage to María Lay Berlucheau produced children whose surname was Bacardi Lay, and so on. However, in North America, the second surname, or matronymic, is frequently dropped, unless there is special significance attached to it, as in the case of Bacardi.

The name Bacardi originally bore an accent on the final syllable and was pronounced Ba-car-*di*. American customers came to mispronounce the brand in the early years of the twentieth century, when it first became popular in the U.S.; they shifted the emphasis to the second syllable — Ba-*car*-di. Now almost everybody pronounces it that way, including most of the family, and the accent has disappeared.

Prologue

Lyford Cay, the Bahamas. July 1988

Lyford Cay is one of the world's most exclusive enclaves. Developed by the Canadian industrialist E.P. Taylor — who, this summer afternoon, lies dying within its well-guarded perimeter — it is a place where Prince Rainier of Monaco and the Aga Khan come to get away from it all. The membership of the Lyford Cay Club has been called "close to a global Social Register." It includes Fords, Rockefellers, Vanderbilts, and Mellons, names indelibly etched on the roster of capitalist achievement.

Close to Lyford Cay's main gate, set back among the bougainvillea, palms, and flaming royal poincianas, is the comfortable but not ostentatious house of José M. (Pepín) Bosch. Built in the shape of a flattened "A," the house is arranged around a big central room beneath a large skylight. A set of glass doors leads out to a conservatory, which looks out on the glistening waters of an inlet where majestic yachts are moored. The living room is colorfully furnished and slightly cluttered. Its walls are filled with paintings that reflect Bosch's eclectic taste — rugged landscapes, windy seascapes, floral arrangements, still lifes, portraits — executed in styles from romantic realism to surrealism to soft-focus kitsch. Everywhere there are objets d'art, mementoes, and photographs. A shelf in the study holds a Cuban banknote encased in plastic. The banknote bears Bosch's signature. Nearby, on the wall, is a framed article from *Time* magazine. Dated March 19, 1951, the article, headed "An Honest Man," begins, "The best Finance Minister Cuba ever had resigned last week."

Pepín Bosch is now ninety years old. He sits surrounded by these reminders of his past, wearing a natty, red-striped, guayabera-style shirt, yellow pants, and beige leather shoes. He is tiny and frail, and there is a midget hearing aid tucked into his ear, but his blue eyes are bright. Pepín Bosch still has all his marbles.

"Castro was afraid of Che," says Bosch, "jealous of Che, because Che was an anarchist. Castro had Che killed. Fidel is a bad boy. He is not restricted by any principles. I said to him, 'You must not be afraid of elections if you do a good job.' Of course he didn't like that."

Pepín Bosch was the head of the Bacardi rum empire when, three decades ago, he gave Fidel Castro a piece of his mind. Bacardi is today the world's largest liquor brand, outselling Smirnoff vodka, Johnnie Walker Red scotch, Gordon's gin, and the thousands of other brands. The empire that produces and markets Bacardi has global sales of more than 20 million cases per year and net profits of well over $100 million. But it is not a multinational in the normal sense. Indeed, it is not one company at all, but five — in the Bahamas, near Lyford Cay; Puerto Rico; Miami; Mexico; and Bermuda — with dozens of subsidiaries from Australia to Spain. It has no holding company or home. Its most precious asset, its trademark, is held in a lawyer's office in the tiny European principality and tax haven of Liechtenstein.

The invisible force that holds this palm-tree empire together is the five companies' common shareholders, an intensely private group of several hundred family members about whom — although they appear in the *Forbes* 400 "Great Family Fortunes" — very little is known. A mystique has always surrounded both the family and the Bacardi product. Few people are aware that Bacardi is a family company and that the family comes from Cuba. Bosch masterminded this greatest of Cuban exile success stories, but he is no longer one of the Bacardi number.

Pepín Bosch would rather talk about Cuban history than the Bacardi business or family. "It would be very difficult," he whispers, "for a businessman in the United States, or Canada, or Britain, to understand what business has to endure in South America or in certain parts of Europe. We did not have a tradition of George Washington or Thomas Jefferson."

He would rather speak of his plans for revitalizing Cuba after the demise of Fidel Castro than the reasons why he no longer has any connection with Bacardi. "My friends and I, we believe that we will see the destruction of Communism, but you cannot accomplish that unless you bring a better living for the people. Cuba cannot live out of sugar. In that I agree with Che Guevara, but he was not smart. You have to have a plan. You have to ask a sacrifice from some people. I don't expect to arrive in Havana and go to my home and kick out the people who are there. I do not expect the Bacardi stockholders to go over there and kick everybody out. The thing has to be well organized. And I think I have a plan."

He would rather discuss Angola, or his continuing involvements in exile organizations such as the Miami-based Cuban American National Foundation, than the present performance of the empire he built or the internal wrangles that beset it. He would rather talk of happier prospects: the imminent fall of Fidel, for example.

As afternoon turns to evening in July 1988, Pepín Bosch's words sound like those of a Cuban exile who refuses to let his dream die. The notion that Fidel Castro might fall seems as farfetched as, say, the suggestion that the Communist party of Hungary might vote itself out of existence, or that the Berlin Wall might come down. But Pepín Bosch has always had a way of making his dreams come true.

He does not care to dwell further on the past. "Because of my age," he says, "talking about the past keeps me awake at night. So many friends tell me that I should write, telling what I have done, and I always say that it would be too much of a hardship. If I should try to tell you my story, I would not sleep well . . ."

CHAPTER ONE

Rum and Revolution

"We knew that they were copies of
copies of portraits that had already
been considered unfaithful during
the time of the comet . . . "
GABRIEL GARCÍA MÁRQUEZ, *THE AUTUMN OF THE PATRIARCH*

Santiago de Cuba. 1830

Pepín Bosch's grandfather-in-law, Facundo Bacardi y Maso, founder of the Bacardi dynasty, was fifteen when he first set eyes on the ancient and picturesque Spanish colonial city of Santiago de Cuba. Born in Sitges, in Catalonia, in 1815 (the year of the Battle of Waterloo), he came as part of an immigrant wave to a booming island economy.

The largest and strategically most important of the Caribbean islands, Cuba is shaped like a sinuous shark. The tail sits across the entrance to the Gulf of Mexico and the snout projects eastward toward Haiti and the Atlantic. Its colonial history, like that of all South America and the Caribbean, began under a delusion. Columbus, in 1492, imagining he had reached Japan or mainland China, sailed along Cuba's northern coast looking for the splendid cities and gold-roofed palaces described by Marco Polo. Early settlers also came lured by dreams of gold, but Cuba's gold mines were soon exhausted, and the island evolved into a way station for those moving on to the Americas.

In the eighteenth century, Cuba's fortunes improved dramatically. Columbus is believed to have brought the first sugarcane to the Western hemisphere, but it was almost 300 years before the mass importation of slaves made possible widespread cultivation. Between 1763 and 1860, Cuba's population grew almost tenfold, to 1.3 million. Partly this growth was due to a boom in immigration, of which the Bacardis were part; but many souls came unwillingly, snatched from the villages of Senegal and the Guinea Coast or sold by the village chieftains.

Santiago de Cuba — at the southeast end of the island, the shark's mouth — was one of the oldest cities in the New World. Founded in 1514 by the adventurer Diego Velázquez, it had been moved to its present location, nestled beside the deep pouch of a magnificent natural harbor, within a beautiful mountain bowl, eight years later. Its first mayor was perhaps the most famous of all the conquistadores, Hernán Cortés, who set out from Santiago on his fabulous conquest of Mexico.

The city's first settlers had to contend not only with searing summer heat, epidemics, and hurricanes, but with raids by both freebooters and squadrons from other European countries trying to establish Caribbean bases. The construction of El Morro, the fortress that still towers above the narrow entrance to the winding channel that leads to the harbor, did not guarantee the city's safety. In 1662, the Welsh pirate Henry Morgan descended with his terrifying band and lived there for a month before looting the city. He stripped Santiago's church of its bells, captured all the ships in the harbor, and headed off with the scornful claim that he could have defended El Morro himself with a gun and a good dog. By then, Havana, at the far end of the island, had long superseded Santiago in importance as a staging ground for expeditions to, and trade with, other parts of the Caribbean and the Americas.

Santiago was a typically Spanish colonial city. Its narrow, cobbled streets were flanked with red-tiled houses, their thick walls punctuated with ornately carved, Moorish window screens. These screens hid marble-floored courtyards, where fountains played and hibiscus and bougainvillea flowered. The city was doubly attractive to the Bacardi family since a colony of fellow Catalans already formed an important part of its commercial life.

Santiago's cultural life, by the time the Bacardis arrived, had been enriched by a powerful French influence. That influence grew out of the influx of French colonists from the neighboring Caribbean island of Santo Domingo (later split between Haiti and the Dominican Republic) following the slave revolt there in 1791. These transplanted French colonists brought blood-chilling tales of rape, murder, and destruction by their former slaves. They also brought ballet classes, drawing lessons, and polite society. They set up theaters and an opera house; they developed coffee plantations. More French immigrants had come to Cuba from New Orleans after the Louisiana Purchase in 1803, and from Europe after the Battle of Waterloo. Faithful slaves brought by French colonists from Haiti, and others imported later, introduced the voodoo cults, whose power spread beyond the black community. Santiago evolved as a unique blend of Spanish colonial history, French culture, black magic, and political intrigue.

Facundo Bacardi's older brothers founded a hardware store. Facundo, after working in the store, struck out on his own as a merchant and wine importer. In 1843, at the age of twenty-seven, he married Amalia Lucía Victoria Moreau, a *santiaguera* of French descent. The Bacardi-Moreau marriage produced six children. Four survived to form the branches of the present Bacardi family tree: Emilio, Facundo, José, and Amalia — Pepín Bosch's mother-in-law.

The Bacardi Moreau family grew to the steam-driven beat of the Cuban sugar industry, which was becoming the most mechanized and productive in the world. By 1850, sugar accounted for more than four-fifths of the country's exports. A decade later, Cuba was responsible for one-third of the world's production. The boom resulted in greatly increased supplies of molasses, sugar's syrupy by-product, and in the potential to distill spirits from that molasses.

Rum was originally a harsh, manly, working-class drink, produced by crude methods. Molasses was diluted with water, then fermented through the addition of yeast. If the fermentation was sluggish, according to one account, "a dead animal, a large piece of meat or some other fancied corrective would be pitched into the offending vat." Once the fermentation process had transformed the sugar in the molasses into alcohol, the alcohol — because its boiling point is lower than that of water — could be distilled from the mixture by heating the concoction in an alembic, or still, a metal retort whose origins lay in alchemy. The alembic drew off and condensed the vaporized alcohol. The alcohol could be refined and mellowed through filtration and storage in barrels, where chemical interaction took place between the alcohol and the wood. Finally, rums of different ages could be blended to produce a unique and potent drink.

Rum's early history is spiced with buccaneers, the slave trade, and the might of the British navy. Henry Morgan, the brigand who looted Santiago, appropriately gave his name to a brand. The pirates in *Treasure Island* drank themselves to death with rum. The British Empire was built on rum-driven naval power. Rum also played a crucial part in the triangular trade — with molasses and slaves — that flourished between the Caribbean, New England, and Africa in the eighteenth and early nineteenth centuries.

Facundo's first involvement with rum seems to have come through selling the product of an Englishman, John Nunes, who had set up a small distillery in Santiago in 1838 to compete with rums from

Jamaica and Martinique. In 1862, in partnership with his brother José — who provided the money — and a French wine merchant named Boutellier, Facundo bought Nunes's tin-roofed distillery on the Calle Matadero for 3,500 pesos. According to recent versions of Bacardi corporate history, the little plant was home to a colony of fruit bats. Amalia suggested to her husband that the bat be used as a trademark — important as an identifying symbol in an age when most consumers couldn't read.

The "bats in the distillery" version of the birth of the Bacardi trademark is just one of a number of versions. According to another, the bats lived not in the distillery but in a tree outside and "would come with great clattering of wings each night into the kitchen and eat the molasses from which the rum was made." Another variation suggests that the bat symbol was acquired through confusion rather than adoption. According to this tale, the Bacardi brothers sold the rum of John Nunes from their general store in gallon containers that had been originally used for a brand of imported olive oil that bore a bat trademark. As a result, the public began asking for the *ron del murciélago*, the rum of the bat.

Perhaps the confusion story was superseded by the more graphic fixed-assets version because it was a better yarn; perhaps it was elided, consciously or unconsciously, because the Bacardi trademark is now a valuable, indeed almost sacred, commodity, and the notion that it was co-opted, by accident and without payment, might cause Bacardi's lawyers to wake up sweating. Whatever the origin, it was from the little distillery near Santiago harbor that the Bacardi bat took symbolic flight, on its way to becoming "the most famous bat in the world."

A key tenet of the Bacardi mythology is that Facundo developed a "secret formula" for a new, smoother type of rum. The details are lost in the mists of time. Bacardi rum certainly evolved as a more refined product than that of its Caribbean neighbors. This gentler quality was eventually at the root of its success, since it proved ideal for making cocktails, which became fashionable in Cuba and the United States around the turn of the century. Because of its success, it developed many local imitators, thus shaping the evolution of a uniquely "Cuban" rum.

As a symbol of the company's vitality, Facundo's second son, also named Facundo, planted a coconut seed in front of the factory. El Coco was lovingly tended, and expansions to the factory would always be made around it. Fifty years later, upon hearing that the tree would survive the old plant's demolition, a happy Facundo wrote to his elder brother Emilio: "If that palm tree could speak! How many things it would be able to tell! Not all of them would be joyful."

The tree would grow in a climate ruled far more by politics than by business. As Cuba's second city, far from the seat of government in Havana, Santiago became the gathering place for those who sought to challenge the island's rulers. Pepín Bosch would become very much part of that heritage.

The ongoing revolutions of Europe, with their lofty ideals, had infected the island, and that infection proved particularly strong for Facundo's eldest son, Emilio Bacardi Moreau, Bosch's wife's uncle, and the dominant family figure of his generation. As a boy, following the earthquake of 1852 in Santiago and the subsequent cholera epidemic, Emilio had been taken to Barcelona, where he stayed until 1857. There, under the supervision of his godfather, Daniel Costa, he developed the literary and artistic tastes that — along with revolution and the rum business — would dominate his life.

From the time he started work in the little office on the Calle Matadero, at the age of eighteen, Emilio also devoted much time to what became a prodigious literary output. His writings ranged from history and historical novels to essays and journalism. Some of his first published work was written on the backs of ledger pages from an earlier, bankrupted business of his father — fitting symbol of the two sides of Emilio's life. He also started to become involved in the ongoing, often bloody, political struggle that was playing havoc with the Bacardis' commercial activities.

Cuba was slower to move toward independence from Spain than the South American nations of the Spanish empire. It did not join those nations in the great revolutionary wars that began in 1808 and, in just a few years, swept the colonial power from the mainland. This was partly because Cuba represented a last outpost in Spain's struggle with the South American nations and was heavily garrisoned. But Cubans were also slow to take up arms because they feared that independence might leave them vulnerable to a black-led revolt, such as the one in Santo Domingo.

Following a coup in Spain against Queen Isabella in 1868, revolutionary sentiment in the eastern half of the island came to a head. On October 10, 1868, Carlos Manuel de Céspedes, a farmer from an old colonial family, freed the slaves from his sugar mill, raised the *grito*, or cry of rebellion, and marched toward the nearby town of Yara with shouts of "Viva Cuba libre" (Long live free Cuba) and "Independencia o muerte" (Independence or death). The ensuing war lasted ten years and was marked by terrible brutality on both sides.

The Bacardis' loyalties were split. Facundo Bacardi y Maso was a Spaniard by birth and felt loyalty to his homeland, but his children were *criollos*, born in Cuba. Emilio, in particular, felt a fierce commitment to the land of his birth. When Spanish troops arrived to recruit young Emilio to the anti-rebel "volunteers," he, according to family lore, "threw the gun they gave him into the street." Instead, he became a *laborante*, or underground worker, for the rebels in Santiago, collecting money and distributing revolutionary periodicals. The distillery on the Calle Matadero became a front, from which "customers" carried off cargo more dangerous than rum.

Some of the most dramatic events of the war of 1868 – 78 unfolded within sight of El Coco. In 1873, a number of alleged revolutionaries were captured aboard the ship *Virginius*, brought into the city, and executed close to the distillery. Emilio's brother Facundo would remember all his life the image of two stiff legs sticking straight up from the funeral cart as it carried off the bodies.

In 1878, the Cuban rebels ran out of steam and signed the Treaty of Zanjón. They had fought a long and bloody war for very little. Yet the Ten Years' War would become sanctified in Cuban history as the first great struggle for Cuban freedom. It was rhetorically characterized by José Martí — regarded today as the greatest of Cuban patriots, and certainly the most grandiloquent — as "that wonderful and sudden emergence of a people apparently servile only a short time before, who made heroic feats a daily occurrence, hunger a banquet, the extraordinary a commonplace."

There was a good deal less romance for those caught in the middle. As Santiago had come under siege and the island's sugar mills had been burned, Bacardi's raw materials and markets had been thoroughly disrupted. Still, in 1876, while the war raged on, the Bacardis had managed to take their rum to the Centennial Philadelphia Exposition, where the halls were filled with works of industrial wonder: locomotives "capable of hauling 670 tons at 40 miles per hour"; giant hydraulic presses and "magneto electric" machines; huge French lighthouse lenses of 400,000 candlepower; rock drills and atmosphere gas engines and ice-making equipment and printing presses. There were also consumer products: elegant carriages, carvings from the

Orient, fine ceramics and luxurious cloths; indeed, displays of almost every manufacture imaginable, from paintbrushes and drugs to Miss Philbrook's "Equipoise Waist" corset. Jamaica rum was reckoned to be the best in the world, but Bacardi won a gold medal in its category.

That same year, there was another cause for family celebration: Emilio Bacardi Moreau married María Lay Berlucheau, another *santiaguera* of French descent. They would have five children who survived to maturity. The first was born in 1877, the year Facundo handed over the business to his sons Emilio and Facundo. This greater business responsibility did not stop both brothers — particularly Emilio — from becoming more deeply embroiled in politics.

Despite the end of war, revolutionary feeling remained high in Santiago. In August 1879, following a tumultuous meeting in the city, a group of revolutionaries headed once more for the hills, thus starting the so-called Guerra Chicita (Little War), which lasted a year. Both Bacardi brothers were implicated and arrested. Facundo was subsequently released, but Emilio was taken out to the dungeons of El Morro, and from there transported, with other prisoners, via Puerto Rico, into exile in Spanish North Africa. He returned to Cuba in 1883, the year his youngest brother, José, joined the business.

On March 9, 1886, Facundo Bacardi y Maso, the founder, died at the age of seventy-one. Among the icons on display throughout the Bacardi empire is a reproduced portrait of him. Painted in the naive style, it shows a square-faced man with a benevolently firm set to his mouth. In fact, nobody knows what Facundo looked like. The portrait was commissioned long after his death by Pepín Bosch.

The manufactured portrait is, at one level, simply an attempt to recreate the likeness of a man; the filling in of history for a family — and a brand — to which history is important. But it is also a reminder that the past is always created at some later date.

The portrait of Facundo is a measure of how little is known of him. He may not have shared the fervent revolutionary sympathies of his sons, but neither did he quash them. He is said to have been highly formal, typical of the Spanish businessman of the period, a man who never appeared in public without stiff collars and cuffs and shiny black shoes, and who was never seen, even by his children, in shirtsleeves. A person of few words, he was reportedly given to pacing the portico of his house, deep in thought, between the time he returned home from the distillery and dinner. His gift to his family, and history, was a brand of rum whose success would grow beyond his wildest imagination.

After the patriarch's death, a new company was constituted with the three brothers — Emilio, Facundo, and José — as equal partners. In the 1880s, recognition brought certain paradoxes to the business. The friction between the demands of commerce and of revolution began to show. Politics did not prevent Bacardi from sending its rum to industrial expositions in the land of Cuba's oppressor; it won gold medals in Madrid and Barcelona. Moreover, in the burgeoning Spanish commercial world, one of the most sought-after distinctions was the right to display a royal coat of arms on one's product. This honor was as eagerly sought by Bacardi as by any company — despite the fact that the head of Bacardi had been imprisoned once (and would be again) by the Spanish monarchy. In 1888, María Cristina, as princess regent for the future Alfonso XIII, appointed the Bacardi company purveyors to the Spanish royal household.

Four years later, in 1892, came a marketing man's dream. Little Alfonso, who was of such sickly nature that he could not live amid the fetid humors of Madrid, fell ill with the grippe. According to Bacardi lore: "The Royal physicians, aware of its many gold medals and high quality, administered Bacardi rum to the prince. That evening, for the first time in days, he fell into an easy sleep. By morning the fever was on the wane." The royal secretary wrote a note thanking the company "for making a product that has saved the life of His Majesty."

Saving the future king's young life seemed a strange boast for a company whose head continued to plot against Spanish rule. Catalans — and the Bacardis were proud of their Catalonian heritage — had opposed the Bourbon succession of which Alfonso XIII was the latest fruit. The Bourbons' best-known contribution to Spanish history had been their abject surrender of the country to Napoleon. The Spanish had thrown them out in 1868, although they had subsequently had them back, *faute de mieux*, in the shape of Alfonso's father, Alfonso XII. The young Alfonso XIII would grow up to connive in the seizure of power in 1923 by General Miguel Primo de Rivera, thus subverting the constitution, losing the monarchy, and helping precipitate the Spanish Civil War. Alfonso XIII's son, having given up claim to the Spanish monarchy, wound up making two unsuccessful Cuban marriages and hanging out in Sloppy Joe's bar in Havana, touching American tourists for money and downing non-medicinal amounts of his father's lifesaver.

But, of course, the boast of manufacturing "the rum that saved His Majesty's life" was not an invitation to weigh history, just as the plaque in the Bacardi Corporation museum in San Juan that reads *BAC-ARDI . . . EL REY DE LOS RONES: EL RON DE LOS REYES* (Bacardi . . . The king of rums: the rum of kings) was never meant to invite an examination of the benefits of monarchy. Rather, kings were invoked as the most discerning of consumers, with almost limitless wealth and the widest range of goods at their disposal. And the quality of being a lifesaver was pretty useful for any product, no matter whose life was saved.

Despite these restorative powers, and despite winning more gold medals at such industrial exhibitions as the great Universal Exposition of 1893 in Chicago, Bacardi foundered in Cuba's disastrous economic climate. In 1894, the company was again reconstituted. The three sons took a new partner, Enrique Schueg, Pepín Bosch's father-in-law. Enrique was a Cuban of French descent, the youngest of five children who had been brought up on a coffee plantation not far from Santiago. The Schueg family had known Facundo Bacardi y Maso, and when they had decided to return to France, they had left him in charge of remitting income from their remaining Cuban possessions.

Enrique — who had a lifelong limp resulting from a bicycle accident in France when he was fourteen — had decided in 1883, after the death of his mother, to return to Cuba. He had sold the family coffee plantation, which had fallen into disrepair, and gone into business with the Bacardis, first in cattle-raising, then in the Santiago rum operation. He married Amalia Bacardi Moreau in 1893 and the next year became a full partner in the business. His timing could hardly have been worse. In 1895, all commercial activity on the island was thrown into turmoil again as the final struggle for Cuban independence broke out.

CHAPTER TWO

Answered Prayers

*"Why, these people are no more fit
for self-government than
gun-powder is for hell."*
U.S. BRIGADIER GENERAL RUFUS SHAFTER

Santiago de Cuba. 1895

In April 1895, José Martí strapped on his revolver and, with some difficulty, landed a boat that had lost its rudder on a rocky beach at Playitas, east of Santiago. This inauspicious arrival, under a red moon, signaled the start of the final struggle for Cuban independence from Spain.

Martí had become the inspiration for the independence movement. A poet, journalist, revolutionary, and dreamer, he is described, without hyperbole, by the British historian Hugh Thomas as having played "a sacramental role in Cuban history." Martí sought to infect Cubans — from exiles in New York, Tampa, and Key West to Cuban businessmen like the Bacardis — with his grandiose visions, and eventually he recruited two of the heroes of the Ten Years' War, Antonio Maceo and Máximo Gómez. With Gómez, he issued a manifesto promising a "civilized war," an oxymoron curiously Cuban in its optimism. Cuba, they promised, would be a republic "different from the feudal and theoretical ones of Hispano-America." Cuba, after all, was different from countries where revolution had foundered. This difference was due to the "civic responsibility of its warriors; the culture and magnanimity of its artisans; the appropriate and up-to-date use of a vast number of skills and riches; the strange moderation of the peasant, seasoned by both exile and war." Martí promised a new economic system.

To Anglo-Saxons, rooted in an altogether more pragmatic — Latins would say mundane — tradition, Martí's prose appears inflated and nebulous. Revolutionary aspiration was, as usual, tightly linked to the well-turned phrase and the classical allusion. Pseudonyms and noms de guerre were taken from Plutarch's *Lives*. Nobody thought it pretentious to don the name of a famous Athenian general or orator.

Shortly after the separate landings of Martí, Gómez, and the brothers Antonio and José Maceo, Martí, riding a conspicuous white charger, was killed in one of the war's earliest skirmishes. The campaign was thus deprived of its greatest pamphleteer and orator. But Martí's death ensured his own unsullied revolutionary status and gave the cause a great martyr.

Emilio Bacardi Moreau was a devout follower of Martí, whom he had gone to visit in New York, and fully shared his aspirations. He also shared the considerable risks of being a revolutionary, joining secret societies, and publishing seditious literature. He became the principal agent and treasurer of the revolution in Santiago, and the *santiagueros* got down to the time-honored, cloak-and-machete business of clandestine rebel support, an activity that had been honed over three decades of almost constant disruption and hardship. Emilio set up information systems using matching torn pieces of newspapers to identify messengers. The women set to sewing and to dressing wounds. Bullets were sent out to the rebels in the surrounding mountains of the Sierra Maestra in sacks of rice and *frijoles*. Emilio's firstborn, Emilito Bacardi Lay, became adjutant to José Maceo and then to his brother Antonio, "the Bronze Titan." The more mundane business of running the company was left in the hands of Enrique Schueg, Pepín Bosch's father-in-law, although he too played his part in the revolution.

These were dangerous times. On one occasion, Spanish authorities staged a surprise search of Emilio's house. He escaped possible execution only through the quick-wittedness of his second wife, Elvira Cape (his first wife, María, had died in 1885), who hid incriminating papers in the clothing of their little daughter Adelaida (called Lalita) Bacardi Cape, and of their black cook, Georgina, and then sent them "shopping." Nevertheless, Emilio was detained a few days later and sent to prison once more on May 30, 1896. After eleven months of incarceration in Santiago, during which his wife continued his secret work, Emilio sailed once more into exile. Because Santiago was now so dangerous, particularly for the family of an exiled revolutionary, Emilio's wife also left the country. She took the Bacardi Cape children — and the youngest of the Bacardi Lays from Emilio's previous marriage — to Kingston, Jamaica.

In May 1897, Pepín Bosch's father-in-law was also jailed for his part in the plotting. Enrique was saved only by the intercession of the French prime minister, Gabriel Hannoteaux. In October 1897, Emilio was released and allowed to go to Jamaica to join his wife and children.

With Cuba in turmoil, and no one running the company, Bacardi was now on the verge of collapse.

Enter the Americans.

By 1898, sympathy with the aspirations of the Cuban freedom fighters, combined with a growing nationalistic belligerence, had led the United States to consider intervening on the rebels' behalf. The notion of American intervention had been anathema to Martí, who called the U.S. "the monster" and claimed to despise its "cult of wealth." Ironically, however, although the American intervention was not without materialistic motivations, it was primarily driven by more emotional concerns, urges traditionally connected more with the Cuban than with the American temperament.

History had by now, thirty years after the fact, turned the horrors of the American Civil War into glorious and noble adventure for the young, who were further incited to jingoism by press barons like William Randolph Hearst. Manifest destiny was on all lips when the U.S. was brought into the war for independence by the mysterious explosion of the battleship *Maine* in Havana harbor on February 15, 1898.

Havana may have been witness to the immediate cause of the war, but it was Santiago that saw most of the action and suffered most of the hardships. The Bacardis' hometown grew even more well known in the eighteen months after the American victory because of the presence there of Leonard Wood, one of the war's great American heroes. Wood, a career officer in the medical corps, persuaded President William McKinley — much to the disgust of the regular army establishment — to appoint him leader of the Rough Riders, the collection of "millionaires and cowboys" whose most famous member was the future president Teddy Roosevelt.

The American invasion force, under the command of Brigadier General Shafter — who, at 300 pounds, was not exactly built for jungle warfare — landed on the beach at Daiquiri, east of Santiago. The only major land engagement of the war took place at San Juan Hill, just outside the city. Hearst, who was there, described San Juan Hill as a "splendid fight."

Things were less splendid for the inhabitants of Santiago, who had undergone the trauma of a siege while the Spanish fleet had been blockaded in the harbor, putting out in its disastrous escape bid just before the Spanish land forces were defeated ashore. The city had been almost deserted. Santiago surrendered on July 16. The next day the American flag was raised over the Governor's Palace in the Plaza Reina.

The Spanish-American War spawned a rich mythology. The exploits of Teddy Roosevelt's Rough Riders, the battle of San Juan Hill, and Captain R.P. Hobson's scuttling of the collier *Merrimac* in the mouth of Santiago harbor, in an attempt to bottle up the Spanish fleet, all became essentials of American school curriculum. This "splendid little war" was a clear victory for the U.S. and an equally clear defeat for Spain, which fell under a "cloud of melancholy silence." Those for whom the results would be much less clear were those for whom it had theoretically been fought: the Cubans themselves.

The Spanish-American War and Cuban independence marked a watershed: Cuban politics could no longer be mythologized as a struggle between "good" freedom fighters and "bad" Spanish colonial rulers. Independence ended the romanticized period of heroic opposition to a corrupt and crumbling Spanish colonial regime and heralded a century in which corruption became a domestic affair. The "enemy" often proved to be the Cuban government itself. And in the eyes of many Cubans, the American liberators became, if not the new oppressors, then at least a force that retarded Cuban nationhood.

One of the most powerful myths that grew out of the war was that the Cubans had been shoved from their rightful place in the winners' enclosure by the Americans' muscular imperialism; that the Americans were insensitive and overbearing, and that they never really gave the Cubans a chance to prove themselves. True, the Americans had little time for the Cuban brand of political hyperbole — exotic aspirations cultivated in the secrecy of Spanish repression — but their skepticism was well founded. Many Cubans who actively sought power wanted not to replace the Spanish system, but merely to take over its corruptions for themselves. Those with lofty ideals, such as Emilio Bacardi Moreau, were bound to see them crushed by political realities.

Leonard Wood was appointed governor of Santiago de Cuba and then governor of Santiago province. There was much to be done. Santiago had twice its normal population of 50,000. It was a city of famine and pestilence, above which the buzzards wheeled. The water system had failed. The sewage system was non-existent; the streets were cleaned only by the buzzards, the dogs, and the rain.

Cleaning up such a mess would require Herculean talents, and

Wood possessed them. He understood that the Cubans had been brutalized by the repressions of Spanish rule, and he set out to win them over by example. He worked all day and half the night, organizing, inspecting, persevering even through bouts of illness.

By September 1898, he could write to his wife: "The old town is at last clean, and we are down, so to speak, to modern dirt which, while not attractive, is of a less offensive character than that of 1520." It amazed Wood that the city's underlying gaiety managed to bubble through the war's veil of horror. The Bacardi flowed freely at the Café Venus in the main square. On the veranda of the Club San Carlos, to which many members of the Bacardi family belonged, "exquisites lounged with fatalistic disregard of death or the fortunes of war."

Wood wanted to develop native talent, but it took time to identify that talent, and more time for the talent to come forward. He was delighted and astonished at how enthusiastically "the best of them responded to the practical ideals with which he sought to supplant the poisonous sentimentalism of the agitators." Among the "best" was Emilio Bacardi, who had returned from exile in Jamaica the month after the Stars and Stripes was hoisted in the Plaza Reina. Emilio came back as a much-honored citizen, with irreproachable revolutionary credentials, and threw himself into civic affairs. His outlook differed from that of Wood, but the men developed a mutual admiration.

When, early in November, the "best elements" in Santiago asked Wood to give them a mayor from among themselves, Wood appointed Emilio, "who had proved himself one of the ablest men in the city." Wood, tongue in cheek, referring to Emilio's business interests, noted: "I don't know what my puritanical friends in Massachusetts will think when they learn that I have selected Mr. Bacardi as mayor of Santiago." Shortly after appointing Emilio, Wood wrote to President McKinley: "The temper of the people is excellent."

With Emilio's active support, Wood began public works, repairing streets and asphalting the Calle Aguilera Baja (where the Bacardi administrative offices were destined to become the most important commercial location in the city). He set about reforming the courts, building limestone roads out of the city, setting up a telegraph system, promoting the education of women, and putting an end to bullfighting and public gambling. In December, when Wood was appointed a major-general, the whole town rejoiced, "solemnly proclaiming," as Wood's biographer, Hermann Hagedorn, wrote, "that he was the best governor their province had had since the landing of Columbus." The city council gave him a medal and a parchment.

When Santiago was struck by one of its periodic epidemics of yellow fever, Wood set out to conquer it with the efficiency of a well-run military campaign. He poured tons of corrosive sublimate on the city. He evacuated huge numbers of people. He built a camp of refuge at Boniato, eight miles west of the city. The epidemic retreated, and everybody came out to celebrate the 1899 feast of Santiago with enormous zest.

The shadow of Spain still lay over the land, particularly in Havana. There, the American military government of General John Brooke was reckoned to be falling under the influence of wily Cuban subordinates, inheritors of the Spanish tradition of administrative corruption. They took control of the island's finances, including all funds collected in Santiago. On March 1, 1899, more than 2,000 men were thrown out of work in Santiago because there was no money to pay them. Emilio Bacardi sent a wire to Brooke that his policies seemed "suicide."

Wood, too, disagreed with Brooke's policy thrusts. He wrote to Teddy Roosevelt: "Clean government, quick, decisive action and absolute control in the hands of trustworthy men, establishment of needed legal and educational reforms, and I do not believe you could shake Cuba loose if you wanted to. But dillydallying and talking politics will play the Devil with people of this temperament. Every café loafer and political demagogue floats on top and the great current of public feeling is so covered with this refuse that one is unable to get an idea of its character unless he lives here and mixes with the people."

The problem was that even for the best and most enlightened Cubans, "dillydallying and talking politics" was regarded as a sacred right.

In July 1899, after falling out with the civil governor, Demetrio Castillo Duany, Emilio Bacardi resigned as mayor of Santiago. It was an unfortunate development for the city. Wood wrote to his wife in August: "Things are in a bad way, and officials are rapidly drifting back to old ways."

On December 13, 1899, having won a behind-the-scenes battle with Brooke, Wood was appointed governor of the island, and he left Santiago for Havana. President McKinley told him: "I want you to go down there to get the people ready for a Republican form of government. I leave the details of procedure to you. Give them a good school system, try to straighten out their courts, put them on their feet as best you can. We want to do all we can for them and to get out of the island as soon as we safely can." But Wood subsequently wrote to McKinley: "We are dealing with a race that has been going downhill for a hundred years."

One of the great problems the United States had in its relations with Cuba — as with other Latin American countries — was that it could not see why its own bustling, technocratic, can-do attitude would not be greeted with open arms. Americans brought to all "foreign problems" an air of scientific analysis. They might indulge in a little jingoism, but their approach was without hyperbole. They were congenital problem-solvers. The Cubans had been plotting and planning for decades; plotting and planning were noble activities. But war is not a good training for peace. Cubans could see the value of a man like Leonard Wood, who could organize water supplies, install sanitation, and call in a corps of engineers at a moment's notice to put things straight. Still, for many Cubans, the northerners were robbing them of their political manhood.

There were major temperamental differences between the Cubans and the Americans. Perhaps the most famous piece of North American writing to emerge from or be inspired by the war was a little pamphlet entitled "A Message to García," written by Elbert Hubbard. The tract, which sold several million copies, was based on the delivery of a message from President McKinley to the Cuban revolutionary general Calixto García by a U.S. army lieutenant named Rowan. In fact, the pamphlet did not deal with Rowan's feat in finding García. Indeed, it had nothing to do with the war at all. Hubbard's "preachment" was a reflection on the fact that Rowan simply did what was asked of him. It was a panegyric to those in the business world who could get things done without asking stupid questions, a paean of praise to the Protestant ethic. That ethic had slim roots in Cuba, where every proposed action provided an excuse for seemingly interminable debate. The American culture of levelheaded management was fundamentally at odds with the Cubans' passionate and artistic nature.

Frustrated hopes and political tensions created at the time of independence would haunt Cuban politics throughout the twentieth century. At the same time, closer commercial relations with the U.S. would provide considerable opportunities. These the Bacardis seized with both hands.

CHAPTER THREE

Success at Last

*"The unselfish and the intelligent
may begin a movement — but it
passes away from them . . . Hopes
grotesquely betrayed, ideals
caricatured — that is the definition
of revolutionary success."*
JOSEPH CONRAD, *UNDER WESTERN EYES*

Santiago de Cuba. New Year's Eve, 1901

At midnight on December 31, 1901, as the cathedral clock struck twelve and the national anthem was played, a huge, 25-foot Cuban flag was hoisted above moist eyes and quivering voices in front of Santiago's municipal building. Emilio Bacardi presided, as Santiago's first popularly elected mayor, over the inaugural Fiesta de la Bandera (Festival of the Flag), an emotional tribute to the land for whose freedom Cubans had fought so long — a freedom now imminent.

Five months later, at noon on May 20, 1902, at the Governor's Palace in Havana, Leonard Wood read a letter from President Theodore Roosevelt to the president and congress of the Republic of Cuba, declaring U.S. occupation at an end. He lowered the American flag and, along with the old warrior Máximo Gómez, who had tears trickling down his cheeks, helped raise the lone-star Cuban banner. As it was hoisted, in a moment sadly symbolic, the halyard broke. Following the ceremony, General Wood and his staff boarded a launch out to the battleship *Brooklyn*. But as the *Brooklyn* steamed past Havana's El Morro fortress, Wood's satisfaction at the transfer of authority was tempered by doubts about the Cubans' readiness for power. Because of those doubts, the U.S. had taken what it regarded as a necessary precaution against Cuban inexperience and the possibility of European intervention. It was called the Platt Amendment.

Reluctantly accepted by the Cubans as an appendix to their new constitution, the Platt Amendment gave the U.S. oversight of Cuban foreign loans and treaties, and the right to intervene to preserve Cuban independence and maintain the freedoms recognized under the U.S. constitution. Many Cubans believed it started the republic on the wrong foot, a step from which it never recovered. The Platt

Amendment represented a major curtailment of Cuban authority, while it burdened the U.S. with responsibility for Cuba's political shortcomings.

Cuba's first president was Tomás Estrada Palma, a popular figure who had lived in exile in New York for many years and played a great part in exploiting the New York press for the rebel cause. Don Tomás, as he was known, proved prudent, economical, honest, and courageous. But his main strength was also his principal weakness: he was no politician. He proved incapable of holding off others obsessed by the potential for loot. The loot was considerable.

Independence started under boom conditions, helped by a reciprocity treaty with the U.S., improved access to the U.S. market for Cuban sugar, and the completion of the Cuba Central Railway. But politics quickly returned to patterns of colonial corruption, and the elections of 1904 and 1905 were rigged.

For the first three years of the republic, Emilio Bacardi continued as mayor of Santiago, busying himself with the implementation of enlightened reforms and the more mundane details of municipal order and good government. After setting the astonishing precedent of halving his own salary, he instituted public works and new libraries; he had the cathedral square replanted and beautified; he banished prostitutes; he ensured that all religious beliefs were tolerated; he employed women in the town hall for the first time. With a mind to the potential of the new Panama Canal, he expanded the port. In 1905, the year electricity was brought to Santiago's main square, Emilio, hoping to help solve the new republic's mounting problems, became a candidate for the senate. In March 1906, having been elected a senator, he gave up the mayor's position and took off for Havana.

By then the rot had set in. In August 1906, three months after Estrada had entered his second term, the opposition Liberals "took to the hills," leading the Cuban president to ask for U.S. intervention. Cuba's first republic was brought to an ignominious close. In September 1906, a disillusioned Emilio returned to Santiago. Henceforth, he would concentrate on philanthropy and the rum business.

For its first four decades, the Bacardi business had been dominated by revolutionary politics. Now Bacardi was about to enter a period of unprecedented prosperity, a prosperity significantly due to links with the U.S. When Emilio Bacardi had returned from exile to war-torn Santiago in August 1898, he had found prominent posters for the Cuban edition of Hearst's newspaper. REMEMBER THE MAINE, they read. BUY THE JOURNAL. Everywhere there were commercial symbols of the U.S.: the United States Hotel, the Arizona Saloon, the Chicago Restaurant. American banks and American express companies had appeared. The Americans had brought much to Santiago, but one of the things they had begun to buy and take away was Bacardi rum. Whatever the results of the Spanish-American War for Cuba, it brought the Bacardi name to a wider North American market. The first two decades of the twentieth century saw spectacular growth in the Bacardi business.

The fall of the first republic in 1906 had done nothing to damage demand either at home or abroad for Bacardi rum. The administrative office, on Santiago's Calle Aguilera Baja, was receiving orders from all over the world. In 1910, the company built its first overseas factory, in Barcelona. In 1911, the old alembic, which had served John Nunes for twenty-four years and the Bacardis for forty-nine, was removed and a new one installed. The new alembic would see an explosion of demand for its product.

In 1915, as more gold medals were accumulated from San Francisco and Panama, the old Calle Matadero plant came under the pickax, and a new, much larger facility was begun. The old palm tree, El Coco, considered almost part of the family, was carefully preserved. The new plant was completed two years later, just in time to take advantage of a boom in demand resulting from the First World War, which virtually cut off supplies of European wine, champagne, and cognac from American and Caribbean markets.

In 1919, Bacardi was transformed into a limited liability company, Compañía Ron Bacardi S.A., the name it was to keep throughout the remainder of its history in Cuba. The shares were divided among Emilio and Facundo Bacardi Moreau and Enrique Schueg, each of whom held stock with a par value of more than $1 million. Emilio was the president, Facundo the first vice-president, Pepín Bosch's father-in-law the second vice-president. (The youngest Bacardi Moreau brother, José, had married Carmen Fernández Fontecha, a socialite from a wealthy Havana family, and had pulled out of the business shortly after independence.)

The business had enjoyed seven years of spectacular growth. Its assets had grown twenty-fold, from only 180,282 pesos in 1912 to

3.7 million pesos. The Bacardi complex on the Calle Matadero, with its warehouses and boiler-houses and bottling plant, all fed by rail-drawn tank-cars of molasses from the mills of the interior, was now the economic heart of the city.

Shortly after the corporate reorganization, another major expansion was undertaken. In February 1922, a new distillery was opened amid city-wide celebrations. At the inauguration, the elderly Emilio, with his long, white mustache, his rimless spectacles under his straw boater, and his trademark bow tie, always slightly askew, was clearly Santiago's first citizen. He was cheered by a huge crowd as he stood in the shadow of a gigantic replica of a bottle of Bacardi. That evening, the company sponsored a banquet at the Hotel Venus, where the banquet room was draped with Cuban flags. The high point of the inauguration was the hoisting of the lone-star flag by Emilio and his niece, Enriqueta Schueg Bacardi.

Enriqueta, a striking girl under a broad-brimmed straw hat, was the link to the company's future. Emilio's wartime incarceration and subsequent involvement with politics until 1906 had led to the increasing importance in the company of her father, Enrique Schueg.

Schueg was, by nature, more of a businessman than Emilio. After the Spanish-American War had introduced Bacardi rum to the occupation forces on the island, he had been responsible for increasing Bacardi's international thrust. Emilio remained important as the figurehead, and he was intimately involved with executive decisions, but Schueg was the architect of expansion. Together with Emilio's brother, Facundo, who remained in charge of the production end of the business, the three family members formed a managerial triumvirate.

Family had always been — and would continue to be — particularly important in Cuban society. As a 1935 report by the U.S. Commission on Cuban Affairs noted: "The family displays greater solidarity and strength, and plays a much more important role in the total social organization than the commercialized cultures with which Cuban society is compared."

At the turn of the century, thirty years of economic hardship and political turmoil in Cuba had further strengthened the importance of the Bacardi family ties. This cohesion was not weakened by the family's subsequent success in Cuba's increasingly "commercialized culture." On the contrary, it was strengthened. For example, although the youngest Bacardi brother, José, had pulled out of the business, his children were taken in by the family when he died and were eventually given 10 percent of the equity in Bacardi by the other three branches.

The Cuban family was an open organization that welcomed association through marriage. Children tended to stay attached to the family home. Women held high status and were unafraid to become involved in politics. Elvira Cape, for example, had continued the clandestine struggle for independence while her husband Emilio was in exile for the second time, before shepherding her children to safety in Jamaica. Cuban women seldom became involved in business affairs, but Bacardi welcomed the husbands of many of its daughters. In this way, the business provided the fertilizer for a huge family tree.

Families that see themselves as trees — and take the trouble to have an artist record them as such — have a common interest beyond blood. A family tree is an artificial construct, its trunk formed at the wedding of an ancestor who had something to bestow upon his children. For the Bacardis, that trunk consisted of Facundo Bacardi y Maso and his wife Amalia Moreau. The gift to be nurtured and passed on was Facundo's rum business.

The "tree" as a biological fact would have been there if Facundo had founded no business, but then no descendant would have bothered to have it reproduced, framed, and hung on the wall. In families with no such unifying force, daughters might go off to form new saplings. But with the Bacardis, the daughters were more like the hanging tendrils of the banyan tree, aerial roots that grow subsidiary "trunks," allowing the tree to reach extraordinary size. Like the banyan's tendrils, Bacardi daughters would reach out and take husbands who — by working in the business — formed new buttresses for the tree and sometimes added new vitality to the business. At the time of the Cuban republic, there had not been much to marry into. Twenty years later, things were very different.

Among the other Santiago businessmen who thrived in the post-independence boom was José Bosch, Pepín's father. Like the Bacardi founder, José had come to Cuba from Catalonia in his early teens. Unlike Facundo, he had come without a family, having left home after clashing with his stepfather. José found work in a hardware store in Mayarí, a small town north of Santiago, where he met and married the daughter of a Cuban father and a French mother. They moved to Santiago, where he worked for a company that sold foodstuffs and insurance, and represented a number of steamship lines. Later he moved to a rival company, which was engaged in banking. Eventually he became part owner of the company.

By 1902, his status and wealth were such that he held a banquet in Santiago for the Cuban president, Tomás Estrada Palma. A contemporary photograph shows a courtly, serious, mustached man, bowing to his seated and smiling wife. He went on to buy sugar mills, establish Santiago's trolley car system, and become part owner of the local electric utility. He helped found a local hospital and, along with Andrés Duany, another wealthy landowner and businessman, developed a subdivision on the western outskirts of the city, beside San Juan Hill, into the town's smartest address. Many of the Bacardis moved to roomy houses on the wide, well-planted boulevards of Vista Alegre. For his family, José built Vista Alegre's most imposing residence. The "Bosch Palace" was a magnificent, gabled structure whose many rooms opened off galleries around a two-and-a-half-story, marble-pillared central lobby.

José's son, Pepín Bosch, was born on April 30, 1898, the climactic year of Cuban independence from Spain, and of its new relationship with the U.S. As befitted the son of a wealthy man, and like many other children of wealthy *santiagueros*, Pepín was sent to the U.S. for his education. He went to Villanova College Preparatory School and eventually to Lehigh University, both in Pennsylvania. He was not an avid student. He flunked calculus and left Lehigh after one term. His parents wanted him to return to Cuba, but a rich Spanish friend who owned a shipbuilding company hired him to work in New York, paying him a generous salary plus full board at the swank Astor Hotel. The playboy shipbuilder was famous for his lavish parties. When Bosch's father heard about his son's life, he ordered him to return. He went to work as a timekeeper in his father's sugar mills.

After the American market for Cuban sugar had been secured in 1912, the business had expanded rapidly. The impact was greatest in Oriente province, around Santiago. Huge forests of fragrant cedar, mahogany, and pomegranate were razed by cheap labor brought in from Haiti and Jamaica to provide land for the new sugar mills, the *centrales*. The newspaper *El Mundo* remarked: "If things go on at this rate we'll be sowing cane in the patios of our houses." When the First World War brought a collapse of the European beet sugar industry, the boom reached even dizzier heights.

Pepín Bosch was soon appointed manager of two of his father's mills, in which he was given a percentage of the profits. By the time he was twenty one, he was a wealthy young man. In 1920, as a result of lobbying by the sugar producers, the price of sugar was allowed to find its own level. There followed a mad scramble that became known as the Dance of the Millions. Previously, a sugar price of 5½ cents a pound was thought to have been enough to stimulate the island to prosperity. By February 18, 1920, the price of sugar hit a record 9⅛ cents. A mania set in. In May, the price peaked at an astonishing 22½ cents. Then came the crash. By Christmas it had fallen back to 3¾ cents. The collapse provoked a crisis, worsened by the herd mentality of Cuba's bankers, who, since the start of the wartime boom, had acted as enthusiastic money salesmen, encouraging Cuban planters and farmers to borrow indiscriminately.

Although Pepín Bosch's father survived the Dance of the Millions a wealthy man, Pepín saw his youthful fortune evaporate with the sugar crash. He considered moving to Argentina, the most prosperous and promising country in South America. But his mother begged him to stay in Cuba, and he took a job as a bookkeeper with an American bank in Havana. More important, both for his own career and for the subsequent success of the business, he married into the Bacardi family.

Bosch had known many of the Bacardi children since childhood. Once he had returned to work in Santiago, he became particularly attached to Enriqueta Schueg Bacardi. Each summer, when she returned from college in the U.S., Enriqueta played tennis with Bosch at the exclusive club at Vista Alegre. In 1922, they were married.

Pepín Bosch was not marrying for money. He was a fiercely proud and independent young man, keen to make his own way. The job he had taken in Havana was with First National City, one of the largest and most venerable of the U.S. banks; it had established its credentials by raising over a million dollars for the U.S. in the War of 1812, and later led a consortium to fund the North in the Civil War. Bosch, who knew City Bank's president from earlier dealings in the sugar business, climbed the bank ladder in the 1920s to become head of the collections department. The job required, and further developed, a certain toughness of spirit.

Compact, soft-spoken, and already balding, Bosch was typically Cuban and yet in many ways not Cuban at all. Though he would one day risk his life and his fortune for the elusive goal of Cuban freedom, he was never given to hyperbole. His prose could stand no editing because it possessed a quite un-Cuban leanness. He was a man of very few words, and fewer spare ones.

Bosch wanted no part of the Cuban tendency to blame failure on

American "domination." Many Cubans — almost invariably politicians — professed to despise capitalism and the American "cult" of materialism, but this line was often pure humbug. It came either from people who were rich in the first place or from those who wanted to play on Cuban anti-Americanism for their own — often materialistic — political ends. Pepín Bosch preferred to take the Americans on at their own game. He was a model of the Protestant ethic. Indeed, one of his favorite tracts, which he often quoted to employees, was Hubbard's "Message to García," that paean of praise for men who could deliver the message, "without asking any idiotic questions, and with no lurking intention of chucking it into the nearest sewer, or of doing aught else but deliver it." One of his colleagues described his management style as "positively Anglo-Saxon." Prominent in the house he built for Enriqueta and himself in Havana's exclusive Country Club Park in the late 1920s was a portrait of Thomas Jefferson.

After Cuba had lived through another period of U.S. administration, between 1906 and 1909, José Miguel Gómez, who had fixed the elections for Tomás Estrada Palma in 1905, had been elected president. His administration was summed up by his nickname, El Tiburón (the shark). He began the process of bribing all newspapers and taking a cut from all public projects. He brought back cockfighting and the lottery.

Gómez retired with his fortune and was succeeded by General Mario García Menocal, who set new standards for corruption. During his presidency, from 1913 to 1921, he reportedly accumulated a fortune of $40 million. The U.S., preoccupied by its imminent entry into the European war, and hoping that Cuba would declare war against Germany, did not intervene when Menocal took the 1916 election by fraud.

Under Menocal's administration, the department of public works specialized in hatching plans for imaginary roads and mythical bridges, the funds for which were pocketed. Congressmen were given lottery collectorships, another license to steal money. Emilio Bacardi had achieved much in his long and distinguished life, but his dreams of an honorable Cuban independence would never be realized.

In the summer of 1922, after triumphantly opening the new Bacardi facilities, Emilio fell ill with a recurrent heart condition. On August 28, 1922, he died at his country house, the Villa Elvira in Cuabitas, just outside Santiago. Public events were suspended for two days; cafés closed their doors; the women of the town wore white mourning gowns fringed with black.

His funeral was the biggest Santiago had seen. The cortege started from the Villa Elvira. By the time it reached Santiago's main square, the procession was more than ten blocks long. Heroes of the wars of independence, members of the diplomatic corps, and squadrons of troops, police, and firemen were followed by the people of the town, there to express their affection for Santiago's first citizen. When the funeral carriage stopped in front of the town hall, the coffin was draped with the huge Cuban flag used at the Fiesta de la Bandera. At the cemetery, funeral marches were played; three salvos of rifle fire echoed in tribute. Funeral orations were long and elaborate.

Emilio's death provoked an avalanche of letters, articles, poems, and monographs. Condolences poured in from all over the island — from the recently elected Cuban president, Alfredo Zayas, from the Cuban congress, from the British consulate in Santiago. Those from abroad included one from Leonard Wood, who wrote from Manila: "My wife and I have always remembered with satisfaction and pleasure our stay in Santiago, and among our most agreeable memories is the cooperation of your husband, with his loyal and energetic help in all that he believed was necessary for Cuba.

"With the death of your husband, Cuba loses a great citizen and yourself a devoted spouse. Santiago de Cuba, without Emilio Bacardi, will never seem the same."

The headline in the *Havana Post* declared: "Greatest Cuban Distiller Dead." The report read: "Cuba loses with Bacardi's death, one of the men who constantly worked for her independence and whose efforts were so persistent and fearless that he was deported to the Spanish penitentiary in Ceuta, where he served a long term.

"He was not only a brilliant novelist, but a great historian and few have been able to equal him in the local color of his writings dealing with Cuban customs . . . A true philanthropist, he did much good for the city of Santiago and her people. Nobody could surpass him in his open-handedness when confronted with a deserving cause."

Havana's *El Heraldo de Cuba* devoted several columns to his life, noting pointedly that "the death of the great Cuban is sad, at this time of national uncertainty, in which disinterested, patriotic, and dignified men like him are so necessary." *La Libertad* of Havana declared: "His death leaves an unfillable gap in the ranks of great men."

In the great sweep of Cuban history, Emilio Bacardi Moreau was a minor player, but he was a model of rectitude and good citizenship.

The tragedy of Cuban politics was that there was little place for men like him. His trip to Havana as senator in 1906 had ended with the downfall of the government and the intervention, at the request of president Estrada Palma, of the Americans. His only other sortie into politics, in 1916, as a councillor in Santiago, had ended when he resigned in disgust at the sordid partisanship of municipal affairs.

The post-independence success of the Bacardi business had enabled Emilio to indulge his philanthropy and his love of the arts. He left Santiago a permanent legacy, the most important part of which was the Museo Municipal Emilio Bacardi Moreau, founded in 1899, with the help of funds from Leonard Wood, who sympathized with Emilio's desire to make Cubans aware of their past. The museum had grown in proportion with Emilio's wealth and benefactions, receiving many artifacts that he collected on his foreign travels. Shortly after his death, construction began on a magnificent new neo-classical building for the collection. The building would carry his name on its portico and into Santiago's future.

Emilio also founded the school of Bellas Artes, where Santiago's young writers and painters found a place to develop their talents. The Villa Elvira too had become a gathering place for artists and poets. Emilio's literary output was prodigious. His novels dealt with historical themes. His best-known and certainly most comprehensive work was his *Crónicas de Santiago de Cuba*, published after his death in ten volumes.

Emilio's extensive travels in the first two decades of the twentieth century were a measure of the business's success. In 1912 — the year he was appointed president of the Red Cross in Santiago — he had taken off with his wife on an extended visit to the U.S., France, and Palestine. In Egypt, where he and Elvira sat perched atop camels in front of the Pyramids for a photograph, he purchased a mummy. When he returned to Cuba, customs authorities debated whether the mummy was a work of art or cured meat. It was the sort of debate in which the *criollos* — those born of Spanish parents in the New World — delighted. Emilio was the pride of the *criollos*. He rejoiced in debate and was not a conventional thinker. His wide-ranging beliefs meant that he was sometimes accused of being atheist, Buddhist, or spiritualist. He certainly rejected conventional religion — not surprisingly, given the corrupt form in which it had presented itself in the Catholic church in Cuba. He was that often wonderful and sometimes bizarre product of the nineteenth century, a *libre pensador*, a free thinker.

His memory survives to this day among older members of the family. His daughter Amalia Bacardi Cape would devote much of her life to the memory of the man who read her bedtime stories, subsequently published as *Cuentos de Amalia*. She would preserve his papers and archives, and eventually endow a $1-million chair in his name at the University of Miami.

Daniel Bacardi Rosell, one of Emilio's grandsons, retains vivid memories of his grandfather's townhouse, where, as a child, he was led by Emilio into a room packed with artifacts, including the famous mummy. He would remember all his life once passing Emilio in the vestibule of his house, and then, as children do, snatching a leaf from a plant. Emilio had called him back and asked him how he would like to have his ear pulled off! Daniel said he wouldn't. So, said Emilio, he should never hurt any living thing, not even a plant. The story was treasured as typical of this most gentle of men. His role as a revolutionary in a violent land was in no way paradoxical. The sight of so much suffering had made him wary of causing pain.

The story is told of a charitable visit he made to a mental hospital. One of the inmates cornered him by a high window, suggesting he should jump down to the patio below. Emilio said that might hurt him. The lunatic responded that he'd like to see him do it anyway. Emilio announced he'd do something even better: he'd jump from the patio up to the window! The fascinated lunatic followed him to the safety of the ground floor.

His perceptive sense of humor was also relayed through another tale; somebody had once pointed out a man to him and said: "That man is always saying bad things about you." Emilio replied: "I don't know why, I never did him any favors!"

Emilio's contribution to the success of the Bacardi business is complex and debatable. One obituary claimed that "he spent the last years of his rich life dedicated to the growth and expansion of the giant business of the Bacardi factory." The *New York Times* obituary said that, under his management, "the distilling company bearing his name made its products known around the world." But a letter from an old friend, written to the newspaper *Diario de Cuba* after his death, declared that "he missed his natural vocation. He was born for Art . . . He hated numbers and his bad luck dragged him into the twists and turns of men of business."

After independence, Pepín Bosch's father-in-law, Enrique Schueg, had become the real driving force behind Bacardi. Nevertheless, Emilio's life and work had added inestimable value to the Bacardi name, undertones of patriotism and citizenship that no amount of marketing could achieve. In 1902, during an illness, he had made a will. He noted that his main asset was his share in the family business. Its value at the time — because of the business's debts — was small. These debts, he wrote, would have to be paid off "since all my effort has always been that the name of Bacardi, in spite of a series of misfortunes, should maintain itself with honor." It was that attitude that helped make the name, and thus the brand, so valuable in Cuba. To this day, Emilio is considered the finest flower of the Bacardis. The power of his memory would prove an important factor in the actions taken more than sixty years after his death by his daughter Amalia and his grandson Daniel — actions that would split the family.

Emilio left behind a large family. Toward the end of his life, he was photographed outside the Villa Elvira with fifteen grandchildren. They would all one day be shareholders, and eventually they would appear as old people in photographs on the walls of their own children and grandchildren, all of whom would be shareholders too. Emilio's branch would take pride in producing many Bacardi employees. Some would come to look with a certain disapproval on their wealthier cousins from other, less populous branches, who chose to enjoy life on company dividends.

In years to come, the forked branch from Emilio's two marriages would take up more than half the family tree. Power, however, had already moved to the Schueg Bacardi branch, where it would stay for more than sixty years. Enrique Schueg had been named president on September 2, 1922. Shortly afterward, Emilio's brother, Facundo, had left Santiago for good. Henceforth he would spend his winters in Havana and his summers in Allenhurst, New Jersey. Some said he left because he had wanted the honor of the company presidency himself. He too was known for his philanthropy. Once, having won the lottery, he opened bank accounts for all Bacardi's employees. He died in Havana of arteriosclerosis, leaving two daughters, María and Laura, and two sons, Luis J. and Facundo Bacardi Gaillard.

The passing of the second generation of the Bacardis inevitably led to inter-branch rivalry. The rum business would provide both the gravitational force that kept them together and the battleground where their rivalries would be played out. The success of the company would both strengthen the bond and make the disagreements more heated. Nevertheless, the Bacardis wore wealth easily. They were thoughtful, generous people, both within the family and to outsiders. For ten years after the death of her husband, José Bacardi Lay — one of the twin sons of Emilio — Zenaida Rosell received only half of her company dividends. Enrique Schueg held back the other half without telling her. He invested them, multiplying their value, and then presented her with the nest egg. It was a typical act of family consideration. Unrelated *santiaguera* widows also found unmarked envelopes filled with money slipped under their doors.

By 1926, when Facundo Bacardi Moreau, second son of the founder, died, the Bacardi business had generated an estimated $50 million in revenues. The members of the already extended Bacardi family were among the most prominent and the richest of Santiago's citizens. Their fame and wealth were growing even more quickly, thanks to one of the most perverse pieces of legislation in the twentieth century.

CHAPTER FOUR

Bathing in Bacardi

*"Beginning as a thick, dark brown
drink to make pirates drunk, and
passing through its phase as a
universal medicine, Rum, by the
grace of a family named Bacardi
and of American Prohibition, had
become, in fact, a gentleman's
drink. The Demon was at last
respectable!"*

BASIL WOON, *WHEN IT'S COCKTAIL TIME IN CUBA*

Miami. 1926

Searching faces in the lunchtime crowd for likely prospects, the Pan
American Airlines agent stood at the busy intersection of Biscayne and
Flagler Avenues in downtown Miami. To anybody who looked as if
he or she could afford it, he made his pitch: "Fly to Havana and bathe
in Bacardi Rum!" The invitation was attractive. Prohibition, outlaw-
ing the production, distribution, or importation of beverage alcohol
in the United States, had been introduced six years earlier. Bathing in
Bacardi was legal in the U.S., but buying it was not.

Abraham Lincoln had voiced most succinctly the argument against
Prohibition in 1840, when he was a Whig member of the Illinois state
legislature. "Prohibition," he declared, "will work great injury on the
cause of temperance. It is a species of intemperance within itself, for
it goes beyond the bounds of reason in that it attempts to control a
man's appetite by legislation and makes a crime out of things that are
not crimes. A prohibition law strikes at the very principle upon which
our Government was founded."

Lincoln was much quoted by the pro-liquor lobby, not least for his
reply to a delegation that had come during the Civil War seeking the
dismissal of General Ulysses Grant for drinking too much. "Doctor,"
Lincoln is reported to have said, "can you tell me where General Grant
gets his liquor? . . . For if you can tell me, I would direct the chief
quartermaster of the army to lay in a large stock of the same kind of
liquor, and would also direct him to furnish a supply to some of my
other generals who have never yet won a victory."

In the final quarter of the nineteenth century, the Prohibition movement had gained momentum, largely through the increasing activism of women's groups, particularly the Women's Christian Temperance Union, which was formed in 1874 and declared itself "organized mother love." The pro-alcohol lobby — dominated by the United States Brewers Association — was heavy-handed and reactionary. It opposed women's suffrage because it imagined the majority of women would sympathize with the WCTU. The WCTU had its own extremists, the most famous of whom was Carry Nation, the deranged virago from Medicine Lodge, Kansas, who described herself as "a bulldog, running along at the feet of Jesus, barking at what He doesn't like." The women's Prohibition movement had already engaged in anti-saloon "crusades," but these had taken the form of prayers and picketing meant to shame saloon-owners into closing down. Clad in the armor of self-righteousness, wielding a hatchet, Nation, "a sainted heroine to the church and the drys, a lunatic vandal to the wets," strode forth literally to break up the saloon trade. Her crusade led her through a succession of smashed barrooms from her Kansas home through Wichita, Topeka, Des Moines, Chicago, St. Louis, Cincinnati, Atlantic City, Philadelphia, and New York. In New York, John L. Sullivan, former heavyweight champion of the world and now a bar-owner, had threatened to "throw her down a sewer." When she arrived at his tavern, he hid.

Nation was an inspiration to many, but also a figure of fun. Her semi-weekly newspaper, *The Smasher's Mail*, was subscribed to by wets for its unintentional hilarity. She ended up performing at county fairs and carnivals, delivering her anti-saloon harangue, and appearing in a play entitled *Hatchetation*, which featured a saloon-smashing scene.

The Midwest was the heartland of prohibitionism. As John Kobler points out in his book *Ardent Spirits*, "The entire temperance movement came to reflect a conflict of cultures — agrarian against industrial, the native-born Yankee against the immigrant micks, dagos, bohunks and krauts, Protestants against Catholics and Jews — and by exploiting the prejudices of the rural masses the dry fanatics won their biggest following."

The organization that was most successful in channeling that following, and that ultimately brought about Prohibition, was the Anti-Saloon League, set up in 1895. The WCTU espoused many other causes, but the Anti-Saloon League was single-minded. It chose its name to attack the most vulnerable part of the alcohol empire.

The National Prohibition Act was drafted by the Anti-Saloon

League's Wayne Bidwell Wheeler. A brilliant political manipulator, Wheeler, using funds provided by a number of churches, proved no less willing than the brewers or distillers to buy venal politicians. But the act took its more popular name from the Republican congressman who introduced it to the House, Andrew Joseph Volstead of Minnesota. Volstead was a cadaverous-looking man with a great hairbrush mustache and bushy eyebrows, very much the son of his Norwegian Lutheran parents. In fact, he did not hold extreme views on liquor. He once even uttered the heresy: "I don't know that there's any harm in one drink." Nevertheless, he believed "law regulates morality, law has regulated morality since the Ten Commandments." The Volstead Act was debated for three months before passing the House in July 1919. The Senate debated it, passed it, and returned it to the House, where it was finally adopted on October 10. President Woodrow Wilson, now a sick man, vetoed the act, but Congress overrode him on October 28, and the Volstead Act became law at 12:01 A.M. on January 17, 1920.

The "noble experiment" was a classic example of the law of unintended results. Prohibition not only led to a boom in criminal activity, helping to organize "organized crime," it also made criminals of huge numbers of otherwise law-abiding citizens and led to the deaths of tens of thousands of men, women, and children who drank spirits not intended for human consumption. Ironically, it also gave drinking more rather than less legitimacy, since it led to the equation of alcohol with personal freedom. Illegal speakeasies soon outnumbered the legal bars that had preceded them. The one-gallon still became a commonplace domestic utensil. And imports surged.

The most obvious beneficiaries were the Canadians, who shared a 4,000-mile unguarded border with the U.S. The Canadian government of W. L. Mackenzie King turned a blind eye to beer and liquor exports to the U.S., benefiting enormously from tax revenue. Two of the Canadian companies that came to dominate the global liquor industry in the twentieth century, Seagram and Hiram Walker/Gooderham & Worts, built their empires on sales to the U.S. during Prohibition. Indeed, there was not a major liquor producer in the world that did not either actively promote or tacitly encourage exports to the U.S.

Before Prohibition, in 1916, Bacardi had set up a bottling plant on West Broadway in Manhattan. When the Eighteenth Amendment appeared on the horizon, the company found itself in danger of being left holding 60,000 cases of rum. Enrique Schueg came up with an ingenious way of disposing of this stock. He sold 60,000 shares in the company, then wound the company up and distributed its assets — one case of rum per share — to grateful and thirsty shareholders.

But demand for Bacardi did not dry up. Orders poured into Santiago for delivery to places the rum would never reach, or places where it would rest only briefly before moving on. By the end of the 1920s, the largest importer of Bacardi, according to the alleged port of destination, was Shanghai. There was also a surge of orders from Bermuda, Nassau, and St. Pierre and Miquelon, the French islands in the gulf of the St. Lawrence River between Canada and the United States. From these shipment points, Bacardi became part of the cargo that sat on freighters outside U.S. international marine limits along "Rum Row," between New York City and Boston, waiting for one of the souped-up motorboats that darted out through sparse Coast Guard lines to ferry the liquor ashore.

Bacardi committed no crime in selling to bootleggers, who found a strong demand for their rum, which was generally thought to be cheaper than whiskey and better than gin. As with all the popular brands, however, the Bacardi name was often attached to inferior products. Moonshiners, criminally producing and selling liquor in the U.S., were not concerned about trademark laws. Bacardi was also reckoned to be easy to synthesize, as *Fortune* magazine pointed out, "for the simple reason that few U.S. citizens knew much about it." This brand piracy led to trademark problems after Prohibition.

The great promotional boost to Bacardi came from tourists who visited Cuba during Prohibition. After 1919, Havana became "the unofficial U.S. saloon," a hive of hotels, casinos, and brothels. Bars like Sloppy Joe's and La Floridita became famous, and Bacardi became among the best known of their forbidden fruits.

When Prohibition started, Bacardi had been in the U.S. market for close to fifty years but was not widely known. It was usually served with lemon or lime juice and sugar as the "Bacardi cocktail." Mixing rum with lime and sugar was not a Bacardi invention. Indeed, the concoction was attributed to the British Admiral Edward Vernon, after whom George Washington's home, Mount Vernon, was named. Vernon, whose nickname was "Old Grog," also gave his name to the mixture of rum and water served to British seamen. The British use of lime in their rum is thought to have been the origin of the slang term "limey."

The Bacardi cocktail was promoted as a sophisticated drink. The version served with shaved ice, the daiquiri, was reputedly named by an American mining engineer, Jennings Cox, after the mining area east of Santiago that had been the landing place for American troops in the Spanish-American War.

Many American tourists came into direct contact with Bacardi family members either in Havana or Santiago. In the latter half of the 1920s, these meetings took place in the grand surroundings of the magnificent new Edificio Bacardi, built as a monument to the brand in 1924. Situated on the Avenida Bélgica in Old Havana, just up from the Presidential Palace, the building was designed by Maxfield Parrish, who was much better known as an illustrator of fantasy subjects. His Bacardi building demonstrated a delightful combination of the modern skyscraper form with rich, almost whimsical decoration. When it was constructed, many people thought the Bacardi head office was being moved to Havana, but such a move was never considered by the staunchly *santiaguero* Bacardis. The business never took more than two floors of the building. The rest of the space was sublet, although never, because of rent controls, at a profit.

Covering almost a complete city block, the $1.4-million building was intended as a monument to quality. The ornate black-and-gold wrought-iron screens on the huge ground-floor windows all sported a great "B." The lowest story was clad in rich reddish-brown marble. The upper floors had decorated yellow brickwork. The top floor — and the central turret that rose above it — bore friezes of delicate brown and blue tiles, and glazed panels depicting cornucopia-bearing nymphs. At the pinnacle of the building was a glass sphere surmounted by a bat with spread wings.

The mezzanine floor had a cocktail bar, to which American tourists were invited. They would emerge from the building's imposing triple-doored entrance, hung on either side with hefty gilded lanterns, full of praise for the product and the people who made it. Many then toured the island. One essential stop was Santiago.

Tourists streaming beneath Santiago's El Morro, through the winding channel that opened into the harbor, gasped at the beauty of the city, spread translucent on the hill below its cathedral. Once docked, they found the same labyrinthine charm that had once entranced Leonard Wood. They also found that the city had resisted further Americanization. One visitor described it as "the worst-paved city in Cuba." Everybody remarked how noisy it was. Those staying at the Casa Granda or the Venus in the cathedral square were woken each morning before five by the reverberations of the great cathedral bell. Shouts of newsboys filled the air until the din of traffic and the horns of the buses took over.

For most American tourists, Santiago still reflected the glories of the Spanish-American War. San Juan Hill was a place of pilgrimage. The site where the *Merrimac* was sunk in the mouth of the harbor was pointed out from the heights of El Morro. Visitors were charmed by the city's quaint customs and beautiful women. On Sundays, the locals circled one another in the cathedral square, women going one way, men the other, in the old Spanish custom of the "flirtation walk." Everybody, from Santiago high society to black cane-cutters and maids, turned out in Sunday best. One visitor wrote, "This ceremony is utterly incomprehensible to the Anglo-Saxon but it is life itself to the Cuban . . . The whole thing makes a lustrous, iridescent, incredible pattern of human behavior."

Santiago was a magical city, and the Bacardis were its first citizens. Those who gathered in the bar of the Venus for the first drink of the day at around nine in the morning — a collection of locals plus many Americans, either miners or remnants of those who had stayed on after the Spanish-American War — all drank Bacardi. As a visiting writer noted: "First, second, third, fourth, fifth, sixth and other drinks in Santiago are the same, Bacardi and water, or water and Bacardi. To drink anything else stamps you as a newcomer indeed."

But the Bacardis were far more than a name attached to a drink. American tourists could also visit the magnificent new home of the Museo Municipal Emilio Bacardi Moreau, inaugurated on January 20, 1928. Down one side of the museum was a reconstruction of a typical Spanish colonial street; inside, as well as works of antiquity, were poignant reminders of Cuba's history, including pre-Colombian artifacts and grisly instruments of torture from Spanish times. The belongings of Cuba's great national heroes were preserved like relics of the saints: the urn containing the remains of Carlos Manuel Céspedes, José Martí's tailcoat, Máximo Gómez's spectacles. There was even the little iron bed on which Cuba's first president, Tomás Estrada Palma, had died.

American visitors returned home with golden memories of Bacardi cocktails or daiquiris drunk in La Floridita, or the Edificio Bacardi, or the Bacardi plant. These sun-drenched memories and glowing accounts increased the fashionableness of the drinks, which became particular favorites of women, who ordered them at Jack and Charlie's 21, or any of the myriad other speakeasies in New York. As a visiting writer noted: "Just as the returning Crusaders spread Eastern culture throughout Europe, so have the round-trip pilgrims to the nostalgic Caribbean brought back to America a renaissance of rum."

Beneath the Prohibition image of Cuba as one long fiesta, however, lay the endemic, often violent complications of Cuban politics, as incomprehensible to most Americans as the significance of a dusty tailcoat or a frail pair of glasses in the Bacardi museum. The elections of 1921 had been marked, once again, by fraud. This, combined with the sugar and banking crises, had led the Americans to intervene once more. When they departed, later in 1921, Alfredo Zayas was elected president. Zayas had been one of the politicians who had voted against the Platt Amendment in 1902, and he had been imprisoned for fraud during the early days of the republic. He spent his four-year rule enriching himself and his family — fourteen of whom he put on the government payroll — while the U.S. proconsul, Enoch Crowder, sat on the battleship *Minnesota* in Havana harbor sending Zayas memorandums on everything from electoral reform to the lottery. Zayas nodded and smiled, stuffed his pockets, and quietly stirred up the press to protest these latest examples of "U.S. imperialism."

Zayas was succeeded, in May 1925, by Gerardo Machado. A native of Las Villas province, Machado started out as a butcher (as a result of which he had only three fingers on his left hand) and cattle rustler. He moved into electricity supply and the sugar business, simultaneously becoming involved in politics. He was reckoned to be a smart businessman, and nothing worse than an amiable rogue when he ran for the presidency. "Chico, come and see me!" became his unofficial campaign slogan. He came to office trumpeting great reform programs, and important public works, such as the Central Highway, were indeed undertaken. But official corruption increased.

The U.S. role was, as usual, ambiguous. American investors in Cuba tended to support the government, and to be willingly taken in by Machado's public relations. In the U.S. there was support for Machado's "semi-dictatorial" stance. President Calvin Coolidge went to Havana and declared that Cuba's people were "independent, free, prosperous, peaceful, and enjoying the advantages of self-government . . . They have reached a position of stability of their government in the genuine expression of their public opinion at the ballot box." But in April 1928, Machado used a packed constitutional convention to extend his term for six years, and Cuban politics took a decidedly violent turn.

Pepín Bosch, who now held a prominent position at First National City Bank in Havana, became — like many of his well-heeled friends — deeply involved in the clandestine struggle against the dictator. He became the treasurer of a revolutionary group, which included ex-president Menocal, that plotted to oust Machado. A number of such groups, the most prominent and influential of which was the Directorio Estudiantil from the University of Havana, became active at this time.

By the end of 1930, after more bloodshed and the closing of the University of Havana, the U.S. had to acknowledge the seriousness of the Cuban situation. Cuba's economic problems had been exacerbated in the latter half of the 1920s by a further decline in the fortunes of sugar. Per-capita U.S. sugar consumption had peaked. In 1926, the Central Santa María in Camaguey had been the last sugar mill to be founded in Cuba, and the slow process of state intervention in the sugar industry began. The allocation of quotas by politicians was an open invitation to graft. In 1929, the year of the great Wall Street stock-market crash and the beginning of the Great Depression, the lobbying of U.S. domestic sugar producers led to the Hawley-Smoot Tariff of 2 cents a pound on imported sugar, against a background of falling international prices. Agreements with other world exporters to restrict output were ineffective. By the early 1930s, the price had hit 1 cent a pound. To add to these miseries, 1932 brought the poorest sugar harvest in Cuba since 1915.

Bacardi felt the consequences of these problems, both in the market and in government pressure. In January 1931, a National Economic Commission recommended new taxes on sales and exports of rum. The status of the Bacardi company — and its importance as an employer — were such that it could threaten to move its manufacturing facilities to Mexico if the tax proposals were not withdrawn. There was a good deal of bluff in the claim. Such was the family's might, however, that the secretary of the treasury personally assured the company that the proposed economic emergency bill would not affect the rum industry. Perhaps to give himself bargaining power in future, Bosch's father-in-law, Enrique Schueg, set about giving substance to his threat. This would be the first time political instability would prompt Bacardi's geographical diversification. It would not be the last.

Meanwhile, in 1931, the revolutionary group of which Bosch was the treasurer staged its attempted coup, landing a small force (with a large quantity of arms and ammunition) at the town of Gibara in north Oriente province. The attempt — in which Bosch did not take part personally — turned into a fiasco. The leader of the group of forty volunteers, Emilio Laurent, was a decent and determined man, but also naive. After a brief scuffle with the rural guards at the pier, during which a guard was killed, the expeditionaries took the police station, the telephone exchange, and the town hall. Then they distributed arms to the townspeople. Laurent called the military commander of Holguín, south of Gibara, and asked for his surrender. The commander agreed and immediately telephoned to warn Havana. Machado dispatched an elite military force by rail and a cruiser to blockade the harbor.

The revolutionaries set off for Holguín by train, only to be intercepted and routed by Machado's forces. Though Laurent and others escaped, many followers, along with innocent people from Gibara, were tortured and shot. During the battle, Gibara carried the dubious distinction of becoming the first town in the Americas to be bombed by air. Meanwhile, the backers of the coup began to feel the heat — among them, Pepín Bosch.

Moving the whole Bacardi operation to Mexico would have been virtually impossible. Enrique Schueg and his executives had doubts about Mexican raw materials and about the rum-producing and aging conditions. Besides, tequila was Mexico's national drink. The domestic market for rum, which Mexicans regarded as medicinal, was severely restricted. Nor was Mexico a model of political stability. Indeed, in some ways the country's past made Cuba's revolutionary history look mild. Mexico had been in a state of constant revolution for more than a century.

One key to setting up a Mexican operation was a young Frenchman, Miguel Dorcasbarro, who had an interest in a sugar mill at Vera Cruz. Dorcasbarro had befriended Enrique's son Arturo Schueg Bacardi; when Arturo died during the First World War, it was Dorcasbarro who returned his possessions to Cuba. When Enrique considered a Mexican operation, he thought of Dorcasbarro as a partner. To set up the Mexican company, in April 1931, Enrique sent José Bacardi Fernández, one of the three sons of the founder's late son José.

José Bacardi Fernández and a team of Bacardi blenders and bottlers set up shop in the high mountain bowl of Mexico City, which had been called by Cortés — before he destroyed it — "the most beautiful city in the world." When the Bacardi team arrived, it was already one of the most populous places on earth, with more than a million inhabitants.

José Bacardi Fernández appears on the Bacardi family tree as a bachelor. In fact he had a brief and tragic marriage to a beautiful *santiaguera* lesbian named Marta Durán. He would have little better luck in business in Mexico. The company foundered from the first, and on May 9, 1933, after a six-day bout of pneumonia, José Bacardi Fernández died, leaving behind another woman who claimed to be his wife. She would live many more years as the self-described "Bacardi widow." In business terms, Mexico was an abject failure. Enrique Schueg decided to close down the operation. Since Cuba was still uncomfortably hot for the politically active Pepín Bosch, Enrique asked his son-in-law to go to Mexico City and wind things up.

When Bosch looked at the Mexican operation, he realized it had possibilities. Instead of liquidating it, he decided to attempt to turn it around. In Cuba, Bacardi was sold in wicker-covered gallon jugs. Bosch had the molds of the jugs sent to Mexico, set up a small manufacturing plant, and hired natives to make wicker covers. Then he promoted the notion that, if you bought a jug of Bacardi and several cases of Coca-Cola, you had a ready-made party. The idea was a marketing triumph. Bosch developed Bacardi's Mexican advertising, stepped up production, and broadened distribution. Sales in 1934 of 178,225 Mexican pesos were almost twice those of the previous year. In twelve months, Bacardi Mexico's debts had been paid off. Six months later, Bosch paid the family its first Mexican dividend. He returned to Santiago in December 1934 with a great success behind him. Suddenly, Enriqueta's husband was a potential force in the company.

The Bacardi company was still in bad shape, but its major political problem had disappeared. *Fortune* magazine had noted in 1933, "For a few years after sugar ruined everybody else in Cuba, the Bacardis and President Gerardo Machado were the only prosperous citizens left. Now Señor Machado is dodging assassins and President Schueg of Bacardi is looking for an end to U.S. prohibition to restore the prosperity of his company, which tariffs, taxes, and overexpansion have touched at last."

By the late summer of 1933, the public was in almost open revolt against Machado. The U.S. withdrew its support and sought a diplomatic initiative to secure his abdication. But when the Cuban army turned on Machado, he had no choice but to flee. Early on the morning of August 13, the dictator boarded a plane for Nassau, with five revolvers, seven bags of gold, and five friends in pajamas. That day, the palace was looted. A razorback hog, fattened on better rations than most of the populace, was hauled across Zayas Park to the foot of ex-president Zayas's statue, where its throat was unceremoniously but symbolically slit. Bloody recrimination fell on Machado's supporters. Into the power vacuum came a group of non-commissioned army officers. Their leader was a sergeant stenographer named Fulgencio Batista.

Born in Oriente, Batista had Indian as well as black blood. He had left home at fourteen to work on sugar plantations, then drifted from job to job, helped by his charm and looks (he was nicknamed El Mulato Lindo, the good-looking mulatto). He had joined the army in 1921 and had used the opportunity to study law and learn shorthand and typing. By the time of Machado's fall, he was known for his quick mind and broad interests.

His seizure of power in the confusion after Machado's departure was swift and skillful. Batista did not become president himself, but by January 1935 he was acknowledged as the only source of authority and security in the country. He would remain the most important figure in Cuban politics for a quarter-century until he, like Machado, would steal away with his spoils.

Cuba's economic prospects, meanwhile, began to look up. A 1934 reciprocal trade agreement, guaranteeing that the U.S. would take the Cuban sugar crop at generous prices in return for unrestricted access to the Cuban market, was a boon. In May 1934 the Platt Amendment was revoked, with the exception of the maintenance of a U.S. naval base at Guantanamo. But repeal of the Platt Amendment did nothing to dilute the entrenched, bitter conviction that the Americans had stunted Cuba's political development. The amendment was now being withdrawn — in the eyes of Cuba's vehement critics of the U.S. — only because the Cuban economy was under de facto American control anyway.

The U.S., meanwhile, preoccupied with the Depression, relegated Cuba to an even more blurred spot in its peripheral vision.

Today, in a plot in Miami's Woodlawn Cemetery, just west of Little Havana, stands a life-size marble figure of Emilio Bacardi Moreau's son, Emilito Bacardi Lay, bearded and mustached, with his back to

Calle Ocho, gazing out over the well-tended grounds where other Bacardis and several Cuban presidents are buried. Dressed in a simple uniform with a colonel's two pips on the shoulders, wearing a hat with a swept-back brim, Emilito carries a marble pistol on his right hip and a marble machete on his left. Beside a vase, in which there are always fresh-cut flowers, is a memorial placed there by his widow, Zoila Luyando de Bacardi. On one side of the slab, after brief details of his mortal statistics, are the Spanish words "He always served his country with valor and dignity." On the other is a brief account of his revolutionary record, including the fact that he served as adjutant to "the Bronze Titan," Antonio Maceo, and that he was wounded three times in wartime actions.

Emilito Bacardi lived to a ripe old age but never worked at Bacardi; indeed, he never really worked at all. Once you had tasted the hardships and joys of revolution, it was perhaps difficult to contemplate such a mundane pastime as selling rum.

Conventional wisdom about family business has it that the third generation is where things fall apart. For the Bacardi family, the enervating effects of wealth were exacerbated not only, as in Emilito's case, by simple disinclination to be involved in the business, but also by a spate of personal tragedies. Each of the four branches — those of Emilio, José, Facundo, and Enrique Schueg — lost at least one son.

Of Emilio's other three sons, Daniel Bacardi Lay died in childhood. Of the twins, José had died of influenza during the war, and Facundo — who had risen to be industrial sub-director in the company by the time of his father's death — had died in 1926 of pneumonia.

Of José Bacardi Moreau's three sons, one, José Bacardi Fernández, had died in Mexico of pneumonia. The blonde, stocky, and popular Antón was happy to fill the role of amiable playboy, while the more serious Joaquín would join the business, becoming a master brewer and dedicating himself to the beer operation that Enrique had begun in the 1920s.

The first son of Amalia and Enrique Schueg, Arturo, had died in Europe in 1917 on his way to fight. Both remaining sons, Jorge and Víctor Schueg Bacardi, would be involved in the business. Although Víctor would play an important part in family counsels for many years, his life was marred by alcoholism.

As for Facundo Bacardi Moreau's two sons, the elder, Facundo Bacardi Gaillard, "the third Facundo," died in bizarre circumstances. A popular and charismatic figure, he had joined Bacardi after being educated in the U.S. and had rapidly risen to vice-president. Like most Bacardis, he enjoyed both the social and the sporting life that his wealth brought him. He belonged to all the best clubs in Santiago and Havana and had several boats, including a magnificent yacht, which he used for fishing, always a Bacardi passion. Described in his *Havana Post* obituary as "one of the most popular men in Cuba" and "well known in the United States," he was the source of one of the relished family stories about Prohibition.

Once, visiting New York, he was taken out to dinner by friends, one of whom said he'd take him to a place that served Bacardi. When Facundo tasted the hooch, he said it wasn't the real stuff. Another friend said, "Well, I'll take you to the swellest place in New York. I'm a member there and I *know* they've got the real stuff." So they went to the other high-class speakeasy, a distinguished-looking club with deep pile carpets, a mahogany bar, and a subdued atmosphere. The bartender poured three drinks from a bottle bearing a Bacardi Carta de Oro label. Facundo tasted it and again said it was a fake. The bartender, insulted, called the manager, who was furious. "Let me tell you," he said, "I've been keeping bars for thirty years and know the real stuff. That's genuine Bacardi — I've been selling it for twenty years — "

"I'm sorry," Facundo said quietly, "but I've been making it for longer than that."

Facundo became well known to American tourists who visited Santiago. He'd meet the ships in the harbor and take the passengers up the hill to the distillery where he'd "fill them full of rum." He'd explain that cocktails should be made from the pale Carta Blanca rum, and that golden Carta de Oro was for drinking straight.

But the popular Facundo came to a sticky end. According to an article in *Fortune*, "One day Señor Bacardi accidentally shot himself with a policeman's revolver." This report makes the incident sound like a mild prank gone wrong. In fact, the prank went very wrong. According to press reports, Facundo was gravely wounded in Santiago's Café Rialto "by the accidental discharge of a revolver belonging to José León, a policeman . . . Señor Bacardi jestingly removed the policeman's revolver from the holster and in replacing it the weapon was discharged, the bullet entering the abdomen and lodging in the spinal column." A later report declared he had been "accidentally wounded . . . while joking with a local policeman over a revolver."

A week after the shooting, having contracted double pneumonia, the founder's grandson and namesake died at age forty. At his bedside were his mother, Ernestina, his brother, Luis J., and his two sisters, María and Laura.

The branch had lost not merely a loved one but a candidate to head the company. Luis J. now took over that aspiration. A remote and somewhat eccentric man, with few interests or friends, Luis J. Bacardi Gaillard had a Howard Hughes-like fear of infection, which caused him to rush off and wash his hands with alcohol if he was ever forced to shake hands with anyone. Although he was vice-president of the Cuban company from 1933 to 1936, and held various positions in other subsidiaries, he never worked full-time. But he and his sisters controlled 30 percent of the company, which made him a powerful force in company affairs.

Enrique Schueg's power was, for the moment, unquestioned, but Luis J. saw himself as the successor. Perhaps that day would come sooner rather than later, for Enrique was now in his early seventies. Throughout the 1930s, Enrique would lean increasingly heavily on a non-family member, José Espín, his executive assistant. (Espín's ultimate claim to fame in Cuban history was that his daughter, Vilma, would marry Raúl Castro — Fidel's brother and second-in-command — and become the most important woman in the Communist regime.) Luis J. and Espín became close, but their relationship with Pepín Bosch, their rival for power, was never good.

After the fall of Machado and the rise of Batista, the immediate business challenge facing the company was how best to take advantage of the post-Prohibition market. That challenge was given by Enrique to his son-in-law. Henceforth Bosch, more than anyone else, would be responsible for building the Bacardi empire. His relationship with the entire family was often strained. He never tired of reminding family members — primarily through his *lack* of consultation — that family was family and business was business. In effect, he was telling them that he was prepared to make them rich, but could do so only if they stayed out of the way.

CHAPTER FIVE

The Barons of Booze

*"This is so much bullshit. If I only
told the truth, I'd sell
ten million copies."*

SAM BRONFMAN, ON BEING SHOWN THE HISTORICAL ADDENDUM TO
SEAGRAM'S 1970 ANNUAL REPORT

Washington. December 5, 1933

At the end of Prohibition, the U.S. liquor market was chaotic. The twenty-nine newly wet states (nineteen states had decided to stay dry) all had different liquor laws. To prevent distillers from controlling their own outlets, Franklin D. Roosevelt's administration ordered that the industry be structured on a three-tier system. Liquor producers and importers, Washington ruled, had to sell to wholesalers, who then sold to the trade. Many of those who had been involved in bootlegging went straight. Liquor became the only business in the U.S. in which one of the licensing requirements was — and still is — the provision of a set of fingerprints.

From the chaos emerged a handful of men and companies that would dominate the U.S. market and thus, statistically, the liquor world, for the next fifty years. These enterprises — the American companies Schenley Distillers Corp. and National Distillers Products Corp.; the Canadian liquor giants Seagram and Hiram Walker/Gooderham & Worts; and the granddaddy of them all, the Edinburgh-based Distillers Co. Ltd. (DCL) — gained a running start because they had that most precious of commodities: aged whiskey.

The pre-Prohibition American liquor industry had been first and foremost a bourbon and rye whiskey industry. In 1913, the American public had consumed 135 million gallons of native whiskey, ten times more than all other spirits combined. Whiskey stocks had soon dried up, and since quality whiskey was expensive and difficult to make, domestic bootleg producers began supplying the market with substitutes, most notably bathtub gin. Passable gin could be made and sold more cheaply than the worst whiskey. A generation of younger drinkers had been weaned on gin, and a whole new category of drinkers — women — preferred it to whiskey. The liquor companies wondered whether gin might have affected the tastebuds of America permanently. But they had no doubt that whiskey would roar back as America's most popular drink.

Schenley was the brainchild of Lewis Rosenstiel, an obsessive, hair-trigger entrepreneur who frequently called senior employees in the middle of the night with ideas that couldn't wait for dawn. Rosenstiel had been in whiskey before Prohibition and had continued legally during the dry years through medicinal sales, warehousing and whiskey "receipts," that is, claims to warehoused stock. Medicinal sales were one of the great loopholes of the Volstead Act, and doctors unsympathetic to the Eighteenth Amendment prescribed whiskey freely. Rosenstiel is also reported to have engaged in the less legal activity of jobbing booze out of St. Pierre and Bermuda. Schenley was described as "the craziest, the damnedest, the quickest, the shrewdest outfit in American whiskey."

The man with whom Rosenstiel would joust all his life for the dominant position in the U.S. industry was Seagram's Sam Bronfman. A brilliant marketer obsessed with quality, "Mr. Sam" was dubbed by *Fortune* "one of the last great tycoons, a vestigial reminder of the gone days when a Vanderbilt or Rockefeller could actually start from scratch and create a family fortune of more than a hundred million dollars."

Bronfman had been brought up on the Canadian prairies, where his immigrant father had worked his way from peddler to hotel-owner. The transition from the hotel to the liquor business was a natural one. The Bronfmans started in the interprovincial mail-order booze trade, exploiting a loophole in Canadian dry laws. Sam Bronfman persuaded the scotch giant DCL to become a partner in his operation, which was built around a distillery he had bought in Kentucky and had transported by river to Montreal. In 1928 he merged his operation with a venerable distilling operation based in Waterloo, Ontario: Joseph E. Seagram & Sons Limited. The new firm was called Distillers Corp.-Seagrams Ltd.

Bronfman and his family made a fortune during Prohibition by supplying U.S. bootleggers. Some loaded their Studebaker "Whiskey Sixes" at Bronfman prairie "boozoriums," fortress-warehouses on the U.S. border in North Dakota and Montana. Some came and went in small boats across the Great Lakes or border rivers. Some brought seagoing ships to Bronfman warehouses on the Atlantic seaboard at Halifax, or on the islands of St. Pierre and Miquelon.

As long as liquor bought in Canada for export bore a B-13 customs document, with a non-U.S. destination stamped on it, that was fine with Canadian authorities. Eliot Ness, of "Untouchables" fame, called

B-13s "the Canadian print job." Ottawa even provided tax rebates on exports. In 1936, without admitting liability, Bronfman settled for $1.5 million claims by the U.S. Treasury for duties on liquor allegedly shipped to the U.S. during Prohibition.

Bronfman — "I don't get ulcers, I give them" — was as mercurial as Rosenstiel. Renowned for his irascibility, he was inclined to throw things at people who annoyed him. He was described by *Fortune* as having "a soft voice, an almost natural suavity and casualness, impeccable manners, and a range that extends, when required, to indelicate language." In short, old Mr. Sam cussed like a trooper.

Sam Bronfman's great Canadian rival was Harry Hatch. Hatch was another tough character who had started out in the saloon and liquor-store business and then parlayed the clandestine skills of liquor exporting to the U.S. into a legitimate business empire. He gained control of the Toronto-based distiller Gooderham & Worts in 1923, and three years later put it together with the larger Hiram Walker, of Walkerville, Ontario, to form Hiram Walker/Gooderham & Worts.

Hiram Walker produced Canadian Club whiskey, one of the world's first great brands. The company's eponymous founder, an American entrepreneur and philanthropist, had moved his fledgling distilling operation across the river from Detroit partly because of threats from a powerful temperance movement in Michigan. He created Walkerville — then east of, eventually part of, Windsor — as a model community, and constructed a magnificent Renaissance villa headquarters on the Detroit River. In the 1920s, the refinement of the building stood in marked contrast to the skulduggery surrounding its business.

The "Windsor-Detroit Funnel" became one of the major transshipment points for booze imports into the U.S. Much of the highest-quality hooch was produced by Hiram Walker. Walker executives could sit in their riverside offices and watch boats large and small, with export papers for Cuba or some other unlikely destination, travel the short distance across the Detroit River. In winter, booze-laden jalopies crawled across the ice like ants. Overhead, Al Capone's fleet of converted bombers made their frequent runs. A great deal of the booze was shipped across the Great Lakes in a fleet of small boats that became known as "Hatch's navy." Those who piloted these boats were regarded less as criminals than as popular heroes. Like Bronfman, Harry Hatch demonstrated his real business genius after Prohibition, building the world's largest distillery, at Peoria, Illinois.

Building an image: Don Facundo Bacardi y Maso. Or is it? Pepín Bosch had this portrait manufactured many decades after the founder's demise. (BACARDI IMPORTS)

Bat's cradle: The little tin-roofed distillery on the Calle Matadero, birthplace of the Bacardi empire, with the coconut tree planted by the founder's son Facundo. (BACARDI & COMPANY LIMITED)

A revolutionary for all seasons: José Martí was the literary inspiration for Emilio Bacardi and virtually every subsequent Cuban activist. (UPI/Bettmann Newsphotos)

Can do: Leonard Wood, who appointed Emilio Bacardi mayor of Santiago, was the spearhead of the U.S. "adventure in altruism" in Cuba. History wouldn't see it that way. (UPI/Bettmann Newsphotos)

Fruits of success: The Villa Elvira, Don Emilio's country house at Cuabitas. For fifty years, Bacardi children would play under the mangoes in its huge grounds. (Roberto del Rosal)

Branching out: Don Emilio with his grandchildren outside the Villa Elvira shortly before his death in 1922. Descendants of his two marriages would take up two-thirds of the Bacardi family tree. (BACARDI IMPORTS)

One new plant, one old: The first rebuilding of the factory on the Calle Matadero. The renovations were made around the famous coconut palm, which had now become almost one of the family. (BACARDI & COMPANY LIMITED)

Don Enrique's "pretty little fiancée": The Hatuey beer plant in the San Pedrito district of Santiago. Hatuey would become the most profitable part of the Bacardi empire in Cuba. (BACARDI IMPORTS)

Triumvirate: The founder's sons Emilio, left, and Facundo, and their brother-in-law, Enrique Schueg, below. Emilio was the figure-head; Facundo was the manufacturer; Enrique opened new markets. (BACARDI & COMPANY LIMITED)

The Museo Municipal Emilio Bacardi Moreau was part of Emilio's legacy to Santiago, a constant reminder of the status of the city's first family. It still contains the Egyptian mummy Emilio had to import as "cured meat." (AUTHOR'S PHOTOGRAPH)

The Edificio Bacardi in Old Havana, designed by Maxfield Parrish, was another symbol of the family's status. American tourists were brought here for free cocktails during Prohibition. (AUTHOR'S PHOTOGRAPH)

Sam Bronfman of Seagram: Having sold to bootleggers from prairie "boozoriums," this Canadian went on to become the "whiskey king of America." He was greatly admired by Pepín Bosch. (MICHAEL MCCORMICK)

Lewis Rosenstiel of Schenley: Rosenstiel distributed Bacardi in the U.S. after Repeal. He wasn't happy when Pepín Bosch took over U.S. distribution via Bacardi Imports in 1944. (AP/WIDE WORLD PHOTOS)

Harry Hatch of Hiram Walker: After Repeal, he built the world's largest distillery at Peoria, Illinois. His company would form close links with Bacardi; for a majority of the Bacardis, too close. (HIRAM WALKER/ALLIED VINTNERS)

Seton Porter of National Distillers: Yale class of '05. Not quite as rough and tough as his colleagues, but he held half the U.S. domestic whiskey stocks when Repeal came. (UPI/BETTMANN NEWSPHOTOS)

Pepín Bosch, who was married to Enrique Schueg's daughter, Enriqueta, first made a name for himself with Bacardi by turning around the floundering Mexican operation. He never looked back. (BACARDI CORPORATION)

Seat of power: The Bacardi company's administrative offices on Santiago's Calle Aguilera Baja. When Pepín Bosch became head of Bacardi, he astonished everyone by putting his desk in the middle of the ground floor. (BACARDI & COMPANY LIMITED)

Dwarfing El Coco: By the end of the Second World War, the Bacardi plant on the Calle Matadero had been rebuilt yet again, dominating the local neighborhood. (LEÓN ARGAMASILLA BACARDI)

Flag waving: The Modelo brewery, outside Havana, was a spectacular success. Beer provided most of the funds for Bacardi's overseas expansion in the 1950s.

Dictator: Fulgencio Batista seized power in 1952, claiming if he didn't, someone else would. His coup was welcomed by many. But the Bacardis had had a long-running feud with the former army sergeant. (AP/WIDE WORLD PHOTOS)

Backing the wrong horse: Daniel Bacardi Rosell, here at the Santiago office in 1957, was, like most of the family, a stout supporter of Fidel Castro. Three years later, Castro would seize the Bacardi business in the name of the revolution. (DANIEL BACARDI)

To Rosenstiel, Bronfman, and Hatch, image was very important, both to market their products and to separate themselves from the skulduggery of Prohibition. This concern with image was reflected in their head offices. Hatch had acquired his magnificent headquarters for Hiram Walker on the Detroit River, replete with polished brass, oak paneling, marble fireplaces, and delicately carved and sculpted classical references. Not to be outdone, in 1928, Sam Bronfman had built Seagram a miniature feudal castle in Montreal, complete with portcullis. Rosenstiel bought the stately old New York Club, across from the Public Library, just off Fifth Avenue in Manhattan, with its brass chandeliers, parquet floors, and travertine fireplaces, and added gilt ceilings and Georgian furniture.

The fourth of the four major North American liquor barons was perhaps less concerned with the trappings of class. He already had them. Seton Porter, the man behind the post-Prohibition success of National Distillers, was a Yale graduate, class of '05. Blond, dapper, and a smooth hand on the tennis court, he had been sent in by his brother's firm of engineering consultants, Seton & Porter, to examine the financial wreckage of U.S. Food Products Corp. The company had previously been the Distilling Co. of America, which, under the name of the Whiskey Trust, had controlled much of the Kentucky whiskey-manufacturing business at the turn of the century. When Porter took control in 1924, the company had subsidiaries that made alcohol, yeast, and maraschino cherries; it also held a fair share of the medical-prescription whiskey business. Most important, its warehouses held around 9 million gallons of whiskey (almost all of it belonging to others via warehouse receipts). Porter reorganized and sold subsidiaries, paid off debts, and, most important, bought back the whiskey. He also started distilling when liquor manufacture was permitted once more in 1929. By the time Repeal came along, he controlled almost half the American domestic whiskey stock.

The final key element in the post-Prohibition market was the looming presence of the greatest whiskey-maker of them all, Distillers Co. Ltd., which controlled barley-based scotch whiskey (as opposed to the North American rye whiskey and corn-based bourbon varieties). DCL produced 70 percent of all the whiskey made in the British Isles. The company had been formed in 1877 by the consolidation of six Scottish distilleries. Between 1919 and 1925 it had been greatly expanded by the addition of John Haig & Co. Ltd., Sir Robert Burnett & Co. Ltd., Buchanan-Dewar, Ltd., and John Walker & Sons Ltd.

Capitalized at over $60 million, Distillers was the largest liquor producer in the world and, according to *Fortune* magazine, "one of the stoutest trusts in commercial history." All Britain's most famous whiskies (Dewar, Johnnie Walker, White Horse, Black & White, John Haig) and its most historic gins (Gordon, Burnett) fell under its aegis.

DCL's venerable board members — many of whom shared their names with their famous brands — were rarely seen in public without top hat and tails; they seemed to divide their time between the whiskey trade and the race course. Dewar's chairman, and a prominent DCL board member, Lord Woolavington, for example, had owned two winners of the Epsom Derby.

Partnership was crucial to the liquor industry. Companies bought whiskey stocks from each other and formed corporate alliances. In the wake of Prohibition, DCL formed a partnership with Seton Porter's National Distillers to build the world's largest gin distillery, in New Jersey. DCL was already a partner with Sam Bronfman's Montreal-based operation. However, the Scotsmen balked upon hearing that Sam Bronfman was planning to go into partnership with Lewis Rosenstiel after Prohibition. Rosenstiel was considered a man prepared to cut corporate corners — and throats — to achieve his business aims. William Henry Ross, DCL's octogenarian chairman, who had risen from a Scottish farm and a junior clerkship to preside over the most exalted board in the liquor world, declared, "I think you should know that we will not, under any circumstances, be associated with Mr. Rosenstiel." Bronfman quietly bought out the DCL interest in his own company but abandoned his courtship of Rosenstiel when he discovered that Schenley was bottling its Golden Wedding brand "hot" — straight from the still, without aging.

Harry Hatch too had formed links with DCL, with whose leaders he shared a love of horse racing. But like his North American colleagues, Hatch had some problems with the haughty lords of scotch. When DCL threatened in the late 1930s to cut off supplies of the grain whiskey that Hiram Walker used in the production of its Ballantine's brand, Hatch built a plant at Dumbarton to manufacture his own scotch.

After Repeal, U.S. whiskey demand was expected to soar to around 200 million gallons a year. Total U.S. stocks — a small amount from before Prohibition, but mainly distilled since 1929 — stood at only

20 million gallons. Canada, primarily Hiram Walker and Seagram, held 48 million gallons, while the British Isles held a treasure chest of some 170 million gallons, more than 100 million of which sat mellowing in the warehouses of DCL.

Of the U.S. stocks, around 10 million gallons were held by National Distillers, 5 million gallons by Schenley, and the rest by a variety of smaller companies. U.S. stocks were far more valuable than overseas stocks, primarily because of a $5-a-gallon import duty imposed by the U.S. government. After Repeal, the U.S. whiskey market quickly became a strategic battlefield: how best to use existing stocks while cranking up production and plotting future strategy.

Existing stocks could be stretched by blending them with neutral grain spirits (all scotch whiskeys are blended, but from different straight whiskies). Americans initially feared that the U.S. version of blending really meant cutting — that is, adulterating — the product, but Sam Bronfman did a brilliant job of selling blends, and Seagram's Five Crown and Seven Crown brands leapt to the top of the market in the mid-1930s.

Bronfman, Rosenstiel, Hatch, and Porter also set about securing agencies for liquor imports. Indeed, one reason DCL was courted so assiduously by the North Americans was that they hoped to gain the agency rights to its famous brands.

In the U.S., the Kennedy family fortune was considerably enhanced by Joseph Kennedy's success in gaining agency rights to some of the greatest British brands. Joseph Kennedy's father, P.J. Kennedy, a Boston Irish immigrant, had made his fortune as a saloon-keeper and liquor importer before going into politics. The wealth of Joseph's wife's family, the Fitzgeralds, had also come from the Boston saloon trade. During Prohibition, Joe Kennedy — who made a fortune in stock manipulation, most of it from shorting the market ahead of the crash of 1929 — was the subject of many rumors linking him to bootlegging. He certainly had access to huge supplies during the 1920s.

With Repeal at hand, Joseph Kennedy saw huge profits in distributorships. In September 1933, he sailed to England to negotiate for some of DCL's greatest brands. Shrewdly, he took with him Franklin Roosevelt's son, Jimmy, whom he knew would be regarded in London as a kind of American Prince of Wales. After two months of negotiations, he returned with the agency rights for Haig & Haig and Dewar. He obtained two huge "medicinal" permits from Washington, which he used to stockpile his warehouses, ready for December 5, the day

Prohibition ended. The import company he formed, Somerset Company, became one of the largest agencies in the U.S. and produced income of around $1 million annually. The Bacardis and the Kennedys never did any liquor business, but their political paths were destined to cross after John F. Kennedy became president of the United States three decades later.

After Prohibition, imports were the most brand-conscious, and profitable, part of the U.S. liquor market. Because Bacardi had become well known during Prohibition, through bootlegging and through American visitors to Cuba, it was among the most sought after of the imports, perhaps *the* most sought after apart from scotch.

Not long after Repeal, Enrique Schueg had appointed a son-in-law of the late Emilio to open an office in New York City. William Julius Dorion, the nephew of a former president of Guatemala, had married Adelaida Bacardi Cape, who, as a child, had had her father Emilio's incriminating papers secreted in her clothing during the final war for Cuban independence. Dorion had given his occupation as "chemist" and his address as 511 Park Avenue, New York. Following their nuptials at the Ansonia Hotel, which was particularly favored by the Santiago community (the Duany family occupied almost a whole floor), the young couple had sailed off for an extended honeymoon in Europe.

Dorion had established a suite of offices in the Chrysler Building, the gleaming art deco fantasy on Lexington Avenue, and courteously received streams of supplicants, offering them Bacardi cocktails and committing to nothing. He was called, by a journalist of the day, "perhaps the world's happiest sales manager. His job seems to be the tactful refusal of orders." When Pepín Bosch arrived in New York, it was to take over from Dorion (who remained involved in Bacardi's North American operations).

Rather than taking quick advantage of the enormous volume of orders, Bosch decided to link up with one of the industry giants to build the market for Bacardi in a more orderly manner. The company he chose was Rosenstiel's Schenley, which, as well as having some of the most popular whiskey brands such as Old Quaker, Cream of Kentucky, Golden Wedding, and Wilken Family, had already acquired a group of prestigious imports in its portfolio, including Noilly Prat, B&G wines, and Dubonnet.

Bosch did not deal directly with the abrasive Rosenstiel; instead he saw Schenley's president, Harold Jacobi, who was considerably more *simpático* than Schenley's major shareholder. During a negotiating session that lasted from ten one morning until two the next morning, Bosch and Jacobi hammered out a deal whereby Schenley would take Bacardi, via Schenley's wholesalers, into every corner liquor store and bar in the U.S.

Bosch had a commission arrangement with Bacardi: he received 20 cents a case for rum sold. He went about his promotional work, cooperating closely with Schenley, with gusto. He traveled the country, visiting accounts, dreaming up ways to make them take and sell more Bacardi. He designed promotional displays. He oversaw advertising in scores of newspapers and magazines. He concocted a portable bar so that his marketing men could teach bar-owners how to make Bacardi and other cocktails. He also became prominent in the broader business arena. Within months of arriving in New York, he was elected president of the Cuban Chamber of Commerce in the United States.

Bacardi started holding promotional cocktail parties for celebrities every afternoon — as it did at the Edificio Bacardi in Havana. These took place at Schenley's bar on the first floor at the old New York Club, where Bacardi had arranged for Jack Doyle, the former bartender of Sloppy Joe's in Havana, to be installed. Within its walls of Italian fumed oak, with murals by the biting satirist William Gropper behind him and a circular blocked-leather bar around him, Doyle dispensed Bacardi cocktails by the thousands, explaining that the secret of the iced version was to shake the flaked ice until it looked like sherbet.

In 1938, the Bacardi office was moved to the thirty-fifth floor of the Empire State Building, where a new bar was also installed. Since hefty original murals were the fashion, Bacardi hired a Cuban artist named Gattorno to execute a bucolic scene. In the middle of the mural was a goat. As a promotional gimmick, the Bacardi staff told a reporter from the New York *World Telegram* that a real goat had been taken to the thirty-fifth floor as a model and had escaped, causing great consternation before its recapture. The story — a minor fabrication by the standards of contemporary journalism — duly appeared but had a bizarre aftermath.

Al Smith, the popular governor of New York and the president of the company that owned the Empire State Building, saw his own promotional opportunity. He called the Bacardi Bar and said he'd like to meet the goat. Bacardi employees set off on a frantic search of farms around New York for a goat that looked like the one in Gattorno's picture. Thus life followed art, and myth gave birth to history. The real goat even escaped briefly.

Post-Prohibition demand for liquor proved to be much lower than expected. The projected whiskey market of 200 million gallons proved wildly optimistic, as did import projections. The industry's expectations had ignored the impact of the crash of 1929 and the subsequent depression. Nevertheless, rum did better than most categories. In the first two full years after Repeal, 1934 and 1935, Bacardi shipped 214,000 cases to the United States, but Schenley sold only 174,000 of them, leaving a fat and expensive inventory of 40,000 cases. Bacardi reduced its shipments over the next two years and by the end of 1937 the inventory was down to a more normal 8,000 cases. Finally, annual sales of Bacardi in the U.S. had started to rise.

As well as fighting to gain market share in the 1930s, Bacardi also became involved in legal struggles over its most valuable asset: its name. The Bacardi name had been much abused during Prohibition. The first efforts to protect the trademark after Repeal involved simple, often crude attempts to steal the magic word. In 1934, for example, the American Bacardi Rum Corporation appeared, its founders having installed a former cab driver named Pedro Ambrosio Bacardi as president.

The best known — or at least best publicized — of the disputes was fought over the Bacardi cocktail. A case was brought against a hotel and a restaurant chain that had been using rums other than Bacardi in their Bacardi cocktails. Bacardi went to court to establish its contention that a Bacardi cocktail could be made only with Bacardi. So important was the case that Enrique Schueg came north — his last trip outside Cuba — to testify. Enrique's son Víctor Schueg Bacardi also appeared, as did Luis J. Bacardi and Bartolo Estrada, an old friend and golf partner of Pepín Bosch who went on to head Bacardi's U.S. operation.

The case was long and often hilarious. Sacred texts, such as *Seventeen Hundred Cocktails by the Man Behind the Bar*, were consulted. A mathematics professor was called, and a former Cuban liquor inspector, both of whom added nothing but confusion. When Enrique Schueg took the witness stand, he was asked, "Well, how is this Bacardi rum of yours made?" "Oh," he replied, shocked, "that is my secret."

Bacardi called forth squadrons of bartenders to establish how they made Bacardi cocktails. Men who had served long years behind the exclusive bars of Paris, New York, Palm Beach, Monte Carlo, and Havana were asked to impart the secrets of their trade. These world-wise purveyors of the hard stuff all solemnly affirmed that no self-respecting barman would serve anything else in a Bacardi cocktail. The court's decision: a Bacardi cocktail is not a Bacardi cocktail unless made with Bacardi rum.

The company's New York lawyer in the case was a gifted young man named Stewart Maurice. Maurice went on to fight numerous other trademark infringements in the years after Prohibition. He thwarted the Boston-based racket that filled old Bacardi bottles with bad rum. He stopped the sale of rebottled Bacardi rum under the name Ron Samba, because the label said the rum had been made by Bacardi. He moved against names that were too close, like Delcardi and Bicardi, as well as attempts to appropriate the name for unrelated products, such as Bacardi Evening Slippers. Maurice would remain the company's trusted counsel for decades, and would eventually become corporate secretary of Bacardi Imports, Inc.

Apart from the battles of the market and the battles of the trade-mark laws, Bacardi's principal concern in the 1930s was that, despite the close trading relationships between Cuba and the United States, rum was still subject to the liquor-import tariff of $5 a gallon. It thus made eminent sense to manufacture within the U.S. Pepín Bosch began scouting locations. The choice he eventually made led to one of the company's greatest successes.

It also led to the longest and toughest legal case Bacardi had ever fought.

Pepín Bosch first thought of distilling Bacardi in Pennsylvania, where he had studied, where he had political contacts, and where, in 1934, the Bacardi Corporation was set up. Under state laws, all officers and directors of liquor corporations had to be Americans. Concerned that political interests in the state might try to seize control of Bacardi, and having little faith in politicians of any stripe, Bosch decided to search for another manufacturing site.

He looked at New Orleans, Florida, and the Virgin Islands. Finally he lit on the U.S. territory of Puerto Rico. Though not a state, Puerto Rico enjoyed tariff-free entry of its products into the U.S. Like Cuba, it also had an abundant supply of Bacardi's ultimate raw material, sugarcane. Unfortunately, it shared another prominent Cuban feature: corruption.

Puerto Rico had been discovered in 1493 by Christopher Colum-bus, and colonized by Juan Ponce de León, who was later mortally wounded searching for the fountain of youth in Florida. The island was not as rich in resources as Cuba, nor was its history as exotic or bloody. An island of subsistence farmers and sugar, tobacco, and coffee planters, it served primarily as a Spanish outpost, guarding the Carib-bean sea lanes. Its position at the prow of the Antilles, sticking out into the Atlantic in front of its larger neighbors, Santo Domingo and Cuba, made it particularly vulnerable. Successful attacks by raiders such as Sir Francis Drake had caused the Spanish to turn San Juan into the most heavily fortified city in the Caribbean. Its El Morro fortress, with its immensely thick crenellated walls, juts into San Juan Bay like the jaw of some enormous, mythical creature.

In the nineteenth century, as the Spanish empire crumbled, the independence movement in the island was relatively weak. Puerto Rico's transfer from Spanish to American jurisdiction after the Span-ish-American War of 1898 was a sideshow to the military and political battles in and over Cuba. The joyful welcome extended to the American occupation force was much less equivocal than in Cuba. The island was claimed by the U.S. as "an indemnity for the expenses of the 'just war' that had liberated Cuba." It was later suggested that the Americans had obtained their colony by mistake. Certainly Puerto Rico was never to figure prominently in the American consciousness, a fact that has played a powerful part in the chronic frustration of the island's politicians. It became a new constitutional animal, an unin-corporated territory, and in 1917 Puerto Ricans were granted U.S. citizenship.

Considerable economic advantages flowed from this U.S. connec-tion. The island paid no federal taxes and its goods were exported to the mainland duty-free. But the well-meaning American administra-tors — come to implant the American Way — aroused the same resentments as they had in Cuba. Meanwhile, incessant debate about the island's political relationship with the U.S. fed an ongoing national identity crisis and an almost Swiftian politics based on the question of Puerto Rico's status.

Unlike Cuba, Puerto Rico did not flourish in the first three decades of the twentieth century. But it was hit just as hard by the global depression of the 1930s, by which time it had become the poorhouse of the Caribbean. The island's politicians, whom American governors found absurd or irritating, displayed the Spanish colonial penchant for favoring hyperbole over action. They also stood between the Americans, with their genuine desire to help, and the island's needy masses.

Pepín Bosch arrived in San Juan on February 22, 1936, to study the potential for a Bacardi rum plant on the island. He visited the governor, the treasurer, the secretary of agriculture, and most of the government's highest officials. He was warmly received: he was coming, after all, to invest money and provide jobs.

The Bacardi Corporation was registered in Puerto Rico a month later. On April 6, 1936, it was given a license to carry on business by the island's treasurer. Rights to use the Bacardi trademark and labels were granted by the Cuban parent. With the government's help, Bosch found a building on San Juan's sea wall, the Malecón, and in May a team of Bacardi distillers and blenders arrived from Santiago. These included Enrique's son Jorge, and two grandsons of Emilio, Guillermo Rodríguez Bacardi and Pedro Lay Bacardi. Guillermo Rodríguez and Pedro Lay spent the rest of their lives on the island.

Bosch's group went about importing equipment and began distilling in July 1936. The first batch of Bacardi rum was distilled in Puerto Rico in January 1937. By the middle of that year, more than $600,000 had been invested in Puerto Rico. But by then Bosch had also run into the bane of Latin American politics. He was told by a senior politician that, unless he came up with a substantial bribe, a law would be passed to make it impossible for Bacardi to manufacture in Puerto Rico. Bosch had never paid a bribe, and he turned the man down.

The Alcoholic Beverages Law of May 15, 1936, prohibited the use, on Puerto Rican-produced rum, of any internationally known brand name that was not produced in Puerto Rico before February 1, 1936. The law was blatantly discriminatory, since it applied only to Bacardi rum. This law was superseded by another that contained the same trademark restrictions and also prohibited exports in containers larger than one gallon, effectively blocking bulk shipments of rum to be bottled elsewhere.

The government claimed that the law was intended to protect the "renascent liquor industry of Puerto Rico from all competition by foreign capital so as to avoid the increase and growth of financial absenteeism." The buzzwords of socialism and nationalism were solemnly intoned to mask corruption. Puerto Rico was subject ultimately to U.S. law, however, and when this revised act was passed, on May 15, 1937, Bacardi filed for an injunction in U.S. District Court against the treasurer of Puerto Rico.

The law was severely criticized in an editorial in the San Juan newspaper *El Mundo*, whose editor, Angel Ramos, became a friend and ally of Bosch. The editorial declared the law was stupid, because it sought to punish the Bacardi trademark for being successful. Ramos pointed out that 300 people would receive employment at a new Bacardi plant; a million dollars a year would wind up in the island's Treasury; Puerto Rico's name would be promoted abroad, particularly in the United States, which would help tourism. The law would destroy all these possibilities.

Bacardi won the first round in the legal battle. The District Court decreed that the laws were "an unreasonable and arbitrary interference with the enjoyment of property, are not a valid exercise of the police power, and violate the due process clause of the Constitution of the United States and the Organic Act of Puerto Rico and are invalid." Bacardi was also awarded costs. But the decision was overturned by the U.S. Circuit Court of Appeals. The case went to the Supreme Court of the United States, where Bacardi's right to use its trademark on Puerto Rican rum was finally established. The bulk-export restrictions remained in force, however, and Bosch agreed that Bacardi would not sell its Puerto Rican rum in the domestic island market. It would not compete with smaller local producers. It would only export.

The perversity of the Puerto Rican government's attempt to prevent Bacardi from manufacturing on the island became evident over the years. Bacardi Corporation became the island's biggest generator of tax revenue. Puerto Rico became the home of the world's largest rum-manufacturing plant, and one of the most attractive production facilities in the world. Ultimately, the company even helped Puerto Ricans in their elusive quest for identity.

But Bacardi Corporation also provided the setting for some of the family's most bitter and traumatic internal struggles, including the battle many years later that split the family apart and besets it to this day.

CHAPTER SIX

From Pimpernel to Politician

"Believe me, I am going to create
the most honest government
that it is possible for a
criollo to do."

CUBAN PRESIDENT CARLOS PRÍO SOCORRAS

Santiago de Cuba. 1939

On the eve of the Second World War, American visitors to Santiago de Cuba were still charmed by the city's quaintness and beauty, but Cuban politics were less comprehensible than ever. The multicolored walls of Santiago were plastered with political posters. In Havana, presidents — mostly puppets of Batista — came and went. No one paid much attention. In 1939, there were more important developments taking place in Europe for Americans to worry about.

Many Cuban property-owners had reluctantly thrown their support behind Batista's de facto rule because he offered stability. Then he moved sharply to the left, attracting the support of the Cuban Communist party. "Advanced" labor laws were enacted that proved costly for employers. Cuban entrepreneurs joked that it was "easier to get rid of a wife than a worker."

In the 1930s, Pepín Bosch was a distant but keen observer. He had become the Scarlet Pimpernel of the Bacardi organization: turning Mexico around, spearheading the drive into the post-Prohibition U.S. market, setting up the Puerto Rican operation, undergoing lengthy cross-examinations in trademark cases. This led to some resentment back in Santiago, to pockets of desire to cut Pepín Bosch down to size. A showdown came over an order — from Enrique Schueg's executive assistant, José Espín — to increase rum prices in the U.S. and Mexico.

Bosch told management it was a bad idea. He had deliberately set a low price to gain market share. If the price were raised, it would give Bacardi's competitors more room to maneuver. Luis J. Bacardi and José Espín were adamant; so was Bosch; Enrique just wanted to avoid trouble. Bosch said: "Look, if you want to raise the price, go ahead. The result will be failure, but then you'll forget that you ordered me to do it, and you'll blame me. So I quit." To the family's astonishment, he took off for the golf course.

Almost immediately, things began to go wrong at Bacardi. The injunction in the company's favor in the Puerto Rico court case, which Bosch had been spearheading, was reversed. The Mexican operation started to lose money. The Bacardis realized they needed Pepín Bosch, and he was asked to return. He agreed, but only for a year. He said he'd help straighten out the legal problem and the price mess, but then intended to leave for good. He told the family he didn't like the way the company was being run.

Bosch had been away only for six months. In that time, he had got his golf handicap down to 18 and had proved himself indispensable to Bacardi. Within three weeks of his return, he had appealed the reversal of the Puerto Rico case, sending it to the Supreme Court. Within three months, Mexico was making money again.

But the company's problems were not over. Its main difficulties developed in Cuba, where the labor situation was deteriorating. Luis J. Bacardi and José Espín had installed a policy of doing things "by the book," and Bacardi's relations with the *batistiano* labor unions had soured. Union leaders regarded their willingness to take on Bacardi as a sign of their commitment to their workers, who had genuine grievances. They had held down their wage demands at the time of Machado because Bacardi was deeply in debt. When the debts had been paid off, the wage increases to which they felt entitled had not been forthcoming. This had led to more frequent — and more public — strikes.

In 1943, Batista, who had been elected president in 1940 in what Hugh Thomas called "the first reasonably honest election since that of 1912," became personally involved in Bacardi's labor problems. During a wildcat strike, he intervened on the side of the workers. Bacardi took him to court and had his decree overturned, whereupon Batista issued a new decree. Again Bacardi refused to comply, contending that the decrees were invalid and infringed constitutional rights. Batista had an intervenor enforce the decrees above the company's protests. In the end, the company won its case, but good employee relations are not achieved through legal battles.

Once again, Pepín Bosch was called to the rescue. When he arrived back in his hometown, he found graffiti accusing the Bacardis of being fascists. He sat down with labor leaders and persuaded them of his good intentions. He increased wages and bonuses and introduced benefits beyond those in Batista's legislation. If a worker had medical problems that couldn't be treated locally, the company flew him to a specialist in the U.S. If a worker died, the company helped pay for the funeral. Before Bosch, the traditional Christmas bonus for a worker had been 5 to 15 pesos, plus a bottle of rum. Under Bosch's regime, such bonuses were eventually paid monthly.

Bosch knew it was pointless to take an adversarial attitude to labor. Why not guide and educate the workers you have instead of firing them? Bosch's paternalistic attitude worked wonders for labor relations and helped establish him as head of the company. He was appointed first vice-president, the de facto chief executive — but not without a fight. Luis J. Bacardi, despite his hold on 30 percent of the company's stock, now saw his dream of control slipping away. He challenged Enrique, but could not marshal sufficient votes. Víctor Schueg was reportedly so incensed by Luis J. Bacardi's challenge that he turned up at a shareholders' meeting carrying a pistol.

Bosch — not from any great liking for Luis J., but out of recognition of his powerful equity position, and perhaps even with a little sense of rubbing in his victory — suggested that they work together. He would give Luis J. his title of "first vice-president," and he suggested they get a partners' desk so they could work face to face and he could teach Luis J. everything he knew. Luis J. was not interested in learning what Pepín Bosch knew. He went into exile in Havana and did not exchange a word with Bosch for thirty years.

José Espín, meanwhile, was kicked upstairs, to the second floor, and put in charge of trademarks. Bosch could not fire Espín, because he remained close to Luis J., who, although gone, could not be forgotten. He still held 30 percent of the company's equity. That ownership gave Luis J. seats on the family board, which traditionally had two members each from the branches of Emilio, Facundo Bacardi Moreau, and the Schueg Bacardis, and one from that of José. Luis J. nominated his two nephews, Adolfo Danguillecourt Bacardi and Luis Gómez del Campo Bacardi, to his Facundo-branch board seats. Pepín Bosch knew they were on the board to keep an eye on him — to remind him that 30 percent of the ownership was waiting for him to put a foot wrong.

The success of Pepín Bosch became inextricably linked with the success of the Bacardi family. Bosch developed a goal that, despite Luis J.'s opposition, made Luis J. and his descendants, and the rest of the family, rich. Bosch decided he would make the Bacardis wealthier than the Guinnesses, the exotic, eccentric British family who were, by the early 1940s, more famous for spending the dividends of their beer empire than for working in it. The price Bosch demanded for making the family successful was that he would be the boss.

He set about stamping his unique style on the business. Instead of moving into an office, he took a desk in the middle of the main Bacardi office on the Calle Aguilera Baja. When not traveling, he could be seen working long hours, not only by all the employees but by people on the street outside. Apart from wanting close contact with — and surveillance over — Bacardi's employees, he had another reason for wanting prominence. A proud man, he was sensitive to the fact that he was and would always be — despite his wife's status as a grand-daughter of the founder — a hired hand. He held his position only as long as a majority of family shareholders supported him. He had already demonstrated that he was not afraid to quit. His desk in the middle of the office said to the Bacardis: "If you are unhappy with me, you know where to find me." Rather than building or buying a house, Pepín Bosch rented one outside town, on the hill at Punta Gorda, looking over the channel of the harbor. It was as if he was emphasizing that he was ready to move again if things were not done his way, as if to tell the Bacardis they were as much on trial as he was.

Bosch's reign almost ended before it started when, in 1946, he became a victim of the jinx that had taken so many of the third generation of Bacardis. On the October 10 holiday that marked the beginning of the Ten Years' War, the first great struggle for Cuban independence, Bosch and Joaquín Bacardi Fernández were preparing to put out in Bosch's yacht from the Santiago docks. There was engine trouble. The captain was tinkering below when leaking petroleum fumes ignited. The boat exploded. The captain was killed. Joaquín was tossed into the harbor; he received no serious physical injuries, but his life was endangered because he swallowed some of the harbor's noxious waters. Bosch was thrown onto the jetty, his leg badly smashed. Enriqueta called the commander of the U.S. base at nearby Guantanamo, who was a friend. The commander provided a plane to take Bosch to Havana; another plane was chartered to take him to a specialist in Boston. He underwent numerous operations to save his leg, and his life.

Labor relations had improved so much under his management that the union leaders sent him a telegram in hospital, telling him there would be no work stoppages while he was away. That year, Enrique Schueg had a stroke, and Bosch — once he returned from his own hospitalization — was even more firmly in charge. Like his father-in-law, he would walk with a limp for the rest of his life. Indeed, a joke would later go around Santiago. Whenever anybody was seen with a limp, someone would say, "There goes a future president of Bacardi."

The way Bosch dealt with his injury demonstrated his iron resolve. Guillermo Mármol, a young lawyer from an aristocratic Santiago family, remembers going with Bosch to visit the Cuban prime minister, Carlos Prío, in his Havana office not long after Bosch had returned from hospital. Bosch could hardly walk and should have been in a wheelchair. With grim determination, he made the effort to climb the stairs to Prío's second-floor office. He told young Mármol, "I will arrive at the office of the prime minister on my feet."

This will was concealed beneath a manner always deferential and soft-spoken. When he set pen to paper, Bosch was a man of few words. Indeed, he was famous for his terse handwritten memos. Executives' hearts would go into fibrillation when they recognized his writing on the envelope. Few people remember Bosch ever losing his temper. "Would you mind doing this, if it's not too much trouble?" he would ask, although it was a particularly dense employee or family member who failed to realize that no choice was being offered. Those who questioned Bosch's decisions had their knuckles rapped, but few dreamed of questioning him. His talents and track record were faultless. His thought processes were a mystery and a wonder to all those who worked in the organization. He was always throwing off new plans. He might be enthusiastic about a scheme one minute and abandon it the next; he always had another to take its place. He had a brilliant business mind and a photographic memory. Most important, he kept the dividends growing.

His aura, which he cultivated, was important, because one of his most difficult tasks was managing the family, the ever-present owners. He had to deal with constant requests to raise dividends or give children jobs, and he could easily have spent his waking hours listening to suggestions on how to run the company. This led him to enhance his natural aloofness and to cultivate a manipulative style; he became masterful at subtly juggling personalities and family interests while disclosing little information about the running of the company.

Bosch brought many members of the family into the business — that was expected by the family — though he usually told them to get experience elsewhere first. He oversaw the development of dozens of young family members but never left them in any doubt that he knew what was best for them. Occasionally, of course, some young rebel resisted being dispatched to the front office or the warehouse in Mexico or Puerto Rico. But such opposition was rare. Bosch was held in awe; besides, if you disobeyed him, you risked expulsion from the company, which was almost like being expelled from the family. "Bosch controlled through an almost mystic process of terror, love, appreciation, and loyalty," recalled one family member. "You put all those together and they don't sound right. But it worked."

Some family members claimed he was harsh with them and didn't listen to them, but nobody ever called him uncharitable. Over the years, Bosch paid for the educations of dozens of young people who could not afford it themselves. Once, the receptionist in the Santiago office told Bosch a girl wanted to see him. He had her sent in. The girl announced that she had just graduated from high school and saw three possibilities in her life: to study in the United States to be a bilingual secretary, to try to get a husband who would take care of her, or to take a wealthy lover. After this blunt assessment of her prospects, she said, "I've heard that you pay for the education of kids, so I'm here to see if you can send me to Columbia University, because my family cannot afford it." Bosch told her to draw up a budget. Soon she was on her way to the U.S.

If you caught Víctor Schueg early enough in the day, he could be the wittiest and most insightful man in Santiago. Once he began to tipple at the Club San Carlos, or the Club 300, or in the Casa Granda, trouble developed, trouble that sometimes led to the trashing of bars and to Víctor's ejection. Nevertheless, he was a powerful director. As well as having a bond with Bosch as joint representative of the Schueg Bacardi interests, he also had a personal bond. Víctor, according to one family member, helped teach Bosch "how to deal with the Bacardi boys." He became one of Bosch's staunchest colleagues.

The second of Bosch's key family associates was Daniel Bacardi Rosell, son of Facundo Bacardi Lay. Daniel's father was one of the twin sons of Emilio's first marriage; he had died of pneumonia when Daniel was a teenager. There were similarities in the lives of Daniel's father and his uncle José. Both married women named Rosell; both had two children, a boy and a girl; both girls produced sons who worked in the business. José's daughter Zenaida married a *santiaguero* named José Argamasilla Grimany, who became an executive in the company.

Young Daniel had gone to the public school in Santiago, then to the University of Havana, where his late father had wanted him to study law. While Daniel was in pre-law, Machado closed down the university; Daniel was sent to learn English and study in New Jersey and wound up doing a general business course at a private academy in Philadelphia. When the University of Havana was eventually re-opened, Daniel's mother, Caridad Rosell Fernández, wanted him to resume studying law. He told her it was time to go to work; he returned to Santiago and asked Enrique Schueg for a job. Enrique suggested he first get some experience, perhaps in a bank. Instead, Daniel bought a truck and went into the haulage business.

The way in which Daniel eventually did land a job with Bacardi says a good deal about family businesses in general and about Bacardi in particular. One day in 1935, Daniel was climbing the stairs to the second floor of the company's head office on the Calle Aguilera Baja when he ran into Antón Bacardi Fernández, one of the three sons of the founder's third son, José. Antón, a personable playboy, had no desire to work for a living. He felt it diplomatic to appear willing, however, and so he too periodically pestered Enrique for employment.

The day Daniel met him coming down the stairs, Antón was wearing a long face. He had taken his persuasive powers too far: Enrique had actually given him a job. Not only was the pay low, he told Daniel, but they expected him to turn up every day, and in the morning too! Daniel said he'd love such a job. Antón said, "Why don't you have it?" Daniel, elated, suggested they tell Enrique at once. "Oh no," said Antón, "you do it. I have an appointment." And he disappeared. So Daniel went on up and mentioned he had just run into Antón. Oh yes, said Enrique, and proceeded to tell Daniel that he had finally given in to Antón's entreaties. A job would be good for him, give him some responsibility, help him settle down. Daniel had to break the news as tactfully as possible that Antón didn't want the job, but that he himself would like it instead. Ah, *la familia*. Enrique shrugged and told Daniel he could start the next day.

Daniel was a short, dapper man, self-effacing but wry, with the easygoing air of commercial royalty that marked the Bacardi family. His wife, Graziella Bravo Viñas, bore him nine children. "The first five are the worst," he liked to say. The story is still relished of his coming home early one morning from an all-night, company-related revel. Graziella greeted him at the door sternly: "This is not the time to be coming home." "You are right," he said, "this is the time to be going to work." And he turned on his heel and went to the office. Daniel was a card. But he was also fiercely dedicated to the business, which Graziella regarded as a rival for his affections, as if it were a mistress.

Daniel became a protégé of Víctor Schueg, whom he greatly admired, and worked his way up the company. In 1948, Bosch appointed him head of the Santiago operation. Through the 1950s and 1960s, Daniel was effectively the number two man in the Bacardi empire.

The third family member close to Pepín Bosch was Joaquín Bacardi Fernández, brother of the jobless playboy Antón and of José, who had made a mess of Mexico before joining those of the third generation who died young. The Bacardi Fernández boys symbolized three themes of the Bacardi family: tragedy, industry, and the carefree joys of wealth. José had a short but tragic business and personal life. Antón lived to have fun, cruising around Santiago and enjoying his inheritance to the full. Joaquín devoted himself to the business. In particular, he devoted himself to beer, taking a degree in chemical engineering at Harvard before doing a stint at the Brewing School of Copenhagen. Joaquín was particularly proud of this qualification and came to be known as "Joaquín the brewer."

Bacardi had first become involved in beer in the early 1920s, when Enrique had persuaded his reluctant partners to buy the almost defunct Santiago Brewing Co., in the San Pedrito district on the north side of the city. Bacardi set about modernizing the facilities to take on the Havana brewers. As ever, quality was key. The company secured a new water supply by sinking an artesian well, replaced the old wooden vats with tanks of steel, and imported German brewmasters.

The beer was called Hatuey, after an Indian chief who had led local resistance to Diego Velázquez in Oriente in the early sixteenth century and had ultimately been burned at the stake. Over the years his name had become synonymous with the struggle for Cuban independence.

Enrique decided Hatuey would be a premium-priced beer. He had no intention of taking on the other domestic beers on the basis of price, so he looked for what today is called a niche. In fact, the niche would eventually grow to occupy more than half the Cuban market, but Enrique was prepared to build the brand slowly, concentrating on the local markets of Santiago and Camaguey, "dejando al tiempo lo que es del tiempo" (leaving to time what is the work of time). Enrique referred to Hatuey as his "pretty little fiancée." Joaquín Bacardi Fernández would become its chaperon.

In character, Joaquín was as different from the popular and spendthrift Antón — who was always buying a round for the bar or tipping the orchestra to keep playing at the end of the evening — as two brothers could be. Joaquín was, well, a little *careful* with his money. Joaquín was not considered *pesado* (that is, tiresome or boorish, the opposite of *simpático*); rather he was regarded as a bit eccentric, part of the Bacardis' rich diversity.

The family poked gentle fun at their financially careful relative. Pepín Bosch used to tell a ribald joke about visiting a New York sex specialist to have a transplant. It had cost $40,000 but was a great success. When Joaquín found out, he declared that he too wanted the operation, and he headed off for New York. The next time Bosch saw Joaquín, he asked if he'd had the operation. "Yes," Joaquín replied, "but it was a disaster." Since he offered no explanation, Bosch, when he was in New York, went to see the doctor. The doctor told him Joaquín had refused to pay the $40,000, had bargained and bargained, and finally claimed he could afford no more than $400. The doctor couldn't guarantee the results, but Joaquín had told him to go ahead. "And so," the doctor told Pepín Bosch, "for $400 I gave him your old one!"

Bosch regarded Joaquín with personal affection and, if not as an inspired manager, as a solid and dependable one. The men also shared the bond of almost having been killed when Bosch's yacht blew up. For Joaquín's part, his attitude to Bosch was summed up by another family member: "He was terrified of Pepín."

When Pepín Bosch took control of Bacardi, business — despite the labor problems in Santiago — was booming. The Second World War, like the First, was resulting in another surge in demand for Bacardi. European imports had been cut off, and the American distillers were geared for the production of industrial alcohol. These restrictions did not apply to Puerto Rico's distillers, and the island's government saw its rum industry as an increasingly important source of both economic growth and tax revenue. (The U.S. excise taxes on Puerto Rican rum sales were returned to the island's government.)

The hazards of shipping were greatly increased. Bacardi's Puerto Rican operation assembled a small fleet of boats, the "Bacardi navy." Two were sunk by U-boats — one while carrying machinery destined for San Juan, the other while bearing a consignment of rum for Hong Kong. Still sales and profits soared. By the early 1940s, both the Puerto Rican and the Mexican rum operations were making more money than those in Santiago. In 1943, Puerto Rican sales hit $10 million.

In 1944, Pepín Bosch decided to cut out the middleman and take control of U.S. imports. On April 10, Bacardi Imports was created, with offices at 595 Madison Avenue. This meant ending the relationship with Schenley. Lewis Rosenstiel and Pepín Bosch did not part on the best of terms. Years later, at a function at the University of Miami to honor Rosenstiel for his donations to the medical school and the school of oceanography, the head of Bacardi Imports, Bartolo Estrada, always a perfect gentleman, said to Rosenstiel, "Good evening, Mr. Rosenstiel, I bring you greetings from Mr. Bosch." Rosenstiel fixed Estrada with a glower and said, in front of the assembled wives: "Bullshit. Bosch never sent me any greetings!"

Bacardi Imports was created in boom conditions — the company's U.S. rum sales in 1944 were $13.1 million — but the market suffered a severe hangover after the war. Dozens of new producers had sprung up in Puerto Rico, and quality control had gone by the board. To sell the flood of Puerto Rican rum, the import agents pressured the wholesalers, and the wholesalers pressured the liquor stores, to encourage customers to buy Puerto Rican rum as part of a package: if you wanted a bottle of scotch, you had to buy two bottles of rum. The lower standards combined with these forced purchases left a bad taste in the mouths of American consumers. When unrestricted sales of whiskey and other imported liquors were again permitted, Puerto Rican rum, including Bacardi, paid the price.

Bacardi Imports' sales dropped by half in 1945 to $6.7 million. In 1946 they edged up to $7.5 million, but the next year, when imported spirits again became freely available, they went into free fall. Inventories of Bacardi swelled. In 1947, the Puerto Rican operation sold Bacardi Imports only $1 million worth of rum. Pepín Bosch did not panic. Instead, with an eye on the longer term, he led Bacardi Imports through the painful and expensive process of taking back excess stocks from the liquor stores, thus salvaging goodwill from the Puerto Rican rum hangover.

Mexico, meanwhile, had also enjoyed the wartime boom but had not suffered such a severe subsequent reaction. Sales in 1942 surpassed 1 million Mexican pesos for the first time, and by 1946 they had hit M$8.6 million. In 1947, when whiskey and cognac also reentered the Mexican market, sales dropped to M$7 million, but the next year they were up again to M$7.8 million. By 1949, they were up to a new record of M$8.8 million, and in 1950 they surged to M$10.7 million. By then, Bacardi had become the second-selling Mexican spirit after tequila.

In the U.S. market, Bacardi remained a small player. The industry was still controlled by the big four players that had emerged in the wake of Prohibition: Seagram, Schenley, National Distillers, and Hiram Walker. The mantle of "whiskey king of America" was, in the immediate postwar period, wrested from Rosenstiel by Sam Bronfman, whose marketing and merchandising expertise, along with his success in selling whiskey blends, had survived a wartime challenge by Schenley for the industry top spot.

From Repeal in 1933 to the end of the war in 1945, the U.S. liquor market became increasingly dominated by brands. The top ten brands now accounted for about the same proportion of the market that the top fifty had accounted for a decade before. Of those ten brands, Seagram and Schenley each controlled three. Seagram had Seven Crown, Calvert Reserve, and Four Roses; Schenley's big sellers were Schenley Reserve, Three Feathers Reserve, and Golden Wedding. The rewards of success were enormous. Seagram's 1947 sales were $618 million and its profits $43 million. Nobody mentioned Pepín Bosch in the same breath as giants such as Bronfman and Rosenstiel. But Bosch was determined that, one day, they would.

From the middle of the Santiago office, Pepín Bosch supervised the affairs of the growing Bacardi empire as a stream of managers and family supplicants sought audience. His desk would be covered with the latest sales figures from New York and Mexico City, with production statistics from San Juan, with blueprints for new operations. Like some great conjurer, he knew how to keep all the plates spinning.

Not long after he returned to Santiago, Bosch decided that an area of great potential for the company was his father-in-law's "pretty little fiancée," Hatuey beer. Production capacity at the 20-acre Hatuey plant at San Pedrito had multiplied five-fold between 1927 and 1940, and the beer now had almost one-third of the Cuban market. When Bosch took over, the product was well known (Hemingway's hero in *To Have and Have Not*, Harry Morgan, says, "I had black bean soup and a beef stew with boiled potatoes for fifteen cents. A bottle of Hatuey beer brought it up to a quarter"), but it wasn't making any money. Bosch set out to tighten operations and financial controls. Then he began to think about expansion.

He decided to build a new brewery to supply the Havana market. The site he chose was El Cotorro, ten miles from Havana. It was served by both road and rail, and had an excellent water supply. The new brewery would be called Modelo, and it would indeed be a model of technology and aesthetics. This latter was an area in which Bosch's wife, Enriqueta, had become prominent.

Enriqueta was universally liked for her kind and sympathetic nature. She was seen as the route to Pepín Bosch's ear, and family members often approached her to intercede with her husband when they wanted a job for one of their children or some other favor. She also helped plan the grounds around new plants and had much to do with the fact that Bacardi's facilities were invariably showpieces.

In December 1947, the company opened the Modelo plant, a temperature- and humidity-controlled monument to technology, filled with stainless steel and burnished copper, set amid acres of mahogany, teak, white oak, and eucalyptus. It was a success without precedent. In the first year of production, to June 1949, the company produced 3.5 million litres of beer. From January to December 1950, it produced 22 million. Expansion plans were drawn up almost as soon as it opened. Most important for the family, it brought a flood of dividends. Bosch might have been held in awe by some, in terror by others, but his business genius was evident to all.

By the end of the 1940s, Bacardi's prospects were excellent. The American market was beginning to pull out of its Puerto Rican rum hangover, to the benefit of both Bacardi Imports in New York and Bacardi Corporation in San Juan. Bacardi Mexico was moving from strength to strength. In Cuba, the success of the El Cotorro brewery eclipsed all else; and Bosch was planning another brewery, in Manacas, to supply the central part of the island.

Bacardi and Hatuey were made by companies that took obvious pride in their country. The emphasis on Cuban achievement in their advertising was more than a sales pitch. Hatuey was advertised as "La Gran Cerveza de Cuba" (the great beer of Cuba), and the Modelo plant as "un orgullo nacional" (a national pride). Bacardi rum's advertising at the end of the 1940s featured the slogan "¡Qué suerte tiene el Cubano!" (How lucky the Cuban is!) Some ads featured the island's natural beauties, its cigars — Winston Churchill, Jean Sibelius, and Edward G. Robinson were cited as Cuban-cigar-smokers — and its sugar industry. Others celebrated Cuba's champions: José Raúl Capablanca in chess, Ramón Fonst in fencing, Kid Chocolate in boxing. They rejoiced in Cuban music and, of course, in the national sport, baseball.

Bacardi's rum and beer brands often celebrated Cuban nationhood jointly. On October 10, 1949, large ads were placed commemorating Carlos Manuel de Céspedes's freeing of his slaves, and the *grito*, or cry of rebellion, that led to the first war of Cuban independence in 1868. The ad featured upreaching hands with wrists bearing broken shackles. The caption consisted of the words attributed by Emilio in his *Crónicas* to Céspedes when he freed his slaves: "As from this moment, you are as free as I am . . . " And in May 1950, a large ad celebrated the hundredth anniversary of the Cuban flag, "la bandera más linda del mundo" (the most beautiful flag in the world).

As well as advertising in periodicals and on radio, Bacardi and Hatuey promoted themselves at social events. Courses in cocktail-making were given at exclusive Havana clubs, including the Miramar Yacht Club, the Vedado Tennis Club, the Havana Biltmore, and the Country Club. Competitions were held, and the inventors of new cocktails — invariably attractive young debutantes — were featured in Bacardi advertising.

Ernest Hemingway, whose Cuban villa was close to El Cotorro, personally promoted Bacardi by consuming huge volumes of Papa Dobles — two and a half jiggers of Bacardi White Label, the juice of half a grapefuit, and six drops of maraschino, placed in a mixer and served foaming in a goblet — in Havana's La Floridita bar. When Hemingway won the Nobel Prize for literature, he was given a reception at Hatuey. Local fishermen — the spiritual heirs of Santiago, the hero of *The Old Man and the Sea* — were invited.

The thoughts that went through the simple Santiago's mind as he fought his epic battle in Hemingway's novel never touched upon Cuban politics. Santiago was far more concerned with Joe DiMaggio. Another example of America's egocentric view of the world? Perhaps, but then most Cubans did indeed tend to push politics to one side, just as they ignored the big, scabby-headed buzzards that sat on Cuban fences waiting for fortune to feed them.

Like the buzzards, however, political turmoil was a constant factor in Cuban life. In the 1950s, it began to consume the nation.

Cuban politics came to call on Pepín Bosch in the smiling form of Carlos Prío Socarras, El Presidente Cordial. In 1950, Prío asked Bosch to become his finance minister. The invitation had all the appeal of signing up for a kamikaze squadron. A more thankless task than guarding Cuba's coffers from Cuba's politicians could hardly be imagined. Senator José Alemán, who had been education minister between 1946 and 1948, was once asked how he had managed to get so much money out of the Treasury. "In suitcases," he had replied.

For most Cuban professionals and businessmen, politics had become something to suffer, not something in which to participate. Honest government had been a noble ideal for Emilio, the *libertador*; now it seemed a delusion, the unrealistic dream of crusading radio politicians like the *santiaguero* Eduardo Chibas, leader of the opposition Ortodoxo party. Chibas described Prío's government as a "scandalous bacchanalia of crimes, robberies, and mismanagement." His inflammatory Sunday-night radio performances attracted huge audiences. The singularity of his stance was summed up by Rolando Masferrer, one of Santiago's most notorious gangster politicians, who admitted, "Only Chibas is not a gangster," adding, "And he's mad." Most Cubans treated their politicians with a shrug. They embraced the mythical glories of their history all the more passionately as the present grew more frustrating.

Batista had not fixed the 1944 election and had left for Daytona Beach, Florida — albeit with considerable booty — a generally respected public figure. That election had been won by Ramón Grau San Martín's Auténtico party. Under Grau's administration, public office continued to be synonymous with corruption. Lottery collectorships were a license to steal money. Bogus jobs were created, the salaries siphoned to political office-holders. Contractors made payoffs for work without tender. Cash was simply stuffed into pockets — or suitcases. Meanwhile, Grau's interventionist policies proved disastrous. Price controls failed, leading to shortages. Public works projects fell apart.

Grau had been succeeded in the 1948 election by Prío, who represented a considerable difference of style but not of substance. Hugh Thomas wrote of Grau: "A Puritan air of hypocrisy dominated his relentless pursuit of other people's money. Prío, on the contrary, enjoyed whatever he laid his hands on." Prío, "difficult to dislike and difficult to take seriously," made few bones about his attitude toward politics as the route to personal wealth. He entered office with suitcases at the ready.

Political life had, by the late 1940s, become a violent contest for the spoils of power. Activists at the University of Havana — whose number included a young law student named Fidel Castro — toted guns and were not frightened to use them. Indeed, Prío encouraged gangsterism, allowing the political mob virtually to shoot its way into government positions, particularly the police force. Pepín Bosch's reluctance to become part of such an administration was not difficult to understand.

Bosch declined Prío's offer, explaining tactfully that he had many problems with the Bacardi business. Prío would not take no for an answer. Eventually, he summoned Bosch to the Presidential Palace and said: "I am the president of Cuba, and I order you to be secretary of the Treasury." It was not so much a threat — Bosch was not susceptible to those — as an appeal to his sense of public spirit. Bosch reluctantly acquiesced. He moved back to his Havana house at Country Club Park, with its prominent portrait of Thomas Jefferson. As his executive assistant, Bosch took the Bacardi lawyer Guillermo Mármol, who had become one of his closest confidants.

Bosch's signature began to appear at the bottom of Cuban banknotes. He took the fiscal responsibility this implied more seriously than Prío could have imagined. Announcing a drive to collect back taxes, Bosch declared: "Everyone will pay, without exception or privilege." He was as good as his word, badgering even his own family. Prío himself would eventually tell the story of the industrialist who had gone to the Treasury to try to get out of paying $18,000 in profit taxes. He emerged in a daze, having paid $120,000, then "went around telling everyone that at last there was a man in the Treasury who wouldn't let him get away with anything."

Far from pleasing politicians, of course, Bosch enraged them. He was harassed by congressional committees, sometimes being questioned until three in the morning. Meanwhile, he still had the responsibility of running Bacardi — which, he told colleagues, he did between seven and eight in the morning.

Shortly after Pepín Bosch went to Havana as secretary of the Treasury, a long-anticipated and yet still epochal event occurred: Enrique Schueg, his father-in-law and still titular president of the Bacardi company, died. Since his stroke four years earlier, Schueg had taken no part in the business. He had slipped into a gentle senility, reverently tended in his big house and chauffeured around the narrow streets of his beloved Santiago by devoted servants and family. He died one of Santiago's most honored citizens. France had bestowed upon him the Legion of Honor for his wartime support of the Free French forces. Cuba had given him the Order of Carlos Manuel de Céspedes and the Order of Commercial Merit. He had also received decorations from the Belgian government, whose consul in Santiago he had been for almost fifty years.

His funeral could be compared only to that of his brother-in-law,

Emilio, thirty years earlier. Thousands of mourners filed past Enrique's coffin. His benefactions to the Catholic church were recognized by the officiation over the ceremonies of Archbishop Monseñor Enrique Pérez Serantes — who would go on to play a significant part in Cuban history — assisted by the Sisters of Mercy and all the city's priests. Several trucks were required to carry the wreaths, which included floral tributes from President Prío and other members of the government. Pepín Bosch flew down from Havana to lead the funeral cortege along with Santiago's popular mayor, Luis Casero, who had proudly continued the Fiesta de la Bandera on New Year's Eve.

The procession made its way to Céspedes Park. The municipal band played. Casero made a short speech, noting that Enrique left behind, "in his illustrious family, worthy successors to his hard-working and irreproachable life."

Enrique Schueg had been eighty-eight, the same age as the Bacardi company. He had been associated with it for sixty-six years. A director and major shareholder since 1894, he had been president since the death of Emilio in 1922. With his own death, the matter of succession, which had already been decided de facto seven years before, would be made official.

Early in March 1951, Bosch was summoned to a congressional committee for yet another grilling, this time to explain his plans to reorganize a run-down government workers' retirement fund. He told the committee he had an alternative engagement; he had to attend a Bacardi board meeting. At that meeting, he was elected president. At last he had the title that went with the responsibility. Keen to escape the opprobrium that his honesty was bringing upon him in Havana, citing "doctor's orders," he withdrew from public life.

Bosch had certainly done his job. Taking over the Treasury, he had inherited a deficit of $18 million. Fourteen months later, when he stepped down, Cuba had a $15-million surplus, its largest on record. During his time as finance minister, Bosch had been one of the few politicians to speak to, and answer questions from, the rebellious students at the University of Havana. He could do that because he was one of only a handful of politicians in the previous fifty years with nothing to hide.

Bosch's political epitaph, in the Havana newspaper *Alerta*, declared: "Bosch took office to the profound disgust of the politicians, and leaves accompanied by their broad smiles as they wait outside the ministry doors to assault the Treasury he guarded."

But much worse than a raid on the Treasury was soon to come.

CHAPTER SEVEN

Taking to the Hills

"According to legend, a white-faced
king named Quetzalcoatl would
come one day from the waters of the
East to release the people from their
appalling need of human sacrifice.
The arrival of Cortés at Tenochtitlán
seemed to the Aztecs to correspond
to the legend. When they discovered
their mistake, it was too late."

GEORGE PENDLE, *A HISTORY OF LATIN AMERICA*

Santiago de Cuba. February 19, 1954

One morning, Daniel Bacardi's family chauffeur, a man named
Rodríguez, rushed into the kitchen of the big family home in Vista
Alegre clutching a sealed envelope. Bursting into tears, he announced
that Daniel's son, little Facundo Bacardi Bravo, had been kidnapped
by three men at knifepoint. Facundo's mother, Graziella, ripped open
the envelope and discovered a ransom note, which said the money
was needed to finance the revolution against Batista. She called
Daniel, told him what had happened, and read the note to him. He
told her not to panic and arranged to meet the chauffeur. Once he
had spoken to the chauffeur, he suggested they both go to the police.
The chauffeur said no; the note had said that the authorities should
not be called.

But the note had come in a sealed envelope, and nobody had told
the chauffeur what was in it.

In the meantime, Bacardi children in Santiago and Havana found
themselves whisked from their classrooms without explanation. They
searched their minds for something they might have done wrong,
wondered if somebody had died. Facundo's sister, María Hortensia,
who had been dropped off at her own school before Facundo that
morning, was questioned by police. Did she remember anything
unusual the chauffeur had said or done? She said he had seemed in a
great hurry that morning. Her school was closer to home, and she
was always dropped off first; but the chauffeur wanted to go so early
that she'd suggested they take Facundo to his school downtown, then

drop her off on the way back. But no, the chauffeur had said: she must be dropped off first. She also remembered a remark a few days earlier that she had found strange. The chauffeur had been going to take a group of the children shopping downtown. It was usual to dress up for such an occasion. Little Facundo had looked scruffy, and his sisters had clucked at him. The chauffeur had said, "He can dress any way he wants, because he's Daniel Bacardi's son."

The chauffeur was taken in for a form of questioning very different from that experienced by María Hortensia. Interrogation — particularly for such a crime — meant torture. Child kidnapping was virtually unthinkable in Cuban society, which revolved around the family and idolized children. Rodríguez refused to admit guilt or to name accomplices; within hours, he had been murdered. Daniel and Graziella Bacardi were horrified, not merely at the crime but because they had now lost what might be the only link to their son.

Word of the kidnap, meanwhile, spread instantly. Fingers that were not dialing were moving over rosary beads. Virtually the whole of Santiago closed down as groups were organized to search for the boy. Such was the clout of the Bacardis that, within hours, thousands of members of the Cuban army, national police, and rural Guardia were combing the Santiago countryside. Later the same day, the boy and a single kidnapper, Manuel Echevarría, were apprehended by an army squad. The boy was unharmed. Echevarría's tongue loosened much more quickly than the chauffeur's had. The link was that Echevarría's sister had been the chauffeur's fiancée.

The story given to the newspapers — thus, for example, it appeared in the *New York Times* — was that Echevarría had implicated the chauffeur. When word had come that the boy had been found and he himself implicated, the chauffeur had "tried to break from police custody." As a result, "He was shot and killed as he tried to escape."

In fact, this form of police execution was a fixture in many Latin American countries. In Mexico, it was called the *ley de fuga*, or law of escape. Given the nature of the crime, there was little sympathy for the chauffeur's fate. It was subsequently reported that "the police had to fight off crowds intent on lynching Echevarría as he was taken to the city prison."

Nobody took the kidnapping of any child, let alone a Bacardi, lightly, but the fate of the chauffeur said something troubling about the underlying culture of Cuban society: it was sentimental on top, sinister underneath. And it was becoming more violent by the day. The fact that the bogus ransom note had mentioned that the money would be used for revolutionary purposes was significant, and disturbing. Many crimes had been committed in the name of revolution. Many more would be.

ᴬᵀᴬ

For the young members of the growing family — those who carried Bacardi as their first name and those who had Bacardi mothers or grandmothers — to grow up as part of the family in Santiago was, as one of them put it, "to have been born with a golden passport."

Santiago was still a city that believed in magic. When simple supplicants would come to mayor Luis Casero for some favor, they might first go to the market and purchase a potion in which to bathe, in order to add power to their petition. When he detected the smell, Casero, a kindly man, would always try extra hard to help someone who had gone to such trouble. It appealed to Casero's sense of humor that, when they got what they wanted, they seemed more grateful to the local practitioners of voodoo than to him. But the fact was undeniable: magic really worked in Santiago. No family had been dusted with more of it than the Bacardis.

Santiagueros didn't defer to the Bacardis just because of their wealth; they genuinely liked and embraced them. "Ah," people would say, with a smile and a reverent tone, "so you are a grandson of Don Emilio," or "you are a daughter of Daniel Bacardi." Doors would be opened, paths smoothed, merchandise wrapped and delivered with nary a mention of sordid cash. When a new consignment arrived at the Santiago branch of the luxurious department store El Encanto, the store called up Daniel's wife Graziella and offered to send the whole kit and caboodle up to Vista Alegre so that she and her relatives and friends had first choice.

Bacardi children played in the huge gardens of old Emilio's Villa Elvira, with its bounteous mango trees and its fountains and its old cannons from the Spanish-American War. They treated the country club as a home away from home. There weren't even chits to sign; the bills were magically paid. There were servants to dress them, chauffeurs to take them to school. But the Bacardis were taught never to be arrogant, never to make demands, never to abuse their privileged positions.

The Bacardi women were all well educated and cultured and gracious. Most had attended schools in Europe or the U.S. or Canada. None were directly involved in the business, but they were prominent in local charities and the arts. Emilio's daughter Lucía Bacardi Cape, known as Mimín, was an accomplished sculptor. His granddaughter, Zenaida Bacardi Rosell, had taken to poetry and wrote most lyrically about the family and the business. Pepín Bosch's wife, Enriqueta, had taken a prominent role after the war in bringing adequate paving to the city; she was always concerned with Santiago's beautification. Although some found the company almost a rival for their husbands' affections, the overwhelming majority clearly saw it as the source of their wealth, security, and status.

Each summer, for three months or so, most of the families moved from their big houses downtown or in Vista Alegre, taking everything except the kitchen sink (but including the refrigerator) to one of the summer compounds around the city. Some went to Siboney, with its lovely beach, east of the city, but most made their way to Ciudad Mar, close to El Morro by the entrance of Santiago harbor. There they sortied out from summer homes on the island of Cayo Smith, or the hill at Punta Gorda, to play in the waters of the Bathing Club, where spectacular tropical fish darted about their bronzed young bodies. It would never occur to them not to play with the children from Cayo Smith's little fishing village, who watched with awe and perhaps envy as their Bacardi playmates disappeared into the local store and emerged laden with Coca-Cola for the whole gang — accomplished, of course, without any money having changed hands; just a pencil mark and a smile. Blessed children indeed.

But the political overtones of little Facundo's ransom note were a sign of the violent changes taking place in Cuban society. By 1954, Cuban politics had taken one of its perennial turns for the worse. While Pepín Bosch had been in the government, Prío's administration had come under sustained attack from Eduardo Chibas, but it had been the gangster Rolando Masferrer's assessment of Chibas that in the end proved most accurate. Chibas launched a mistaken attack on the minister of education, Aureliano Sánchez Arango; instead of backing down when he could produce no proof of his allegations, he made a final broadcast and then shot himself while still on the air. Many believed that he did not intend to kill himself, but he died ten days later, on August 15, 1951. Hugh Thomas wrote that Chibas "accomplished in his own death the destruction of Cuban political life."

As its candidate for the 1952 election, Prío's Auténtico party chose Carlos Hevia, who ran the Bacardis' El Cotorro brewery. Hevia, an old revolutionary colleague of Pepín Bosch, had taken part in the abortive 1931 coup attempt against Machado of which Bosch had been treasurer. Hevia had also been interim president of Cuba, for just seventy-two hours, in 1934. Though personally uninspiring, he had been director of supplies and prices during the war, and in Prío's cabinet he had been secretary of state, minister of agriculture, and president of the development commission. Pepín Bosch supported him financially but also likely found him a less than exciting candidate.

The left wing, in particular the Communist party, which Hevia had severely criticized, accused him of being a puppet for the political interests of Prío and the business interests of the Bacardis. The head of the Cuban Communist party, Francisco Calderio Blas Roca, wrote: "The candidacy of Hevia is not only the candidacy imposed by the Presidential Palace, it is a symbol of the surrender to imperialism, since Hevia is the nominee of Annapolis and the Bacardi Rum Company, which has long since ceased to be Cuban, being more American than Cuban."

The statement was demagogic drivel. Bacardi was an internationally known company built entirely with Cuban money and mostly with Cuban talent. But the Bacardis were capitalists, and capitalists had long been fair game for any unfounded political slight, and not just from the Communist party. Hugh Thomas, for example, writes offhand-edly: "Hevia was now forty-eight, an engineer and, *though closely connected with the Bacardi Rum Company*, believed to be honest" (italics added).

Thomas never explains why close connection with the Bacardi Rum Company should indicate dishonesty. Plainly, no explanation was thought necessary. Perhaps it never even occurred to Thomas that he was slandering the Bacardis. They were capitalists, and thus automatically guilty of something or other.

The 1952 elections were never held. On March 10, 1952, backed by the army, Fulgencio Batista seized power once more, claiming that he was concerned that if he did not take control, Prío would. Of Prío, it was said that he "fell like a rotten fruit . . . he was as inept for crime as he was condescending towards criminals." The coup was bloodless, and Batista's move was accepted in most quarters with some relief. Compared with the intervening eight years, his own previous regime looked like a model of honesty and good government.

The U.S. recognized Batista's government, but then it would have been difficult to do otherwise, since he came to power with no resistance. "The people and I are the dictators," Batista explained. But for the Bacardis, Batista was anathema, not merely because of the historic antipathy between them but because he had seized power illegitimately. Once again, members of the family were about to enter the dangerous world of clandestine politics.

The July Fiesta was always the biggest event in Santiago's social calendar. There were huge, elaborate floats; beautiful *mulata* dancers performed; streets were closed and decorated, with a prize from the Bacardi company for the best; sales of Bacardi rum and Hatuey beer skyrocketed. A label from a bottle of Hatuey or Bacardi gave you a vote in choosing the Carnival queen. "Con Bacardi," declared an ad from the times, "siempre es alegría, Fiesta y Carnaval" (With Bacardi, there's always joy, fiesta, and Carnival). There was also a frisson of danger, so naturally the Bacardi girls — who were raised as delicate flowers and strictly chaperoned — were not permitted to attend. They had to make do with a Carnival ball at the country club, and perhaps a little well-ordered celebration in a street especially closed off for the purpose in Vista Alegre. For the Bacardi boys, of course, it was different. And the Bacardi men; well, they just disappeared for three days. Daniel Bacardi, as head of the distillery, and head of the company in Pepín Bosch's absence, felt obliged to commit himself as fully as possible to the proceedings.

"This is a scandal," Daniel's wife complained to a friend, a Jesuit priest. "Look at Daniel and all those other men who should know better — taking drinks with everybody, chasing those *mulatas*, riding on floats. People will lose respect for them."

"Forget it, Graziella," the priest replied. "Everybody loves them for it."

By the last day, July 26, the strain always began to tell, and that was one of the prime reasons for what happened very early that morning during the Fiesta in 1953. While most of Santiago was sleeping off late-night indulgence, a group of young revolutionaries made an assault on Moncada, a sprawling, low-rise, crenellated barracks on the eastern side of the city. The attack was bungled, and Batista's troops, even with their hangovers, repelled it. The surviving attackers were hunted down, and many of them tortured and killed. One who survived — partly because of the intercession of the man who had presided over Enrique's funeral, Archbishop Monseñor Enrique Pérez Serantes, partly because his wife, Mirta Díaz-Balart, came from an important family, and partly through sheer luck — was the leader of the bungled expedition, Fidel Castro.

Moncada was a rash attack on a military installation by zealous young terrorists. But its importance in the mythology of Cuban history is enormous: it gave its date, *26 julio*, to a political movement; it provided the movement with martyrs; and, perhaps most important, it gave a platform to the man who would dominate Cuban politics as no man had ever done before.

To *santiagueros*, Fidel Castro was a local boy. His background was well-heeled, though he did not exactly come from a "good family." His father, Angel, was a ruthless, self-made plantation-owner who had carved out an estate north of Santiago in the valley of Birán, described by Andrew Duany, scion of the prominent family that held huge landholdings adjacent to those of Angel Castro, as "a refuge of criminals, gamblers and cult leaders who were not accepted or wanted elsewhere." The voodoo cults found fervent followers in the valley, while, wrote Duany, "representatives of the clergy, justice and civilization seldom took it upon themselves to enter this hostile terrain." Birán could be reached only by dirt roads. The journey was long and dangerous. Nobody would dream of venturing into the area alone or unarmed. Angel Castro ruled his kingdom with a rod of iron, and his workers lived in feudal conditions, receiving not money for their labors but IOUs that could be redeemed only at Angel's company store.

Juan Prado was a young Cuban who, before joining Bacardi in 1951, worked for the local subsidiary of the U.S. soap company Procter & Gamble. His first sales territory was the region surrounding Palma Soriano, a little town northwest of Santiago. The territory included Angel Castro's plantation.

One of Prado's sales lines was candles, which, along with kerosene lamps, were the only form of lighting in most of the area. Prado's company had a sales contest for candles, which Prado was desperate to win. Having looked through the sales records, he decided the only man who might buy in the volume he needed was Angel Castro. Taking a companion and a revolver, he climbed in his jeep and headed for Birán. Although he did not personally know Angel's son Fidel, then engaged in gangster politics at the University of Havana, they had mutual friends. This gave him an advantage in dealing with the father, who would be pleased to chat with someone who knew of his "crazy" son's doings. Prado arrived after the arduous drive and was given dinner in the huge dining hall where all the workers and managers ate. The next day they talked business.

"I'm here on a long shot," said Prado, "but to be honest with you,

I am in a sales contest for candles, and I looked in my book, and you haven't bought any for some months and I thought you must be low, and I wondered if I could sell you some."

Angel Castro looked at his big, handwritten ledger. "How many cases do you need to win the contest?"

"Five hundred."

"Send them to me," said Angel Castro. "If I can't sell them, I'll stop selling kerosene!"

Rigging markets wasn't too difficult when you owned the company store. Such was the environment in which Fidel Castro gained his first experience of capitalism.

Despite this primitive background, Fidel Castro had been sent to Dolores, the local Jesuit school in Santiago, and afterward to the major Jesuit academy in Havana, Belén, both of which were attended by many members of the Bacardi family and company employees. He had become a full-time revolutionary while studying law at the University in Havana and had participated in several upheavals — including the bloody riots in Bogotá, Colombia, in 1948. Like many of his fellow students, he was out to make a political name for himself.

Castro not merely survived the attack on Moncada, he used the subsequent trial, even though it was secret, as a platform. According to revolutionary mythology, Castro treated his captors and accusers to a two-hour lecture, building "history's case to justify taking up arms against tyrants." He cited the English, French, and American revolutions, along with St. Thomas Aquinas, John of Salisbury, Martin Luther, John Calvin, Montesquieu, Jean-Jacques Rousseau, John Milton, John Locke, Thomas Paine, French and German jurists, Honoré de Balzac, and, of course, the ultimate Cuban source, José Martí. A version of this lengthy exposition of high-sounding principles was smuggled out and subsequently published as *History Will Absolve Me*. This document, as Tad Szulc writes in *Fidel: A Critical Portrait*, "remains to this day the fundamental and legendary document of the Cuban revolution, the venerated scripture of the rebel movement."

The Moncada incident caused uproar in Santiago and marked the beginning of a period during which the city became increasingly unsafe. But there was little doubt that the attack had its heroic attractions for the *santiagueros*, including the Bacardi family. One detail of the incident unreported in subsequent Cuban revolutionary histories is the identity of the man who paid for the funerals of thirteen young revolutionaries killed by Batista's troops. It was Pepín Bosch.

Fidel Castro was given fifteen years in prison and taken off to the penitentiary on the Isle of Pines, thus following a noble Cuban tradition — shades of Emilio Bacardi Moreau — of imprisonment for political beliefs.

Batista, meanwhile, grew lazy in his dictatorship. Like some bizarre figure from a novel by Gabriel García Márquez, he spent much of his time on trivial matters, listening to tapped telephones, playing canasta, and watching horror movies. He eradicated political gangsterism, and the economy boomed; but civil unrest mounted, marked by sporadic bombings throughout the island. Santiago's popular ex-mayor, Luis Casero, was among those arrested and imprisoned.

Castro, far from being persecuted in prison, was almost indulged by the Batista regime, which seemed confident because the economy was healthy. In Havana's bustling Vedado district, the new Havana Hilton, the financing of which Pepín Bosch had helped organize, was the most prominent symbol of a new building boom. The *Havana Post* described Cuba as bidding for the position of the "Las Vegas of Latin America." The old Hotel Nacional — another hotel in which Bacardi held an interest — opened a casino in 1956. Eartha Kitt, Lena Horne, and Nat King Cole were all regulars in the Havana nightclubs.

So secure did Batista feel that, in 1955, under a general amnesty, he released Castro, who immediately moved to Mexico to continue plotting. On December 2, 1956, Castro returned on the overloaded motor yacht *Granma*, with an "invasion force" of eighty-three people, including the Argentinian doctor who — once he was safely dead — would become the patron saint of modern Cuban revolution, Che Guevara.

There had been considerable disruptions in life in Santiago ahead of the attack. The local student leader, Frank País, an ally of Castro, carried out a series of commando raids in the city toward the end of November as part of a softening-up process. Civil life had been brought virtually to a standstill. Still, like Moncada, the *Granma* invasion turned into a fiasco. Bad weather delayed the landing. The yacht ran aground. Castro's force and his allies on the island were virtually wiped out. Castro's actions again seemed theatrical, almost quixotic, but again he survived. Along with a handful of followers, he made his way into the mountains of the Sierra Maestra, whose misty blue peaks rise to the west of Santiago.

In 1957 and 1958, teenage members of the Bacardi clan joined their schoolmates in secretly collecting money for Castro and his romantic figures in the nearby mountains. José Espín's daughter Vilma became a messenger for the Castro forces. If family members became too enthusiastic — as did, for example, Roberto del Rosal, a great-grandson of Emilio — they were packed off to school in the United States. Younger family members were sent to Havana. Santiago was simply not safe.

Even those who were not politically committed found themselves involved in the struggle. In Havana, Guillermo Mármol, the Bacardi lawyer who had served Pepín Bosch in government and whose advice Bosch now frequently sought, agreed to act as driver for Aureliano Sánchez Arango — the former Prío minister — who was planning a coup. Sánchez, a onetime Marxist, was known to be honest and brave. Mármol drove him to clandestine meetings at little houses in the Havana suburbs, but refused to go inside in case he met anybody he recognized. Guillermo Mármol knew that Cubans were bad at keeping secrets.

Mármol did not discuss these involvements with Pepín Bosch. In fact, Pepín Bosch did not agree with Sánchez Arango's politics. Nevertheless, when Sánchez Arango asked Mármol to help him find the money to get out of the country, Mármol approached Bosch, specifying only that the money was for the anti-Batista cause. Bosch handed over cash without question.

Mármol also delivered cash from Bosch for arms shipments to Felipe Pazos, an important figure in the Castro revolution. Pazos had been a student revolutionary against Machado in the early 1930s and had lived in exile from 1930 to 1933. He was considered the outstanding economist of his generation; he had worked in the fledgling International Monetary Fund. Prío, with whom he had been a student revolutionary, appointed him president of the Cuban national bank from 1950 until the Batista coup, during which time Bosch was also finance minister. Pazos's son, Javier, was active in University of Havana student politics in the 1950s, which was perhaps part of the reason why Felipe lent his support to the 26 July Movement.

Pazos played a crucial intermediary role in starting the U.S. media coverage that was to make of Fidel Castro a cross between Robin Hood and Lawrence of Arabia. Pazos approached Ruby Hart Phillips, who had been the staff correspondent for the *New York Times* in Havana for twenty years, suggesting that a correspondent be sent into the Sierra Maestra immediately after the *Granma* fiasco to interview

Castro and thus prove he was not dead. Phillips arranged for a *New York Times* editorial writer named Herbert Matthews to travel to the Sierra. He was helped and encouraged by *santiagueros*, including Pepín Bosch, who realized the importance of the American media.

Matthews, in his subsequent dispatches, did far more than prove that Castro was alive. His enthusiastic coverage earned him the title "Father of the Castro Revolution." It also led to his being reviled as one of the greatest journalistic dupes of all time.

🦇

Herbert Matthews was following a powerful tradition of American proactive journalism in Cuban affairs. Its greatest exponent had been William Randolph Hearst. Hearst had not only played a crucial part in stoking public opinion in favor of American intervention in Cuba back in 1898; he and his staff had practiced a brand of "gonzo" journalism that has probably never been equaled. The mind-boggling level of Hearst's involvement was exemplified by a message he sent to one of his London journalists after the outbreak of the Spanish-American War. If the Spanish tried to send a relief fleet to Manila, he instructed, then the journalist was to purchase a ship and scuttle it in the Suez Canal.

After U.S. troops landed near Santiago in the summer of 1898, Hearst had visited the rebel general Calixto García. García (to whom the famous "message" had gone) presented him with a tattered flag and assured him that the *Journal* had been the "most potent influence" in bringing U.S. military assistance to Cuba. At San Juan Hill, one of Hearst's ace reporters had taken part in the charge and been wounded. The reporter related what happened next, in his own purple prose: "Someone knelt down in the grass beside me and put his hand on my fevered head. Opening my eyes I saw Mr. Hearst . . . a straw hat with a bright ribbon on his head, a revolver at his belt, and a pencil and notebook in his hand . . . Slowly he took down my story of the fight. Again and again the ting of Mauser bullets interrupted. 'I'm sorry you're hurt, but,' his face was radiant, 'wasn't it a splendid fight? We must beat every paper in the world.'"

By the 1950s, Hearst's involvement was universally reviled in liberal American media and academic circles as having promoted the worst kind of U.S. "imperialism." Herbert Matthews went to the Sierra carrying this guilt as part of his intellectual baggage. Perhaps he saw a chance to set history straight.

Matthews was not the only important U.S. journalist to be courted by Pepín Bosch for the anti-Batista, pro-Castro cause. Another was Colonel Jules Dubois of the *Chicago Tribune*, who also played a seminal role in shaping American opinions about Castro. One incident, recounted by Dubois, clearly indicated the source of Fidel Castro's support.

In June 1957, Dubois flew to Santiago, where he was met by his "old friend" Pepín Bosch. Dubois later wrote: "'It is fortunate you came tonight,' Pepín said, 'because this morning a couple of Fidelistas killed a soldier who was riding in a bus. Your arrival might prevent the police and army from snatching four boys from their homes and killing them in reprisal.'"

That same June evening, a clandestine dinner was held at the otherwise deserted country club at El Caney, just outside Santiago, in honor of Dubois. Present at the dinner were Pepín Bosch; Daniel Bacardi, then president of the Santiago Chamber of Commerce; Judge Manuel Urrutia, who was destined to be Castro's first president (he had been a judge at Castro's trial after the 1953 raid on Moncada, and had dissented from conviction); Father José Chabebe, a prominent Catholic priest and head of the Catholic Youth Movement; the president of the University of Oriente; the presidents of the local Rotary and Lions Clubs; the heads of the Santiago medical and bar associations; and other prominent local businessmen.

At one end of the oblong table, Dubois noticed an empty chair, with a place setting and a card: "Reserved." The toastmaster, Fernando Ojeda, a Santiago coffee-exporter, made a point of explaining to Dubois, in front of the assembly: "One of our compatriots had planned to attend this dinner in your honor tonight, but he sent his regrets that he could not make it. We can understand that and we accept his excuses because he has engaged in an important mission for Cuba. His name is Fidel Castro."

Despite his own vulnerability, and that of the Bacardi company, Pepín Bosch made little secret of his opposition to Batista. The dangers of his stance were becoming apparent.

Earlier in 1957, on March 13, a group of revolutionary students from a group called the Directorio Revolucionario had stormed the Presidential Palace in Havana (at the time, Batista was reportedly reading *The Day Lincoln Was Shot*). The shirtsleeved young attackers came in two waves, in cars and a delivery truck. Armed with a map of the palace given them by ex-president Prío, they fought their way to the second floor but could not find their way to the third, to which Batista had retreated. The students were routed and their leader —

who had seized a local radio station — was killed. The shooting could be heard clearly from the Edificio Bacardi; police even believed the shooting may have come from there. Juan Prado, who was then sales manager for Bacardi in Havana, remembers climbing to the building's tower to watch the action.

The aftermath of that attack produced an interesting example of the psychology of dictatorship. Eusebio Mujer, head of the confederation of trade unions and a stout supporter of Batista, went to the palace to "congratulate" Batista on his survival. Some business leaders, not wanting the unions to gain further advantage, or simply seeking to curry Batista's favor, followed suit. Soon the trickle of corporate well-wishers turned into a flood. Hugh Thomas wrote: "The aftermath of the attack on the palace had two characteristics; first, the sympathy which the business world, the upper classes in general, and foreign commercial interests showed toward Batista was remarkable. The leaders of all these communities called on Batista during the next few weeks to condemn the attack; so did the National Association of Sugar Mill Owners, . . . the Veterans of the War of Independence, the Cuba Banking Association, the Insurance Companies, American and Spanish businessmen, property owners, coffee and cattle-breeders' associations, rice growers, cigarette and cigar manufacturers, even fishermen."

For this assessment, Thomas apparently relied on Batista's own account (in his book *Cuba Betrayed*). But, of course, once a few groups visited Batista, a psychological pressure built on other groups to follow. Soon it became clear that *not* to congratulate Batista would be construed — under the subtle but potentially fatal pressures of dictatorship — as a sign of opposition. Indeed, more than subtle pressures: businessmen were *summoned* to the palace to congratulate Batista. Thomas's misreading is made abundantly clear by what happened to Pepín Bosch when he didn't join the procession of well-wishers.

Batista dispatched a senator to ask for a letter of congratulation and support from Bacardi's president. Bosch refused. The senator asked if Bosch would be willing to express his "goodwill" toward Batista in an interview with one of the journalistic hacks Batista kept on the government payroll. Again Bosch refused, saying that anybody who had seized power deserved to have to watch his back. In that case, he was told by the senator, the government "could not guarantee his safety." Bosch told the senator he had no fear; they wouldn't dare to kill him.

Such was the climate in which the "remarkable sympathy" of the "business world, the upper classes in general, and foreign commercial interests" toward Batista was displayed.

Batista indeed lacked the courage to attack Bosch directly. But he could bring other pressures to bear, including increased taxes. Bosch and the Bacardis became concerned that Batista might seek some excuse to expropriate them. For this reason, in 1957, the Bacardi trademarks were clandestinely moved from Cuba.

Later that year, while Bosch was in Mexico ironing out problems at a new plant, Batista's soldiers appeared at Bosch's home in Santiago. There they found Bosch's younger son, Carlos Bosch Schueg, nicknamed Lindy (after Charles Lindbergh, to whom he had been presented as a baby in Havana). An eccentric young man whose first love was farming, Lindy had gone into a pig and chicken business with American partners in Santiago. The soldiers who arrived at the house wanted him to come along with them. He was not being charged, but in those days charges were not necessary. He called one of his American partners, who came with him to Moncada, where he was detained. Taking him into custody was meant to force his father back to the island.

News of Lindy's incarceration spread quickly. His uncle, the formidable Víctor Schueg, raised hell, and other important connections came into play. It was not possible to contact Bosch, however, since there had recently been an earthquake and communications with Mexico had been disrupted. Guillermo Mármol volunteered to take the news to Bosch in person.

On hearing what had happened, Bosch betrayed a rare flash of rage. He and his wife returned at once to Santiago via Havana. By the time he got home, Lindy had been released. Nevertheless, Bosch went to the commander of the barracks and said, "I am here. What do you want with me?" The commander replied that he wanted Bosch to lead an uprising against Batista. Bosch, sensing a trap, said he knew nothing of military things. He returned to his house, packed, and left the country, telling Lindy that he must leave too.

By July 1957, with Castro ensconced in the mountains nearby, Santiago was in a state of near-open war between the 26 July Movement and the police. Smart residential districts such as Vista Alegre were acknowledged as strongholds of the 26 July Movement. When Castro started broadcasting from the Sierra over Radio Rebelde, his most devoted listeners could be found huddled round their expensive Zenith sets at the Vista Alegre tennis club.

A new U.S. ambassador, Earl Smith, was appointed in July 1957. Almost immediately, he decided to visit Santiago. The day before he was due to set out, however, the local revolutionary student leader, Frank País, who was still only twenty-three, was shot. Such was the power of the 26 July Movement in Santiago that its members were able to come openly to País's lying-in-state at the house of his fiancée, América Telebauta.

The *batistianos* were eager to suppress any form of demonstration for Smith's benefit. However, the women of Santiago, coming downtown as if on a shopping expedition, gathered in the cathedral square and greeted Smith's motorcade with cries of "Libertad! Libertad!" Smith was appalled at the brutality of the police, who turned fire hoses on the women, many of them well-dressed and middle-aged, and muscled them into police vans.

Frank País's funeral was followed by a general strike, which Daniel Bacardi, as head of the local Chamber of Commerce, helped organize. After several days, *batistiano* soldiers burst into Daniel's house in Vista Alegre and demanded that he sign a document telling the populace to go back to work. His wife hustled the family into a back room, where they spent most of the night praying. Daniel refused to sign, but a notice appeared in the paper the next morning over his signature telling the workers the strike was over.

Life in Santiago grew more and more difficult. Army and police patrols were regularly fired upon. Flags with 26 July insignia appeared mysteriously over public buildings. Strikes became frequent. But the critical factor in the fall of Batista was, as with every major development in modern Cuban history, the United States.

When a naval revolt in Cienfuegos was put down with U.S. equipment — including B-26 bombers, which had been supplied only for defence purposes — there was great consternation in the U.S. State Department. The halting of arms supplies now became the principal issue in U.S. – Cuban relations. Ambassador Smith was still a Batista supporter, but he found his own embassy staff in Havana openly hostile to the dictator. The CIA, he discovered, were practically *fidelistas*.

In March 1958, the U.S. stopped shipping arms to Batista. This withdrawal of U.S. support marked the beginning of the end of his regime. In April, Castro called an unsuccessful general strike, which damaged his credibility and raised Batista's hopes. But when Batista launched an unsuccessful offensive against Castro in the Sierra, his own credibility was undermined.

The Castro forces engaged in a round of kidnappings. By November, the war had also begun to have a major impact on the economy. To terrorism, which came mainly from urban guerrilla units unconnected with Castro, Batista responded with repression. Even those with no liking for Castro began to favor him as the only clear alternative. Meanwhile, the reports of Matthews *et al.* in the American media had established Castro as a popular hero. Castro, for his part, mollified moderate political leaders by assuring them he would restore the 1940 constitution, which had been drawn up under Batista but never implemented. He also promised free elections. In the meantime, the election Batista called for 1958 was a massive fraud even by Cuban standards. By then nobody was taking much notice of elections.

Pepín Bosch, though he had channeled resources into the Sierra early on, now had misgivings about Castro. Such was the level of support for the guerrilla leader, however, that Bosch was not able to voice these misgivings among most Cubans. His views were shared by a number of experienced U.S. diplomats, such as his friend William Pawley, the former U.S. ambassador to Brazil and Peru and founder of Cubana Airlines.

Pawley had been deeply concerned at the prospect of Castro, whom he regarded as clearly a Communist, coming to power. In November 1958, six weeks before the takeover, he had persuaded a group of senior State Department and CIA officials that Batista should be persuaded to capitulate to a caretaker government. One of the five members of that provisional government would be Pepín Bosch.

Pawley held a secret three-hour meeting with Batista on December 9. As Pawley said later in testimony to a U.S. Senate subcommittee: "I offered him an opportunity to live at Daytona Beach with his family; that his friends and family would not be molested; that we would make an effort to stop Fidel Castro from coming into power as a Communist, but that the caretaker government would be men who were enemies of his, otherwise it would not work anyway, and Fidel Castro would otherwise have to lay down his arms or admit he was a revolutionary fighting against anybody only because he wanted power, not because he was against Batista."

Pawley was asked at the Senate subcommittee whether the new government containing Bosch would have been unfriendly to Castro. He said yes.

Nevertheless, Pawley had not been able to back his offer with the official approval of the U.S. government. He was authorized to say only that he would *try* to persuade Washington to approve. Batista may also have balked at the idea of handing over power to longtime foes such as Bosch. He turned Pawley down.

On December 17, 1958, Ambassador Smith told Batista that the U.S. no longer believed he could maintain effective control, and Batista's thoughts turned to flight. Less than two weeks later, on New Year's Eve, Fulgencio Batista fled his country, leaving it to the fate William Pawley had predicted.

Bacardi's Santiago plant was already witness to an ill omen: the coconut tree, El Coco, planted almost one hundred years before by the founder's son Facundo, and around which Bacardi's plant expansions had always been made, was dying.

CHAPTER EIGHT

From Dream to Nightmare

*"One does not establish a
dictatorship in order to safeguard a
revolution; one makes the revolution
in order to establish the dictatorship."*

GEORGE ORWELL, *1984*

Santiago de Cuba. January 1, 1959

During mid-morning, the first reports reached Santiago that Batista had fled. The word spread like wildfire: Fidel Castro was coming! Elation swept through the city, not least through the factories, offices, and homes of the Bacardi family. The tyrant was gone; all waited for his nemesis, the symbol of a nation's often-dashed hopes. Castro was about to take his rightful place at the head of the table.

That evening, Castro led his triumphant columns of bearded warriors — the *barbudos* — and female commandos into the city. The rebels' first stop was the Moncada barracks, bloody birthplace of the 26 July Movement. The barracks surrendered without a shot. The entire population turned out to cheer, to catch a glimpse, perhaps even to touch the hem of Castro's olive-green uniform.

Later, outside the reception in the municipal building, the crowd waited in Céspedes Park, whose gardens had been laid out by Emilio Bacardi. There, fifty-seven years before, as the city's first popularly elected mayor, Emilio had instituted the Fiesta de la Bandera. The intervening years had brought enormous commercial success to the company, but the political frustration had been felt as keenly by the Bacardis as by any Cubans. If any family had revolutionary credentials it was the Bacardis. They had never kowtowed to Batista. They had donated money to the rebel cause. Now, at last, the dreams of Emilio Bacardi might be realized. By a son of Oriente province. And on New Year's Day.

Family members crowded in the windows of the Club San Carlos to listen to Castro's first speech. Nobody could have been more proud when Castro called Santiago the "bulwark of liberty." Nobody could have been more gratified or surprised when he declared it would become the new capital of Cuba. Castro promised free elections, free speech, a free press, land for the landless, and restoration of the 1940 constitution. He also called for a general strike.

After the speech, along with the other citizens of Santiago, the Bacardis bowed their heads as Archbishop Pérez Serantes, after praising Castro and his *barbudos* for their triumph, prayed for everlasting peace in Cuba.

Later the same day, January 2, leaving his brother Raúl in Santiago, Castro set out up the island's central highway for Havana on what would prove a triumphal march, lasting five days and nights.

As Hugh Thomas wrote: "For an emotional, generous and optimistic people such as the Cubans, Castro's capture of power, with its air, self-conscious no doubt but irresistible, of re-enacting the wars of independence, redeeming Martí's failure and Céspedes's before that, gave a superb thrill of self-congratulation and pleasure. For much of both South and North America, weary of the seemingly endless if often worthy steppes of the Eisenhower era, Castro's victory also afforded a moment of romance, a splash of sunlight, an echo of an heroic age long before even Martí — the era of the conquistadors."

The North American media played up these heroic images, continuing their role as handmaidens and midwives to the revolution. Jules Dubois received the first post-revolutionary interview with Castro, in the town of Holguín, then followed him up the island with scarcely disguised enthusiasm. Dubois's scoop miffed Herbert Matthews, who felt that, since he had provided such sterling service in promoting Castro via the *New York Times*, he deserved the honor of the first interview. This didn't prevent Matthews from writing an editorial congratulating the American and British governments on their hasty recognition of Castro. The Castro regime, Matthews wrote, had "pledged itself to honor all international obligations, to hold new elections within a maximum of two years, and to protect foreign property and investments." Ed Sullivan flew from New York to interview Castro in the Provincial Palace at Matanzas for his Sunday-night CBS Television program.

Not everybody viewed Castro's accession with unalloyed joy. Pepín Bosch had returned to Havana as soon as word had come of Batista's flight. Since there were no commercial flights to Santiago, Bosch set off for Santiago by road, accompanied by two carloads of Bacardi and Hatuey executives from Havana. Control of Cuba was still in doubt. Roads had been landmined. The journey was not without its perils.

Since Bosch was traveling east and Castro west on the same

highway, a meeting was inevitable. Castro's armored caravan was due in Manacas, where Bosch had opened another successful Hatuey brewery in 1952, at around the same time as Bosch's little convoy. The general manager of Manacas, Augusto ("Polo") Valdez Miranda, a lawyer and former revolutionary from the period of Machado, had known Bosch since that time and had been deeply involved in anti-Batista politics. Some members of Bosch's party imagined they would wait to meet Castro. Most were excited by the prospect. Bosch was opposed to the idea. "I don't know who he is," he said. "Let's go." Circumventing the oncoming hordes, they headed on to Santiago.

Other members of the family were enthusiastic about meeting Castro. At the Havana end of Castro's triumphal march, at the Modelo brewery at El Cotorro, management prepared a victory lunch for the conquering hero. Employees placed a banner across the brewery fence welcoming Castro and thanking him for their liberation. The factory's siren heralded his approach with long, deafening blasts. But Castro sped right past the plant, leaving disappointment in his wake. Nevertheless, Joaquín Bacardi, "the brewer," told Dubois that day: "It is the most marvelous thing that I have ever seen or expected to see in my life . . . Cuba is now free and I hope it will remain so for many years."

At El Cotorro, local television cameras caught up with Castro. Thenceforth his every move through jostling crowds was transmitted to a breathless Havana. The convoy, with its captured Sherman tanks on trailers and its buses full of exhausted *barbudos*, now became becalmed in the sea of welcome. Castro switched to an expropriated helicopter for the final few miles into the suburbs of Havana.

Peals of church bells mixed with factory whistles and ships' sirens. Eyewitness Ruby Hart Phillips, in her book *The Cuban Dilemma*, wrote: "The crowds cheered themselves hoarse, threw confetti, waved small flags and held up placards with words of welcome. The wave of joy which swept the city as the column moved toward downtown Havana was almost tangible. Never before had any Cuban or probably any hero of the Western Hemisphere been given a welcome such as this."

Among the crowds was a great-grandson of Emilio, young Adolfo Comas Bacardi, who had recently moved with his family into a big house in the new Biltmore suburb to the west of the city. The teenage Adolfo cheered and cheered, and then rushed home to watch the rest of the spectacle on television.

At a televised mass rally that evening, a white dove perched on Castro's shoulder. Hollywood couldn't have done it better. Castro's assumption of power seemed almost miraculous. No government overthrow had been invested with such magic since Cortés's conquest of Mexico against overwhelming odds more than four hundred years earlier. Cortés's victory had depended significantly on the Aztecs' belief that he was a god whose arrival had been foretold in local mythology. Castro, too, cheered into Santiago and Havana without bloodshed, assumed an air of almost superhuman invulnerability. The *barbudos* did not arrive as bandits, as so many "revolutionaries" had in the past. They did not drink or loot. They came with Father Chabebe's blessed medallions and rosaries round their necks.

Cortés had had prophecy going for him; Castro had the *New York Times* and CBS. Just as the newspapers of Hearst and Pulitzer had stirred up sentiment for the Spanish-American War sixty years earlier, so American newspapers — and now television networks too — had stirred up sentiment for Castro, who played them like a violin. He and his *barbudos* were portrayed as a priesthood, ready to cleanse the nation of corruption and bring freedom and honor. Cubans, too, had enchanted themselves with Castro's image. Like the men at the banquet in Santiago, they projected their fondest hopes into the empty chair.

Television proved enormously important in securing Castro's almost mesmeric hold on the Cuban people. As Andrew Duany wrote at the time: "The first appearance of Fidel Castro on the television screens produced an almost magic effect throughout Cuba. The vision of the men in arms on that triumphant January day electrified practically every Cuban and when the bearded Fidel spoke from the barracks of Camp Columbia, with a white dove playing on his shoulder, he seemed for a while to be a true modern Messiah."

To the Cuban population, the notion that Castro might adopt Communism seemed ridiculous. His political program, as far as he had recently expounded one at all, was far from radical. Indeed, it seemed nebulous. He promised only to be true to the revolutionary spirit of the past. "This time," he said, "it will not be possible to say, as on other occasions, that we will betray our dead, because this time the dead will continue in command."

How could Cuba have known, amid the euphoria, that the dead in question would turn out to be Lenin and Marx?

Castro had been as surprised as anyone by Batista's flight, and his first reaction had been not joy that Batista had gone, but outrage that he himself might be robbed of power. Batista's departure created a vacuum into which others than himself might well have moved. Castro had called the general strike to cripple the country until he could seize control. His declaration that Santiago would be the new capital sprang only from uncertainty about Havana's loyalties. Once he had secured Havana, Santiago was conveniently forgotten.

At that first reception in Santiago, many who had been at the dinner for Dubois eighteen months earlier, such as Daniel Bacardi Rosell, had been disappointed that the conquering hero had not greeted them with open arms. Indeed, Castro had treated them coldly, talking over their heads, even turning his back on them. The businessmen and professionals tried to persuade themselves it was just injured pride. After all, they had sent money and made sacrifices, but how could these compare with the sacrifices of the *barbudos*? They took comfort that one of their number, Manuel Urrutia, was due to be declared president.

Manuel Jorge Cutillas, a great-grandson of Emilio and a young chemical engineer working for Bacardi as well as lecturing at the University of Oriente, had listened to Castro from the second floor of the Club San Carlos. He had looked in awe at Batista's tanks, now like big docile animals come to Castro's heel, and witnessed another piece of history after Castro's triumphant entry into Santiago. As a member of the university faculty, he attended the swearing-in of Cuba's new president.

The inauguration of Manuel Urrutia took place in the university library. Cutillas found himself among heroic leaders of the *barbudos* but was shocked to see Bonifacio Asa, the former head of Batista's secret police, still wearing his blue uniform but now sporting an armband of the 26 July Movement.

On January 10, Father Chabebe — who had been at the "empty chair" dinner for Jules Dubois — was at a banquet to honor the U.S. vice-consul in the city when a fellow priest approached his table and whispered: "Please come with me, Father. Four Batista officers are to be tried and executed tonight. We will be needed."

Father Chabebe was disturbed. How could one know, before a trial, that the verdict would be guilty and the sentence death? When Chabebe went to the municipal court, he found five rebel "judges," only one of whom had any knowledge of the law. They paid little attention to the proceedings, chatting among themselves or with Castro's brother Raúl, who dropped in. Eventually, death sentences were pronounced for all prisoners. They would be carried out at once.

Manuel Jorge Cutillas and his wife, Rosa María Dubois, were staying with his parents in Vista Alegre at the time because the Villa Elvira was not felt to be safe. They were awoken that night by volleys of gunfire from the nearby firing range in the San Juan Hills, where Father Chabebe was hearing the confessions of those condemned at the tribunal, and others, before they were shot at the edge of an open pit. The sporadic gunfire kept Cutillas and his wife awake for the rest of the night. The next day, he saw in the newspaper that "war criminals" had been sentenced to death by a revolutionary tribunal and shot. Among them was the man Cutillas had been surprised to see at Urrutia's inauguration, Bonifacio Asa.

Cutillas was shocked, not that Asa had been executed but that Castro had first recruited him to work for the new, "magnanimous" revolutionary government. What game was Castro playing? For the first time, a nagging disquiet entered Cutillas's mind.

In March 1959, his disquiet grew when forty-four Batista airmen, accused of war crimes, were acquitted at a trial in Santiago. Castro declared a retrial, installing the minister of defence as the prosecutor. The airmen were all convicted and sentenced to between two and thirty years in prison. Subsequently, their defence lawyers lost their jobs and a number of the defence witnesses were jailed. "Revolutionary justice is based not on legal precepts," Castro declared, "but on moral conviction . . . Since the airmen belonged to the air force of Batista . . . they are criminals and must be punished."

Castro had just declared himself above the law.

Pepín Bosch's doubts about Castro were strengthened by these first months of revolutionary justice and summary execution. They were strengthened further in April 1959, when he was forced to travel with Castro. Shortly after the revolution, the American Society of Newspaper Editors — many still infatuated with Castro's Robin Hood image — invited the Cuban leader to the United States. Castro realized that the presence on the trip of such a highly regarded business figure as Pepín Bosch would have great value to the revolution, albeit as camouflage.

Bosch was wary. When Castro's office called him, he refused, saying he had only just returned from exile and had much to do at Bacardi. But Castro insisted and Bosch, aware of Bacardi's vulnerability, felt he had no choice. When he turned up for the flight at Havana, he discovered, while waiting for Castro in the American ambassador's car, that he was to be the only businessman on the plane. Castro arrived two hours late in a worn and wrinkled uniform. His secretary, Teresa Casuso, according to her own later account, cleaned Castro's dirty fingernails on the plane, "while he read comic books."

The flight confirmed Bosch's worst fears. Castro sat beside him and asked for his help. They spoke for two hours. Castro asked Bosch how Cuba might be further industrialized. Cuba had iron ore and molybdenum; Bosch mentioned the potential for specialty steels. Castro seemed interested, but kept asking, "Can we beat the U.S.?" It was an obsession. Speaking of labor, Bosch said that it was dangerous for the government to control unions, as Batista had done and as Castro wanted to do. He also said that Cuba had to have elections; true liberty depended upon it. When he used the word "liberty," Castro got up and stalked off. The two men never spoke again.

Bosch saw that the new Cuban leader hated the United States, and that — despite his strenuous public denials — he was a Communist. While Castro went on his public relations tour, Bosch, feigning illness, flew to New York to warn his associates that Bacardi was going to have big trouble in Cuba. In Washington, he secretly approached Christian Herter, the acting secretary of state, with whom Castro had lunched, and said that he would be prepared to accept an invitation to join Castro's government if he could hasten the dictator's fall. This suggestion — which reportedly went all the way to President Dwight Eisenhower — was turned down. Pepín Bosch was clearly prepared to risk his life to counter the terrible danger he saw facing Cuba.

Castro meanwhile received delirious welcomes wherever he went — except, that is, from skeptical and unfashionably "right-wing" politicians such as Vice-President Richard Nixon, who thought the Cuban leader was either naive about Communism or under the control of the Communists. But Castro kept repeating: "We are not Communists." He reiterated that Cuba would not confiscate foreign-owned private property. Elections, however, would be some time in coming. His slogan — "Revolution first, elections afterward!" — began, with a certain Orwellian cadence, to be heard and read in Cuba. Castro went on to tumultuous receptions in New York, at Harvard, and in Montreal before returning to Havana.

When Bosch returned to Cuba, he quietly told senior Bacardi

executives that he saw problems with Castro. He did not risk outright condemnation, which would have been dangerous. Many family members and executives thought Bosch was wrong and maintained their faith in Castro. He had to be given a chance. Conflicting attitudes to Castro had already created sharp rifts in the family. The Havana dining table of the Comas Bacardis, for example, had always been a joyful free-for-all, to which friends and relatives were invited and where nothing was kept from the children. Within months of the revolution, however, conversation became so heated that talk of politics was banned.

The Bacardis had always felt themselves to be socially enlightened and public-spirited. Some also felt the guilt peculiar to inheritors. Perhaps it was right that they should suffer a little, if it was for the good of the nation, if it was to help the poor, if Cuba was to go its own way. This guilt received plenty of encouragement in an atmosphere increasingly antagonistic to the wealthy, the well-educated, and, especially, the critical.

Castro had made a great show of nominating men and women of impeccable credentials, such as Urrutia, to the new Cuban government. Meanwhile, he had begun a secret agenda. Special task forces had been established. Their first and most important fruit was the agrarian reform law, written without input from the cabinet, including the minister of agriculture. Land reform was a basic tenet of the revolution; at first sight, the reforms appeared to be merely the implementation of this fundamental promise. Under the law, an upper limit was placed on the size of estates, with compensation to those whose land was expropriated. This seized land would be doled out to sharecroppers, or turned into cooperatives by a powerful new body, the Institute for Agrarian Reform. INRA became a kind of institutional Big Brother. Its scope grew far beyond agricultural reform, encompassing public works and education. INRA formed close links with the rebel army, which carried out its bidding.

Che Guevara, a doctor by training, headed INRA's department of industrialization. This, Bosch knew, did not bode well for Cuban industry. INRA was full of *barbudos*, toting guns and, like their leader Fidel, working "guerrilla hours." Force was used to fill gaps in policy; the gaps became wider. The army began to seize property at its fancy. During the takeover of one ranch, a $20,000 breeding bull was killed for a barbecue, a symbol of the fatted capitalist calf being led to the slaughter.

A French agronomist, René Dumont, visited the provincial director of INRA, a young former student of dentistry, in Santa Clara. "He vaunted himself before us to sign a little document every time he needed to acquire such and such an installation, factory, shop . . . Clearly he carried out these expropriations without preconceived plan, on a whim, without seeing if it was really useful and above all if INRA was capable of running it." Eventually, instead of being distributed to the peasants, the seized land was collectivized.

Between June and September 1959, the Cuban political situation changed radically. Most members of the cabinet — in particular those who had opposed the agrarian reform law — were dumped. On July 17, in stage-managed frustration, Castro resigned as prime minister and then went on television to denounce President Urrutia, accusing him of fabricating a Communist "legend." Castro declared he would submit his future to "all of the people" at an anniversary rally on July 26. Peasants were brought into Havana by INRA. Castro spoke for four hours. This, he declared, was "direct democracy." Now Castro promised only that Cuba would have elections within four years. "To hold them sooner would only distract the Cubans from their main task of ending unemployment."

Increasingly, anyone who criticized the regime was denounced as reactionary and counterrevolutionary. By mid-year an extensive anti-Castro underground movement had taken shape. In October, Rino Puig, who worked for Bacardi in Santiago, visited the U.S. naval base at Guantanamo under the guise of his job as a Bacardi salesman. Once inside, he managed to get a private interview with the second-highest-ranking officer at the base. He provided information obtained by the underground on the totalitarian plans of the Cuban government and asked for military supplies to fuel resistance. The officer, though friendly, treated Puig's concerns as alarmist. "I don't really think this is Communism," he said. "To me, this revolution is like a tropical storm: it lashes but it passes."

Castro, meanwhile, was canceling meetings with senior business-men, saying, "I have no message for these gentlemen." In November, Felipe Pazos, who had played an instrumental role in bringing Castro to power and had enabled the Cuban government to present a respectable fiscal front, was ousted as head of the Cuban national bank. His replacement was Che Guevara. With this appointment, wrote *Fortune*, "Fidel Castro's intentions toward the nation he rules became unmistakably clear. Castro means to destroy all free enterprise in Cuba, and to replace it with a system of absolute state control."

By the end of the year, there was outright revolt among some of Castro's best-known and most heroic followers. The most sensational defection was that of the revolutionary leader Huber Matos, who wrote in his letter of resignation to Castro: "It is right . . . to recall to you that great men begin to decline when they cease to be just."

Castro denounced Matos. Matos wrote to Castro, clairvoyantly: "I have the courage to pass twenty years in prison."

The problem for Matos and those like him was that Castro had come to embody the revolution. In this, he belonged to the traditions of *caudillismo* and personalism that were central to Latin American politics. These politics always came down to strong, uncompromising individuals, men on horseback, the inheritors of Cortés and Pizarro and Ponce de León. Political issues were always personalized; despite the incessant debate over ideas, power always wound up in the hands of one man. Checks and balances were anathema to Latins, as were compromise and concession. The people made psychic investments in individuals, which made it correspondingly harder to abandon them once they seemed to be going off track. To abandon Fidel would be to abandon the revolution, despite its increasing stranglehold over public life and its suppression of the media.

By now, Castro's domestic policy came straight from Machiavelli. Heroes of the revolution who might have challenged Castro disappeared. Habeas corpus was suspended. At the trial of Huber Matos, in December 1959, Castro and his brother Raúl made lengthy speeches of condemnation. Matos was forced to give his (unreported) defence speech at six in the morning. No charges were proved. He received the twenty-year sentence he had forecast, during which he would undergo torture of his genitals.

Castro announced that a tremendous campaign against the revolution had been mounted. People should report to the police, he said, "all remarks against the revolution."

Pepín Bosch's New Year's message for 1960 in the Bacardi annual report was a masterpiece of understatement. "The ninety-eighth year in the life of this company is now beginning," he wrote. "Long years of joy and sadness have passed. Some members of this organization have always offered their best and most sincere efforts to their native land so that liberty, democracy, and human rights might be a reality in our country, and we should always offer all sacrifices and risks for our nation without hope that we will receive anything in exchange.

"Nobody can predict the future while it is still unfolding, but I send you all, full of hopes of the best for everyone, this sincere message of good will and joy."

In fact, Pepín Bosch had no doubt about the way the future was unfolding: the country had fallen into the hands of a tyrant. He did not believe, however, that the situation would be permanent. How could the U.S. tolerate what was now clearly a Communist dictatorship only ninety miles from Key West?

By January 1960, there was a foreign exchange crisis; exchange controls were introduced; the inflationary consequences of the revolution's giveaways began to be felt. Anyone who opposed the process was a counterrevolutionary, likely to be shot or imprisoned. Communist printers refused to set newspaper editorials they didn't like, or added *coletillas* (clarifications or, literally, "little tails"). The Communists — as Bosch had feared — took over the trade unions and appealed for a freeze on prices and the abolition of the right to strike. The workers' revolution had turned on the workers.

There was an attempt at rapprochement by the U.S. in January 1960, but at the end of that month, Soviet vice-president Anastas Mikoyan arrived in Cuba, offering much aid, if in vague terms. He also repeated several times: "In Russia no compensation has been paid for property taken over." The writing on the wall was now very clear.

In March, a French freighter, the *Coubre*, bearing arms, blew up — reminiscent of the *Maine* — in Havana harbor. Without a shred of evidence, Castro blamed the U.S. That same month, the U.S. made one more attempt at abasing itself, offering to "apologize" for spy plane overflights and to provide arms, but the realization was now growing in Washington that Castro's hatred of the U.S. was immutable.

In Cuba, anti-U.S. hysteria was echoed by anti-counterrevolutionary hysteria. The mob sought personal salvation in collective barbarity. Cries of "¡Paredón!" (the wall, against which those to be executed were placed) rang in Old Havana. A new reign of terror had dawned.

Television stations were expropriated. Newspapers were burned or closed down. Remarkably, many members of the U.S. media and the academic community continued to embrace Fidel. In April 1960, Castro was invited on CBS Television to declare that there were similarities between the U.S. government, Hitler, and Mussolini in using allegations of a Communist plot as a scare tactic.

As Cubans were incarcerated without trial, foreign intellectuals such as Jean-Paul Sartre and Simone de Beauvoir came to gush over the revolution. As prisoners underwent torture, a Fair Play for Cuba Committee was set up in the U.S. Impressionable young American students were smitten by the idea of "taking to the hills." Posters of Che began to appear on dormitory walls at American colleges.

In May 1960, the last of the free, critical press died. The plates of an article calling for free elections, and signed by 300 of the Havana *Diario de la Marina*'s 450 staff, were broken by union thugs. The police refused to do anything. The editor fled and the paper was closed down.

A couple of days later, in the last free paper, the *Prensa Libre*, a critical article appeared by the respected columnist Luis Aguilar. A *santiaguero* who knew the Bacardis well, Aguilar had written bravely, and with increasing disillusionment, about the course of the revolution. At the head of his last column, he placed two quotes. The first was Voltaire's "I thoroughly disagree with what you say, but I shall defend to the death your right to say it." The other was Mao's "I want a hundred ideas to germinate in my country, and a hundred buds to sprout."

The article was a moving epitaph to free speech in Cuba. "Now," wrote Aguilar, "the time of unanimity is arriving in Cuba, a solid and impenetrable totalitarian unanimity. The same slogan will be repeated by all the organs of news. There will be no disagreeing voices, no possibility of criticism, no public refutations. Control of all the media of expression will facilitate the work of persuasion, collective fear will take charge of the rest. And underneath the sound of the vociferous propaganda, there will remain . . . the silence.

"This way leads to compulsory unanimity. And then not even those who have remained silent will find shelter in their silence. For unanimity is worse than censorship. Censorship obliges us to hold our own truth silent; unanimity forces us to repeat the truth of others, even though we do not believe it. That is to say, it dissolves our own personalities into a general, monotonous chorus. And there is nothing worse than that for those who do not have the herd instinct."

The article carried a *coletilla* declaring that for those who did not like "totalitarian unity" there was always "*paredón*, prison, exile, or contempt." On May 15, most staff members signed a statement supporting the paper. The following day, on the grounds that the paper was attacking "truth, justice, and decency," it was closed down.

After the 1960 sugar harvest had ended, the last under free

enterprise, all the land owned by the mills was seized by INRA. In mid-year, the University of Havana — traditionally the seat of political opposition — was taken over. The issue now was not so much whether Castro would seize foreign and Cuban companies, but when.

In February 1958, Castro had written: "I personally have come to feel that nationalization is, at best, a cumbersome instrument. It does not seem to make the state any stronger, yet it weakens private enterprise . . . Foreign investments will always be welcome and secure here."

In June 1960, Castro demanded that three of the oil industry's "Seven Sisters" — Shell, Esso, and Texaco — refine Soviet oil. The oil companies refused and were expropriated, along with other U.S. assets worth a total of around $850 million.

To this point, the U.S. responses to Castro's vituperative attacks and expropriations had been astonishingly mild. Eisenhower had refrained from the one obvious economic reprisal, ending U.S. purchases of Cuban sugar. Although the U.S. had paid close to double the world price for the 3.2 million tons of Cuban sugar it had taken in 1959, Che Guevara had characterized these purchases as economic imperialism. Now, at last, the quota was ended. Buying sugar had been economic imperialism; now cutting off the purchases was economic imperialism.

On August 6, the American-owned utilities — the Cuban Telephone Company and the Cuban Electric Company — the oil refineries, and all the sugar mills that had been only "intervened" — that is, whose management had been taken over but whose assets hadn't been seized — were formally expropriated. That same month, Cuba's Catholic bishops formally denounced the Cuban regime. Castro declared: "Whoever condemns a revolution such as ours betrays Christ and would be capable of crucifying Him again."

On September 18, 1960, Castro went to New York to attend the United Nations. His reception in the U.S. was far less enthusiastic than it had been in April 1959. His address lasted four hours and twenty-six minutes; the U.S. press found it "absurd and full of lies." Castro had to fly back on a borrowed Soviet airliner when his own was impounded under writs of attachment obtained in Miami against Cuban debts.

Liberals in the U.S. still maintained that the U.S. had "driven" Castro toward Communism. But the debate about whether he was a Communist, and when and how he had become one, was largely barren. As *Fortune* noted in September 1959, "Whether Castro himself is a Communist is a point not worth arguing about. If he wrecks the Cuban capitalist system, Communism will almost certainly follow."

The basic tenet of Communism is government ownership of the means of production. Most of the foreign-owned part of the economy had been seized. Now it was the turn of the Cuban capitalists.

Expropriation: Atlas Shrugs

*"For months past, every provision
had been prepared for by countless
speeches, articles, sermons,
editorials — by purposeful voices
that screamed with anger if anyone
named their purpose."*

AYN RAND, *ATLAS SHRUGGED*

Havana. October 13, 1960

As he drove by the Presidential Palace, heading home from his office in the Edificio Bacardi, the Bacardi lawyer Guillermo Mármol noticed that the lights were burning late. People crowded the narrow streets of Old Havana, milling about in confused concern. The whole town was buzzing. That day, U.S. President Eisenhower had announced a ban on exports to Cuba, except for medicine and some foodstuffs. As Mármol drove home along the winding seawall, he felt a sense of foreboding.

Next morning, Mármol was woken by a telephone call from a friend. The friend told him to switch on the radio. Mármol's foreboding grew stronger. A list was being read of names of companies whose assets were to be seized under a new law. There were almost four hundred of them: all the banks (except for two Canadian ones); all the remaining private sugar mills; sixty-one textile mills; sixteen rice mills; eleven cinemas; thirteen large stores; and eighteen distilleries, among them Bacardi. With the stroke of a pen, the Bacardis had lost the $76 million in assets they had accumulated in Cuba over almost a century.

The news came as no surprise to Mármol, or indeed to any of the Bacardis. It had been expected for months. Pepín Bosch had not stayed for the final act. Three months earlier, in July, he had stepped quietly into Mármol's office in the Edificio Bacardi, closed the door behind him, and told his old friend that he had cleared his papers, was leaving Cuba, and would not be back while the present government was in power. Besides immediate family and Mármol, Bosch had told no one of his plans. The only item he had left on his desk was another note from Fidel Castro, asking for his help. Bosch had not been prepared, in Lenin's famous dictum, to manufacture the rope for his own hanging.

The immediate reason for Bosch's departure was unrelated to Bacardi. A law passed the previous November had given the Castro government control of every phase of the oil business. Bosch was president of an oil-exploration company he had put together with American colleagues. INRA had seized all the oil companies' geological records, presumably in the belief that socialist fervor would be better at finding oil than geological experience ("Cuba Regains Petroleum Riches" had read the headline in the government newspaper *Revolución*). But the *barbudos* preferred the shortcut to wealth. When they discovered that Bosch's company had several million dollars on deposit at Manufacturers Trust in New York, they presented a cheque in that amount to Pepín Bosch for his signature. Bosch refused, claiming he had fiscal responsibilities to the company's shareholders, who might sue him. The *barbudos* had left grumbling. Although there had been no direct threats against him, Bosch knew it was time to leave.

Batista had salivated over the prospect of owning a piece of Bacardi but had lacked the political will to seize it. Fidel Castro had the political will; he had had only to find the pretext. Bacardi's fate had undoubtedly been sealed even before Castro marched into Santiago in January 1959; it had merely taken Castro twenty-two months to build his case. Like their fellow Cuban capitalists, the Bacardis were now enemies of the people and had to be taken over in the name of the people. Cuban capitalists had been backed into a corner from which any attempt to escape was construed as a sign of guilt. All that remained was for the sentence to be read.

The preamble of Law 890 declared: "It is evident that . . . [economic] development cannot be achieved except through adequate planning of the economy, expansion and progressive standardization of production, and national control of the country's basic industries."

Calling the need for national control "evident" took the issue of expropriation beyond the messy area of debate. The preamble went on to claim, however, that private companies *deserved* to be expropriated. Far from conducting themselves in a manner "consistent with the objectives and aims of the revolutionary transformation of the national economy," Cuba's large private companies had instead sabotaged production and siphoned money out of the country. These "selfish and anti-national practices" weren't all. The "liquidation" of the "privileges" of "certain economic groups" had caused these groups to react "violently," to ignore and violate laws, "even going so far as to finance with ill-gotten money groups of counterrevolutionaries in open alliance with international financial imperialism."

By now, of course, these charges were in many cases true. Bacardi employees and former employees, such as Rino Puig in Santiago and Augusto Valdez Miranda in Manacas, were indeed active in anti-Castro groups, with Pepín Bosch's support. Valdez Miranda had quit Bacardi and gone underground soon after the Castro coup but had stayed in close touch with Bosch, helping to raise money for arms for rebel groups in the Escambray region. He had left Cuba by sea in July 1960, with a price on his head.

The "duty of the Revolutionary Government," Law 890 decreed, was to "liquidate the economic power of the privileged interests that conspire against the people, by proceeding with the nationalization of the large industrial and commercial companies that have not adapted themselves nor will ever be able to adapt themselves to our country's revolutionary reality." Now it was just a matter of waiting for the *barbudos* to arrive.

The managing director at the Bacardi office in Havana was Armando Pessino, who was married to Elena Gómez del Campo, a granddaughter of Facundo Bacardi Moreau. Pessino had already sent Elena and the children to Miami. When word of the expropriations came that Friday morning, he arranged to meet Juan Prado, the sales manager, at ten at the Miami bar, a few blocks from the Edificio Bacardi. Pessino had a plane reservation later that day. He gave Prado the keys to his Porsche and asked him to put it away for him. They shook hands and Pessino left. Prado went to the Edificio to wait. He called Santiago and spoke to Daniel Bacardi Rosell, head of the company in Pepín Bosch's absence. Daniel told him that, if the *barbudos* came there, he should tell them the head office was in Santiago.

It was naval officers who turned up at the Edificio to carry out the expropriation. Prado explained that this was just a branch office; the navy men shrugged and settled in anyway. Prado asked for a receipt, almost a counterrevolutionary request in itself. He wasn't a family member, just an employee; if he didn't have something to show them, family members might think he'd stolen their goods. They gave him a chit, which he eventually delivered to Pepín Bosch.

The expropriators asked Prado to work for them. Taken by surprise, he said he'd have to think about it. Then he booked a flight to Santiago to confer with Daniel. Next day, when he got on the plane, the same naval officers were aboard.

By going to the wrong office, the government forces had given the Bacardis an extra twenty-four hours in Santiago; but little could be done. Castro's militia had stationed themselves at the gates of the Bacardi plants as soon as Law 890 had been announced. Still, the impact did not hit young Manuel Jorge Cutillas until the morning of October 14, when he drove out of the plant to the University of Oriente. At the gates, he was stopped by the militia and told to open the trunk of his car. He felt angry. It was as if he had been stopped at his own front door to make sure he wasn't stealing his own possessions. They searched his trunk again when he came back in the afternoon. The next day, the navy arrived.

Daniel Bacardi had been a great supporter of Castro, and he clung to his faith until the bitter end — Pepín Bosch had left him behind as the cheerful front man. But it was hard for him to hide his feelings when the expropriators turned up. He, too, asked for a receipt, and was told he'd be given one later. Then he went to Víctor Schueg's house. Daniel and Víctor did not speak. They broke into tears and wept — for themselves, for their families, for Bacardi, for Cuba.

Castro's Institute for Agrarian Reform had begun its program of seizure of property and industry in the naive belief that all it needed to run them was physical control of assets and revolutionary fervor; that operations would magically continue with the *barbudos* working guerrilla hours at the helm. The INRA people had no idea of the importance of experience because they *had* no experience. They found out, after their initial binge of expropriation, that good intentions weren't enough. Human capital was, however, much harder to hold than a sugar plantation or a manufacturing plant; the revolutionaries would have to take pains to keep it.

Operations at the Bacardi plant in Santiago continued almost as normal. After the initial turmoil, the new *fidelista* general manager called in the technical staff to announce that he had no intention of running the plant differently. "This plant has been taken over by the people of Cuba," he said, "and we rely on you to make it run. Whatever you say has to happen in this plant happens, and if you have any trouble with any worker, here's my direct line. Call me."

"What about the union?" asked one of the engineers.

"Forget about the union," said the manager. "We are the union."

When Juan Prado returned to the Edificio Bacardi, he was again asked to stay on. Now Bacardi belonged to the people; the revolution needed him; they all had to work together. Prado told his new bosses he was upset; he had worked for the family a long time. Over the next few days, a stream of visitors tried to persuade him to carry on, to convince him that staying was best for Cuba. Of course, many of them believed that it was. Prado, afraid to state flatly that he wanted the hell out, continued to temporize. At last, the head *fidelista* at Bacardi in Havana said, "What about working for another nationalized organization? They need people over at Coca-Cola." Sure, said Prado, but first he needed a little holiday.

A couple of days later he slipped out of the country.

Many family members had already left Cuba. Now, the thoughts of those who remained turned to departure. Getting out, however, was becoming increasingly difficult. Until the expropriation, many family members had told themselves: "This can't be happening." They didn't want to be forced out of their homes. Now, their principal Cuban assets having been taken, the largest part of their wealth lay outside Cuba. Most decided to leave because of concern for the safety of their families; some left to fight. Whatever their motivations, flight from the regime, in the prevailing climate, was equated with guilt; with attempting to "steal" assets, albeit their own; with not being "good Cubans." Thus there was little open discussion about departure, even between different branches. Plans were kept to one's immediate family.

Not long after the expropriation, the Comas Bacardi family was woken up at home in Havana by a group of musicians. With them was Daniel, who announced he had assembled the band to serenade his mother. Daniel appeared tipsy. He arranged the musicians on the patio outside the dining room and told them to play. Then he came and sat with the family, and it became obvious he was completely sober. Speaking softly amid the serenade, he said he was planning to leave Cuba, though as yet he didn't know how. He wanted to know what the Comas Bacardis planned to do. They said they too would be leaving.

A week later, Daniel took off for Spain. A few days after that, the Comas Bacardis also began to leave.

Some of the Bacardis' departures were touched with pathos. The second son of Manuel Jorge Cutillas had been born with a heart defect. He had been taken to heart specialists in Havana but they had been unable to do anything for him. Now Cutillas planned to use a trip to a heart specialist in the U.S. as a cover for the exodus of his immediate family. But on November 9, three weeks after the takeover, his son died. The tragedy increased the family's desire to leave. Saying they wanted a holiday to recover from their bereavement, they went to Havana and managed to get exit permits. But when Cutillas looked at his, he realized it wasn't signed. The lawyer handling the details for the family said it was an oversight; but when the permit was returned, the government official wanted to see Cutillas. Full of trepidation, Cutillas presented himself. The official asked what he did for a living. Cutillas, not wanting to divulge that he was not only an employee of the recently expropriated Bacardi business but also a member of the family, said he was a teacher at the University of Oriente. The official asked what he taught. Cutillas said chemical engineering. In that case, said the official, he would need special permission from the rector of the university: the revolution could not afford the loss of teaching talent. The official took Cutillas's passport and said he would have to bring back a letter. Cutillas smiled and said certainly, no problem, knowing it would be impossible. The recently appointed rector was a devout Communist.

Cutillas tried frantically to contact anybody in Havana who might be able to help, including a commander in Castro's army whom he had known in Santiago and who was now an aide to Fidel. Nobody returned his calls. Cutillas decided to go back to Santiago. Boarding the plane, he spotted the commander he had been trying to contact. "Hey, Manuel Jorge," said the commander, all smiles, "¿Cómo estás? By the way, I got your message, but I've been so busy that I haven't been able to call you." The men sat together for two hours on the plane. Not once did the commander ask what Manuel Jorge had wanted. He knew.

In Santiago, Cutillas made contact with the anti-Castro underground. Those attempting to leave the island without papers were subject to jail sentences or even the firing squad, but Cutillas was consumed by a desire to escape. He worried that it might be weeks or even months before he could get out; but almost immediately he got a call. Would he like to go for a ride the next morning, perhaps do a little hunting? He would be picked up at four in the morning. His contact said, "Just come as you are."

In the morning, after a tearful farewell with his parents, and having arranged to have his wife and family fly from Havana, Cutillas was driven to a point near Guantanamo Bay. There, without even a change of clothes, he boarded a dilapidated 70-foot cargo boat along with half a dozen others, former *fidelistas* who had become disillusioned with Castro and were leaving the island to fight him. In darkness, they headed east in heavy seas toward the windward passage between Cuba and Haiti.

Just before dawn, the sparsely equipped, rusty, and unarmed vessel was raked by a searchlight. Cutillas, scrambling to hide, felt his heart pound. He feared they had been spotted by the Cuban coast guard; but the beam came from a U.S. destroyer, which plowed by without offering a challenge. As the weather worsened, the boat began to take on water in mountainous seas. The bilge pumps failed. Cutillas and his fellow escapees found themselves bailing for their lives, wondering if they'd traded a possible execution for a certain drowning. The captain turned south and ran with the storm, which lasted for more than twenty-four hours. Finally, when everyone was near total exhaustion, the winds abated.

Although the weather was still bad, the captain turned the prow north once more. The passage was tempestuous and marked by further engine trouble. By the time they reached the Bahamas they were moving through calm waters under a cloudless sky. Cutillas and the others laughed and joked giddily, enjoying the exhilaration of having escaped Castro and survived the storm. Six days after they set out, they landed, sweat-stained and weary, near Miami.

Most family members left Cuba by more conventional means, many undergoing the indignity of being strip-searched to make sure they were not attempting to "rob" the revolution of their possessions. The cost of safe departure was the "gift" to the state of all material goods save one suit of clothes and a few small objects — a ring, a watch, a locket.

The treasures of the Bacardi museum in Santiago had already been given to the Cuban people. Devoted *fidelistas* noted that the family's big houses would make wonderful schools and public buildings; others realized they would make wonderful homes for themselves. Raúl Castro reportedly took over Pepín Bosch's house at Punta Gorda. The Bosch Palace in Vista Alegre became a prison for a while. Daniel's big home in Vista Alegre, which he had rented from the developer Andrew Duany, became the Russian consulate. Emilio's old home, the Villa Elvira, became a center for "psychiatric research" and then a restaurant.

Although they made the Bacardis' exodus difficult, the revolutionaries were not sorry to see most of them go. Their presence was an embarrassment, since there really was no "revolutionary" case against them. Once they had gone, the regime could say that the Bacardis were just capitalists who had followed their money, people with no commitment to the revolution or to Cuba.

Not all the Bacardis and their associates left immediately. Guillermo Mármol worked quietly and unobtrusively in the Edificio Bacardi, helping to get exit papers for Bacardi employees, particularly technicians, whom Pepín Bosch needed for new plants he was planning.

Others who had stayed to fight Castro found they had stayed too long. Juan Prado's brother José, who had fought Batista, wound up spending nine years in jail. Rino Puig, the Bacardi salesman who had tried to pass information to the U.S. forces at Guantanamo, with his brother Ñongo, became part of an island-wide anti-Castro network that included former members of Castro's rebel army. But Castro's secret police penetrated one of its cells, and a week after the expropriation, on October 22, 1960, when Puig knocked at the door of a safe house near Havana, he was greeted by the barrel of a machine gun. He was arrested and condemned to fifteen years in prison.

Resistance to Castro was hunted down and exterminated with a ruthlessness not seen even in the times of Machado. By the time of the October expropriations, there were far more Cuban political prisoners — perhaps 10,000 — than there had ever been under Batista.

Originally, it seems, the Castro regime had assumed that Cuban capitalists might continue to create wealth while simultaneously having slices taken off their hides. As one Castro official said in September 1959: "We need those people because they have brains and connections, *and no matter how much you take away from them, they'll always be able to find more.* Cuba has to have new industries, and they will be the ones to find the cash. They're sitting on their money just now, probably waiting until things settle down. One of these days they won't be able to resist the tax advantages Fidel is offering people who invest in industry. Then their money will come out of hiding and go to work for Cuba" (italics added).

Pepín Bosch had not been sitting on the Bacardis' money. The aspect of his stewardship for which the Bacardis were now profoundly grateful was that he had established extensive holdings outside Cuba. Bosch had prepared the company well for the trauma of expropriation; ironically, he had expected the expropriator to be Fulgencio Batista.

Bosch's main thrust in the 1950s had been to expand Bacardi's overseas operations. The funds for this expansion came primarily not from rum but from Hatuey beer. Largely because of the success of the Modelo brewery, beer was generating twice as much net profit by 1954 (around $1.6 million that year) as the Santiago rum business. The third brewery, built at Manacas in 1953, made beer profits even more dominant as the decade went on. By 1959, Hatuey was selling 10 million cases annually and had more than 50 percent of the Cuban beer market. This success provided funds for major expansions in Mexico and Puerto Rico, and for a new plant in Brazil. The expansion was accompanied by improvements in Bacardi's technology, which better enabled the company to produce a standardized product in different locations, thus preparing it for statelessness.

A key figure in introducing the new technology was Juan Grau, a charming and brilliant young MIT-educated chemical engineer. Grau was born in Santiago and grew up with members of the Bacardi family, such as Manuel Jorge Cutillas and Adolfito Danguillecourt Bacardi. He had also been a classmate and friend, at the Belén Jesuit College in Havana, of Fidel Castro. Castro was then a lanky, round-faced youth renowned for his memory and his single-minded determination to master any sport or activity he tried. Grau and his classmates used to laugh at his crazy antics, calling him El Loco.

Grau was hired by Pepín Bosch in 1950 as technical director of the Santiago distillery. Grau also taught part-time at the University of Oriente, a job he eventually handed on to Manuel Jorge Cutillas. In 1954, Bosch asked Grau to go to Mexico to help design and build a new distillery. Since Bosch had turned the operation around more than twenty years earlier, Bacardi had become well known in the Mexican market; but real success came in the 1950s, after Bosch hired Ernesto Robles León to run the company. Robles León, a lawyer, was a tall, eloquent, charming, aristocratic figure with slicked-back hair and a pencil mustache. He possessed the all-important quality of *presencia*, a word that means so much more than the English "presence." *Presencia* goes with a jut of the jaw and puff of the chest; with a gesture of the hand, like a flamenco dancer's; it's the proud sidelong glance of the matador asserting himself in the face of horned death; it carries overtones of *machismo* and *dignidad*. Although he had no marketing experience, Robles proved to be a genius at selling rum and at dealing with government, which in Mexico was a very important part of business life.

Despite Facundo's "secret formula," the Bacardi rum in Mexico had never been the same as that produced in Santiago or Puerto Rico. Now Bosch wanted a new distillery that would produce identical rum. The site he chose was 100 miles south of Mexico City, amid the rich sugarcane fields of the Atencingo Valley, within sight of the mighty volcanic peak of Popocatepetl (beneath which Malcolm Lowry's consul played out his tragedy in *Under the Volcano*). Called La Galarza, the plant was on the site of an old sugar mill and hacienda.

Juan Grau constructed a pilot plant and began a lengthy examination of the differences between the Mexican and Santiago products, which were felt to be due to the different soil conditions in which the sugarcane grew. The fruit of his labor appeared in 1956 when the plant opened, although it took another two years before all production problems were finally ironed out.

Bosch loved new installations. None was more lovely than La Galarza. Its molasses tanks, boilers, and distilling columns sat on a hill amid a floral effusion: purple-flowered jacarandas and fire trees, bougainvillea and cactus, African junipers, graceful cypresses and clipped Indian laurels, *mate* trees that clung to the carefully preserved old buildings. Ducks and geese floated on a millstream. A beautiful little chapel, built in 1696, became the scene of dozens of weddings and christenings of Bacardis and Bacardi employees. There was a big walled orchard, and an old converted guesthouse with towering ceilings, use of which became one of the perks of Bacardi executive status in Mexico.

Even before the Mexican distillery was finished, Bosch, spurred by the deteriorating conditions in Cuba, had hatched even grander plans for Puerto Rico. In the early 1940s, the Puerto Rican government had been encouraged by U.S. administrators — remnants of President Franklin Roosevelt's interventionist Brain Trust — to adopt state ownership as the route to growth. These policies had failed, and the administration had switched to a more successful program of private incentives under Operation Bootstrap. This reliance on private initiative was accompanied by the requisite political distaste, which Puerto Rico's much-admired governor, Luis Muñoz Marín, summed up thus: "For Puerto Rico's development to take place, we must allow three hundred sons of bitches to become millionaires." Within this more accommodating — if still resentful — environment, which offered low-cost loans and other advantages, Bosch planned a major expansion.

During the Second World War, the Bacardi operations had been moved into the stately Puerta de Tierra building, just east of Old San Juan, which had served, among other uses, as a jail and a tobacco-processing plant. In 1937, the year after he had first gone to the island, despite his legal battle with the island's government, Bosch had purchased a tract of mangrove swamp across the bay from Old San Juan at a place called Cataño. At the time, some in the company called the purchase "Pepín's Folly." During the war, however, while deep approaches were being dredged for the U.S. naval base in the harbor, Bosch persuaded the navy and the dredging companies to dump the dredged material on his property rather than taking it out to sea, thus increasing his usable acreage.

In the mid-1950s, when Bosch decided Bacardi needed a major new plant in Puerto Rico to supply the U.S. market, U.S. sales had still not climbed back to wartime levels. Nevertheless, in January 1958 — the year in which U.S. sales at last surpassed those of 1944 — Bacardi opened the new showpiece distillery, which Governor Muñoz Marín christened "the Cathedral of Rum." Following another expansion, masterminded by Juan Grau, in 1959, the distillery's capacity grew to twice that of the plant in Santiago. To serve the growing Spanish market, another new Bacardi factory had also been built at San Feliu de Llobregat, Barcelona. Bosch was making sure that Bacardi did not have all its eggs in one basket.

Pepín Bosch's trip to Washington with Castro in April 1959, which persuaded him that Bacardi's days in Cuba were numbered, prompted another round of overseas construction. The Mexican operation had continued to flourish under Robles León, so Bosch decided on an even more spectacular expansion on 75 acres of land at Tultitlán, 20 miles north of Mexico City.

For the Tultitlán complex, Bosch commissioned some of the world's foremost architects. Several years earlier he had approached Ludwig Mies van der Rohe, the leading exponent of the German Bauhaus school. Bosch asked Mies, whose starkly rectilinear International Style had swept American architecture in the 1940s, to design a new head office in Santiago to celebrate the company's centenary. To the uninitiated — and to those of an iconoclastic bent, such as Tom Wolfe — Mies designed repetitious boxes. His somber style seemed at odds with the florid effusions of the Caribbean. Bosch, however, had been impressed by Mies's Illinois Institute of Technology campus in Chicago.

Another factor in Bosch's hiring of Mies might well have been that Sam Bronfman had used him to design the Seagram Building on Park Avenue in Manhattan to celebrate that company's hundredth anniversary. (The unsophisticated Bronfman didn't like the design for the Seagram Building. He preferred the Disneyland style of Seagram's Montreal headquarters. But his daughter, Phyllis, who was attuned to the avant-garde architectural attitudes of the day, persuaded him that he was an old fuddy-duddy.)

Bosch may have caught a little avant-garde fever himself, but he really *wanted* a one-story building with no internal walls, which happened to be in Mies's repertoire. "My ideal office," Bosch wrote to Mies, "is one where there are no partitions, where everybody, both officers and employees, see each other." So it had been since 1944, when puzzled Bacardi employees had first seen Bosch's desk in the middle of the Santiago office.

Mies gained "inspiration" — the uninitiated might regard it as basic homework — while staying in Havana. The salt-laden air persuaded him to use reinforced concrete rather than steel. The blinding Caribbean sun persuaded him that glass greenhouse walls might not be appropriate. The building he scrawled on a notepad — even Bosch acknowledged that "Mies could not draw" — was a single large space 130 feet square and 18 feet high. The roof extended 20 feet beyond the walls and was suspended by two columns on each side. The building was partially enclosed by screening brick walls and set on a podium.

It speaks volumes about the ethereal nature of modern architecture that Mies designed the building before he ever saw Santiago. In fact, the design was never implemented because it proved unsuitable to the Santiago climate. (Mies eventually created what Pepín Bosch regarded as his Bacardi building — except in steel rather than reinforced concrete — in the form of the Berlin National Gallery. A decade later, Bosch used essentially the same design for the offices of Bacardi International in Bermuda.)

Bosch turned to Mies once more for the main building at Tultitlán. Mies designed an airy, open-plan, two-story building with the second floor arranged in balcony form around the glass-walled ground floor.

The bottling plant at Tultitlán — a series of great, airy, billowing vaults — was the work of a Mexican architect, Felix Candela. A Cuban architect, Saenz Cancio y Martín, produced yet another architectural vision in the canopied reception building. The buildings faced each other across a central reflecting pool. (Because of Mexico City's pollution, the pool eventually had to be covered, becoming Founders Plaza.) In the background were huge storage facilities for the barrels of rum. Eight gardeners tended the spectacular grounds, which featured, among other floral delights, more than 30,000 tulips and dahlias.

The presence of so many styles in one place reflected Bosch's eclectic tastes, but somehow the whole thing worked. Most important, the complex, which was inaugurated in August 1960, announced that Bacardi prided itself on quality. It was not in business for the fast peso. Of course, as Bosch knew, quality is the surest way to pesos. Bacardi's Mexican operation became the first to surpass sales of 1 million cases a year.

Juan Grau stayed in Mexico until 1959, then worked on the major expansion in Puerto Rico, briefly returning to Santiago — which was still in the first flush of revolution — to help Manuel Jorge Cutillas with the distillery expansion there. In the meantime, Bosch's visionary gaze had fallen on Brazil. He asked Grau to build a new plant at Recife, then manage it. Recife, which sits almost at the eastern tip of the country, had been chosen partly because there was local sugarcane, but also because Bacardi would receive tax breaks for putting a plant there. Perhaps that was one reason why things didn't turn out well.

Like most business geniuses, Pepín Bosch saw the big picture and looked at things in often surprisingly simple ways. His hopes for the Brazilian market were based on arithmetic: Mexico was selling 1 million cases; Brazil had twice as many people, so it would sell 2 million.

Juan Grau had misgivings the moment he turned up with his wife and children in Recife, in February 1960. The site on which the plant was to be built — a sandbar by a river — was being leveled with the help of donkeys. Grau's first concerns were water supply and the disposal of molasses slops. This latter question was particularly important. The slops could be used as fertilizer, or put into landfill, or dumped at sea (when diluted sufficiently, they become part of the food chain). But they could not be dumped into smaller bodies of water, because they would suck out the oxygen and kill marine life.

No problem on either count, Bosch assured Grau. He pointed to a water pipe coming from town, then indicated a waste disposal plant across the river. "I have had a word with them," he told Grau, "and they will take your waste." Grau was left with a blueprint and an order for the main distilling equipment. He had no valves, pipes, or pumps, and no engineer; and he didn't speak a word of Portuguese.

Six months into the project, when the plant was beginning to take shape, Grau crossed the river to see about hooking into the waste disposal plant. "Ah yes," said the man in charge, "I remember that old man with the bald head coming to see me." He asked Grau about the waste — specifically, its biochemical oxygen demand (BOD), a measure of the amount of organic matter in the sewage. Heavy sewage from a town might run 200 parts per million. Grau announced that the Bacardi waste contained 20,000 parts per million. The sewage-processing manager was aghast. Eventually, a special barge had to be built to dump the wastes in the Atlantic twice a day.

Despite these hurdles, Grau had the plant up and running in eleven months. The first bottle of Bacardi came off the lines on October 16, 1961, at 7:30 A.M. Pepín Bosch was waiting to sign the label. The celebration was spirited, but the tribulations of the Recife operation were not over. The first shipment destined for Rio traveled the 2,000 miles along the Atlantic coast over unpaved roads. The cases of Bacardi had not been sealed, allowing sand to get in; when the shipment arrived, all the labels had been rubbed off.

Bosch was always prepared to make mistakes. He often told Bacardi employees: "You cannot bat a thousand. But .400 is all right, if it is the right .400." Brazil would prove a particularly tough inning. But at least it had helped pull the ballgame from Cuba.

In Havana, Fidel Castro and his fellow leaders appeared to retain the astonishing belief that Cuban capitalists would willingly sacrifice themselves on the altar of revolution not merely until but even *after* all their assets had been seized. This attitude was encapsulated in a meeting between Che Guevara and Julio Lobo, who had been Cuba's greatest sugar producer and trader, had given large amounts of money to the anti-Batista cause, and had uttered the fateful words: "We didn't care who overthrew Batista providing someone did."

Lobo had stayed in Cuba until the bitter end. Finally he had been summoned to see Guevara, who told him that the revolutionary auditors had pored over his business accounts and found no irregularities. He had therefore been "left till the last." Now Lobo's time had come.

"We are Communists," Guevara said, "and it is impossible for us to permit you, who represent 'the very idea' of capitalism in Cuba, to remain as you are." Lobo's choice was to disappear or else "integrate" with the revolution. He asked what form this "integration" might take. Guevara proposed that Lobo become general manager of the Cuban sugar industry under the revolutionary government. Naturally, Lobo would lose his estates, though he might be allowed the proceeds of his favorite mill.

Lobo asked for time to consider the offer and returned home. He instructed his secretary to take all she could from the banks and bury it in a secret passage beneath his office in Old Havana. The next day, however, his house was sealed and guarded. Lobo left the country on October 13, the day before the mass expropriations of Law 890 were announced.

Guevara sounded like one of the villains from Ayn Rand's novel *Atlas Shrugged*, which had been published in October 1957 to outraged reviews from the same liberal establishment that was now cheering on Castro. A monumental work — part steamy soap opera, part adventure story, part philosophical treatise — *Atlas Shrugged* described an America of the not-too-distant future in which liberal/socialist forces were on the point of bringing the country to its economic knees. Like Castro's fans, Rand would have regarded Fidel Castro as a Robin Hood. The only difference was that Rand regarded Robin Hood as a villain: "the first man who assumed a halo of virtue by practicing charity with wealth which he did not own."

The capitalist victims of Ayn Rand's book had, by the end, quit the world in which they were despised and yet desperately needed. They made their way to a secret place where talent and application reigned supreme, there to start a capitalist society from scratch. That dénouement might have been psychologically satisfying, but it was somewhat improbable. The Bacardis, too, departed the place that reviled them. Instead of heading for Rand's secret valley, most of them headed for Miami.

CHAPTER TEN

La Lucha and Betrayal

*"I can assure you that this flag will
be returned to this brigade in a free
Havana."*

JOHN F. KENNEDY TO BRIGADE 2506 AT THE MIAMI ORANGE BOWL

Miami. January 1961

John F. Kennedy succeeded Dwight Eisenhower as president of the United States on January 20, 1961, and in the weeks following the inauguration Miami buzzed with the imminence of military action against Cuba. The year before — with Che Guevara claiming that the U.S. sugar quota amounted to "economic slavery" and declaring economic war on the "monopolies" of the North — Eisenhower had accepted a recommendation to arm and train an assault force of Cuban exiles in Guatemala. Kennedy knew of this Guatemalan base before coming to power but developed misgivings when given full details of the invasion plans. During his campaign, Kennedy had talked tough about eradicating the "cancer" of the Castro regime; once in office, he began to vacillate. His uncertainties reflected the intellectual tenor of the times.

Pepín Bosch was deeply disturbed by the potentially enervating effects on U.S. policy of the small but influential group of pro-Castro liberals in the U.S. media and academe. Public opinion in the U.S. had now turned against Castro, but die-hard supporters remained, including Herbert Matthews of the *New York Times*, whom Bosch had courted in the fight against Batista. Matthews had made a personal commitment to the regime. That didn't stop Bosch from trying to win him over to the anti-Castro cause. On March 15, 1961, he wrote a flattering note to Matthews: "To Fidel you are the equivalent of an army division, so winning you away will be quite a victory." Matthews refused to be "won away." In his book *The Cuban Story*, published that year, he noted the "fierce" attacks on himself and the *Times* from "former Cuban friends and admirers," including Bosch. He also quoted Bosch's letter, adding self-righteously: "All that could 'win me away' are the facts, the truth, the real developments in Cuba."

Bosch considered Matthews impervious to "the real developments." He found it inconceivable that, despite the expropriation of virtually every major private company in Cuba, the question of whether Castro was a Communist was still being debated by American liberals. A letter in the *New York Times* on March 8, 1961, was typical of the attitude that drove Bosch and other exiles to distraction. "It is important for the American people to understand," wrote the American socialist Corliss Lamont, "that when such regimes put into effect radical measures, as well as establishing close diplomatic and economic relations with the Communist bloc, this does not mean that they are Communist-controlled or are becoming Communist. Yet most organs of public opinion in our country, many government officials and large segments of the population in general tend to cry 'Communist' when indigenous and militant nationalist movements abroad go to the Left.

"A prime example of this unfortunate tendency in the United States is seen in the constant use of the term Communist in reference to the Cuban Government headed by Fidel Castro."

Castro's actions, said Lamont, had been the result of the Eisenhower administration's treating it like a "pariah," and of the "hostile actions" of American business and government interests. Calling the Castro regime Communist, he said, was just a "matter of propaganda and political strategy."

So incensed was Pepín Bosch by Lamont's letter, and by Herbert Matthews's continuing support of Castro — with its impact on *New York Times* editorial policy — that he wrote a long rebuttal, which he placed as an ad in the *Times* on March 24. Bosch's letter was more than a scathing rejoinder; it contained astonishing allegations about what was going on in Cuba. Appearing under the heading "Compañía 'Ron Bacardi,' S.A." and the bat symbol, it was signed "José M. Bosch. President (Former Minister of Finance of Cuba prior to the Batista Administration)."

Bosch noted that Matthews, Lamont, and the *Times*'s own editorial policy sought to justify the "so-called Cuban Revolution" by citing its efforts on behalf of the "long-suffering Cuban peasant and worker." Castro had waged the revolution against Batista, Bosch pointed out, in the name of the constitution and free elections. Castro had repeatedly said he did not want to govern the country after Batista's fall. All this could be found in Matthews's own accounts. Instead of keeping his word, said Bosch, Castro had decided to "communize the country by force and tyranny, by murder and jail terms, and has converted our Constitution into a mere piece of paper."

Bosch ridiculed the assertions of Matthews and Lamont that Castro was not a Communist since he did not receive orders from Moscow. How could they know without tapping his telephone? What definition of Communist were they using? Bosch wrote: "It is my understanding that if a Government claims itself to be Marxist (as the Cuban government has claimed); if it attacks the United States and all freedom-loving countries as Imperialistic and Capitalistic; if it claims that the Soviet Union is the only true friend of the Cuban revolution; if it maintains the Communist Party, as the Cuban government does; if it places known card-carrying Communists in all key posts in the government; if it persecutes religion; sows hate and fear instead of trust and friendship; slaughters all political opponents whether they be teen-age students, peasants, workers or women; destroys all law, courts of Justice, the rights of private property, and repeatedly violates the Bill of Human Rights as incorporated in the Charter of the United Nations — it is my understanding that such a government is a Communist government. If it is not, then I have no sense."

Bosch reported his conversation with Castro aboard the flight to Washington just after the revolution on April 15. It was evident then, he said, that "Castro hated the United States and everything that it stood for." Why? Because the U.S. "proved the falsehoods of Communism, not with theory or words, but with facts." Of the criticism the U.S. had attracted for cutting off the sugar quota, Bosch wrote, "It seems inconceivable to me that the United States should be expected to place several hundred million dollars a year in the hands of an avowed enemy of this country by continuing the purchase of Cuban sugar."

Then came a startling assertion. "Just recently," Bosch wrote, "I have received confidential information that in the western part of the island of Cuba, specifically in the vicinity of the town of Soroa, Province of Pinar del Río, an installation is being finished that has required hundreds of tons of portland cement, and has led observers to conclude that a rocket-launching pad is being prepared for use by the Soviet Union. Many reports of other secret military installations are being received continuously in my office. Do the American people not realize that these installations may be used to pinpoint atomic destruction to any part of the United States, and that a military base in Cuba would be invaluable to the Soviet Union, not only because of its military value as a base at the very back door of the U.S., but also because of the prestige that this would give the Russians?"

Bosch suggested that neither Matthews nor Lamont knew what was really going on in Cuba; or perhaps they didn't wish to know. Castro, he said, had destroyed Cuba's national wealth "and practically everything of material and spiritual value in my country." The Communists were "attempting to permeate the hearts of my people with hate and fear as Lenin, Stalin, and Beria did to their people. Tyranny accompanied by the most vile murder and torture is attempting to break the spirit of Cuba." Bosch ended: "Let all good men come to the assistance of their neighbours, the Cuban people, in this their hour of need, so that tyranny may be banished from this continent never more to raise its ugly head."

The liberal establishment, of course, pooh-poohed the letter. Bosch was just bleating because he'd lost his company. He was speaking out of self-interest. And all that ridiculous ranting about Stalin, Lenin, and Beria! But the clearest sign of paranoia was his ludicrous assertion that the Russians were establishing nuclear missile sites on the island. Why, it looked like he'd picked up that wacky notion from Graham Greene's recently published novel *Our Man in Havana*. In the book, a hard-up Havana-based British vacuum-cleaner salesman signs on with British intelligence. Lacking any real material, he fabricates the story of a giant installation in the mountains from which a secret weapon may be launched. Pressed for details, he sends a drawing of a vacuum-cleaner attachment!

But life had a way of following art in Cuba. Castro had forecast in January 1961 that the U.S. would invade Cuba before Eisenhower left office, and had ordered a general mobilization. The "excuse" for the invasion, he said, would be the false accusation that Cuba was constructing secret rocket-launching pads. Thus, in the eyes of Castro's die-hard supporters, Bosch was merely laying the groundwork of lies for the invasion to follow.

It was widely known among the exile community in early 1961 that a brigade of Cuban exiles — known as Brigade 2506, after the serial number of the first volunteer who died in training — was being trained for an invasion of Cuba. But in April, as Pepín Bosch's indignant letter appeared in the *New York Times*, anger and confusion welled among the exiles at their Guatemalan base. The Cubans' U.S. mentors told them that forces in the Kennedy administration were trying to block the invasion: they might be ordered to abort it. So opposed to this derailment were the U.S. military advisers that they even suggested, if worst came to worst, that the Cubans should go ahead anyway, and that the American advisers would willingly become prisoners and present the Cuban exiles with the full plans for the assault.

The attack was finally, and reluctantly, given the go-ahead, but under circumstances of almost guaranteed failure about which the Cuban brigade knew nothing.

The Cuban army officer who led the assault was a quiet, wiry twenty-nine-year-old, José ("Pepe") Pérez San Román. "Fight fiercely," he said on the eve of the action, "but protect the civilians and respect the prisoners. On to victory!" he cried. "Freedom is our goal; Cuba is our cause; God is on our side!" His fellow freedom fighters cheered wildly. The force slipped ashore in the pre-dawn of April 17 at three locations at the Bay of Pigs, some hundred miles east of Havana on the south side of the island.

God may have been on their side, but the American administration was a less certain ally. The Cuban brigade was doomed because the Kennedy administration had decided that, ostensibly to preserve "deniability" about U.S. involvement, its promised U.S. air cover would not be provided.

The Castro forces, ever alert, were soon on the scene. Their own small but unopposed air force wreaked havoc. By late morning the situation was desperate. In mid-afternoon, Pepe Pérez San Román radioed his last message: "Am destroying all my equipment and communications. Tanks are in sight. I have nothing to fight with. Am taking to the woods. I cannot wait for you." U.S. advisers listening to this message aboard the U.S. flagship reportedly cried. Pérez San Román dispatched messengers to his fellow commanders, ordering them to take to the woods until the air cover came. With his staff officers and forty-six men, he headed into the Zapata swamps and awaited the promised support.

Close to 1,200 Cuban exiles were captured; 114 died in combat or perished in the subsequent ordeal, and 60 were seriously wounded. The prisoners were paraded publicly and "interrogated" by Castro before the television cameras in Havana as part of a show trial. The men were ultimately ransomed by the U.S. in return for $62 million in medical equipment.

The Americans had achieved the worst possible outcome by their actions — or lack of them — at the Bay of Pigs. Castro was handed the excuse to execute most of the "counterrevolutionaries" he had in custody, and to make as many as 100,000 more arrests. On May 1, 1961, amid the anti-American hysteria, he declared Cuba a socialist state and announced that, since the revolutionary regime directly expressed the will of the people, there would be no more elections. Castro boasted that he had beaten not merely a small band of Cuban exiles, but the might of the U.S. (A huge billboard was placed overlooking the beach at Playa Girón, at the mouth of the Bay of Pigs, proclaiming it to be the site of "the first great imperialist defeat in Latin America.") Such was the down payment on the cost of Kennedy's lack of political conviction. The full price would not become apparent until eighteen months later.

By most accounts, the Cuban Missile Crisis started on October 15, 1962, when photographs taken by a United States U-2 spy plane provided "indisputable evidence" that the Soviet Union was constructing missile sites on the island. Why had it taken twenty months for the U.S. to confirm what Pepín Bosch had claimed to know back in April 1961? Had Bosch made it all up? Had life followed Cuban "paranoia"? Was Bosch's intelligence network superior to that of the U.S? Or did the Kennedy administration know what was going on but take all that time to summon the courage to do anything about it?

Again, by most accounts, there followed a week of deliberations, after which, on October 22, Kennedy announced a naval blockade of Cuba. Fingernails were chewed for six more days as the world "teetered on the brink of nuclear destruction." On October 28, Soviet leader Nikita Khrushchev agreed to withdraw his country's missiles from the island.

The affair was subsequently portrayed in the U.S. as a tough-minded stand by the young president, a kind of High Noon in which the black hats had been forced to back down. In fact, Kennedy had paid an enormous price for the alleged withdrawal of the Soviet missiles. Among other elements of the pact he made with Khrushchev was a non-invasion pledge, which virtually guaranteed Castro's safety and made outlaws of those Cuban exiles who, like Pepín Bosch, still sought to overthrow him from the U.S.

The third act of what Cuban exiles regarded as the Kennedy betrayal came two months after the missile crisis. At the Orange Bowl in Miami, at a ceremony to welcome back the ransomed survivors of the Bay of Pigs invasion, President Kennedy was given the flag of Brigade 2506. Jackie Kennedy, softly, in Spanish, expressed her "wish and hope" that someday her own son would "be a man at least half as brave as the members of Brigade 2506." Cubans chanted "Guerra!

Guerra!" but the Kennedy – Khrushchev pact had guaranteed there would be no *guerra*.

The final, vein-popping piece of evidence of Kennedy's betrayal of the Cuban exiles emerged in Arthur D. Schlesinger Jr.'s *A Thousand Days*, in which he disclosed that Kennedy said to him, just before the Bay of Pigs: "If we have to get rid of these 800 men, it is much better to dump them in Cuba than in the United States, especially if that is where they want to go." Kennedy had already been warned, according to Schlesinger, that there was a "disposal problem" with the men of Brigade 2506. The U.S. role in the Bay of Pigs was not to back the anti-Castro Cubans, then, but to deliver them to their destruction.

Brigade 2506 as a "disposal problem;" the missile crisis as sellout (the U.S. did not even negotiate on-site inspection); the Orange Bowl as a cheap PR stunt. Betrayal after betrayal. As T.D. Allman says in his book *Miami*: "That rendezvous in the Orange Bowl really had been a turning point in history. This wasn't because of what the president had promised; it was because Kennedy's pledge meant nothing."

To be sure, with the exception of Herbert Matthews, there was no shortage of mea culpas from key figures in the American media about how wrong they had been about Castro. Two of the most respected journalists who had covered the revolution, Ruby Hart Phillips of the *New York Times* and Jules Dubois of the *Chicago Tribune*, subsequently wrote books bitterly denouncing the Castro revolution. But they made sure that people like the Bacardis received their share of blame for being duped. "The Castro revolution," wrote Phillips, "is a classic example of how a small minority can seize a country under the guise of a 'social revolution' with the fervent assistance of the would-be 'liberals' in the wealthy and property-owning middle classes. Blinded by emotion and hypnotized by the personality of one man, these classes were led down the road to Communism."

Jules Dubois, too, noted that he was only one of many who had been duped. What about the "empty chair" dinner thrown in his honor at the Santiago country club? Hadn't virtually the entire establishment of the city appeared as Castro's supporters, including Pepín Bosch and Daniel Bacardi? Dubois had written of that incident in his book *Fidel Castro: Rebel Liberator or Dictator*, completed mere weeks after Castro's arrival in Havana in 1959. That book had included a letter from Castro, which declared: "Every person in the society of free nations — and even those who are oppressed under the heels of dictators — has a right to express his or her opinion. Under the tyranny of Fulgencio Batista that right was denied to the people of Cuba.

"It is the duty of every newspaperman to report the news, for only with freedom of the press can there be political freedom."

Dubois had finished that book on March 7, 1959. He asked: "Can a man who is so imbued with such a missionary zeal to see others free degenerate into a dictator himself?" At the time, Dubois plainly thought not. Now, however, Castro's letter prompted another question: Could there ever have been a more consummate liar than the Cuban dictator?

In *Operation America: The Communist Conspiracy in Latin America*, written four years later, Dubois attempted to set the record straight. He wrote: "Prior to the general exodus of refugees from Cuba, Castro approved the methodical destruction of every vestige of opposition. The initial step was to instill terror, and this was done through the execution wall and the firing squad which, at first, punished the killers of the Batista regime. Then those who might become obstacles in the path of Communist advances were liquidated on trumped-up charges by drumhead 'people's courts' while Communist claques overran the courtrooms."

Exiles such as Pepín Bosch needed little reminding of their complicity in Castro's victory. Indeed, their examination of the part they had played in their own downfall became obsessive. Like besotted cuckolds, they had been blind to infidelity, refusing to see the obvious until it was too late. Now, like wounded lovers, they kept returning to the emotional scar, reviewing the evidence with forensic morbidity. How could Castro have deceived them so? When had he decided to deceive them? Had he always been lying? How could they have been such fools?

What appalled and astonished Bosch and his fellow exiles most was that *any* support for Castro remained. If anything, this support grew stronger on the university campuses of the radical Sixties. For every Ruby Hart Phillips or Jules Dubois, who had been there and seen it, there was a bonehead academic — Dr. Milton Eisenhower, for example, the former president's brother — who set out to extirpate the sin of American "imperialism" and exonerate the Castro regime by writing books about how bad things had been under Batista, knowing little about that regime, never having visited Cuba, and not having bothered to learn Spanish. Many who did visit the country in the

1960s went, like travelers to Stalin's Russia in the 1930s, with their minds made up. The conventional liberal wisdom, with its Orwellian mantra — right bad, left good — blinded whole groups of men and women. In the words of Todd Gitlin, a radical student leader at the time who became a professor of sociology at the University of California at Berkeley: "Cuba was the revolutionary frontier, the not-yet-known. Here, apparently, was the model of a revolution led by students, not by a Communist Party — indeed in many ways against it. The triumph over a brutal American-sponsored dictatorship had been improbable, dramatic, hard to categorize." Gitlin's use of certain words — "apparently," "not-yet-known," "hard to categorize" — betrays his eagerness to persuade his readers that nothing was obvious at the time. Of course, these are the words of someone who did not see what was going on in Cuba because he did not want to see.

By the conventional liberal wisdom of the self-delusive 1960s — as of the self-delusive 1930s — Communism was no enemy. And of course, the antics of Joseph McCarthy's witch-hunt in the early 1950s had even linked Communism, ironically, with the preservation of free speech — a ludicrous association, as the Castro experience clearly showed. At a time when universities used "ideological pluralism" and "moral relativism" as excuses for supporting any regime but that of the United States, the phrase "anti-Communism" was almost invariably prefixed by the word "mindless."

The Cuban exiles, with their passionate approach to politics and loose adherence to facts, proved easy targets for academic superciliousness. The exiles fed their hatred on every rumor, true or not, about Castro. Each bizarre story was passed around, embellished, upheld. To those in exile, the key to these stories was their psychological truth. Castro was the embodiment of evil. To continue giving him the benefit of the doubt was to them a kind of insanity; it was like claiming that a rapist had merit because he had not murdered his victim, or that Hitler couldn't have been all bad because he liked dogs. There came a point at which weighing the merits of any case became itself unreasonable, an act not of evenhandedness but of psychopathology. To suggest that people who had been dispossessed, whose friends and relatives had been tortured or murdered, were the wrong ones to judge — because they had been too close to the action, too personally involved — was not just infuriating, it was perverse. It implied that those with more "objectivity" were able to regard dispossession, torture, and murder as so many "necessary evils" in the cause of the greater good, a fallacy demonstrated time and again in revolutionary history since the Reign of Terror.

Cuban exiles noticed, meanwhile, that their more "broad-minded" pro-Castro opponents, confronted by irrefutable evidence of the economic disasters wrought by the regime, retreated into vague rationalizations: "It's better than it was before," or "Look at what Castro's done for medicine and education," or — the one that sent the mercury right out of the exiles' thermometer — "The people may not be free, but at least they have food."

One of the Cubans' problems, in exile as it had been in Cuba, was political unity. Old supporters of Batista, and those who had once fought them as *fidelistas*, although now both anti-Castro, made uneasy Miami bedfellows. Initially, the CIA persuaded the exile groups to unite under the name Frente Revolucionario Democrático. The FRD presented lengthy position papers and impassioned speeches, and worked on a new Cuban constitution, but the group turned out to be an exercise in frustration. It was absorbed into the Cuban Revolutionary Council, but this group too proved ineffective.

In 1964, a frustrated Pepín Bosch, who was now dividing his time among his homes in Recife, Mexico City, and Miami, stepped directly into the fray. He provided $75,000 to finance a referendum among Cuban exiles "designed to underpin a representative coalition against Castro." The referendum failed to create a voice for a single Cuban community, but it did become important in the ongoing fight with Castro, both in public relations and — more controversially — military terms.

From the Bosch-funded referendum, an organization was formed called RECE (Representación Cubana del Exilio). Bosch provided the office and paid the salaries. The original RECE executive group included one of Pérez San Román's commanders from the Bay of Pigs, Erneido Oliva González, and a young man involved in a related operation that never landed on the island, Jorge Mas Canosa. Canosa went on to become the most influential and often controversial figure in Cuban exile politics through another organization supported by Bosch, the Cuban American National Foundation.

At the outset, Bosch asked Mas Canosa's uncle, "Polo" Valdez Miranda, the long-time revolutionary who had overseen the Hatuey brewery in Manacas, Cuba, to run the RECE office. Valdez Miranda organized a newsletter sent both to Cuban exiles and, from locations outside the U.S., to Cubans still on the island. He also engaged in activities that, in light of the Kennedy-Khrushchev pact, were — at least officially — frowned on by U.S. authorities. Partly funded by Bosch, Valdez Miranda and Mas Canosa plotted military raids on Cuba.

Among RECE's recruits was Tony Cuesta, another exile from Santiago. Backed with RECE money, Cuesta launched an attack from two speedboats in Havana harbor. He machine-gunned a police station, a hotel, a radar installation, and the house of Osvaldo Dórticos, then president of Cuba. The raid cost Cuesta his sight, his left hand, and twelve years in Cuban jails. RECE also equipped a number of small assault forces that landed in Cuba, at least one of which was meant to assassinate Castro with cyanide-tipped bullets.

Bosch's subsidy of armed action against Castro was considered nothing of which to be ashamed, nothing to conceal, although it forced him to hire bodyguards in the 1960s. Evil that used force had to have force used against it. But RECE's forces were pathetic compared with the considerable resources at Castro's disposal. After 1970, when the effectiveness of Soviet surveillance equipment rendered such invasion suicidal, RECE became primarily an organ for disseminating news.

Slowly, the Cuban exiles were coming to terms with the fact that they were not going home. President Kennedy had installed generous financial assistance for the exiles. Much of that help was contingent on their moving from Miami. But many stayed.

Miami had started out as a place to get away from it all, a city carved from flat swampland early in this century as a middle-class, middle-brow holiday resort and retirement destination. When the Cuban exiles arrived, they had no intention of staying; it was merely the closest point to home. They hadn't come, as the author Nestor Carbonell said of many exiles, "pulled by the American economic dream, but as refugees pushed by the Cuban political nightmare . . . Most of us focused primarily on the liberation of our homeland. There was no thought of permanent U.S. residence, much less of citizenship. Our plans in Miami were tentative, temporary . . . Optimism was often sparked by U.S. policy statements on Cuba, or by epic pronouncements trumpeted by exile leaders with dashes of wishful thinking."

This obsession with going back made the exiled Cubans quite

unlike other immigrant groups. Their attitudes aroused resentment among Miami's various ethnic communities. The white middle class felt as if a group of strangers had burst into their homes speaking a foreign language, and, without so much as a by-your-leave, taken positions by the window with a pair of binoculars, consumed by events unfolding at a dimly perceived and less understood distance. The black communities were upset because industrious but impecunious Cubans were prepared to take low-paying jobs and do them better.

In the mid-1960s, it became apparent that the imminent liberation of Cuba was a pipe dream. The exiles began to regard themselves no longer as refugees but as immigrants. Despite this sublimation of exile fervor into commercial achievement, the hurt — and the dreams of its reversal — remained strong. If anything, the Cubans nurtured their wounds because of the apparent unwillingness or inability of their American hosts to understand them.

It was the Cuban Missile Crisis that first made this vociferous, gesticulating, and passionate people a source of uneasiness to Americans. As T. D. Allman notes: "For Miami's 'real' Americans in December, 1962, the liberty of Cuba, no matter how desirable abstractly, was something for which they had no intention of risking, or even disrupting, their lives." These "real" Americans thought, perhaps, like Hemingway's Harry Morgan, "It's the Cubans run Cuba. They all double cross each other. They sell each other out. They get what they deserve. The hell with their revolutions."

The assassination of John F. Kennedy in November 1963 intensified the Americans' grave disquiet over U.S. involvement with Cuba. Although the official explanation, then and now, was that Kennedy had been killed by the solitary Lee Harvey Oswald, there would always remain disturbing theories that others — and a much larger conspiracy — were involved. Amid the suggestions that Russians, Texas oilmen, the CIA, Lyndon Johnson, or the Mafia had masterminded the hit, there remained nagging questions about Cuban involvement. Had Fidel Castro merely returned the favor for Kennedy's involvement in plots to assassinate the Cuban leader? Or were Cuban exiles repaying the president for his betrayal of their cause and their homeland?

Miami, which over the past thirty years has been transformed into an almost Cuban city, provided the caldron that kept the struggle, *la lucha*, boiling. "Real" Americans, meanwhile, had bigger problems to absorb them during the 1960s and 1970s — chiefly, of course, Vietnam. Many Cuban exiles were as outraged by that war as the radical left, but for a different reason: Why did the U.S. think it so important to halt the march of Communism 13,000 miles away when it had allowed it 90 miles from its own doorstep?

For his part, Pepín Bosch was determined that the Bacardi empire, far from being crippled by expropriation, would thrive. Entrepreneurial spirit could not be thwarted by the mere seizure of assets. The essence of Bacardi's success lay not in the ownership of gleaming plants or stocks of aging rum; it lay in the mind of Pepín Bosch. He may have thrown himself wholeheartedly into the fight against Castro — every few weeks, he called Polo Valdez Miranda at RECE's little Miami office and asked the same question: "What do you think of the Cuban situation?" — but he did not neglect business. In fact, business achievement became, for Bosch and the Bacardis, a critical part of *la lucha*. Success would be the best revenge.

CHAPTER ELEVEN

Survival and Success

"But he that filches from me my good name
Robs me of that which not enriches him
And makes me poor indeed."
SHAKESPEARE, *OTHELLO*

New York. February 15, 1961

On the morning of Wednesday, February 15, 1961, at the Manhattan offices of Bacardi Imports at 595 Madison Avenue, Pepín Bosch stood before the first Bacardi shareholders' annual meeting outside Cuba. Welcoming family members, he said he regretted that the Castro government had made this meeting outside their homeland unavoidable. The important point was that they, and the company, had escaped.

A corporation is a legal entity located not where its assets happen to be but where its articles of association — a kind of corporate birth certificate, outlining the parameters of its existence — say it is. Bacardi's articles, drawn up when it was reconstituted in 1919, had, with foresight, made the company mobile: its location was either Santiago or wherever the board of directors chose. Before Bosch left Cuba for the last time, in 1960, the board had moved Bacardi's headquarters to the offices of Bacardi Imports.

At the New York meeting, a new Bacardi board was elected for a two-year term. Its family members were Bosch as president; Daniel Bacardi Rosell as first vice-president; Radames Covani, the husband of Emilio's daughter Marina Bacardi Cape, as second vice-president; Emilio's daughter Adelaida Bacardi Cape; and the two nephews of Luis J. Bacardi, Adolfo Danguillecourt Bacardi and Luis Gómez del Campo Bacardi.

Bosch had already held one board meeting outside Cuba, on November 25, 1960. There he had explained that — since Bacardi's New York lawyers, Rogers, Hoge & Hills, had confirmed the Castro government's actions to be "illegal and invalid" — a letter had been sent to the company's distributors explaining what had happened and telling them action would be taken against anyone dealing in Bacardi rum exported from Cuba. Rogers, Hoge & Hills had been instructed to take all necessary steps to preserve worldwide trademark rights.

Typically, the first item on the agenda at the New York shareholders' meeting was to approve what Pepín Bosch had already done.

To strengthen the message in the letter, Bosch had dispatched the former Havana sales manager, Juan Prado, to visit Bacardi agents in Europe. "Explain that our company has been confiscated," Bosch had told Prado, as they walked along a Miami street. "But only in Cuba. We are not finished elsewhere. We are still alive and want all the business we can get." Prado was to tell customers their needs could be supplied from the Puerto Rican and Mexican plants. He took off for Europe with a scribbled list of names and addresses. Some were incomplete, since the company's records had been seized in Cuba.

Bosch had shifted Bacardi to New York because the company had an office there, and also to be close to the company's New York lawyers. Since the company was primarily concerned with licensing Bacardi's other operations, however, there was little reason to be in Manhattan, or indeed anywhere in the United States, where taxes were high. Bosch considered moving the company to Mexico before deciding on the tax haven of Nassau in the Bahamas. Before the Castro coup, Bosch had already set up one Nassau subsidiary to hold the Bacardi trademarks, fearing that Batista might try to expropriate the company. Shares in the new Nassau-registered company were distributed, pro rata, to family members on the basis of their holdings in the Cuban company. Bosch also decided to put a distillery on the island of New Providence, where Nassau is located.

The hundredth anniversary of the original Bacardi company, on February 4, 1962, came fifteen months after Cuban expropriation. It was sandwiched between the Bay of Pigs fiasco and the Cuban Missile Crisis. Still, it was a less melancholy occasion than it might have been. Thanks to Pepín Bosch's vision and strategic planning, the company now had modern plants in Puerto Rico, Mexico, and Brazil, and another planned for Nassau. It exported to a hundred countries. Mexico had just surpassed 1 million cases a year. Puerto Rico wasn't far behind, having shipped 850,000 cases in 1961. Most of that went to Bacardi Imports in New York, which that year sold more than 700,000 cases.

Meanwhile, although *la lucha* was not going well on the political front, Bacardi continued its fight with the Cuban government. Bosch had no intention of letting the *fidelistas* steal Bacardi's Cuban-supplied overseas markets or its foreign bank accounts. Most important, he couldn't allow Castro to steal the company name.

Bosch had already moved the trademarks — that is, the legal right to use the Bacardi name and bat symbol — out of Cuba, but that did not stop the Castro government from trying to usurp those rights. Ironically, the Communists attempted to use capitalist law courts to assert their claim to what they had — in the name of the people — stolen.

Many Bacardi employees and lawyers were involved in the trademark fight, but two stood out. One was Roberto Pujals, who had been Bacardi's lawyer in Santiago. He'd had a very successful practice in Cuba, where his clients had included Texaco, the Nicaro nickel company, and several American-owned sugar mills. He had also been a partner in a thriving Santiago flour mill. As the Castro government expropriated each of his clients, he ceased representing them. By the time it came to the Nicaro nickel company, he was concerned that, if he resigned again, he would be seen as a counterrevolutionary. He went to Nicaro and begged them to fire him, which they obligingly did. He had left Santiago in November 1960, the month after the Bacardi expropriation. Bosch hired him as Bacardi's corporate secretary.

The other key figure in the trademark fight was Alfred (Pete) O'Hara, who had joined the Bacardis' law firm of Rogers, Hoge & Hills after heading the civil division of the U.S. Attorney's office in New York City. O'Hara's style, sometimes brusque and undiplomatic, was summed up in a typically terse, although tongue-in-cheek, memo he received from Pepín Bosch. "Dear Pete," said the note. "A Kissinger you're not." O'Hara's first task had been to assemble the huge volume of paperwork needed to reconstitute the company in the Bahamas. He and Pujals became legal marines, ready to fight the Cuban government wherever it attempted to sell the Bacardis' rum.

The Castro government first tried to establish ownership of a bank account held by Bacardi in New York with the Bank of Nova Scotia. Bacardi was tipped off; the company brought suit and won a judgment establishing its existence as a refugee corporation and its entitlement to the property it had owned in Cuba. This judgment was a powerful precedent that O'Hara was able to use in other jurisdictions. Another persuasive legacy of the Manhattan case was that, although costs had been awarded against Cuba, the Castro government had never paid them. O'Hara made sure that lawyers acting for the Cuban government in other jurisdictions knew this. Castro's foreign lawyers thus became nervous not only over their fees, but over their potential liability for damages.

The Bacardi legal strategy was straightforward. In most jurisdictions, a trademark is registered with customs authorities, who impound imports if the trademark's owner has not given permission for its use. The Bacardis retained loyal employees in Santiago; whenever a shipment of rum left port, its destination was transmitted to the Bacardis via the U.S. naval base at Guantanamo. Every time a cargo of rum from Cuba turned up anywhere in the world sporting the name Bacardi, the lawyers were there to challenge its validity.

The Guantanamo information pipeline proved highly effective. Thanks to a cable from the base, for example, local authorities were waiting when a cargo turned up at the giant Dutch port of Rotterdam. Dutch laws are tough on illicit imports, and the captain of the ship — in the absence of legal advice — dumped his cargo over the side.

O'Hara, warned that a shipment was headed for London, set off to England to hire local counsel. Sure enough, some weeks later, 1,000 cases of rum, under the name Compañía Ron Bacardi Nacionalizada, turned up at the London docks. O'Hara made sure they were seized by customs officials. Subsequently, the Cuban government brought suit to establish its right to expropriate the brand name. Thus was launched the first in a series of expensive and protracted legal battles fought in courtrooms from Manhattan to Tokyo, and from Tel Aviv to the Dutch Antilles. Bacardi won every case, either by adjudication or default. The only case that went to trial was in Israel, where the Bacardis spent more money fighting Castro than they could hope to gain from rum sales for the ensuing century.

O'Hara began working virtually full-time for Bacardi on the trademark fight and on the formation of new companies and the distribution of their shares among family members. He handled the legal side of setting up Bacardi International in Bermuda to handle the bulk of Bacardi's non-U.S. activities. Apart from Bosch, he was the only individual who came close to understanding the complexity of the Bacardi empire. That knowledge would one day make him critically important to Bacardi.

With the election of the Progressive Liberal Party in the Bahamas in 1967, Bosch became concerned once more about political stability. The black-dominated PLP advocated stricter government control of the economy and increased Bahamian ownership. As a result, O'Hara had to go through the whole trademark-moving process again. The new home of the precious trademark was the tiny, mountainous principality of Liechtenstein in central Europe, where, said Bosch, "they have beautiful laws." O'Hara had to manage the paperwork of reassigning the trademark rights in 117 countries.

O'Hara, like most who worked with him, held Pepín Bosch in awe. The lawyer was amazed by Bosch's grasp of business detail, and by the huge volume of information about the company he kept only in his head. O'Hara once had an appointment with Bosch in New York to deal with a long list of complex trademark matters. He had set aside the whole day. Bosch arrived at nine and was gone by ten-thirty. He had an answer to every question. "Mr. Bosch," O'Hara asked, "wouldn't you like to have a memorandum with respect to the matters that we've reached a decision on today?" "No thanks," replied Bosch, tapping his cranium, "it's all in here."

O'Hara would sometimes be summoned to meet Bosch in Recife, but usually he was asked to visit Bosch in Nassau. Bosch invited him out on his yacht to fish. Like a Saudi prince, Pepín Bosch did business in his own time. Eventually, he'd get to his agenda.

O'Hara was fishing with Bosch one day off Nassau while a Cuban radio commentator was vilifying his host as a traitor. Bosch listened with delight. O'Hara, because of his role in the trademark case, already had a recurring nightmare of being hijacked to Havana; he wondered if they shouldn't perhaps throw a towel over the name of the boat. Cuban MiGs were just a few minutes away. Bosch wouldn't dream of concealing the proud Bacardi name. He seemed to thrive on the Communists' hatred of him.

Bosch rarely betrayed anger but, as with most Cuban exiles, the mere mention of Fidel Castro was enough to raise his blood pressure. The Mexicans tended to be sympathetic to the Castro regime, largely because of the deep anti-Americanism that ran through their own history. One day, seeing "Viva Fidel" daubed on the side of a truck bringing rum from La Galarza to Tultitlán, Bosch called up the plant manager and told him that, if the culprit would identify himself, Bosch would be glad to buy him a one-way ticket to Cuba. On another occasion at La Galarza, spotting a copy of *Time* with Castro on the cover, Bosch angrily seized it and tossed it in a wastebasket.

Bosch was sixty-two when Castro seized Bacardi's Cuban assets, an age when many men relish the thought of retirement, but he felt he was just beginning. As well as taking a consuming interest in the ongoing fight with the Castro regime, Bosch flew constantly around the Caribbean heart of the empire and on longer sorties to New York,

Recife, and London. He usually descended unannounced, which kept everybody on their toes. He shepherded former Cuban employees and family members into jobs within the empire. Because of the Cuban losses, and Bosch's desire to spend every available dollar on expansion, he reduced dividends. Some family members found they had to work for the first time. Parts of the family still harbored old resentments, but none could deny Bosch's Moses-like role in delivering them from Castro.

The booming world economy, the trend toward lighter spirits, brilliant advertising — all played a part in Bacardi's extraordinary growth. A fierce dedication to, and identification with, the product by Bacardi employees was also important. The company developed and attracted talented technicians and sales and marketing people, as well as outstanding executives. But it would have been a very different story without Pepín Bosch. He was the solar mass around which the satellite operations revolved, the energy source that drove the system.

The U.S. market, served by Bacardi Imports with rum made by Bacardi Corporation in Puerto Rico, had suffered for many years from the aftertaste of the poor rum shipped during the Second World War. Indeed, it was 1957 before Bacardi returned to the sales levels of 1944. From that point, however, the company never looked back.

In 1963, Bosch decided to move Bacardi Imports to Miami. There was inevitable resistance from company executives, most of whom had now lived in New York for more than twenty years. But Miami was the centre of *el exilio*, in whose dramas Bosch continued to play a leading part. He also wanted to bring Bacardi Imports closer to the empire's Caribbean heart, and to reduce his own considerable traveling time. To mark the move, Bosch decided to erect another landmark structure. Always on the lookout for the unusual, he took his inspiration from plans he had seen for a building in Buenos Aires. The structure's mass was suspended from above. But what made Bacardi's new building on Biscayne Boulevard in Miami really distinctive was the great floral pattern on its sides. It was executed in blue and white *azulejos* tiles, designed by a Brazilian artist, Francisco Brennand. The ground floor of the building was dedicated to a Bacardi art gallery.

The building was not very practical, and almost the antithesis of Bosch's favored open plan: employees were spread over six floors, and communication was made more difficult by the lack of internal stairways. But staff meetings in the top-floor conference room, which featured Gattorno's mural with its mythical goat (transported from the New York office) and a spectacular view of Biscayne Bay, told a tale of continuous success. The growth of sales at Bacardi Imports was so rapid that staff soon overflowed the building, leading Bosch to erect an even more bizarre structure, a block on a fat, orange-tiled stalk, with stained-glass walls and no windows. Eventually, a low-rise office building on the corner of the block had to be taken over too. The hodgepodge of architectural styles lacked unity, but the headquarters with its manicured gardens was an arresting advertisement for the company.

In some ways, Bosch's outrageous notions — sticking great floral patterns on the side of a building hanging from space, and constructing a stained-glass cube lollipop — prefigured the very "Cuban" structures later built by the Miami-based firm of Arquitectónica. Arquitectónica's most famous building is a huge condominium on Brickell Avenue with a 50-foot cube cut from the middle, in which sits a Jacuzzi, a palm tree, and a bright red spiral staircase. Miami architecture was described by Joan Didion in her book *Miami* as a style "which appeared to have slipped its moorings," but it indicated a boldness that was a key element in putting Miami and *cubanismo* on the map.

A critical factor in the success of Bacardi Imports was brilliant advertising. The man behind Bacardi's U.S. ad campaigns was Bill Walker, a fast-talking, chain-smoking advertising ace who reveled in dreaming up new ways to sell the product. Walker had entered the business in Detroit in 1949 with a firm called Brook, Smith, French & Dorens. He stayed with the agency as, over twenty years, it underwent various mergers and reorganizations, becoming part of Ross Roy, then Rumrill-Hoyt, and ultimately part of the Saatchi & Saatchi empire. When he was transferred to New York, he was appointed a junior account executive on Bacardi rum. In the 1950s, Bacardi Imports had no marketing or advertising staff of its own, so Walker's agency ran these functions.

Faced with the continuing image problems of rum in the U.S. market, Bacardi, on Walker's advice, decided to play down that its product was rum at all: it was Bacardi. This in turn helped with the second element of the company's strategy: to take market share from *all* the other spirit categories' leading brands: a little from Smirnoff, from Canadian Club, from Jack Daniels, from J&B. In the mid-1960s, under the guidance of Luis Lasa, who was then in charge of advertising, Walker set out to establish that Bacardi was the most "mixable" of spirits, a "one-brand bar."

Lasa was also important to the company's growth. As a young man, he had gone from high school to work at First National City Bank in Havana. There he had first come across Pepín Bosch, who was dividing his time between working for the bank and plotting against the dictator Machado. In later years, Lasa continued to see Bosch through their joint memberships in national advertising and industrial associations in Cuba. Lasa became an advertising and sales executive with the Cuban subsidiary of Colgate-Palmolive. He left Havana under threat of arrest in 1960 and headed for Miami. Colgate had asked him to move to New York, but he wanted to stay close to Cuba, sure he would soon return. He worked for a couple of years with the Cuban Refugee Center, as a volunteer, then as an employee. By 1963, when he realized he wasn't going back to Cuba, he considered rejoining Colgate and moving to Manhattan. When Bosch heard this, he asked Lasa to join Bacardi Imports.

Lasa had turned fifty, a relatively advanced age at which to enter a new business; but he went about his work with the indomitable enthusiasm that had become the trademark of Cuban exiles. He started at the bottom, traveling from store to bar to restaurant as a "missionary," persuading people to sell Bacardi. It was a tough job. He was not permitted to buy drinks for potential customers: such inducements were against the law. Everything depended on his personality and persuasive powers. After six months, he was put in charge of promotion. A year later he was put in charge of advertising. He was then given a large sales territory, and eventually he was made responsible for national sales. He bustled around the country, revving up the salesmen, working with distributors. He hit the big markets — New York, California, Illinois, and Florida — but traveled to the boondocks too. There wasn't a liquor-store shelf or a bar display anywhere in the country in which he didn't take a passionate interest, and he knew each of Bacardi's more than 200 distributors by name.

One of the most important steps in the growth of Bacardi was the decision, in the mid-1960s, to approach the mighty Coca-Cola company about joint advertising. Rum-and-Coke, the Cuba Libre, though it had been around since the turn of the century, was now seen as central to Bacardi's "mixability" thrust.

The Coca-Cola empire had origins as humble as those of Bacardi. The product had originated as a "proprietary elixir" developed by a pharmaceutical chemist named John Pemberton in a cast-iron kettle over an open fire in his backyard. The concoction had emerged by mistake when the syrup had been accidentally mixed by a drugstore owner with soda instead of tap water.

Coca-Cola first went on sale in 1886 in the Atlanta drugstore where it had been made. In 1891, Pemberton sold the rights to Asa Candler, and the next year Candler formed the Coca-Cola Company and registered "Coca-Cola" as a trademark. By 1895, the product was being sold all over the U.S. In 1899, Candler was approached by two entrepreneurs, Benjamin Franklin Thomas and Joseph B. Whitehead, with a plan to bottle Coca-Cola, which was then being sold primarily as a bulk syrup that drugstores diluted. Thomas, ironically, had first noticed the potential for bottled soft drinks while serving the year before in Cuba in the Spanish-American War. Candler granted Thomas and Whitehead the rights for the U.S. (with the exception of New England, Mississippi, and Texas), and the franchised bottling business was born.

Coca-Cola's success was remarkable, not least because its principal ingredients, extracts of the coca leaf and the cola nut, were virtually unknown. Its taste was therefore indescribable. The central theme of its advertising was that it was "delicious and refreshing." By 1914, a share of Coca-Cola stock, issued with a par value of $100, was worth $17,000; Candler was reportedly worth $50 million.

In 1919, the Candler family sold out to a group of Atlanta businessmen, headed by Ernest Woodruff. Under Woodruff's son, Robert Winship Woodruff, the company enjoyed even greater success. Woodruff emphasized bottled sales, in the curvaceous container, developed in 1915, that became part of the company trademark. He also took the product into world markets. By the Second World War, Coca-Cola and the wholesome imagery developed in its advertising had become part of the fabric of the American way. During the war, Woodruff issued an edict that every American serviceman should be able to buy a bottle of Coca-Cola for 5 cents, "wherever he is and whatever it costs the company." Dozens of plants were built and shipped overseas to serve combat troops. Woodruff saw the business as a cooperative effort based on independent franchisees, supported by more advertising money than had ever been spent on any product. What started as a thirst-quencher had become, by the 1960s, a symbol of America itself.

In 1965, Coke's agency, McCann-Erickson, launched the famous "Things go better with Coke" campaign. Luis Lasa decided to approach the Atlanta giant to see if it was willing to acknowledge publicly that one of the things with which Coke went best was Bacardi. Given Coke's squeaky-clean image and the fact that it had promoted itself during Prohibition as "The Great National Temperance Beverage," it was not likely to be an easy task.

Luis Lasa and Bill Walker made an appointment with Coke's marketing head, Fred Dickson (later president of the company). Bacardi-and-Coke was a popular drink, they pointed out, and there could be mutual advantages in a joint advertising campaign. The Coke people were concerned about Bacardi's distribution. Lasa bet them that they couldn't find a bar or liquor store that didn't have Bacardi. A deal was cut that same day. Elated, Lasa and Walker headed for Atlanta airport, where they went into the bar for a celebratory drink. "Two Bacardi-and-Coke," they said. "Sorry," said the waiter, "No Bacardi." "Well, give us a Coke." "Sorry," came the reply. "No Coke." The next day the place was swimming in both products. And it made *such* a good story, another little psalm in the bible of brand mythology.

The first fruit of this union appeared, amid the cornucopia of ads for the American dream, in the May 20, 1966, issue of *Life* magazine. The upper portion of the ad featured a photograph, the bottom part a signed affidavit. In the photo, two soldiers in U.S. Cavalry uniform sit on either side of a civilian under a lamp at a barroom table. On the table is an empty Coca-Cola bottle. The soldier on the right, a sergeant, is about to pour from a bottle of Bacardi into the civilian's iced glass of Coke. The other soldier, an officer, waits with glass extended. Beneath the picture are the words "So *that's* how 'Rum & Coke' was invented!"

The affidivit, sworn and signed before a "notary public of the State of New York," declares: "FAUSTO RODRÍGUEZ, being duly sworn, deposes and says:

"In 1899 I was employed as a messenger in the office of the U.S. Army Signal Corps. I became friendly with a Mr. [name blanked out], who worked in the office of the Chief Signal Officer.

"One afternoon, in August, 1900, I went with him to the [name blanked out] Bar, and he drank Bacardi rum and Coca-Cola. I just drank Coca-Cola, being only 14 years old.

"On that occasion, there was a group of soldiers at the bar, and one of them asked Mr. [name blanked out] what he was drinking. He told them it was Bacardi and Coca-Cola and suggested they try it, which they did.

"The soldiers liked it. They ordered another and toasted Mr. [name blanked out] as the inventor of a great drink.

"The drink has remained popular to the present time."

The words "Sworn to before me this 24th day of October, 1965" are followed by the notary's signature.

Beside the affidavit are the words: "And *how* Mr. R! It's now the #2 rum drink. Most are made with Bacardi rum, because we make Bacardi dry and light bodied. That's one reason people buy about as much Bacardi as all the other rum brands *combined!*"

The bottom line of the ad reads: "Drink BACARDI rum — enjoyable always and *all* ways."

The Bacardi-and-Coke ad raised questions about the uneasy ties between brand advertising, history, and politics. One intriguing omission from the ad was the more common name for rum-and-Coke, which in most versions of the invention of the drink became the whole point of the story. For proprietary reasons, the company was keen to promote "Bacardi-and-Coke" rather than "Cuba Libre." But Cuba Libre — "Free Cuba" — was a loaded and emotive phrase in the mid-1960s, those first traumatic years after Castro had seized power and Cuban exiles felt so terribly betrayed by the U.S. administration. Brands abhor controversy, and this was an issue to avoid.

The ad was set in an historical never-never land. No hint is given of where the men are. From their uniforms, they might be in a Wild West saloon, perhaps the bar at Fort Apache. Only the name of the witness, Fausto Rodríguez, gives the game away: the bar is in Havana, and the soldiers are members of the U.S. occupation force after the Spanish-American War.

And who was Fausto Rodríguez? Although he may have worked as a messenger for the American armed forces in Havana at the turn of the century, he spent most of his life working for Bacardi. Before he retired, he became well known as head of Bacardi's publicity in New York — his nickname was "Mr. Bacardi." Fausto Rodríguez had spent his whole life telling and retelling the rum-and-Coke story, and it didn't usually come out the way it did in the ad. Sometimes in his tale his role would be to assist his American friend — who was inclined to get roaring drunk — back to quarters. Sometimes Fausto would turn up not as a humble messenger in the Signal Corps but as the personal Mercury of the U.S. governor, Leonard Wood. The bar was the old American Bar on the Calle Neptune, and its proprietor, Barrio, was said by Fausto to have mixed Bacardi with the first shipment of Coca-Cola to arrive on the island, and given the drink to the young messenger to sample. Fausto never claimed he said, "Sorry. I'm only fourteen — I'll just have a Coke." Rather, he told his listener that he

Pepín's folly? Bosch was criticized when he bought swamp land on Puerto Rico's San Juan bay, but the site became home to the world's largest rum plant, christened by Governor Muñoz Marín "the Cathedral of Rum." (BACARDI IMPORTS)

SOB: Pepín Bosch, right, with Governor Luis Muñoz Marín of Puerto Rico in 1958. Marín had said, "We must allow three hundred sons of bitches to become millionaires." Bosch had been glad to oblige. (BACARDI CORPORATION)

Down from the mountains: Fidel descended to a tumultuous welcome in Santiago when Batista fled Havana on the morning of January 1, 1959. The Bacardis cheered, but their days were numbered. (UPI/BETTMANN NEWSPHOTOS)

Presencia: Ernesto Robles León, right, a lawyer with a powerful personality, made a success of Bacardi Mexico in the 1950s and 1960s. Then he made the mistake of falling out with the Mexican government. (BACARDI MEXICO)

Corporate culture: Pepín Bosch pouring the first yeast culture into the pilot plant at Recife, Brazil, in 1960. He knew Bacardi's overseas plants were crucial to the company's survival. (BACARDI)

Billowing vaults: Pepín Bosch created a flamboyant display of architecture at Bacardi Mexico's headquarters at Tultitlán. The reflecting pool eventually had to be paved over because of pollution. (BACARDI MEXICO)

Art for art's sake: The Miami headquarters to which Bosch moved Bacardi Imports in 1963 was arresting — suspended from above, and flanked with floral blue-and-white tiles. The only problem was moving between floors. (BACARDI IMPORTS)

Fighting fit: Pepín Bosch was close to retirement age when Bacardi was expropriated in Cuba, but he fought Castro both in the law courts and — more controversially — with arms. (NEW YORK TIMES)

Trompe l'oeil: The mural for the new museum at the Puerto Rican plant, painted in 1966, was an unintentional reminder that there was more to Bacardi history than met the eye. (BACARDI CORPORATION)

So <u>that's</u> how "Rum & Coke" was invented!

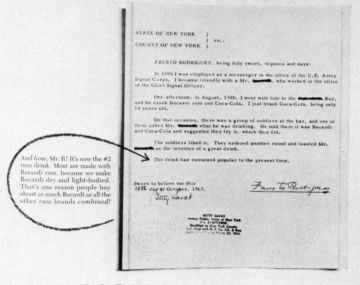

And *how*, Mr. R! It's now the #2 rum drink. Most are made with Bacardi rum, because we make Bacardi dry and light-bodied. That's one reason people buy about as much Bacardi as all the other rum brands *combined!*

DRINK **BACARDI**® RUM—ENJOYABLE ALWAYS AND <u>ALL</u> WAYS

A Cuba Libre by any other name: The copy never mentioned Cuba, and the Coke bottle was an anachronism, but this 1966 Bacardi-and-Coke ad in *Life* was a turning point for "The Mixable One."

Something to laugh about: Luis Lasa became one of the stars of Bacardi Imports in the 1960s and 1970s. He and Bill Walker negotiated the joint advertising deal with Coca–Cola. (Bacardi Imports)

Hands on: Jorge Bosch, Pepín's son, marks the two-millionth case of Bacardi bottled in Puerto Rico for sale in the U.S. Later Jorge fell out with Pepín and found himself back at school. (Bacardi Corporation)

Traveling case: The two-millionth case reaches Miami. Sales manager Gustavo Quiñones is on the left. Eddy Nielsen, right, would take over from Bartolo Estrada, middle, three years later. Sales would continue to soar. (Bacardi Imports)

Something cooking: Bosch had just resigned from Bacardi over opposition to his plans to bring in an "outsider." But he was preparing a little surprise for the family. (NEW YORK TIMES)

Another wedding in the wings? Eddy Nielsen, left, with Romy Martínez at Lucía Nielsen's wedding. A worried Nielsen knew Martínez was helping Bosch find a buyer for his Bacardi stake. (ROMY MARTÍNEZ)

Successful suitor Cliff Hatch, Sr., was delighted to buy Pepín Bosch's stake in Bacardi. Bosch told him that once he went, there would be a flood of family sales. There weren't. (HIRAM WALKER/ALLIED VINTNERS)

found the mixture good. That very evening, so Fausto's tale usually concluded, the new concoction was served to U.S. soldiers accompanied by a toast from Barrio: "¡Por Cuba libre!" The toast was taken up, and *that* was how the drink was invented.

The rum-and-Coke story was just that: a good story. What did it matter if the shapely trademark Coke bottle on the barroom table was an anachronism, invented fifteen years after the meeting was meant to have taken place? Who cared if it really happened that way at all? Advertisements, even those featuring signed affidavits, were not to be confused with history. Something along those lines had happened, and the story didn't hurt anybody. It became another part of Bacardi brand mythology. As with "the rum of kings," the story was not an invitation to delve into the complexities of Cuba's past. And, of course, Americans had been drinking not Cuban but Puerto Rican Bacardi for almost thirty years. Unlike the rituals of *revolución*, *exilio*, and betrayal that defined — and in some cases scarred — Cuban emigrant consciousness, the Bacardi brand image, like the Bacardi company, was mobile and mutable.

Bill Walker hatched other ads using uncontroversial bits of brand "history." For a daiquiri ad, he had an actor portray Jennings Cox, the American mining engineer credited with the cocktail's invention, authentic right down to a (photostatted) copy of an 1896 *New York Times*. He used another actor as the Devil to promote "devilish drinks."

In 1967, Walker developed the "Bacardi party" and "Bacardi mini-party" ads, both with the punchline "Bacardi rum — the mixable one." These were followed by the "Bacardi party to go" campaign, featuring a tray of Bacardi light and dark and all kinds of mixes. Present at the shooting of this ad, Walker decided the tray looked too new, and "distressed" it by beating it with his shoe. The incident graphically indicated Walker's hands-on — or rather, feet-on — dedication to his favorite product.

Walker also hatched effective ads based on the themes of moderation and calorie-counting. The classic moderation ad featured rows of bottle caps of soft drink mixes, plus a steering wheel of the same size. "Bacardi Rum mixes with everything," it declared, "except driving." He put together an effective series of ads based on a diet "quiz," pointing out that a Bacardi drink had fewer calories, and sometimes less alcohol, than some specified equivalent. But the most successful theme was always "the mixable one." Those ads, with clean backgrounds and tight scripts, emphasized the rum's mixability, versatility, smoothness, and fun. Bacardi martinis, Bacardi screwdrivers, Bacardi and tonic, Bacardi straight — you could have it any way you wanted it.

And more and more people wanted it. Sales hit 1 million cases in 1964, 2 million in 1968, and 3 million in 1971, when the gentlemanly Bartolo Estrada retired and handed over the presidency of Bacardi Imports to Eddy Nielsen, a grandson of Enrique Schueg.

The 1960s also saw the beginning of a rapid growth of Bacardi's international markets. Government tariffs and trade agreements continued to influence the direction of the burgeoning empire. The most important new production facility built in the 1960s was the one near Nassau, on New Providence in the Bahamas. The plant exported to the U.K. without quota restrictions or duties under "Imperial preference." Since the trademarks were also still held on the island, New Providence became the site of the empire's central quality-control laboratory.

Nassau was the first great distilling venture begun after expropriation. It was a joint effort involving many of the company's best talents. Daniel had been appointed president of Bacardi & Company Limited when it was set up in 1958. The treasurer — and manager-treasurer of Bacardi International Limited, with which Bacardi & Company shared offices — was Orfilio Peláez, a Cuban lawyer who had been both a student leader and a union organizer before becoming a vice-president in the Puerto Rican operation and then treasurer of the main company in Santiago. The man in charge of installing the new plant, with the title of production engineer, was Richard Gardner. He had become a master brewer at Hatuey in Santiago before going to Brazil to help Juan Grau with the Recife plant. The plant superintendent was Manuel Jorge Cutillas. Nassau, opened in January 1965, had a capacity of 1 million cases a year.

The man who first pointed out to Pepín Bosch that those cases, and many more, could be sold worldwide was Juan Prado, the former Havana sales manager. Prado had realized there were bigger European markets to be tapped when he'd crossed the Atlantic as Pepín Bosch's emissary to persuade Bacardi agents to stay with the company after the Cuban revolution. He'd allowed himself three days in each country. Most Bacardi agents agreed at once to stay with the company, so he had time on his hands. Since he had no cash, he spent his time visiting local customers. Everywhere he went — Holland, Belgium,

Germany, Denmark, Norway, Finland, Austria, Italy — people wanted to know about the Cuban situation. As he told the story, he found himself getting orders. He knew there was a potential gold mine in these markets. At the end of the trip, he wrote to Orfilio Peláez suggesting a sales push in Europe.

But the push was sacrificed to other priorities, and Prado was dispatched to organize sales in Brazil. At first, he was told by Bosch to prepare for the return to Cuba. After the Bay of Pigs, however, it was obvious that the return was not imminent. Prado stayed on in Brazil.

A couple of years later, Bosch sent Daniel Bacardi to look at the European market. Daniel confirmed Prado's assessment of untapped potential. Bosch met with Prado in Rio de Janeiro. "Juan," he said, "you once recommended that we appoint a man to develop the international market. Why don't *you* go and do it?" And so Prado joined Bacardi International.

In 1962, Bosch's son, Lindy, after unsuccessful business ventures in Miami, had reluctantly asked his father for a job. His father — perhaps also reluctantly — had given him one with Bacardi International in Nassau. Lindy knew little about the business but worked enthusiastically. In 1965 his father decided to move him and Bacardi International to the tax haven of Bermuda, the picturesque, fishhook-shaped little British colony 600 miles off the east coast of the U.S. There Lindy Bosch was joined by Prado and by Eduardo Cutillas, Manuel Jorge's younger brother, a big, bear-like man who had an accounting background and had worked for the company in Santiago before the revolution. Joaquín Bacardi Fernández, "the brewer," was appointed presidential figurehead. This small handful of employees set about building international sales.

Like Luis Lasa in the U.S., Juan Prado placed great emphasis on travel. The logistics of Bacardi International were complicated. It handled orders from all over the world and passed them along to the plants in Nassau, Recife, Mexico, or Puerto Rico. The distance between the rum supplies and the markets was as much as 10,000 miles. To be closer to its markets, Bacardi set up branch offices in London in 1967 and in Sydney in 1968.

When Prado made his initial sortie, Britain had been the only country in which he had had problems persuading Bacardi's distributor to stay with the company. The distributor, Hedges & Butler, was headed by a very proper Englishman named Tavenot who, in Prado's recollection, "wore a morning suit in the office and never smiled during business hours." Tavenot refused to give Prado a commitment. Eventually, when Pepín Bosch visited him, Tavenot agreed not to deal with the Communists.

In Britain, as in the U.S., Bacardi began to promote Bacardi-and-Coke. Coca-Cola had been regarded as part of the American commercial invasion of Britain; but in the 1960s the soft drink, and the idea of mixing it with Bacardi, began to catch on. The widespread appearance of ice in bars helped the promotion of "long" drinks; the advent of mass budget travel to Spain, where Bacardi was sold cheaply, was also important. Many British tourists returned from a week on the Costa Brava and ordered a Bacardi Cuba Libre at the local pub, even if they didn't know what the phrase meant. Prado, like his counterparts in the U.S., was not pushing the Cuba Libre, wanting the drink to catch on under the proprietary name of Bacardi-and-Coke.

Bacardi International found the theme of mixability, so successful in the U.S., less effective elsewhere. In the mid-1960s, the company decided to push Bacardi's association with the "three S's," sun, sand, and sea — with perhaps a hint of a fourth "S" in the bikini-clad models who adorned the ads. Billboards, magazine ads, and television commercials were shot in hundreds of locations, from Mauritius to Hawaii, but the place was never specified. The world of Bacardi became a ubiquitous, sun-drenched wonderland of vacation leisure, the liquor industry's equivalent of Marlboro Country.

Regional variations were developed for different markets. In Germany, Bacardi was positioned, under the company's local distributor, Charles Hosie, as an imported specialty drink of exotic origin. Germany also provided the best example of breaking with the country-of-origin tradition. The German market had originally been supplied from Cuba, later from the Bahamas and Trinidad, and ultimately from Martinique. Germany also became the center for duty-free sales, bottling rum from Recife. Great advances were also made in the technologies of shipping and bottling. Casks gave way to stainless steel containers, and eventually to bulk tankers.

Among the new distilling operations opened in the early 1970s was one in Canada, at Brampton, northwest of Toronto. Pepín Bosch decided to take one of the two giant Canadian liquor companies, Hiram Walker — whose head, Cliff Hatch, Jr., he knew well — as a 25-percent partner. Alberto Bacardi Bolívar, one of the three sons of Joaquín "the brewer," was installed as president of the new company, which was called FBM (for Facundo Bacardi Maso) Distillery Co. Ltd.

He was later joined by two other family members, León Argamasilla Bacardi and Roberto del Rosal. Argamasilla and del Rosal shared Emilio Bacardi as a great-grandfather. Their fathers, José Argamasilla Grimany and Luis del Rosal Rosende, had been important executives in Santiago, like Alberto's father.

The short, stocky, and ebullient León Argamasilla Bacardi, whose mother, Zenaida, had inherited her grandfather Emilio's poetic inclinations, and whose brothers, José (Tito) and Amaro, also worked in the business, was appointed blender. Roberto del Rosal became chief financial officer. Del Rosal, who had taken part in an aborted landing related to the Bay of Pigs invasion, was returning to the business after a period in the wilderness, having balked at Pepín Bosch's order to go to Venezuela.

León Argamasilla was renowned for his outspokenness. One day he was introduced, at a social function, to the Cuban consul in Toronto. The consul, all smiles, said that he'd like to visit Bacardi's Canadian plant. Argamasilla fixed him with a cold stare and asked, in his strong Cuban accent, "But who would show you around?"

The consul looked embarrassed. Argamasilla laid it out more clearly for him: "You are my enemy."

Unused to such blunt talk, particularly in a country that had traditionally been sympathetic to the Cuban revolution, the consul started preaching the party line about how much Fidel Castro had done for the Cuban people: just look at all those improvements in the quality of medical care and education.

Argamasilla shot back that Cuba could have had all those things without the imposition of a Communist dictatorship and the suspension of personal freedoms.

"The U.S. makes many mistakes," replied the consul defensively.

"But not," responded León Argamasilla Bacardi, "as many as you."

Just to make sure it was sinking in, León repeated his message: "You are my enemy."

During the 1960s Bacardi International moved its Bermuda operation several times. By 1970, it was time for it to have its own Pepín Bosch-inspired landmark. Bosch originally planned to build a five-story structure on the western outskirts of Bermuda's opulent, pastel-colored port capital, Hamilton. The building had been designed for him by Ricardo Eguilior, a well-known Santiago architect who had designed industrial facilities and homes for the Bacardis in Cuba, as well as the Nassau plant. But planning authorities turned down the design because Bosch wanted decoration on the building similar to that of the Bacardi Imports building in Miami.

Bosch decided to reproduce a version of the Mies building that had been designed for the Santiago office but never built (although Eguilior remained the official architect). As usual, Bosch involved himself in every aspect of the building's furnishing. Mies's harsh style seemed at odds with the joy and color of *cubanismo*, but Bosch set about putting his own florid and eclectic stamp upon the single-story, glass-walled structure. For the vestibule — which faced over fountains, a waterfall that changed color, and a rolling lawn to the street — he commissioned a Cuban artist, Félix Ramos, to paint a 37-by-16-foot mural of a rural Cuban scene — the family's lost home, with its misty green mountains and towering royal palms. The painting was flanked by great traditional Dutch chandeliers.

Inside the building, the tall, glass-walled executive offices faced a large central area. For the ceiling of this area, Bosch had the stars of the night sky above Santiago on the date of the company's creation — February 4, 1862 — reproduced in "Plexiglas crystal Lumacubes." Each office was given a "thematic frieze" and matching carpet representing some part of the world. The carpets were hand-woven in Puerto Rico; the theme wallpaper and drapes were manufactured in England. The furniture was mostly of traditional antique styles — Georgian, Regency, Hepplewhite, or William and Mary. Abstract paintings — including spidery prints by Paul Klee — completed the aesthetic smorgasbord. And yet somehow the concoction created an imposing and pleasing effect.

When the building was opened, in May 1972, almost 300 guests, including many family members and senior company executives, flew in from forty-six countries. There was much to celebrate. The success of Bacardi rum had, in the thirteen years since the Castro revolution, provided a compelling bond for the Bacardi family. It had also produced a great deal of money. In 1960, the year of expropriation, Bacardi had sold 1.7 million cases of rum worldwide. By 1972, the figure had climbed to 7.8 million. The family's dividends had soared.

But an issue easily ignored thirteen years earlier was now pressing. It was the issue with which entrepreneurs often have the greatest problem, because it forces them to face their own mortality. The issue was that of management succession. Pepín Bosch's small physical stature had always belied his power, but he was now seventy-four. His face had, in old age, taken on an almost cherubic quality. His little frame, tottering on its weak leg, seemed suddenly frail.

Who would look after the business when he was gone?

CHAPTER TWELVE

Dropping the Pilot

*"Every time I read the life of a great
man, I skip the last pages because the
end is always disagreeable."*

EULOGIO CANTILLO, A GENERAL IN THE CUBAN ARMY UNDER BATISTA

Puerto Rico. 1968

By the late 1960s, Bacardi Corporation had become the showpiece of the Bacardi empire, not only because it owned the largest rum plant in the world but also because, in 1962, Pepín Bosch had sold 10 percent of its equity to the public. Bosch believed it was sound policy to have local shareholders. He also felt that creating a public market for the stock of at least one of the companies would give family shareholders an opportunity to sell shares if they needed money (and not bother him for loans — requests he usually turned down). A public quotation also meant that Bacardi Corporation could use its shares to acquire other companies. Finally, perhaps, was the element of ego. As one executive put it, "Going public was like a debutante's coming-out ball." Everybody could admire how big and profitable the company had grown.

The Puerto Rican plant also became a tourist attraction. In 1962, a great open-sided pavilion was built, with a sweeping winged roof, overlooking the bay and Old San Juan. In 1966, as part of further production expansions, a little museum was added. The highlight of the museum, covering an entire wall, was — and remains — an arresting trompe l'oeil painting, depicting, with a self-referential twist, a wall. The painted wall displayed trick portraits, photographs, certificates, and newspaper clippings of important events in the company's past, as well as artifacts associated with the rum business.

To one side, a painted window looked out onto a vista of palms under fluffy white clouds against a bright blue sky. Along the top of the wall was a mock-wooden sign, with its famous slogan: BACARDI . . . EL REY DE LOS RONES. EL RON DE LOS REYES (Bacardi . . . the king of rums. The rum of kings). To the left of the sign, five bats were frozen, with their shadows, in mid-flight. The wall's center was dominated by a sheet of paper, apparently curling up at the edges, on which was portrayed the Bacardi family tree. It was a very big tree.

The mural raised intriguing questions about history. The pictures on the wall were portraits of portraits; the photographs were doubly reproduced; the certificates were forgeries. They were forceful reminders that the events of the past are filtered more than once in the telling, and that things are not always as they at first appear. Tour parties, however, did not come to reflect on the mutations of history. They were taken into the "Cathedral" to see the fermentation and distilling processes. Then they were guided into the bottling plant — where, in 1967, a line capable of 2,500 cases a day had been installed — to witness the clattering marvels of automation. Finally, they were escorted back to the pavilion for their complimentary daiquiris and Bacardi-and-Cokes.

Outside shareholders got to look at the company in another way. Public quotation meant — under the rules of the Securities and Exchange Commission, the Washington-based investment watchdog — that Bacardi Corporation had to issue financial reports, providing a window into the otherwise intensely private organization. For the most part, these reports, as they grew glossier and thicker, told the story of a march to financial glory. When the company had gone public, in 1962, its sales had been $26.5 million and its earnings $2 million. Eight years later, in 1970, sales and earnings had more than trebled, to $84 million and $7.2 million respectively.

The company's 1968 annual report had contained, apart from financial results, the most significant announcement in the Bacardi empire in a quarter century: that of Pepín Bosch's retirement. "The Board," said the report, "respectfully accepted Mr. Bosch's decision and expressed its deep appreciation and admiration for his 34 years of continuous loyal service. His many friends and associates recognize that the Company's present position of financial soundness and preeminence is due in very large part to the efforts of José M. Bosch, whose untiring devotion to the best interests of Bacardi and its stockholders will always be revered."

Pepín Bosch was now seventy. Two years earlier, a double intimation of mortality had hit him when both his brothers-in-law, Víctor and Jorge Schueg, had died. The time had come to pass on the reins. But, as one family member remarked, "the notion of Pepín Bosch retiring was like the idea of God retiring." It was impossible to imagine.

Succession in family business rarely goes smoothly. To want your children to succeed you, to carry on tradition, to maintain the honor of the family name — these are all part of a genetic drive. But that drive is peppered with psychological complexity, a mighty clash of desires and doubts: the difficulty of the patriarch's recognizing his own mortality; the problems of children measuring up to a successful father; the conflict between the meritocratic ideals of entrepreneurial capitalism and the non-judgmental aspect of family affection. For Bacardi, these complexities were multiplied by the age of the business, the size of the family, and its members' deep emotional attachment to both the empire and the Bacardi name. Bacardi had come to have a quite different meaning as a brand than as a symbol of family heritage. To the family, Bacardi meant the rich history and the pleasant life of Cuba, and above all Santiago. It meant family unity. Ownership of the name went not merely with a comfortable life; it went with the very essence of being. The Bacardis weren't like some of the Rockefeller clan, who — succumbing to anti-capitalist history, which saw their brilliant ancestor as a "robber baron" — dropped the family name. The Bacardis were intensely proud of everything for which the name stood. To the company, however, the brand had developed different meanings for different markets: mixability here, sun, sand, and sea there. The one thing the brand *didn't* stand for — except perhaps among the exile community in Miami — was Cuba, with its political complications and personal resentments.

The ownership and management of Bacardi, too, had inevitably grown apart. At the beginning, the business had been all Bacardis. Now, although the family tree had blossomed, the proportion of family members in the company's growing workforce had fallen (although they still occupied senior positions). The family members, as owners, were nevertheless keen to see a family member in control.

Pepín Bosch had not founded Bacardi, but the empire had enjoyed its greatest success under him. Not only had he built it into a multinational with a global brand, he had rescued it from the grasp of Communism. He had made the family rich. But his solipsistic style — the rule among corporate empire-builders — had made training a successor difficult. Indeed, his "Message to García" management approach had rendered any form of executive development problematic. What was most prized during his long tenure was the ability to carry out — better still anticipate — his orders. Bosch was prepared to take advice, but you had to make sure he had asked for it. Moreover, the empire's broad geographical reach and loose corporate structure — which had evolved largely for tax reasons — made it even more of a solar organization, with satellite subsidiaries and asteroid employees revolving around Pepín Bosch.

Bosch's style had nevertheless generated great loyalty. Nobody doubted his devotion to the business. There had been few departures from the organization. One that occurred in the mid-1960s, however, was telling. Pepín Bosch had told the technical whiz Juan Grau that he wanted him to manage the Brazilian operation. Grau had not only found himself in Recife with a co-manager, but had discovered that they were both there merely to execute Pepín Bosch's orders. Bosch for his part thought Grau had insufficient experience to manage alone. The situation was complicated because Grau, whose father had died at around the time he joined Bacardi in 1950, looked upon Bosch as a father figure. Once Grau had balked at the management arrangements in Brazil, however, that was the end of him. He reluctantly left the company after fourteen years. Although he would return ten years later, his departure clearly showed that when there was a conflict between emotional attachments and the company — the company inevitably being identified with the edict of Pepín Bosch — the company came first. Indeed it could be no other way. Being an ersatz son of Pepín Bosch was no easy thing if you also worked for Bacardi.

Being his genetic son was even harder. Both Jorge and Lindy Bosch had played out their childhoods in the shadow of Bacardi, following their father through the peregrinations that had led him to Santiago as head of the organization. They had played in the garden of the little production facility on the Calle Cedro in Mexico City; they had "helped" their father in Puerto Rico, fixing metal bottle caps at the building on the Malecón in Old San Juan; they had been taken by the hand by their grandfather, Enrique Schueg, to see deferential New York bankers, just so that old Enrique could practice his English.

Before joining Bacardi, Jorge had studied chemical engineering. Lindy, the younger, more sensitive, and less self-assured boy, had, with his father's encouragement, pursued a career in farming in Santiago, but had been forced, with a young family to support, to seek a job in the company as well.

After the Castro coup, Pepín Bosch had sent Jorge to Puerto Rico, where, in 1963, he was appointed president. Jorge had reveled in his job, but there were rumblings that he didn't work hard, didn't have to. Bacardi Corporation's success was a function of the success of the theoretically independent Bacardi Imports, which sold most of its production. There was also grumbling about whether Jorge would have enjoyed the eminence he did if it were not for the influence of his father. There were even greater doubts about Lindy, whom his father had installed as executive vice-president of the international operation in Bermuda. Like Jorge, he was well liked personally, and regarded as sincere, honest, and hardworking; but he wasn't an executive decision-maker. He himself acknowledged that he tended to get bogged down in details. Sometimes, in his uncertainty, he substituted bluster for leadership.

That Pepín Bosch was felt to have anointed his two sons aroused inevitable resentments, although nobody would dare express these to him. Moreover, as long as their father was around, Jorge and Lindy were seen less as succession material than as indirect instruments of control.

If Jorge Bosch was ever to have a chance to prove himself, Pepín Bosch would have to leave. In 1968, it seemed that Jorge's chance had finally come. But Bosch's idea of retirement was made clear in an article that appeared in the *New York Times* in March 1970. He was quoted as saying: "I've slowed down somewhat of late . . . I'm on the road only five months a year now. I used to travel about twice as much before." "Mr. Bosch's present pace of travel would tire many a younger man," declared the article. This was not a conclusion that the septuagenarian Bosch found objectionable. The headline was: "Retired? Not Chief of Bacardi." Not everybody was so happy about that — Jorge Bosch, for example.

Jorge found that his father was still directing him, and they clashed. One bone of contention was Jorge's executive habits. His leased Learjet, which Bosch regarded as overindulgence, even decadence, was a particularly sore point. Perhaps Pepín Bosch had privately concluded that his son just didn't have it. You had to be hungry; Jorge wasn't hungry.

In 1972, evidence of Jorge's lack of "hunger" — even basic attention — came to light. It was discovered that both sales and profit figures of Bacardi Corporation for November 1971 had been double-counted, because of an "inadvertent error." This led to an embarrassingly public hauling-down of 1971 sales and profit figures by $5.3 million and $3.2 million respectively. Jorge Bosch hadn't prepared the accounts himself, of course, but as chief executive he was responsible.

Since Jorge had been a great fan of computerization, and the "inadvertent error" had been made by the data processing department, his father considered him even more culpable.

For Pepín Bosch, this was the last straw. He descended upon San Juan and, in front of the board of directors, stripped Jorge of his powers. Jorge disappeared — at his father's suggestion — into the Harvard advanced management program. He didn't even say goodbye to his fellow executives at Cataño. The next year, Pepín Bosch reappeared as chairman of Bacardi Corporation. When, after Harvard, Jorge attempted to return to his office in Cataño, perhaps feeling he had paid for his error, his father told him to take an office at Bacardi Imports in Miami, which didn't entirely please Imports president Eddy Nielsen. Pepín Bosch then assumed the title of president of Bacardi Corporation, although he did allow Jorge to assume the title of chairman.

Bosch's effective firing of his son tellingly showed the uneasy fit between corporate demands and family life. The issue was not so much that he had fired his own son, but whether his son should have been president of Bacardi Corporation in the first place.

No explanation was offered in Bacardi Corporation's annual reports for these executive musical chairs. In a later corporate history, written for Bacardi Corporation's fiftieth anniversary, the whole shuffle was dismissed in a single sentence: "Bosch had returned to the presidency following the interim term of his son, Jorge, from 1963 to 1974." Eleven years as president and still only "interim"?

Lindy meanwhile was titular head of a flourishing organization, although Bacardi International's success was due largely to the talent of key executives such as Juan Prado. Lindy may never have thought of himself as a candidate for the highest office, but when his father told him bluntly that he would never succeed him, it hurt nevertheless. At one stage, Bosch had thought about hiring a senior British executive from Bacardi's U.K. importer, Hedges & Butler, to run Bacardi International, but Lindy had said he wouldn't accept him. The Englishman would have had to operate with Pepín Bosch above him and Lindy beside him. His position would have been untenable.

The sensitive souls of the family recoiled at this unpleasantness, but did so in comfort thanks to the cash machine Bosch had created for them. By 1974, the market value of Bacardi Corporation alone, of which the family owned about 90 percent, was some $330 million. More important, the 200 or so family shareholders were splitting around $6 million in cash dividends from Bacardi Corporation — not a fabulous income, but enough to keep the wolf from the door. And then, of course, there was income from the other four companies.

Following Jorge's ouster, Bosch installed Arturo Manas, Jr., as the day-to-day manager of Bacardi Corporation. Manas was a tall, smooth fellow whose father, a stockbroker, Bosch had known in Cuba. Manas spent so much time commuting to see Bosch at his rambling home at Lyford Cay that he came to be regarded as little more than a messenger. They joked at the Cataño executive offices about the "seventeen-cent decision," seventeen cents being the price of a stamp on a letter from Nassau. Bosch was back in control.

Again, there were behind-the-hand criticisms of Bosch's management style, but before long his value to the empire was again forcefully proved. One of Bacardi Corporation's major problems had always been with Puerto Rico's militant labor unions; production was frequently stopped by lengthy strikes. The company was also vulnerable to work stoppages in the transportation industry, since virtually all its production was shipped to the U.S. One way of partially insulating itself from these disruptions was to ship in bulk to Florida and bottle the rum there. However, bulk exports were still banned under the legislation introduced to thwart Bacardi in Puerto Rico in the late 1930s.

Bosch believed he could now persuade Puerto Rico to change these restrictions. With this in mind, he purchased a tract of land in Jacksonville, Florida. Then Bacardi Corporation, with Bosch lobbying in the background, set about changing the bulk export rules. Bottling facilities would remain on the island, Bosch argued; only increased demand would be met by U.S.-bottled rum.

As part of his lobbying effort, Bosch went to visit Sam Bronfman, the great patriarch of the Seagram empire, at his mock medieval Montreal offices. It was June 1971, just weeks before Bronfman's death. Seagram had a Puerto Rican rum, Ronrico, which was subject to the same bulk export restrictions as Bacardi. Bosch hoped to persuade Bronfman to support his lobbying effort with the Puerto Rican government. Bosch admired Bronfman, but Bronfman had no great liking for Bosch. He made a point of not liking any of his competitors; indeed, he took a certain curmudgeonly delight in not liking anybody. Moreover, Bosch had just done a deal with Seagram's great Canadian rival, Hiram Walker/Gooderham & Worts, under which the Canadian company became a partner in Bacardi's Canadian operation. Bronfman turned Bosch down.

Bosch eventually got his way; in 1975 bulk exports were permitted. By then Bosch was engaged in another lobbying effort, this time over tax exemptions available for new plants. He was incensed that Bacardi Corporation, which generated more tax for the island than any other company, received no part of the exemption.

Again, Bacardi's argument was couched in terms of the advantages to Puerto Rico of giving the company a tax break. Just as a tax break would stimulate new industry, so it would stimulate existing industry. These tax advantages could be passed along to the consumer, stimulate sales, and generate more excise revenue for the island.

The politicians — still embracing the son-of-a-bitch-millionaires attitude of former Governor Muñoz Marín — said they would give Bacardi nothing. Bacardi's pleading for tax exemption was a thinly concealed bid to raise profits; the island didn't need the company; Bacardi was just bluffing. Affairs came to a head when Bosch appeared at hearings in the legislature. Again, the politicians believed he was bluffing. Their attitudes, he said, did not make him very happy. He was going to order at once, he announced, that a distillery be built at Jacksonville, Florida, where there was already a bottling plant. The company was leaving Puerto Rico.

Bacardi got its tax exemption. Ironically, the island that forty years before had attempted to use discriminatory legislation to keep Bacardi out now passed discriminatory legislation to keep it in.

Pepín Bosch had taken on a national government in a trial of strength, and won. But he was not getting younger, a fact of which he was cruelly reminded on October 25, 1975, when his wife of more than fifty years, Enriqueta, died. Her death, after a long battle with cancer, was more for Bosch than a personal tragedy. She had always been an important conduit between her husband and the family members, many of whom were intimidated by him. Her illness had reduced that role; her death removed not only a point of contact, but also a point of emotional attachment. The gap began to widen between Pepín Bosch and the Bacardi family.

On the day of Enriqueta's funeral, young León Argamasilla Bacardi, the stockily built little blender from Bacardi's Canadian operation, happened to meet Pepín Bosch shortly after getting off the plane in

Nassau. Bosch's first question to León — "What are you doing here?" — spoke volumes about his strained relations with the family. León said that, of course, he was there for Enriqueta's funeral. "Oh," said Bosch, "come with me," and took him on errands before returning with him to his house at Lyford Cay.

When Bosch turned up with León at his house, other family members wondered if it meant something. Was León part of Bosch's succession plan? Was he the chosen? Succession was preoccupying more and more people, yet nobody knew what Bosch was planning.

One alternative Bosch considered was an outright sale of the business. He solicited an offer of around $600 million, but the family expressed no interest in selling. How could they sell their heritage? Some thought Bosch had no intention of selling but had solicited the offer merely to emphasize the growth in the value of the business under his leadership.

Seeing no successors in the family, the only solution, he decided, was to bring in an outsider, a professional executive to manage under his tutelage. This was by no means an unusual idea. Indeed, some business experts, such as Professor Harry Levinson of the Harvard Business School, expressed the view that professional management was the *only* way to go for family businesses. In a 1971 article in the *Harvard Business Review*, Levinson had written: "Where there are multiple and complex family relationships and obligations in a company, and particular problems about succession, the best solution is a transcendent one. The family members should form a trust, taking all the relatives out of the business operations while enabling them to continue to act in concert as a family . . . In general, the wisest course for any business, family or nonfamily, is to move to professional management as quickly as possible." Levinson added: "I know of no family business capable of sustaining regeneration over the long term solely through the medium of its own family members."

Not all academics agreed with Levinson's bleak view of family managerial development and his belief in professional management. Another Harvard Business School professor, Louis B. Barnes, and a Harvard alumnus, Simon Hershon, published an article in the *Harvard Business Review* of July-August 1976, in which they pointed out that "the main problem with this rational argument is that most companies lean more heavily on family and personal psychology than they do on such business logic." To treat families as an unfortunate business problem to be resolved with scientific management, they argued, and to believe that the sooner the guys with the MBAs arrived the better, was to misread the very nature of most businesses.

That family businesses inevitably faded into "widely held public companies managed by outside managers with professional backgrounds" was, they argued, a myth. The myth had been planted by Berle and Means's classic *The Modern Corporation and Private Property*, which had been written in the 1930s and greatly influenced the way people — or rather academics — thought about business. According to Berle and Means, ownership of major U.S. companies was becoming widely diffused; control was increasingly falling into the hands of managers who owned only a small fraction of the company's stock. The myth had been enhanced by the even more influential popular economist John Kenneth Galbraith, who created the concept of the "technostructure" of industry as a faceless and impersonal system.

In fact, this was not the case. Of the estimated 1 million businesses in the United States, wrote Barnes and Hershon, 980,000 were family-owned or -controlled. The proportion of professionally managed companies naturally increased with a company's size — size usually correlated with longevity, and family influence usually decreased over time — yet a large number of the biggest companies remained under family control. In 150 of the companies in the Fortune 500, controlling ownership was retained by an individual or a family. These were not the genetic remnants of the business dynasties of the nineteenth century, but included many new faces.

Barnes and Hershon concluded that the question of whether a family business should stay in the family was academic: "It is apparent that families *do* stay in their businesses, and businesses stay in the family." The answer, then, was to manage transition. "For this to happen," they wrote, "'the old man' must face the decision of helping the company live even though he must die. If he can do this, the management of transitions can begin. In effect, a successful family transition can mean a new beginning for the company."

Pepín Bosch did not see family transition as a viable alternative for Bacardi. The family would see no other alternative as viable.

Bosch confided in few people, but one man who had always been a confidant was the lawyer Guillermo Mármol. About three months after Enriqueta died, Bosch asked Mármol to meet him in Bermuda.

After dinner at the Hamilton Princess, across from Bacardi International's head office, they went for a stroll. Bosch told Mármol he had employed headhunters to find a professional manager to whom he planned to offer a five-year contract, and who would operate under his supervision.

The man chosen was Thomas E. Singer, an executive vice-president with the Gillette Company in Boston. Singer, born in Austria and educated in the U.S., had wide international experience. He had served in both the U.S. army and the Department of State, and he spoke fluent Spanish, French, and German. He had worked with Gillette for almost twenty years, running subsidiaries in West Germany, the U.S., France, and England.

It seems not to have occurred to Bosch that the family might be unenthusiastic about having an outsider run the company. Instead of calling a family meeting and laying out his plans, Bosch spoke only to a few key family members. He would not even reveal the outsider's name, claiming he could not do so while the man was still employed. Bosch, it seems, assumed the family would go along with his plans. Hadn't everything he'd done in the past been in their best interests?

Family members might have used the word "dictatorial" to describe Bosch's management style, but he was no dictator. His position was in no way analogous to that of his great nemesis Castro; Bosch depended ultimately on the democratic vote of the family. There had been no election campaigns for thirty years in Bacardi, but there *had* been regular elections; the forms of corporate democracy had always been followed. Bosch's position had never been challenged because he had done a brilliant job. But the degree to which he had developed the company and enriched the Bacardis was not represented in his personal shareholdings. Indeed, he had always seen to it that shares in new companies or expansions were distributed in historic proportion among the different branches.

Enrique Schueg had had 30 percent of the 1919 company. As one of his four children, Enriqueta Schueg, Bosch's late wife, had inherited around 7.5 percent of the subsequently expanded empire. Bosch himself, in more than forty years, had accumulated no more than 3 percent of any of its corporate parts. Moreover, when Enriqueta's will had been drawn up, Bosch, in an extraordinary gesture, had insisted that her fortune, including the Bacardi shares, go to their sons, Jorge and Lindy. He told his wife he did not need the money; since the boys were one day going to inherit it all anyway, it may as well go to them at once. Bosch also had in mind that he might, after Enriqueta's death, marry again, and that it would trouble his conscience to enjoy a new life with his late wife's money.

After Enriqueta's death, Bosch and his sons controlled no more than 11 percent of any of the main Bacardi companies. Ultimately, his position depended on acceptance by a majority of the family shareholdings. Of the four branches, his own — the Schueg Bacardis — had always supported him. He had kept the support of the abundant branch of Emilio through his long relationship with Daniel Bacardi Rosell. The smaller branch of José, now represented only by Joaquín Bacardi Fernández and his sons, had also supported Bosch. The one major source of potential dissent had always been the 30-percent stake held by the descendants of Facundo Bacardi Moreau. This branch was still controlled by the aging Luis J. Bacardi Gaillard, whom Bosch had deposed more than thirty years earlier.

If the family was to throw up an alternative to Bosch's professional manager, who would he be? There was only one candidate of the right age and with sufficient experience: Eddy Nielsen.

Nielsen looked and sounded an unlikely Cuban. In fact, he had been born in America, the son of a Norwegian physician, also called Edwin Nielsen. His mother was Lucía Schueg Bacardi, the second daughter of Enrique Schueg and Amalia Bacardi Moreau, the only daughter of the founder. After college in New England, Nielsen had spent four years in the U.S. army, then returned to Cuba to work briefly with Bacardi before going to run the Schueg Bacardis' ranching, water-pumping, and salt interests near the U.S. naval base at Guantanamo. Following the Castro revolution, expropriation, and exile, he had — at Pepín Bosch's request — rejoined Bacardi, working first in its Mexican operation and then in the empire's U.S. import arm.

Nielsen was a soft-spoken and courtly man in his early fifties, but he looked younger. He had learned most of what he knew about the business, and perhaps some of his low-key, affable management style, from Bartolo Estrada, from whom, in 1971, he had taken over as president of Imports. When he had joined Imports, Estrada had told him, "Look, Eddy, I want you to be your own man and develop your own style. But you might as well watch the way I operate, because it seems to have worked for me." After Nielson became president, one of his most significant moves had been (with Bosch's approval) to persuade the advertising genius Bill Walker to join the company. Under Nielsen, Bacardi Imports had continued to enjoy spectacular success. Nielsen may have been American by birth, but he had a Cuban background, spoke Spanish, had an impressive track record. Most important, he was family.

Nielsen had been one of the few people to whom Bosch had revealed his plans about bringing in the outsider. Nielsen had been surprised and shocked. He felt there was a great deal of family talent in the company — including himself — that might be locked out of top management by Bosch's decision. He decided to come up with an alternative that would address the family's concern about outsiders and also keep them better informed about corporate developments.

As word of "the outsider" ran round the Bacardi clan, Nielsen became the focus for revolutionary conspiracy. His most important backers were Luis J., his nephew, Adolfito Danguillecourt Bacardi, and their big chunk of Bacardi stock. At a family meeting in Madrid, it was decided that the family did not want an outsider to head the company, even under Bosch's supervision. Bosch's old supporters, Daniel and Joaquín, did not want it; the younger generation of family managers in the company did not want it; the overwhelming majority of shareholders did not want it.

Nor did they want Bosch to leave. They acknowledged his achievements. But there had to be an orderly change of management, and control had to be kept in the family. Bosch's autocratic style had built the company, but more organization was needed, more consensus, more democracy. Eddy Nielsen was the man who would achieve all this.

The family wanted Bosch to stay as the figurehead, the company's "grand old man." For the fiercely proud Bosch, who had ruled unquestioned for more than thirty years, there was only one response. He resigned, retired to Lyford Cay, and brooded bitterly about the ingratitude of the family. Family members felt bad but believed Bosch had been high-handed and insensitive to the fact that Bacardi was, first and foremost, a family business.

Ironically, 1976 was the fortieth anniversary of Bacardi's presence in Puerto Rico. In acknowledgment of his critical role in founding and building Bacardi's operation there, Bosch had been presented with the key to the city of San Juan. Now he felt the family had taken the keys to his company away from him.

The immediate managerial problem created by Bosch's departure was to find a new head for Bacardi Corporation. The New York lawyer Pete O'Hara was recruited as a stopgap chief executive. Expecting to hold the position for no more than six months, he retained his partnership at Rogers, Hoge & Hills and his New York office. But O'Hara liked the job, and the high profile it gave him. He never moved to Puerto Rico but became chief executive and then chairman; he stayed with the company for ten years.

Under O'Hara's name, a brief statement appeared in the 1976 annual report: "On May 28, Mr. José M. Bosch, who founded Bacardi Corporation in 1935, returned to retirement. Mr. Bosch had previously retired in 1969 as an active member of the management. He resumed an active role in the corporation in 1972 but indicated several times, as he did at the corporation's annual meeting in April 1976, that he intended to retire once again. His contributions to the success of the corporation are immeasurable and sincerely appreciated by all of us who had the benefit of association with his genius and wisdom."

Bosch's protégé, Arturo Manas, Jr. — who had been slyly dubbed at Cataño his "messenger" — also disappeared from the roster of executives.

A story in the *New York Times* in August 1976 suggested that the empire, following Bosch's "retirement," would now try "collective leadership." It put forward Manuel Jorge Cutillas as a possible successor to Bosch, but made no mention of Eddy Nielsen and offered no hint of the circumstances of Bosch's departure. Bosch, whose smiling face illustrated the story, estimated Bacardi assets to be worth about $700 million. He was quoted as saying, "When I look back, I get the greatest satisfaction from the fact that despite this incessant expansion I leave the company without debts, bonds and debentures." The only hint of discord came in a quote from an unidentified "insider." "If it were not for him, many Bacardis would have to actually work for their living today."

Bosch betrayed no hint of bitterness, but bitterness was there and would not disappear with time. More than a decade later, it bubbled out in another quote Bosch gave the *Times*. "The Bacardi family is not without its frictions, of course," said the story. "Mr. Bosch claims that the desire for privacy among those Bacardi heirs who have not worked at the company — or at much else — is well founded. 'They always wanted to stay out of the limelight,' he said. 'It was different with me. I have pride in what I accomplished. They have no reason for pride. They never produced anything.'"

Perhaps Bosch was by then disgruntled that the Bacardi empire had *not* crashed after his departure. It remained a dynamic organization, with more potential than he may have realized. In the meantime, however, Pepín Bosch had a final shot for the family.

Within a couple of months of his wife's death, Pepín Bosch had sold his house at Lyford Cay and was working on plans for a new one. He knew he would see his wife everywhere in the home they had shared, and he did not want to dwell morbidly on the past. At seventy-seven, Bosch looked resolutely to the future. Once dead, the past, no matter how dear, had to be broken with. There was no point dwelling on it. Lesser men, particularly at Bosch's age, might have wilted under the twin blows of losing, within six months, his wife and control of the company he had built. Not Pepín Bosch. He told the *New York Times*: "I'm looking for a new job." He was smiling, but he wasn't joking.

As for his Bacardi holdings, there was only one course of action. Perhaps it was a matter of honor — of not wanting to share a major investment with ingrates. Perhaps it was simply the logical consequence of wounded ego: an unfounded belief that, after his departure and the rejection of his advice to bring in professional management, the empire could only crumble. Perhaps it was spite. Whatever the reason, Bosch told Eddy Nielsen in 1977 that he was going to sell his stake in Bacardi.

To help him do so, Bosch turned to a young New York merchant banker, Román (Romy) Martínez IV, whose father had been a close friend and confidant of Bosch for many years. Martínez was now with the Wall Street firm of Kuhn, Loeb. Pepín and his son Jorge went to Martínez and said they were looking for a buyer. Bosch explained that he wanted the "right" company. One obvious candidate was the Canadian liquor giant Hiram Walker/Gooderham & Worts, already a partner in Bacardi's Canadian operation. Martínez called the company's Canadian headquarters in Windsor, Ontario. Hiram Walker, it turned out, was very interested indeed.

Hiram Walker was now being run by Cliff Hatch, Sr., son of the founding genius Harry Hatch, who had died in 1946. Cliff had joined Hiram Walker in 1937, when he was twenty-one. During the war he had been a naval commander, hunting U-boats in the North Atlantic. Afterward he returned to Walkerville and rose through the ranks on his merits, becoming president in 1964.

The Hatches had become Windsor/Walkerville's first family. They shared the town with the giants of the North American motor industry, whose headquarters were across the border in Detroit, so they didn't have quite the grip the Bacardis had on Santiago de Cuba. Cliff Hatch had established himself as a pillar of the community. A man of modest tastes and frugal habits, he believed there was room for everybody. He and his competitors might fight in the market, but that didn't mean they couldn't sit down and have a few laughs over dinner. He was liked and admired for his ability to separate the battle for liquor markets from personal friendships. Even Sam Bronfman liked him; when Mr. Sam turned eighty, Hatch was asked to preside over the celebratory dinner.

Cliff Hatch's management style was direct and uncomplicated. He didn't hold with the proliferation of corporate committees, or with piles of policy manuals; he often moaned that business seemed to be sinking beneath a sea of paper. He liked to keep Hiram Walker's organization lean, its margins high. He was, in short, a man after Pepín Bosch's own heart, and he already knew Bosch through the partnership with Bacardi in Canada.

Cliff Hatch's philosophy was to build a core of quality brands — the great assets of the liquor business. People were always coming to him, saying enthusiastically, "I know how to make Drambuie." "Sure," he'd tell them, "but you can't *call* it Drambuie. And that's what counts." Hiram Walker had a stable of five renowned brands — Canadian Club, Ballantine's, Kahlúa, Tía María, and Courvoisier — but was still lagging behind its great Canadian rival, Seagram. Its 1977 sales were flat; those of Seagram were running 7 percent ahead of 1976.

Bacardi, meanwhile, was showing annual sales growth of 25 percent, and closing in on Seagram's Seven Crown and Heublein's Smirnoff as the world's top brand. In the rum business, there was only one brand. Cliff Hatch was delighted to learn that a piece of it might be available. And who knew how big that piece might get once Hiram Walker had a foot in the door?

Cliff Hatch was too much the gentleman to ask exactly *why* Bosch wanted to sell; naturally, though, he set out to gain a clearer idea of what he was buying. Bosch's Wall Street adviser, Romy Martínez, showed him an alluring set of figures. The sales and earnings of Bacardi Corporation for the year to June 30, 1976 — $173.5 million and $14.6 million respectively — were matters of public record, but the rest of the organization's results had previously been top secret. Hatch learned that the empire had sales of around $466 million, and net income of almost $30 million.

Despite Hiram Walker's partnership in Bacardi's Canadian operation, Hatch knew little of the complexities of the Bacardi empire. At first, he imagined that Hiram Walker was being offered a stake in a single holding company, but he soon discovered the fragmented nature of the enterprise. Hiram Walker was in fact being offered shares in the five main companies by the Bosch family: 9 percent of Bacardi Corporation, the main distillery in Puerto Rico; 11 percent of Bacardi Imports, the U.S. import arm in Miami; 8.51 percent of Bacardi & Company, the trademark-owning company in Nassau; 7.01 percent of Bacardi International in Bermuda; and 7.18 percent of Bacardi Mexico. Apart from the indirect stakes in the international companies controlled through Bacardi International, there were also small direct holdings in the Venezuelan and Canadian Bacardi companies. Some other family shareholders joined Bosch and offered parts of their own holdings, bringing the whole bundle to about 12 percent of the empire.

Before long, word found its way to Eddy Nielsen that Bosch was looking for a buyer, and that Romy Martínez was working on the project. At the wedding of one of Nielsen's daughters, Lucía, at the Everglades Club in Palm Beach, Nielsen took Martínez aside for an hour. He was concerned about who Bosch might sell to, and he told Martínez the family didn't want him bringing around any Arab millionaires.

In fact, Nielsen may have had mixed feelings. If Bosch sold out, at least he would no longer be looking over Nielsen's shoulder. The Facundo branch — because of its long feud with Bosch — may also have been glad at the prospect of his sale. Bosch indicated he was prepared to sell to the family, but they decided his price was too steep. And negotiating with him, in the circumstances, would have been difficult.

A deal was quickly cut with Hiram Walker. The Canadian company would pay $45 million in cash for the 12-percent block. Nielsen was told who the prospective buyer was, and Romy Martínez took Cliff Hatch, Sr., and Bud Downing, who would succeed Hatch as Hiram Walker's chief executive, to visit Nielsen in Miami.

Nielsen made clear to the Hiram Walker executives that the family didn't want the Canadian company to buy more Bacardi shares. If Hiram Walker had hopes of gaining control of Bacardi, he told them, they could forget it. Cliff Hatch, ever the gentleman, told Eddy Nielsen that if the Bacardis were adamantly opposed to the purchase, then Hiram Walker would back away. But Nielsen realized that if the Bosch stake was headed for an outsider, Hiram Walker was at least the devil they knew.

Hiram Walker's move attracted largely favorable comment from analysts and the media. "Canadian Club whiskey and Bacardi rum!" wrote *Forbes* magazine. "What an interesting couple. Like a dignified, wealthy old man consorting with a swinging young lady." The irony was that the swinging young lady was a good deal older than the wealthy old man. She was also a little frigid.

Hiram Walker's executives, despite the cool reception, hoped that over time the family would warm to them and permit the Canadian company a larger stake, perhaps even sell out to them. In fact, Hiram Walker went in not merely hoping for but needing a larger share of Bacardi for technical reasons. Under the rules of equity accounting, Hiram Walker could show a proportion of Bacardi's profits in its own profits only if the Canadian company owned more than 20 percent of the rum manufacturer. Bosch had indicated to them that gaining additional shares was not likely to be a problem. Bosch believed that, once he'd gone, other parts of the family would want to sell. This may have been partly vanity, but it was also a necessary selling point. The last thing the Canadians wanted was to be locked into a hostile organization with no hope of either selling out or gaining a larger share.

Over the years, Hiram Walker proved as good as its word. Its executives never pushed their weight around, never rocked the boat, never asked for positions on the boards of Bacardi companies. They were always available to offer advice. At shareholders' meetings, they made a point of standing up among the serried ranks of Bacardis to say how pleased they were with the management of the company.

By not buying out Pepín Bosch in 1977, his successors at Bacardi had made a mistake. Eddy Nielsen would later reflect ruefully: "If we'd had a crystal ball, we'd have mortgaged our souls and gone out and bought it. Hiram Walker had greater faith in our future than we did." They had made a mistake only because the company went on to become even more remarkably successful.

Eddy Nielsen's Brief Honeymoon

"A change came o'er the spirit of my dream."
BYRON, *THE DREAM*

Miami. 1976

Eddy Nielsen sat in his smoked-glass office, overlooking the sparkling blue waters of Biscayne Bay, with a heavy new mantle of responsibility about his shoulders. He was now de facto chairman and chief executive of the empire, the Bacardi family's "Godfather." He came to power committed to a new and more democratic regime. He would bring the family back to the center of power; he would be more accessible; he would create a more formal structure. The last goal was problematic. Bacardi was not a conglomerate in the normal sense. Its holding company had been in Pepín Bosch's mind. This structure was tax-efficient, but it made Bacardi a body without an official head.

From a financial and fiscal point of view, it still made sense to keep all the companies officially separate, but to create a central, representative, family group, Nielsen formed a new company in 1976, INTRAC (for International Trademark Consultants) S.A., with its headquarters in Costa Rica. Its office there was manned by Guillermo Mármol, whose intimate knowledge of the business and amiable personality had helped him survive Pepín Bosch, to whom he had been closely linked for so long. INTRAC would have no assets or operational function, but it would coordinate the activities of the other Bacardi companies. Its board contained seven members, two from each of the three major family branches and one from the branch of José, just like the board of the old company back in Cuba. Nielsen was appointed INTRAC's president.

Anyone who combines the duties of chairman and chief executive has to keep one eye on the business and the other on the shareholders — but the Bacardis were not your average shareholders. How could venerable old family members, who remembered dandling Eddy Nielsen on their knee, not imagine that they had the right to contribute a modest two cents' worth on corporate issues? Familiarity bred unwanted advice — one reason why Pepín Bosch had been so careful not to make himself too available.

Under the reign of Pepín Bosch, the family had felt itself increasingly remote from the business. This had been no accident. Bosch didn't want family interference. The interests of Pepín Bosch and those of the family had coincided in the growth of the company and its dividends, but when a conflict had arisen between the needs of the business and the psychological needs of the family — the dispute over bringing in an outsider to run the show — the family had asserted itself, and won. Family members — for so long in thrall to Pepín Bosch — had rediscovered that they were a democracy after all. They were still close enough that a majority could quickly be organized to impose its will on management. That fact would come back to haunt Eddy Nielsen.

Like Bosch, Nielsen had to balance the interests of the branches. The most powerful branch was now that of Facundo, so long in the shadows during the time of Pepín Bosch. After the sale of the Bosch interests to Hiram Walker, the Schueg Bacardis had less than 20 percent of the empire; the two branches of Emilio still had 30 percent between them, but that interest was spread among far more people than the 30-percent stake tightly held by Facundo's branch.

Facundo's descendants were still represented on the seven-man board by the two nephews of Luis J. Bacardi, Adolfo Danguillecourt Bacardi and Luis Gómez del Campo Bacardi. Adolfo Danguillecourt Bacardi, the son of Adolfo Danguillecourt and Luis J.'s sister Laura, lived in Madrid and described himself as a "business adviser." He had never worked in the company. Luis Gómez del Campo Bacardi, the only son of Laura's sister, María, described himself as a "private investor." Others described him as a playboy. He had worked briefly for Bacardi in Nassau after the revolution. Luis had not been enthusiastic about the job, to which he had commuted from Miami. Subsequently, he had done some informal promotion, supported by Bacardi International, sporting the family name at the haunts of the European jet set, from the royal enclosure at Ascot to the casinos of Monte Carlo, where he spent much of his time. Luis Gómez del Campo enjoyed the good life provided by his Bacardi dividends.

Emilio's branch was represented by Manuel Jorge Cutillas, perhaps the family's most talented executive — Eddy Nielsen singled him out at once as his successor — and Eusebio (Cuchi) Delfin, a grandson of

Emilio and Elvira Cape via Amalia Bacardi, whose husband, also Eusebio Delfin, had been a Havana banker. Cuchi, a lawyer, had never worked in the company.

The Schueg Bacardi branch was represented by Nielsen himself and Víctor Arellano, who had married one of the daughters of Enrique's son Jorge. The Arellano Schuegs lived in Mexico City, where Víctor sat on the board of Bacardi Mexico. The branch of José was represented by Alberto Bacardi Bolívar, who ran Bacardi's Canadian operation and was married to Daniel's daughter, María Hortensia Bacardi. That made their children, of whom María would eventually bear eight, Bacardi Bacardis. Alberto was the prototype of commercial royalty. He had the looks of a Cuban matinée idol and a smile worth a hundred cases of Bacardi. Alberto wasn't proud only of his Bacardi bloodlines. His mother was a descendant of Simon Bolívar, the great South American revolutionary. Alberto had revolution in his blood.

Alberto enjoyed a high profile. Most Bacardis were reluctant to appear in corporate advertising, but both Alberto and his father were featured in Bacardi's Canadian advertising. In one magazine ad, Alberto sat on a desk in front of an old family portrait. "We're not just the name on the bottle," said the ad, "we're the family behind it. In 1862, my great-grandfather created a rum so extraordinarily smooth and light-tasting it soon became the most famous in the world." The portrait behind Alberto was not that of his great-grandfather, Facundo Bacardi y Maso, but of Facundo's second son, Facundo Bacardi Moreau — just a little historical license, fact sacrificed to brand image.

As well as this family board, an executive advisory group was set up: Nielsen, Manuel Jorge Cutillas, and Pete O'Hara, the New York lawyer who now headed Bacardi Corporation.

Central control of the empire raised sensitive regulatory issues. Both the U.S. tax authorities and the Securities and Exchange Commission frowned on coordination between Bacardi Corporation and Bacardi Imports. Due to the favorable tax treatment received by Bacardi in Puerto Rico, it made sense to take profits there rather than in Miami. But the U.S. Internal Revenue Service watched closely for any deliberate skewing of expenses to increase profitability in San Juan. The SEC, meanwhile, was concerned about the intercorporate relations of Bacardi Corporation as a public company. Bacardi Corporation had important trading and licensing relationships with other, wholly family-owned Bacardi companies. It sold virtually all its rum to the

Miami-based Bacardi Imports and received its rights to use the Bacardi trademarks from Bacardi & Company in Nassau. If Bacardi Corporation were controlled by the same people, there was the potential for conflict. License fees, for example, might be set at levels that benefited the companies with higher levels of Bacardi ownership.

In fact, because of the special tax breaks in Puerto Rico, it made sense for Bacardi to skew profits *toward* the publicly traded company. To address the possibility of conflict, however, the notes to the financial statements of Bacardi Corporation's annual report included a little fairy tale under the heading "Ownership":

"The original 'Bacardi' rum business was founded in Cuba in 1862 by Don Facundo Bacardi y Maso. The corporate successors to the 'Bacardi' rum business are owned in large part by descendants of the founder. Management is unable to determine the precise extent of the ownership of such descendants, since these individuals reside in a number of countries, indirectly own stock through corporations or trusts and have many different family names. However, it is management's best estimate that approximately 80% of the Company's stock is beneficially owned, directly or indirectly, by various descendants of the founder. Management has taken the position that the Company is not controlled by, or under common control with, any other person or group of persons. It is possible, however, that the potential for control by various descendants of the founder might be considered to exist."

If Bacardi Corporation's management was "unable to determine the precise extent of the ownership" of Facundo's descendants, it certainly knew the general extent. And it knew full well who represented it: Eddy Nielsen. As for "Management has taken the position that the Company is not controlled by, or under common control with, any other person or group of persons," that had to be only "a position" — analogous, say, to the position that the moon was made of green cheese — because it wasn't true. "It is possible, however, that the potential for control by various descendants of the founder might be considered to exist."

Indeed.

Because of concern about the SEC and the IRS, members of the executive advisory group were not allowed to discuss the affairs of either Bacardi Imports or Bacardi Corporation, even though Eddy Nielsen was chairman of the former and Pete O'Hara chief executive of the latter.

Nielsen reported to the INTRAC board twice a year, in June and

November, in Spain. A shareholders' meeting was held each year, usually in Costa Rica, and Nielsen instituted an INTRAC annual report to keep family members up to date on the group's activities outside the United States.

INTRAC gave the family a formal mechanism through which views could be expressed and information disseminated. The creation of the executive advisory group gave Nielsen a brain trust to help him chart the empire's strategic direction.

The advisory group grew to include the operating heads of the major companies. O'Hara's absentee presidency of Bacardi Corporation led to managerial confusion at Cataño, and Manuel Luis del Valle, a respected local businessman, was eventually picked to succeed O'Hara as president and then chief executive (although O'Hara remained as chairman). Del Valle's parents had known Pepín and Enriqueta Bosch well, and he had been a close friend of their son Jorge. Del Valle became an important part of the advisory group. Its other members were Juan Grau, who had returned to the company in 1974 and been put in charge of the flagging Mexican operation in 1976, and Eduardo Cutillas and Juan Prado, the marketing whiz, from Bacardi International in Bermuda.

Despite the overlapping memberships of Nielsen and Cutillas, the separation of the family board from the executive group was potentially problematic. INTRAC was not the real source of decision-making power. This irked some of its members, in particular Alberto Bacardi. But the discontent was muted because of the empire's success under the new structure.

The three years following Pepín Bosch's departure — 1977, 1978, and 1979 — saw the most spectacular growth in Bacardi's history. In its highest-profile market, the U.S., Bacardi increased sales in each of these years by 1 million cases. No other brand had ever grown by 1 million cases in a year. Bacardi's other markets also surged by a combined total of around 1 million cases in 1978 and another million in 1979. Worldwide sales in 1970 had been 6 million cases. The year Bosch left, 1976, they hit 10.5 million. Three years later, they were an astounding 16 million cases.

Public evidence of increased profits from the booming U.S. market came in the statements of Bacardi Corporation. In 1976, gross sales had been $153.3 million and net profit $12.6 million. In 1979, gross sales were $220 million and net profit $39.4 million. Private profits from the rest of the empire were growing even more quickly. In the three years following Bosch's departure, the family's income had more than trebled.

In 1934, after the repeal of Prohibition, Sam Bronfman had paid for a full-page message in 150 U.S. newspapers: "We who make whiskey say: Drink moderately." In few industries could one imagine companies discouraging customers from using too much of their product; but alcohol was not like other products.

Liquor had always had two faces. One could be found in glossy magazine images of fit, tanned bodies under palm trees; eye-to-eye promise by blazing fires; tuxedoed success in oak-paneled surroundings. The other was found in the twilight zone of overuse and addiction, the personal disintegration and family disruption of alcoholism, and alcohol-linked road deaths. Most drinkers occupied the middle ground — where alcohol represented a relaxant, a social lubricant, a celebration — but the correlation between increased consumption and undesirable side effects had led to a touch of split personality in the industry.

The drys may have been defeated by Repeal, but Sam Bronfman knew that widespread misgivings about alcohol remained. He realized that pre-Prohibition antagonism toward dry sentiment had to be modified. The 1934 ad produced congratulatory letters and telegrams from both wets and drys. The emphasis on moderation and safety became recurrent themes of the industry. Bacardi had contributed its own "Bacardi mixes with everything except driving" ad.

Spending on such "moderate" drinking, slowed only by the war, surged for forty years after Bronfman's ad. Net of taxes, spending had doubled in the U.S. between 1960 and 1970, rising from $3 billion to $6 billion. It had doubled again, to over $13 billion, by 1980.

In this overall growth, Bacardi was a major beneficiary of two trends: the switch from "brown" to "white" spirits, and the continued shift to well-known brands. By 1980, the brown spirit category — scotch, bourbon, and the whiskey blends — had been in decline for close to a decade. Total whiskey sales in the U.S. had peaked in 1971. But this decline had been more than offset by a switch to white, light spirits. Smirnoff vodka was the first great white brand, but Bacardi was an even more spectacular success. Back in 1960, the whiskeys of the Canadian giants Hiram Walker and Seagram had ruled the U.S. market. Seagram's Seven Crown and V.O. were the top two brands;

Hiram Walker's Canadian Club was third. All had been dominant since the end of Prohibition. Of the other seven brands in the top ten, only Smirnoff was white. By 1980, the top two spots had been seized by Bacardi rum and Smirnoff; two other white spirits, Popov vodka and Seagram's gin, had moved into the top ten.

The other major trend benefiting Bacardi was the increasing importance of the major brands. In 1979, the top ten accounted for 25 percent of all U.S. spirits sales (versus 14 percent in 1960). In dollar value, the increase was even more dramatic. The top ten brands in the U.S. had, in 1960, accounted for expenditures of $870 million. By 1980, they accounted for around $4.95 billion. In two decades, the U.S. retail liquor market had trebled in dollar value. Spending on the top ten brands was up by a factor of six.

In 1980, Bacardi ranked seventh among America's largest distillers/importers (after Seagram, Heublein, National, Schenley, Hiram Walker, and Brown-Forman). Its case sales were only one-third those of Seagram, but they were all in a single brand — by now, indisputably, the greatest liquor brand of all time. Bacardi's average annual compound growth over the previous decade had been almost 12 percent, well above that of any of its major rivals. One of every twenty drinks poured in the U.S. was a Bacardi, and the name dominated rum sales as no other brand dominated its category, taking 60 percent of the U.S. rum market. But then the U.S. market, for a variety of reasons, ground to a halt. Liquor had become a "mature" industry in the U.S.; that is, the market was saturated. The U.S. economy was also moving into recession. The U.S. liquor market stood at around 455 million cases in both 1980 and 1981, but in 1982 the market slumped 21 million cases to 434 million. While whiskey sales continued to decline, the growth markets of the 1970s, rum and vodka, turned flat.

The industry's market problems were exacerbated by an increase in anti-alcohol sentiment such as had not been seen since the heyday of the Women's Christian Temperance Union. Neo-prohibitionist fervor was whipped up by a phalanx of lobby groups. One of their thrusts was to equate alcohol with illegal drugs; they described alcohol as "the most abused drug in the U.S." They sought restrictive and punitive measures as a solution for controlling alcohol abuse. The most obvious, and potentially most damaging to the liquor companies, was higher taxes, which — as people clamored over the deficit — offered politicians the opportunity of killing two birds with one fiscal stone.

The antis also sought health-warning labels, further restrictions on liquor advertising, a reduction in retail outlets — particularly in low-income "blighted areas" — and increased legal liability of taverns and restaurants for accidents resulting from alcohol abuse.

The industry, in response, formed the Licensed Beverage Information Council (LBIC) in 1979 to conduct education programs about drunk driving, teen drinking, fetal alcohol syndome, and alcoholism. But it found itself fighting a losing battle.

Surveys by the Distilled Spirits Council of the United States (DISCUS), the industry's Washington-based representative body, proved the effectiveness of the anti-alcohol lobby. One revealed that 38 percent of "media and opinion leaders" believed even moderate drinking should be discouraged; 62 percent supported warning labels; 40 percent believed that health and social problems caused by drinking were increasing; 50 percent were of the opinion that abstinence was healthier than drinking in moderation.

Surveys of the general public revealed results even more alarming to the liquor companies. More than two-thirds believed a couple of drinks daily were not good for health; two-thirds believed liquor was "stronger" and "harder" than beer and wine; 54 percent supported increased taxes to discourage alcohol abuse.

The public refused to believe studies supporting the health benefits of moderate drinking. The industry's displays of concern were treated with skepticism. Meanwhile, a new emphasis on fitness was making hard liquor even less fashionable. Market maturity, neo-prohibitionism, and the spritzer generation were threatening the hard stuff with hard times.

Bacardi faced other difficulties. President Ronald Reagan's "Caribbean initiative" threatened to remove some of Bacardi's competitive advantage by allowing other island rum producers tariff-free access to the U.S. But the company's biggest concern was that it was a one-product company. What if tastes changed? What if a fickle public decided it didn't like Bacardi?

Bacardi's final problem, strange as it may seem, was an increasing pile of spare cash. In 1983, Bacardi Corporation enjoyed a 29-percent leap in net income, to $58.8 million. The other Bacardi companies kicked in profits of over $50 million. Rum sales were generating much more than required for the maintenance and growth of the business in a stagnant industry. The influential New York-based liquor industry magazine, *Impact*, noted: "Bacardi's dazzling 12 per cent average annual compound growth rate during the seventies is clearly a closed chapter in this brand's story."

The big question facing Eddy Nielsen and Manuel Jorge Cutillas was: What would the next chapter be? Both were convinced that the "one-product nightmare" and the spare cash pointed in the same direction. Bacardi, they believed, had to diversify.

Meanwhile, somebody had noticed that, in 1983, the company would ship the 200-millionth case of rum it had produced since it left Cuba. This was cause for celebration. It would also provide management with an opportunity to lay out the empire's new course for the family. A gathering of *la gran familia* was called for Acapulco.

Diversifying into Trouble

*"They show us a winery, a beer
company, lots of things. They look
good, but then I ask, 'What do we
know about wineries? What do we
know more than Budweiser or
Schlitz about beer?' Rum we know
very well."*

PEPÍN BOSCH, IN *FORBES*

Acapulco. 1983

BIENVENIDOS FAMILIA BACARDI read the billboard that greeted the
hundreds of Bacardis and Bacardi employees at the spectacular Acapulco Princess hotel. They had come to celebrate the production of
200 million cases of Bacardi rum since the Cuban expropriation, more
than half of which had been sold, under Eddy Nielsen's stewardship,
in the previous seven years.

Acapulco provided an opportunity to indulge in a little nostalgia.
At the ziggurat-shaped Princess, with its dripping greenery, waterfall-
fed pools, and 480 acres of manicured gardens, microphones were
passed around at lunches and dinners, and familiar old stories were
repeated. At a special ceremony, commemorative bottles were given
to the senior executives and noble retirees. The old guard — Joaquín,
Daniel, and José Argamasilla — were photographed amid their immediate family groups. There was music and dancing and *alegría*.

There was also a little business. The managers from the various
Bacardi operations took the podium to recite their considerable
achievements. The most important presentations were those of Eddy
Nielsen and Manuel Jorge Cutillas, who rejoiced in the company's
history and pointed toward its future. They ran through the whole
saga — the bats in the distillery in Santiago de Cuba, the "rum that
saved His Majesty's life," the concoction of the daiquiri and the Cuba
Libre, the death of the "faithful" palm El Coco at the time of the
Castro revolution, the spectacular success of the post-Castro period.
They told of the sad diaspora of the family and its key employees. They
described the growth of the empire, right up to Bacardi's most recent
plant, in Panama.

Cutillas delivered a panegyric to the trademark. The mark was much more than a commercial reference that distinguished an enterprise. "It is," he said, "the complete representation of what an enterprise is, of what it produces, of its humanity, of its philosophy, of its history and of its constant growth. The trademark that triumphs is always the result of a great human effort." Its most important characteristic was quality.

"What created the phenomenon [of Bacardi's success]?" asked Cutillas. "Was it the decision of men and visionaries who knew how to penetrate the market at the right time? Was it intelligently planned public relations strategies? No, the first thing was a quality product."

There were some who — while agreeing about the importance of quality — might have differed with Cutillas over the reasons for Bacardi's success. Indeed, everybody was acutely aware that the "visionary" behind the empire's achievements, Pepín Bosch, was not there; and they all knew why.

Nielsen and Cutillas turned to strategy. Nielsen declared: "We believe in only one formula — diversification." He said that Bacardi's success had been based on diversification since the days of Facundo Bacardi y Maso, who had diversified into rum manufacturing from his first business as an importer and distributor. The second diversification was into beer, the Hatuey brand. Then geographical diversification had proved enormously important. There were new rum products, with the line being expanded from the original Carta Blanca through Carta de Oro, Añejo, 1873, and, more recently, Solera and Gold Reserve. There had been moves into other spirits, such as the tequilas Don Emilio and Xalisco. There was Nassau Royale liqueur, and O'Darby's Irish Cream. The future would see more new products: cocktails, pre-mixes, and other low-alcohol combinations.

Eddy Nielsen pointed out that in Puerto Rico, Bacardi had become involved in the manufacture of plastic bottle caps and the distribution of electrical equipment and foodstuffs. It had moved into the bulk-tanker business. In Spain, Bacardi had acquired a sugar mill; in Germany, a bottling and distribution business, which also distributed the products of other companies. The companies in Mexico, Canada, Brazil, the United States, and Puerto Rico also distributed other brands of drinks and wine.

Nielsen mentioned that one of the most important diversifications had been the recent foundation of Bacardi Capital Ltd. in Bermuda. Its mandate was to offer financial services to the Bacardi companies. At the same time, it could offer these services to members of the family, shareholders, and others. "In the future," said Nielsen, "it could be the vehicle for diversifying into other areas."

Diversification was the key to the future.

A video was made of the event. On it, a number of family members and key employees are asked about the future of the company. Flushed with the occasion, they were all of one mind: the future would be brilliant.

One of the side visits for family members was to Mexico City and the plant at Tultitlán, with its array of striking buildings. There the family passed under a huge sign. On one side was a slogan: CERRAR FILAS Y SUMAR FUERZAS (Close ranks and add your strength together). On the other side was a poem:

I go with taut reins,
controlling my speed,
because the important thing is not
to arrive alone, or early,
but with everybody,
on time.

What forcibly struck some members of the family was just how *many* of them there now were; they were seeing people meant to be "family" for the first time. Arriving "with everybody / on time" was going to be an increasingly difficult task.

Daniel Bacardi in particular was no fan of diversification. He believed Bacardi should stick to rum. One of every twenty drinks poured in the U.S. might be Bacardi, but nineteen of twenty were not. Meanwhile, the potential in the rest of the world was much greater. Just look at giant markets like France and Japan, which Bacardi had hardly penetrated.

Nielsen and Cutillas saw that view as simplistic. Bacardi's marketing and sales forces were the envy of the industry. But sales in the U.S. had gone flat, and although they were moving ahead in other world markets, they simply could not invest the funds they were generating in the rum business. They had to look for growth opportunities elsewhere.

No, argued Daniel. If you're generating more money than you can use, pay it out in dividends. If you have other projects to put to family members, they can decide if they want to invest individually. Stick to your knitting.

The claim that diversification had been a recurrent theme in the Bacardi empire was tendentious to say the least. Indeed, the remarkable fact about Bacardi's history — the approach that had given it a unique place in the global liquor industry — was how *little* the company had diversified. It had started with one product and stuck to one product. Diversification was not a fact but an aspiration; and now, in management's eyes, a necessity. Nielsen and Cutillas wanted to give it some historical grounding.

True, a number of minor diversifications had already been undertaken. Two would prove particularly problematic: Bacardi Corporation's move into electronics, and the creation of Bacardi Capital. These problems would lead Daniel Bacardi to see himself as a Cuban Cassandra, and he would become the leader of a dissident group.

Eddy Nielsen's thorniest problem with the family would arise a couple of years after the Acapulco meeting. Like Pepín Bosch, he would face a challenge that thwarted his plans because they threatened the family's control of the business. First, however, he would discover that Bacardi mixed with telephone-clock-radios made a very poor cocktail.

As Eddy Nielsen pointed out, by 1983 Bacardi Corporation had already been developing sales of foodstuffs and other liquors in the Puerto Rican market for several years. In 1983, it had also bought two small companies that marketed domestic electrical and electronic goods: wringer-washers, kitchen ranges, television sets and clock-radios, telephone equipment and video cassette recorders.

Guillermo Rosell (distantly related, by marriage, to the Bacardis), who had sold them the two companies, came to work for Bacardi. Later that year, he brought a new, larger venture to Bacardi Corporation's management. He helped persuade them to pay $12 million in cash for Lloyd's Electronics, Inc., a company based in Edison, New Jersey. Lloyd's sold cheap, Asian-manufactured home and portable audio equipment, a line of telephones and telephone-clock-radios, and electronic calculators.

Lloyd's was in trouble. Its 1983 sales of $39 million were one-third what they had been five years before. The company also had credibility problems. It produced the kind of equipment that came free with magazine subscriptions. Rosell persuaded Bacardi that an injection of capital, combined with his own marketing and management skills, could turn the company around.

If Bacardi management did not understand the market for tele-phone-clock-radios, it should certainly have known that credibility cannot be achieved overnight. In 1984, lower bulk sales of rum put Bacardi Corporation's earnings into reverse. Lloyd's exacerbated the problem by turning in a loss. Its suppliers were late with deliveries. Demand for its telephones declined further in a soft market. Compe-tition increased. The U.S. imposed anti-dumping duties on some of its Far Eastern suppliers.

Bacardi Corporation told shareholders in its 1984 annual report that the Lloyd's problem was under control. Management had been reorganized. Relationships with Oriental producers had been "stream-lined." New product lines had been introduced. Overheads had been reduced. Everything was reported to be shipshape.

But it wasn't. Bacardi Corporation's net income rebounded from $46 million in 1984 to $55 million in 1985, but the problems at Lloyd's worsened. Its products weren't selling. Warehouses were overstocked. Intense competition continued to slash, indeed elimi-nate, profit margins.

Bacardi management decided to cut its losses and sell. The 1985 report contained a corporate mea culpa: "Our limited entry into the consumer electronics business has been disappointing. However, we continue to believe diversification is an appropriate and necessary direction, and we shall continue to explore its potential, in particular in areas which most closely relate to our experience and expertise." Lloyd's had lost $5.3 million in 1984 and $5.4 million in 1985, but the problems did not end with the decision to sell. Bacardi Corpora-tion became involved in a dispute with the Lloyd's buyer, which itself ran into financial difficulties. The total cost of the Lloyd's debacle to Bacardi Corporation was close to $29 million.

The Lloyd's affair was an embarrassment for Bacardi Corporation's management. The man who had directly overseen the electronics business was Adolfo Comas Bacardi, but the ultimate responsibility for the decisions to get in and then to cut losses lay with Manuel Luis del Valle. Del Valle was not a man to shirk responsibility. Once he had realized a mistake had been made, he had moved at once to correct it. Unfortunately, it had taken almost three years to solve the problem.

The Lloyd's losses were significant, but not crippling. Nobody had "bet the company," and management had certainly had its strategy focused by the experience. The only company that never made mis-takes, del Valle pointed out, was one that never tried anything new. It wasn't the first time mistakes had been made at Bacardi.

For Daniel Bacardi, however, the Lloyd's affair confirmed his misgivings. They should have listened to him.

For Daniel Bacardi, however, the Lloyd's affair confirmed his misgivings. They should have listened to him.

While the Lloyd's problems had been unfolding, major developments had been changing the global liquor business. The entire industry faced the same problems as Bacardi, but not all companies saw the same solutions. Diversification was one strategy; another was to look for growth through aggressive rationalization, acquisition, and strategic alliances within the industry. One reason why the North American companies looked first to diversification rather than rationalization was the spectre of anti-trust legislation.

Seagram under Sam Bronfman had profited by a move into oil. In 1981, under Sam's son Edgar, the company bought a chunk of the chemical giant Du Pont. This would prove a shrewd move. Hiram Walker too had moved into the petroleum-exploration and natural-gas-transmission businesses. European companies — in particular British ones — had, by contrast, started to concentrate on rationalizing within the industry rather than diversifying outside it. Their interest inevitably moved across the Atlantic, to the world's biggest liquor market.

In the 1960s, the conventional wisdom had been that the multinational company represented the wave of the future. The models were the giant American motor companies. Such multinationals functioned through autonomous subsidiaries manufacturing different products in different countries. Their relationship with their parent was primarily a financial one. But the late 1960s brought dramatic change as companies started marketing "global" products around the world. Ford, for example, now started thinking in terms of a "world car." The result was the Escort. The academic guru of these changes was the Harvard professor Theodore Levitt. He wrote of "a new commercial reality — the explosive emergence of global markets for globally standardized products, gigantic world-scale markets of previously unimagined magnitudes."

Liquor was already globalized to a large degree. But it was in a position to become even more so. The British led the way. Anthony Tennant, head of International Distillers and Vintners, the liquor arm of the British conglomerate Grand Metropolitan Hotels, and the liquor industry's guru of globalization, pointed out in a 1985 speech that in the previous twenty-five years, "consumer wants, tastes and desires have been homogenized by increased international trade, travel and modern communications technology, making the same brand proposition and marketing mix relevant for the first time to all markets." National idiosyncrasies still had to be taken into account, but the liquor world was fast becoming a smaller place.

British and French liquor producers had already begun seeking vertical integration by buying up the importing and distributing companies that held rights to their brands in North America. Thus they gained not merely another level of profits from their products, but greater control over marketing strategy. The first major move came in 1980, when Tennant's IDV bought the U.S. distributors Paddington and Carillon, which held the marketing rights to major brands such as Absolut vodka, Bailey's Irish Cream, Grand Marnier, and J&B scotch.

The following year, the French group Moët Hennessy acquired its U.S. distributor, Schieffelin, thus gaining control of its major champagne and cognac brands. In 1982, Whitbread, a charter member of the British "beerage," acquired Julius Wile, and with it brands such as B&B liqueur, Bollinger champagne, and Dry Sack sherry. Whitbread followed in 1985 by buying Buckingham Corporation, which gave it the leading brand of scotch, Cutty Sark. In 1984, the lord of the scotch business, Distillers Company Limited, brought U.S. sales of both Johnnie Walker Red and Johnnie Walker Black, and its premium gin, Tanqueray, under direct control through the purchase of Somerset Importers (the company formed after Prohibition by Joseph Kennedy). These takeovers were forerunners of the bigger acquisitions that changed the face of the liquor industry in the latter half of the 1980s.

The big liquor companies also started looking at strategic alliances. The aim was either to distribute one another's products or to form joint distribution agreements. Eddy Nielsen hadn't said anything about strategic alliances in Acapulco, but eighteen months later, an opportunity for such an alliance arose. He decided to pursue it.

🦇

Early in 1985, Eddy Nielsen and Manuel Jorge Cutillas began talks with Hiram Walker/Gooderham & Worts, the Canadian company that was their only major outside shareholder and that also held a direct stake in Bacardi's Canadian operation. Having come to know and respect the Hiram Walker people, Nielsen and Cutillas had agreed in principle that they might get closer to their Canadian partners. That, of course, had been Hiram Walker's hope and intention all along.

Hiram Walker still didn't have a large enough stake in Bacardi to equity account, that is, to take a proportion of the rum company's profits into its own bottom line. But it had seen the value of its investment soar. The Bacardi stake it had bought for $45 million was reckoned to have more than quadrupled in value in eight years.

In that same period, Hiram Walker had turned into a very different corporate creature. Inspired partly by fears of a hostile takeover, the Canadian liquor company had merged in 1980 with Consumers Gas — a large Toronto-based natural-gas pipeline utility with extensive petroleum-exploration interests — to form Hiram Walker Resources Ltd. The merger had led to problems. Consumers' exploration subsidiary, Home Oil, had made a disastrous U.S. acquisition that resulted in a $177-million after-tax write-off.

In 1983, Hiram Walker Resources organized yet another defensive merger, this time via a limited share swap with Interprovincial Pipeline (IPL), which transported Alberta oil to its main central Canadian markets. Hiram Walker acquired 34 percent of IPL; IPL took 15.7 percent of Hiram Walker. The Consumers deal had seemed to be based on the "survival of the fattest" principle; the IPL deal appeared predicated on mutual back-watching.

Hiram Walker was still vulnerable. In a business jungle populated increasingly with corporate raiders — and sharp-eyed investment bankers ready to point out likely targets — it appeared a conglomerate ripe for the plucking. Bud Downing, who had succeeded Cliff Hatch as chief executive at Hiram Walker Resources, saw an opportunity to structure a deal beneficial both to his own company and to Bacardi. Why not organize another share swap — similar to the one executed with Interprovincial Pipeline — under which Hiram Walker would gain a larger stake of Bacardi, and Bacardi a significant stake in Hiram Walker? Hiram Walker would be able to equity account a share of Bacardi's profits, acquire a closer relationship with a valuable partner in its liquor operations, and gain a large and friendly shareholder. Bacardi, for its part, would get a stake not only in a more diversified liquor company — offering the potential for mutual strengthening of distribution networks — but also in a company with broad energy interests.

This idea was tossed around in discussions between Nielsen and Cutillas, and Bud Downing and Cliff Hatch, Jr. — who was now running Hiram Walker's liquor operations — in the summer of 1985.

The decision to go ahead was made by Downing, Nielsen, and Cutillas during a fishing trip in July of that year. Investment advisers for both sides began running the numbers, and by December a deal had been roughed out.

Hiram Walker would increase its stake in Bacardi to between 20 and 25 percent. Bacardi would take a sizable minority stake in Hiram Walker in return for a combination of additional Bacardi shares and cash. Bacardi would pay Hiram Walker somewhere between $200 million and $350 million, depending on the valuation of the shares it exchanged with Hiram Walker.

The first family members to learn about the plans — besides Nielsen, Cutillas, and the executive group — were those on the board of INTRAC. INTRAC was not consulted on the wisdom of the deal; it was merely informed that it was being examined. Not all the INTRAC board members were enthusiastic. One who was particularly unenthusiastic was Alberto Bacardi Bolívar.

Apart from Nielsen and Cutillas, Alberto was the only working Bacardi executive on INTRAC, but he was not a member of the advisory board. He felt he deserved more credit than he sometimes received for taking Bacardi's Canadian sales to more than a million cases a year. He bridled at having to report to the Cutillas brothers. Although he sat on the board of INTRAC, he felt he had an insufficient voice in the running of Bacardi affairs. He saw INTRAC as a rubber stamp.

Eddy Nielsen was close to Alberto. Their families saw a lot of each other, and the two men often hunted and fished together. Although he often confided in Alberto, Nielsen did not regard him as a heavyweight. Alberto had a nice life up in Toronto. He did the social rounds; he was on the boards of hospitals and charitable organizations; he was seen at the right cocktail parties.

Alberto did not appreciate being dismissed as a lightweight. Why had he not been more intimately involved in the negotiations? He knew Hiram Walker well. (Because of Hiram Walker's holdings in the Canadian subsidiary, he had Bud Downing, whom he liked and admired, on his board.) He also had misgivings about the proposed deal. He knew that a fabulously wealthy family of Toronto real-estate developers and conglomérateurs, the Reichmann brothers, had been accumulating shares in Hiram Walker. If the Reichmanns used that stake as a springboard to a takeover, they would own more than 20 percent of FBM and 12 percent of the whole empire. If they staged an assault after a "mini-merger" had gone through, the Reichmanns might wind up with an even larger stake. The Toronto brothers were known for their acquisitiveness. In Alberto's opinion, Nielsen and Cutillas weren't taking the Reichmann scenario seriously enough. When Alberto expressed his concerns, however, Nielsen refused to discuss the issue. He believed Alberto simply didn't understand the proposal. The deal would contain a clause under which Bacardi would have first option to buy back its shares in the event of a hostile takeover. Surely that was protection enough.

Alberto didn't like not being taken seriously. He regarded himself as a good executive, indeed a very good one. He had higher ambitions within the empire, and higher ambitions ultimately meant Eddy Nielsen's job, or at least that of his heir apparent, Manuel Jorge Cutillas.

Alberto was a force to be reckoned with. He belonged to a tight family group. His father was now well advanced in years, and his brother Joaquín no longer worked for Bacardi; but his second brother, Jorge, had an important job with Manuel Jorge Cutillas at Bacardi & Company in Nassau, looking after the trademarks, and his sister Carmen kept abreast of things from her home in Costa Rica. Between them, they controlled 10 percent of the empire.

At a meeting in Madrid, the board of INTRAC listened carefully as the proposed mini-merger was outlined. They were asked not to discuss it. Final details had not been ironed out. Alberto kept his concerns to himself, but the jet-setting Luis Gómez del Campo mentioned it to his cousin, Laura Danguillecourt Bacardi, who lived in Madrid. Disturbed at the prospect of the family's losing control, she in turn called her most senior Madrid relative, Amalia Bacardi Cape. Amalia was even more disturbed.

Amalia was one of the three surviving octogenarian daughters of Emilio Bacardi Moreau. To the venerable Amalia, who owned a fat chunk of stock and divided her time between homes in Madrid and Miami, the memory of her father was sacred, almost obsessive. For Amalia, Bacardi was synonymous with the cultured and kindly man who had read her bedtime stories and used the fledgling company in Santiago as a cover for his revolutionary activities; she remembered him as the first popular mayor and the first citizen of the sun-drenched city of her youth. She had lovingly prepared and paid for the publication of a history of her father, *Emilio Bacardi en su tiempo*.

Amalia heard from Laura Danguillecourt of the plan to sell part of the company as she was preparing to come to Florida for the winter. She fretted across the Atlantic and by the time she reached Miami, she had decided on her course of action. The "outsiders" were at the gates; the Trojan horse was about to be admitted; she had to sound the alarm. She had to stop the deal. She and Laura coordinated a round of phone calls and meetings. They found ready support from Alberto and Daniel and their families and had soon organized sufficient family members with enough votes to halt the deal.

Nobody wanted to tell Eddy Nielsen face to face. Just after Christmas 1985, the Bacardi Godfather received two letters, one from Miami and one from Madrid. One began "Estimado Edwin" (Esteemed Edwin), the other "Querido Eddy" (Dear Eddy). Bearing the names of a total of thirty-five shareholders, the letters informed him that the signatories had learned of certain "conversations" he had been having regarding a possible sale of a portion of their family business to another company. Both letters — whose wordings were substantially the same — declared that the undersigned did not wish to reduce their stakes, "whatever might be the price and conditions of an eventual offer." They wanted Eddy Nielsen to relay these thoughts — *No way, José* — to the prospective buyer. They ended by congratulating Nielsen and the other directors and executives for the "excellent results" obtained in 1985. One ended with a "cordial and affectionate hug" — a package of Band-Aids attached to a letter bomb.

Amalia believed she was acting for the good of Bacardi, but then so did Eddy Nielsen. The problem arose over just *which* Bacardi they were fighting for. Bacardi was a word that unlocked a rich array of meanings. Over time, the meanings had grown more diverse. The magic name meant different things depending on where you stood.

For salesmen operating out of Biscayne Boulevard, Bacardi was a product to be peddled; for the lawyers in New York or Nassau it was a trademark to be protected; for the engineers in Puerto Rico or Recife it was a process to be maintained; for the advertising and marketing men in Miami or London it was an image to be promoted; for the senior executives of its constituent parts it was a company to be grown; for Eddy Nielsen and his closest advisers, it was an empire whose strategic direction had to be carefully planned.

For many family members it had a different set of connotations. For the drones, Bacardi was a money machine; molasses went in at one end, dividend cheques came out the other. For the older generation, people like Amalia, who had grown up before the Castro revolution, the name Bacardi conjured up not a business but a whole way of life. Santiago de Cuba was long ago and far away, but Bacardi's symbolic significance had grown in the wake of the Castro coup. Indeed, the company's subsequent struggle with the Communist regime — a crucial part of its history — had given it a broader meaning within the whole Cuban exile community.

For Cubans in *el exilio*, a group that had become a major commercial and political force in the United States, Bacardi was a symbol both of the country they had lost and of the American Dream they had achieved. For the many Cuban-Americans who thrived in a successful commercial present while dwelling in an emotional political past — constantly recalled by media images of their bearded nemesis — the Bacardi bat symbol mocked the Cuban dictatorship. Bacardi had demonstrated that Cubans could take on not only Cuba's Communists, but also the commercial might of the giant British, American, and Canadian liquor companies. Meanwhile the product itself was forever associated with fiestas and carnivals, with sunny days and happier times.

For Amalia and the older Bacardis, selling a portion of the empire would be like selling part of their soul. The wealthy drones could adopt a similarly "noble" stance, knowing the dividend cheques were going to keep coming anyway.

Eddy Nielsen, of course, did not regard himself as a proxy Faust. His concern was to find an appropriate corporate strategy in a stagnant liquor market. But on the basis of rumor, a good part of the family had undermined his managerial authority. The letters had clearly demonstrated that Nielsen's responsibilities far outweighed his powers.

Amalia had not wanted to dent Eddy Nielsen's authority, or to unseat him, just to let him know that the family didn't want its ownership diluted. Nielsen, for his part, strongly resented the implication that he was acting "secretly," trying to put one over. Complex deals always had to be kept under wraps until the details had been resolved; he would then have put the proposal to the family to accept or reject. If Amalia had simply come to Nielsen, he could have told her he had no secret plan. Her fears of losing control were groundless. In the event of a takeover of Hiram Walker, Bacardi could buy back its own shares.

With some embarrassment, Nielsen had to break the news to Bud Downing and Cliff Hatch, Jr. "We can't get an agreement," he told them. "The family just doesn't want to hear about it."

Downing and Hatch were disappointed but philosophical. In fact, the deal would likely never have gone through; it required the approval of Hiram Walker's two other major shareholders, Interprovincial and the Reichmanns. The Reichmanns were not likely to be enthusiastic about a move that might protect Hiram Walker from them.

Hiram Walker's feeling of vulnerability soon proved well founded. A few months after the Bacardi deal fell apart, the Reichmanns mounted an assault, and Hiram Walker Resources became part of a global takeover war that led to the acquisition and dismemberment — or more precisely, and unusually, the dismemberment and *then* acquisition — of the company. In the midst of the battle, HWR's liquor arm, Hiram Walker/Gooderham & Worts, was sold to the British beer, food, and liquor giant Allied-Lyons PLC. If the mini-merger had gone through, Bacardi could have made a killing on its stake in Hiram Walker. Once again, the family had quashed a plan in the belief that the family and the business were inseparable — that you didn't sell part of one any more than you'd sell part of the other.

Once Nielsen had broken the news to the Hatches and Downing, Daniel Bacardi, Cassandra-like once more, and Alberto, feeling vindicated in his own concerns about the mini-merger, decided to make sure Nielsen knew his plans had been rejected. They wanted to rub it in, apply pressure, perhaps even force Nielsen's resignation. This seemed like the moment to strike — bloodlessly, of course. Perhaps Alberto's time had come.

Alberto called a special meeting of INTRAC, a revolutionary move in itself. INTRAC had evolved into a rather sleepy organization; a special meeting was a big deal. Alberto wanted to pass a resolution ensuring that Bacardi would have no further dealings with Hiram Walker. He wanted things in writing. He wanted letters from Hiram Walker too. These demands amounted to an insult, an accusation of bad faith on Nielsen's part.

Alberto had misread the situation. Just as the family had wanted to stop Pepín Bosch from bringing in an outsider but not to overthrow him, now they wanted to stop the mini-merger but not to unseat Nielsen. Once the INTRAC meeting had been called, Eddy Nielsen imagined that Alberto had secured the proxies to supplant him. Despite a proxy-gathering mission to Spain, however, Alberto could not muster support for turning the screw. The showdown — in Eddy Nielsen's Miami office in January 1986 — turned into a comedy of errors. Alberto had enough votes to call the meeting, but not enough to pass the resolution of effective censure over Hiram Walker. He and Nielsen were left looking at each other. It was as if Cassius had turned up to meet Caesar, but forgotten his dagger.

Guillermo Mármol, the general manager of INTRAC, who was also present, found a procedural way out of the mess. Eddy Nielsen's response to the challenge seemed remarkably restrained, but then Eddy Nielsen was American; there was something cooler in his veins. A Cuban might there and then have said to Alberto Bacardi: "You rotten sonofabitch."

In his office above the bay, Eddy Nielsen brooded about the family's lack of gratitude and the ease with which, on the basis of half-digested rumors, it could turn on management. He had worked hard for a decade to keep them together. He had taken trouble to introduce a less autocratic style than that of Pepín Bosch. He had gone out of his way to keep the family better informed, and what had they done to him? They'd made him look like a fool.

CHAPTER FIFTEEN

Bacardi Meets Bonfire of the Vanities

*"Americans were . . . by temperament
'naive,' a people who could live and
die without ever understanding
those nuances of conspiracy and
allegiance on which, in the Cuban
view, the world turned."*

JOAN DIDION, *MIAMI*

Bermuda. February 1986

Pepín Bosch's daughter-in-law Ermina Eguilior — Lindy Bosch's second wife, and the daughter of the Bacardi architect Ricardo Eguilior — admits she was a spoiled child. Once, while visiting the Bosch house at Punta Gorda, she decided to pick some of the flowers in the garden. In fact, she ended up picking *all* the flowers. When her mother saw the destruction, she was horrified, apologizing profusely to Enriqueta and Pepín. Enriqueta said never mind, not to worry, girls will be girls. Pepín Bosch just looked at little Ermina. She would remember that ice-blue stare for the rest of her life. The eyes of Pepín Bosch could be terrible things: surveillance devices, weapons, instruments of judgment.

Pepín Bosch liked to keep an eye on people. Six months after he took control of Bacardi in Santiago, the company's accountants, the Cuban subsidiary of Arthur Andersen, had carried out an audit. The auditor told Bosch it was astonishing how little petty pilfering he'd found; he believed it had a lot to do with Bosch's presence. As Bosch had once written to Mies van der Rohe, his ideal office was one where "there are no partitions, where everybody, both officers and employees, see each other." The Bacardi International building in Bermuda had high, glass-walled executive offices facing onto a big, open central area. There, high on one wall, portraits of Emilio, Facundo, and Enrique Schueg, the second generation's Blessed Trinity, smiled down benignly beneath the Plexiglas crystal Lumacubes of the Santiago night sky of February 4, 1862.

Toward the end of 1985, there was more going on at the Bermuda

195

headquarters than met the eye. A financial hemorrhage was taking place: the gash was no wider than a telephone wire.

☙

Eddy Nielsen had high hopes for Bacardi Capital. At the Acapulco meeting, he had called it "one of our most important diversifications." The operation had been set up in the last quarter of 1983, with Bacardi & Company and Bacardi International as equal owners. These Nassau- and Bermuda-based operations were essentially banks. Between them they reaped the trademark and licensing fees from the other Bacardi companies. They had relatively little overhead. The reason the fees found their way to these palm-treed islands was that they were tax havens, or, as the Spanish put it more colorfully, *paraísos fiscales*, fiscal paradises. By 1983, they had several hundred million dollars in cash. If management can think of nothing better to do with spare funds than place them on deposit, it begins to look as if management is short of ideas; it might as well just pay the funds out to shareholders. Eddy Nielsen and Manuel Jorge Cutillas were eager to show the family they *did* have ideas. Diversification, for example. If you had spare cash to diversify, why not get directly into the financial business, where the really big bucks were being made in the early 1980s? If you could get the right people, the right money managers, blessed breed, they should be able to make your money grow.

Bacardi Capital's five-man board represented the cream of Bacardi management. Apart from Nielsen and Cutillas, there was Manuel Jorge's brother Eduardo, Pete O'Hara, and Nicholas Dill, Jr., a local Bermudian lawyer. If you had suggested they were going into the gambling business, they would have been horrified. Eddy Nielsen stressed that caution and conservatism were key. "You've got to learn to crawl," he'd tell his fellow directors, "before you walk." They got tired of hearing him say it. Eddy Nielsen didn't even contemplate running, let alone hurtling white-knuckled on a roller-coaster.

The man they chose to head the new company was Brewster Righter. His credentials were impeccable. A Harvard graduate enticed away from a promising career at the New York-based electronics giant ITT, he also had trust-company and investment banking experience. He had met the Bacardis while working for ITT's Bermuda-based reinsurance subsidiary. ITT had just moved into the financial field, so Righter was thought to be a good "start-up" man. Subsequently he'd been posted to London. When the Bacardis decided to form Bacardi

Capital, they thought of him. Being cautious people, they hired a headhunter to check him out thoroughly. Righter checked out.

Righter was a tough man with big ambitions. A former marine, he'd been given the nickname Rambo by some of the Bacardis who had seen him hunt, even though the object of the hunt was only doves. He had other nicknames: Rocky, and "Bang It Out" Brewster. He didn't sound like the crawl-before-you-walk type — unless, that is, you were doing it through the undergrowth with an automatic rifle in your hands.

Hired as executive vice-president and chief financial officer of Bacardi Capital, Righter assembled a team of young financial professionals. His number two was Ian Macdonald, who worked with Bacardi International. A Canadian, Macdonald had spent nine years with Coopers & Lybrand, Bacardi International's chartered accountants in Bermuda. The Bacardis thought him solid, reliable, and levelheaded.

Bacardi Capital was given offices in the Bacardi International building, where everybody could see what everybody else was doing. The final quarter of 1983 was devoted to establishing "strategic objectives, policies, programs and relationships" — all the business-school buzzwords. Operations started on January 1, 1984. As start-up capital, Bacardi & Company and Bacardi International each provided $10 million of equity and $60 million of "interest-bearing advances," the bulk of which came from Bacardi International. Then Brewster and his boys were off and running. In many directions. And very fast.

Bacardi Capital co-founded a Swiss finance company and began trading. In January 1985, it bought part of a company specializing in arbitrage. In April, it acquired 75 percent of Financial Options Group Inc., a broker and dealer in foreign currency options on the Philadelphia Stock Exchange. In July, it founded a Cayman Islands – based trust company. In October, it bought three-quarters of a Bermudian insurance company. On January 1, 1986, it bought a reinsurance business.

The Bermudian old guard resented having Bacardi Capital's whiz kids plunked down in their midst. Bacardi International's regular employees felt they were mere milkmaids to a cash cow, providing the raw material with which the whiz kids were going to work their wonders. And Eduardo Cutillas, the board member on the spot, felt uneasy because Righter wanted a piece of the action, a percentage of profits, for himself and his boys. Eduardo — a reticent man who liked to take things one step at a time — worried that a piece of the action might encourage bigger action than prudence might suggest.

आँ

Trading as a principal, for your own account, is by definition a risky business. Financial markets are as close to perfect as markets get. Word about what's moving them up or down — and information about the factors likely to move them up and down in future — is transmitted with breathtaking speed. Movements arise from unexpected new information. Beneath this model of efficiency and rationality lies the beast of mass psychology, a force first chronicled well over a century ago by Charles Mackay in his *Memoirs of Extraordinary Popular Delusions and the Madness of Crowds*. But the lurking beast of mass psychology does not make trading less attractive. The lure of being one jump ahead of the crowd is irresistible; being one jump ahead can be very lucrative.

The principle is simple enough. You buy a commodity or financial instrument in anticipation that it will go up in value, or you sell in anticipation that it will go down. The principle applies to pork bellies, currencies, or bonds. But on these simple markets have been built a huge array of more exotic means of participation, whereby risks and rewards are multiplied. One such is options. You purchase the right to buy or sell an equity, bond, or commodity at a fixed price at a future date. Such instruments are like fairground rides that, by putting a revolving carriage on the end of a swinging arm, which is itself on a rotating wheel, create a whiplash effect, greatly increasing the thrills and spills. If you *think* a commodity or financial instrument is going up or down, you buy or sell it; if you *know* it is going up or down, you buy or sell options. If you're one jump ahead, if you beat the herd, you can make the big killing. Big killings, however, were not what Eddy Nielsen, the Cutillases, and Pete O'Hara had in mind; indeed, it wasn't entirely clear what they had in mind.

At Bacardi Capital, things started to go wrong in the second quarter of 1985. Timothy Hanahan, a young man with four years' foreign-exchange trading experience at Citibank N.A., began to take heavy positions against sterling, based on the assumption that the British currency would continue its decline against the U.S. dollar. Instead, it rose in weeks from $1.05 to $1.40. Hanahan was fired in May. Foreign-currency dealing was taken over by Chris Shane, a Harvard MBA who had been vice-president with responsibility for options and arbitrage at the Toronto investment dealer McLeod Young Weir.

Shane succeeded in turning the foreign currency dealings round. But in the fall and early winter of 1985, he started taking short positions on stocks and bonds, anticipating that interest rates would go up and the equity market down. In the last quarter of 1985, these assumptions proved disastrously wrong.

The firm's auditors, Coopers & Lybrand, had already sounded warnings about the inadequacy of staff and the need for stronger internal controls and procedures, including an internal auditor; but the management of Bacardi Capital felt a full-time auditor was not warranted. Righter couched it in terms of cost savings; but a full-time auditor would just get in the way. Bacardi Capital had big money to make. They didn't have time to wait around for some picky book-keeper.

Nielsen and his fellow board members failed to understand — and were misled about — the risks involved. Righter told them that 80 percent of assets were allocated to low-risk investments. That proved untrue. The board also failed to register the degree of Coopers & Lybrand's concerns, although those concerns were again muted by Bacardi Capital's management.

The board did get wind of potential problems. In an October 1985 memo, Eduardo Cutillas wrote of Righter, who not only was running Bacardi Capital but also was working on the potential Hiram Walker mini-merger: "I find that Brewster is really stretching himself too thin to handle BIL [Bacardi International] day-to-day financial operations and that BCL [Bacardi Capital] is growing very quickly and he should be 100% focussed in that direction."

In another internal memo, written in December 1985, Ian Mac-donald and Luc Duchesneau, another recruit from Coopers & Lybrand, pointed out that certain "facts" suggested "Bacardi Capital Ltd. is currently facing a problem which could compromise the company as a going concern in the future." These facts included corporate losses; traders not fully aware of the risks inherent in their positions; delays in getting financial information; inability to check if policies and investment guidelines were being adhered to; and, finally, the fact that "the company is overly reliant on individuals and the loss of key people would impair the ability of the company to continue to conduct its business activities." Macdonald's name on the memo would prove ironic.

Toward the end of 1985, Chris Shane, who had turned around the currency trading positions only to move the wrong way in bonds, began to show signs of panic. He continued to short bond options, but the bonds persisted in moving up. Twice in the month he doubled up his position. The result was a loss for the final three months of 1985 of around $13 million. Rather than informing the board, Righter attempted financial cosmetics. Getting wind of a projected loss for 1985, he had already suggested to Macdonald in November that every effort be "bent" to achieve appropriate "accounting results," and that "we should front-end as much income as possible and defer expense where feasible."

By the time the real 1985 situation had been revealed to the board, 1986 losses were taking off into the stratosphere. In the first two weeks of the new year, interest rates continued to fall and bond prices to rise. The short positions taken by Shane cost another $3 million. Righter and Macdonald knew they were sitting on a volcano, but they tried to appear calm, hoping the pressures beneath them would subside. Shane resigned on January 20.

Macdonald, with no trading experience, took over. His first week on the job was not auspicious. By January 27, he had taken the company to a short position of $125 million in U.S. Treasury bonds. The market rallied once more, and the company lost another $3 million. Two days later, on January 29, more options were sold, increasing the short position to $250 million. That week, the price went up another point; the company lost another $3 million.

In February, Macdonald began to act more like a gambler at a roulette wheel than a trader. Having bet twelve times on the black, and having seen red come up each time, he kept doubling up. It'll be this time, he told himself. Meanwhile, the dealers — mainly big New York firms — through whom these transactions were being made were making margin calls, demands for cash to cover potential losses, almost daily. Millions of dollars were being wired, in particular to the New York firm of Goldman Sachs. These margin calls, and the need to wire money to meet them, should have set off alarm bells, but it was Macdonald who was authorizing the loans to cover his own trading losses. He was functioning both as the trader and as the financial administrator with borrowing authority, both player and referee. The player was miles offside but the referee wasn't blowing the whistle. He told himself things had to turn around soon; interest rates *had* to go up. He kept selling short.

Macdonald took Bacardi Capital's short position up to a mind-boggling $600 million. Rates kept going down. Bond prices climbed another two points. The company lost a further $12.6 million. On February 14, the short position was bought back, and on February

17, the results of the year's trading to date were reported to the horrified board of directors. Bacardi Capital had, according to Macdonald and Righter, lost $21 million. But the board knew only half the truth. No reference was made by Righter to the $13 million lost in the last quarter of 1985. The board was still being told the loss for the previous year was only $2 million.

At this first board meeting in February, Righter and Macdonald told the board that $21 million was the maximum possible loss for 1986, and that the position had been capped. They also suggested a strategy to recoup some of the losses. But the board was once again being misled. The losses had not been capped. And the strategy to recoup them would only result in further losses.

One day after Brewster Righter and Ian Macdonald appeared before the board of Bacardi Capital, Macdonald returned to his short-selling strategy. Between February 21 and February 24, 1986, the bond market rallied strongly, with the price of U.S. Treasury bonds moving up another four points. In this period, Macdonald took the company short the equivalent of $400 million of Treasury bonds. He lost another $18 million. Shaken, he terminated all positions and closed the program down.

In the words of a subsequent report, "the trading strategies . . . were geared toward assuming larger and larger positions of greater and greater risk with the objective of producing gains to offset prior losses." Trading limits set by the board had simply been ignored.

Toward the end, concerned that they did not know what was going on, the board members had sought outside help. Pete O'Hara called Bacardi Corporation's auditors, Arthur Andersen, and asked if they could send a senior man to Bermuda. Since Bacardi was an important client, Andersen sent its head of international capital markets, Joel Miller. O'Hara didn't give Miller the impression that things had gone seriously wrong — indeed, the board had no idea they had. Miller was simply told the board needed help with some of the complex issues being presented to them.

Miller, an affable but incisive number-cruncher well versed in the ways of financial folly (he had been in Brazil during the commercial banks' lending spree), had attended the February meeting at which Righter and Macdonald claimed the losses for the year were capped. At the second meeting, a week later, after Miller had had an opportunity to look into Capital's complexities — by which time Macdonald had managed to lose another $18 million — he challenged Righter's version of the accounting principles the auditors found acceptable. Miller realized the board was being sold a bill of goods. Righter began to stumble, indeed to break down. The meeting became unpleasant. Eddy Nielsen was not present. On learning what had happened, he chartered a plane from Miami to fire Righter in person.

Righter's lack of supervision of subordinates had been a big part of the problem. While trouble was building, in December 1985 and January and February 1986, Righter had spent a good deal of time outside Bermuda hatching new schemes. He was in Philadelphia discussing making a film on the stock exchange there; he was in Switzerland schmoozing with bankers. Eduardo Cutillas could not claim the same excuse. Millions of dollars were being lost by people he could literally see through the glass-walled offices of the Bacardi International building. They went downstairs to the canteen to eat together. They met after work for drinks. Yet Eduardo wasn't aware of what was going on.

Evidence of more funny business later emerged from internal audits. Righter had authorized the buying-out of a defunct trading account that had belonged to Ian Macdonald's twin brother, David. The account, with the Toronto broker Wood Gundy, was $250,000 in the red. Capital paid $100,000 to Gundy to take over the account, in effect settling Macdonald's brother's debt for 40 cents on the dollar. Eduardo Cutillas confronted Macdonald with the evidence and asked him for an explanation. Macdonald, "troubled" by Eduardo's assertions, admitted he had made "mistakes" in judgment but declared: "I can assure you that they were honest mistakes based upon the available information at the time; that is to say, hindsight often makes things quite a bit clearer."

Macdonald claimed he had become aware of "a possible profitable merchant banking opportunity" in April 1985, but was concerned about "a perceived conflict of interest," because the positions had belonged to his brother's "now delinquent account." "Therefore," he wrote to Eduardo, "it was with great reluctance that I brought the opportunity to Bacardi's and Brewster Righter's attention." Not only was it Macdonald's brother's account, but Macdonald had himself lost money as a guarantor. The whole transaction, in the opinion of one shocked Bacardi Capital board member, "stunk." Bacardi put the matter in the hands of its Bermuda lawyers.

The financial debacle at Bacardi Capital was deeply embarrassing for the board. The senior custodians of the family's fortune had been asleep at the switch. They had failed to understand the risks involved and, despite warnings, had placed too much trust in the honesty of senior management, which had simply lied to them. Eduardo Cutillas's position appeared the least defensible.

In Bacardi's manufacturing and marketing culture, plans were made months, sometimes years, in advance. This approach proved quite unsuited to the second-to-second mentality of trading in financial instruments. As for Bacardi Capital's auditors, they had simply never caught up with events. And now Eddy Nielsen had to break the bad news to the family.

The Bacardi family now consisted not just of different branches, but of family groups within, and sometimes between, branches. Daniel's group was bound first — perhaps foremost — by close blood ties, but its members betrayed a complex mix of motivations. The group consisted of part of Daniel's own branch — that of Emilio — and of the whole clan of Bacardi Bolívars, the children of Joaquín the brewer, and survivors of the "junior" branch of Facundo's youngest son, José Bacardi Moreau. The additional link between Daniel and the Bacardi Bolívars was that his daughter, María Hortensia, was married to Alberto.

From Daniel's branch, his main supporters were from his own family and the family of his sister, Ana María Bacardi Rosell, and his cousin, Emilio Bacardi Rosell. Both these latter groups were based in Puerto Rico.

Daniel's sister Ana María was married to one of the most outspoken members of the family, Adolfo Comas. Adolfo was a doctor from a tobacco family in Pinar del Río, at the far western end of Cuba. Soon after he moved to Santiago to practice, he met Ana María. They were married in 1936. Adolfo eventually gave up medicine and opened a very successful Santiago nightclub, the Bamboo, which became a hub for private celebrations and for promoting the product of his wife's family. Thus he was at once useful to Bacardi but independent of it. This gave him latitude to speak his mind. He had always found Pepín Bosch manipulative, and told him so, although it was perhaps easy to take a high tone when you didn't have to run a business and cope with the family at the same time.

Both the twin sons of Ana María and Adolfo Comas, Adolfo and

Toten Comas Bacardi, worked in the business, Adolfo in Puerto Rico and Toten in Spain. Both were popular and well regarded. At the Acapulco gathering, they'd done a little shtick for the video — "I'm Adolfo and this is Toten." "No, *I'm* Adolfo and this is Toten."

Adolfo Comas Bacardi had been hired by Jorge Bosch in 1967 and had been responsible since 1978 for Bacardi Corporation's domestic distribution division. As a result of the big court case in the 1930s, Bacardi had won the right to use its trademark on rum manufactured on the island, but not to sell locally. However, when other major liquor companies — including Seagram and Hiram Walker — had opened plants on the island, Bacardi had persuaded the government to let them sell there too. Sales had initially been slow, partly because Bacardi, despite its long history on the island, was still regarded as "foreign." However, in the late 1970s, Bacardi had introduced a series of brilliant television advertisements, celebrating the talents of Puerto Ricans. They had also started an Artisans Fair on the grounds of the Cataño plant, which had become an enormous success.

These gestures had appealed to a nation subject to perennial identity crises. Bacardi sales had started to climb. By 1982, Bacardi held 25 percent of the Puerto Rican market, and Adolfo had been rewarded with the vice-presidency of sales and marketing. Adolfo's division also became involved in the domestic distribution of other liquor brands and foodstuffs, and although he had also been responsible for overseeing the move into electronics, he had survived that debacle. During 1986, food and spirits distribution was set up as a separate division and Adolfo was appointed its head. His career seemed to be progressing nicely. Many thought Adolfo was being groomed to take over as head of Bacardi Corporation. But he shared his father's chief characteristic: he was outspoken. He came to share his uncle Daniel's misgivings and found it difficult to keep those misgivings to himself.

Following word of the financial bloodbath at Bacardi Capital, Daniel and his group headed off to a Bacardi International meeting in Bermuda, demanding answers and seeking additional controls. If these were the sorts of mistakes of which management was capable, management had to be reined in.

Manuel Jorge Cutillas and Eddy Nielsen, aware of Daniel's discontent, suggested they meet ahead of the official gathering. Daniel explained that his main concern was still the sale of even a part of the company to outsiders. Nielsen and Cutillas reiterated that they had aborted such plans. Daniel looked skeptical. He presented Nielsen with a letter composed by the working dissidents, suggesting various restrictions on management's use of funds. Such controls were naturally unwelcome to Nielsen and Cutillas. Still, the meeting was relatively cordial. Daniel agreed to hold fire until they had discovered exactly what had gone wrong at Bacardi Capital.

When Joel Miller's bulky and damning report was presented at the end of July 1986, Nielsen sent copies to the shareholders. He held a meeting at his home in Miami and another special shareholders' meeting in Nassau. The dissidents weren't happy with the report. Just as they had suggested that the half-understood Hiram Walker deal was part of a "secret plan" to sell the company — a plan they believed was still in place — they now suggested that Miller's report showed only the tip of the iceberg. Miller, they said, was a close friend of O'Hara's; Arthur Andersen was Bacardi Corporation's auditor. It was all too cozy. They even suggested that O'Hara himself had been involved in trading activities.

The common culture of exile and betrayal that all the Bacardis shared provided fertile ground for these rumors and allegations of clandestine plans. As Joan Didion wrote in *Miami*, speaking of the surviving members of the 2506 Brigade from the Bay of Pigs invasion: "They were all Cuban first, and they proceeded equally from a kind of collective spell, an occult enchantment, from that febrile complex of resentments and revenges and idealizations and taboos which renders exile so potent an organizing principle. They shared not just Cuba as a birthplace but Cuba as a construct, the idea of a birthright lost. They shared a definition of *patria* as indivisible from personal honor, and therefore of personal honor as that which had been betrayed and must be revenged. They shared, not only with one another but with virtually every other Cuban in Miami, a political matrix in which the very shape of history, its dialectic, its tendency, had traditionally presented itself as *la lucha*, the struggle."

For the dissidents, as for many older members of the family, the Bacardi business had not just become the focus of memories of Cuba, it had become almost synonymous with Cuba. Cuba had been sold out before; it could not be sold out again.

The rumors and allegations were passed around the sizable family subgroup, now consisting of a couple of dozen adult members, like particles circling a nuclear accelerator. The more they were repeated, the faster they went; the faster they went, the more weight they acquired, until, in some strange parody of relativity — veracity equals rumor times the velocity of circulation (the Cuban constant) squared — these rumors eventually achieved the momentum of truth.

One issue that came back time and again to confront Nielsen and Cutillas was: Who was going to take the blame? Who was going to *pay*? How could this all have happened within yards of Eduardo Cutillas's office without his knowing about it? Perhaps there was something deeper here. There must have been. Some felt Eduardo should pay with his job. The only reason he didn't, they claimed, was that he was Manuel Jorge's brother, part of the inner circle. Some felt the responsibility rested higher up, with Nielsen and Manuel Jorge. They should pay the price. Whereupon, of course, the dissidents themselves would be pleased to take over.

At the meeting in Nassau, Daniel took it upon himself to look for the real culprits of Bacardi Capital — as if they hadn't been identified in the report — and said he might sue them himself. If nothing was done, he said, management might get the idea they could go around losing $50 million every day. The meeting was becoming less cordial. When discussion turned to the points Daniel had brought up at the meeting back in April, Nielsen said that auditing was being tightened. Toten Comas Bacardi asked who was in charge of auditing at the Bermudian operation. Nielsen said, of course, Eduardo Cutillas. "You mean," said Toten, "the man responsible for losing the $50 million is still in charge?"

Nielsen became annoyed. He was still embarrassed by the challenge over the mini-merger. Now he felt the dissidents were making a thinly disguised bid for power. Hadn't they read the report? If he and the rest of the Bacardi Capital board had been guilty of anything, they'd been guilty of trusting too much. They'd hired people with credentials. They'd checked them out with headhunters. What more could they have done? They'd learned their lesson. Now they'd hired Archie McCallum, the talented and, above all, conservative former chief financial officer of Hiram Walker, to take over Bacardi Capital. They'd also taken on Hiram Walker's former chief executive, Bud Downing, another straight-arrow, down-to-earth Canadian, as a consultant. That was the end of it.

When the discussion moved to the empire's "spare" cash and its possible uses, somebody let drop that a good chunk of money would be needed for the privatization of Bacardi Corporation. The room became electrified. What privatization of Bacardi Corporation? It was the first the dissidents had heard of it.

Another secret plan!

Bacardi Corporation's public status, established twenty years earlier when Pepín Bosch sold a portion of the company's equity to the public, had been of little benefit to the family. The public float of shares was so small that the market was inherently unstable: a purchase or sale of any size drove the price up or down. Going public had not proved an effective way for family shareholders to raise money. Moreover, minority shareholders restricted management's ability to act on behalf of the overwhelming majority: the Bacardis. Having minority shareholders forced the company to maintain the fiction that it was not ultimately under family control. Most family members considered taking the company private an eminently sensible idea. For many, the question was why Bacardi Corporation had ever been public. As Pete O'Hara had put it, Bacardi Corporation was "a little bit pregnant." Either you should be private, or you should be a lot more public. Judging by the negative reaction to the Hiram Walker deal, there was no way the Bacardis were going to agree to allow the empire to become more public. Going private was the only alternative.

In the eyes of the dissidents, however, privatization suddenly became part of management's "secret plan." Why did they want to take Bacardi Corporation out of the public eye? It could only be because they intended to do something that could not bear public scrutiny: a plan to sell! Opposition to privatization became an article of revolutionary faith for the dissident group. Bacardi Corporation's public filings were now seen as precious documents, potentially the only means of gaining information about the company.

The majority of family members had resoundingly rejected any closer association with Hiram Walker and were disturbed by the losses from diversification. They did not, however, want to challenge Nielsen or Cutillas. To undermine them was to shake the stability of the whole family. The Bacardis feared the unseating of the Godfather as the Aztecs had feared the death of the gods. The trauma of Pepín Bosch's departure remained fresh in many minds. The position of Godfather was sacred, and sacrifices were considered worthwhile to maintain the status of its occupant. After all, how great had the consumer electronics and bond trading mistakes really been in the larger scheme of things? Eddy Nielsen had assured them that no more deals like Hiram Walker would be considered. The dividends kept flowing. Best to let the whole thing pass over.

Daniel and his group, however, demanded to be heard. In earlier days, fighting for a political cause, he might have saddled up and ridden off with his rebel band into the Sierra Maestra, armed with guns and revolutionary schemes. But these were modern times, and this was a commercial war. He headed for the canyons of Manhattan, where the big corporate lawyers roam.

CHAPTER SIXTEEN

Heading for the Legal Hills

*"Of a strange nature
is the suit you follow . . . "*
SHAKESPEARE, *THE MERCHANT OF VENICE*

New York. Summer 1986

After the aborted Hiram Walker mini-merger, the Bacardi Capital debacle, and the news of the planned privatization of Bacardi Corporation, Daniel Bacardi Rosell turned to the man whose advice he had sought so often in his life: Pepín Bosch. Bosch still harbored the hurt of his resignation a decade earlier; he undoubtedly resented Eddy Nielsen. Moreover, the mooted privatization of Bacardi Corporation was based on the premise that he, Bosch, had made a mistake in taking it public. It had taken ten years, but now the family — or at least part of it — was turning to him for help.

Bosch was sympathetic to Daniel's concerns and criticisms of management. Daniel wanted professional advice, and Bosch agreed to help. He knew just the man to call: Romy Martínez, the Wall Street investment banker from Santiago who'd acted for the Bosch family in its sellout to Hiram Walker in 1977.

Bosch called Martínez and outlined Daniel's problems. Daniel believed the privatization was an attempt by management to entrench itself and keep information from shareholders. Who, asked Bosch, would be a good lawyer for Daniel to speak to? Martínez said if he was going to get legal advice, he might as well get the best: Sam Butler, senior partner at Cravath, Swaine & Moore.

Cravath, Swaine & Moore is the whitest of white-shoe New York law firms. Its Fortune 500 list of clients includes IBM, Time, and CBS. Since he'd attended Culver Military Academy, Sam Butler had been on the fast track: Harvard College, Harvard Law School, a stint as a Supreme Court clerk, two years in the army, and then to Cravath, where he'd been ever since. Butler wasn't all that keen on the term "white shoe." He preferred to think of Cravath not as the bastion of old-world values, filled with partners who belonged to the Knicker-bocker or the Union Club, but as the ultimate meritocracy. He pointed out that he came from Logansport, Indiana, and that many of his partners had worked their way up the legal ladder from Texas or Minnesota. Still, Butler was indisputably big-time. He was on the board of the New York Public Library and the American Museum of Natural History, and his personal clients included the European Economic Community. Butler didn't usually deal with family matters, but he agreed to consider the Bacardi dissidents' case as a favor to Martínez, with whom he had worked.

Bosch flew to New York to check out Butler. Butler seemed the right kind of man, so Bosch advised Daniel to consult him. Daniel, Alberto, and Romy Martínez made their way to Butler's New York office. Butler helped Daniel refine the list of demands presented to Eddy Nielsen and Manuel Jorge Cutillas earlier in the year. He also drafted a letter to Bacardi Corporation's lawyers, Kelley Drye & Warren — with whom Pete O'Hara was now associated — noting his clients' concerns.

The response to the dissidents' letter was not surprising. Sam Butler described it as a "kick in the groin."

On November 17, 1986, Bacardi Corporation announced a self-tender for up to 2,250,000 shares of common stock at $41 per share, conditional on there being, after the tender, fewer than 300 shareholders. Under SEC rules, if a company has fewer than 300 shareholders, it can deregister — it no longer has to file public financial statements. Bacardi Corporation had something over 500 shareholders but expected that more than 200 would sell. The rebels, however, were preparing a double whammy for Eddy Nielsen. They still insisted on more stringent management controls; if they didn't get them, they planned to block the privatization.

After the meeting at which Adolfo Comas Bacardi first learned about the privatization, he had returned to San Juan and confirmed with Bacardi Corporation's head, Manuel Luis del Valle, that privatization was indeed being planned. He told del Valle that a group of stockholders opposed the plan because of its expense and because they didn't trust management. Hiram Walker had been sold to the British liquor, beer, and food giant Allied-Lyons, which meant that Allied now held Bosch's former 12-percent stake in the Bacardi empire. Perhaps, said Adolfo, the ruling group might resurrect mini-merger plans with Allied?

Del Valle found the Bacardis a warm and sensitive family. He liked

The last family love-in, Acapulco, 1983: Alberto, left, and Eduardo Cutillas, receiving commemorative bottles. Eduardo was later sent to tell Alberto he'd forfeited his right to work for the company. (BACARDI FAMILY)

Adolfo Comas Bacardi and his wife, Olga. Adolfo was on the fast track until he joined the dissidents and lost his job. (BACARDI FAMILY)

Joaquín "the brewer," left, and Daniel Bacardi Rosell. Both were close to Pepín Bosch. Both their families would challenge Eddy Nielsen. Was Pepín Bosch anywhere in the picture? (BACARDI FAMILY)

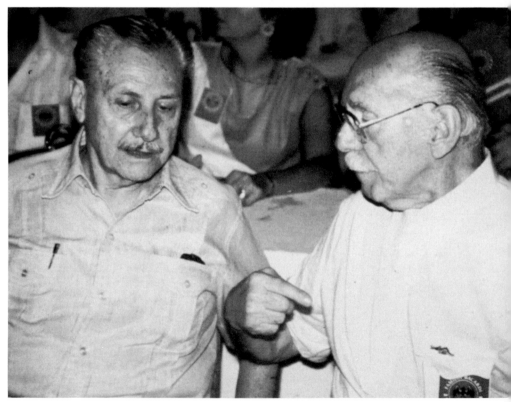

Luis del Rosal, left, and José Argamasilla Grimany, two of the Santiago old guard. Between them, they had five sons working in the company. (BACARDI FAMILY)

We're not just the name on the bottle, we're the family behind it.

Making rum is more than a business when your name is Bacardi.
With us, it's a family tradition.

In 1862 my great-grandfather created a rum so extraordinarily
smooth and light-tasting it soon became the most famous in the world.

Just how he did it has remained a family secret for more than a
hundred years now.

By living right here in Canada, I assure that our present rum
maintains in every respect the taste and quality that made it such a
sensation back in my great-grandfather's day.

You see, keeping an eye on things is another of our family secrets.

BACARDI rum.

Alberto Bacardi

Not just a pretty face: Alberto Bacardi Bolívar liked a high profile, but he didn't
think Eddy Nielsen took him seriously enough. He issued the first direct challenge
to Nielsen. It fell flat. (ALBERTO BACARDI/FBM CANADA)

Jet-setter: Luis Gómez del Campo Bacardi, who liked to sport the Bacardi name at Monte Carlo and Ascot, let the proposed "mini-merger" with Hiram Walker out of the bag. Doña Amalia Bacardi was not amused. (BACARDI MEXICO)

Live wire: Guillermo Rosell, who was related to the family through marriage, plugged Bacardi Corporation into electronics. The family got a nasty financial shock. (BACARDI CORPORATION)

In the dark: Bacardi Capital operated out of the open-plan offices of Bacardi International, under Pepín Bosch's recreation of the February 1862 night sky in Santiago. (BACARDI IMPORTS)

Spat under the bat: Manuel Jorge Cutillas, left, was Eddy Nielsen's chosen successor. Following the Bacardi Capital mess, Daniel Bacardi thought there should be more controls over management. (Bacardi & Company Limited)

Heading for a fall: Luis Echarte had enjoyed a meteoric rise at Bacardi Imports as the protege of his father-in-law, Eddy Nielsen. But the family decided he wasn't *simpático*. (NEW YORK TIMES)

In the thick of it: Bacardi Corporation's board, shortly after firing Adolfo Comas Bacardi. Behind the seated figures of Manuel Luis de Valle, left, and Pete O'Hara are, left to right, George Dorion, Jorge Luis del Rosal, Walter Faulkner, Jerry Lindzon (second husband of Elena Gómez del Campo, of the powerful Facundo branch), and Juan Grau. (BACARDI CORPORATION)

Friends in high places: Isaac Chertorivski, head of Bacardi Mexico, stands with raised hand beside Mexican President Carlos Salinas de Gortari. In Mexico, good government relations are critical. (BACARDI MEXICO)

Family and friend: Juan Grau, right, reckoned the "non-family family" had more fun than the relatives. Manuel Jorge Cutillas probably agreed with him. Grau moved from Mexico to Miami after Luis Echarte's departure. (BACARDI MEXICO)

Adolfo Comas Bacardi and his work. But he had always noted a dangerous hint of rebellion in the young executive. In business, it usually paid to use your head before your heart; it always paid to use it before your spleen. Del Valle told Adolfo it was a shame the family had to fight. He also pointed out that Adolfo, as a member of Bacardi Corporation's management, had to follow the company's policies. The majority of shareholders had approved the privatization plan. If they had decided, as he put it, to go "back into their cocoon" — a decision with which he agreed — then Adolfo had to help implement the plan.

"Look," del Valle told Adolfo, "you've got to play the role of management or the role of a shareholder. But you can't play them both." Del Valle stressed that these were his own views, not ones imposed by the family. If 80 percent of his shareholders wanted him to go private, and one of his managers opposed it, the manager would have to go. Adolfo never seemed to grasp that idea. How could he be fired for protecting, as he saw it, the interests of the whole family?

On October 23, 1986, the elder Adolfo Comas died. Perhaps the son, Adolfo Comas Bacardi, thought it appropriate, in his subsequent actions, to honor his father's uncompromising spirit. Nevertheless, it was Adolfo who, in November, explained the privatization plan to the workers at Cataño. He told them they had nothing to worry about: management had great faith in them. Perhaps he felt this public display of management loyalty made up for his private opposition.

Hoping to cool things down, Manuel Jorge Cutillas asked Adolfo to a meeting with Daniel and Manuel Luis del Valle. The four men met at Manuel Jorge's mother's house in Miami. For several hours they discussed Hiram Walker, Bacardi Capital, and the privatization of Bacardi Corporation.

Manuel Jorge said that Eddy Nielsen, although he might not be the best communicator, had the best intentions. In any case, Nielsen was due to retire from the presidency of INTRAC at the forthcoming annual meeting in Costa Rica. The conversation went round and round, and the particles of paranoia accelerated until the meeting broke up.

In practical terms, the dissidents' opposition to privatization made little sense. Although SEC filing requirements were among the most rigorous in the world, they were still no more than the financial equivalent of an executive mug shot. SEC filings were no more revealing than a smiling face or a business suit. The working dissidents received far more information about the workings of Bacardi as managers and board members of Bacardi Corporation and the other Bacardi companies. Moreover, if they didn't like management policy, they had ready access to all the shareholders. Amalia had shown how easy it was for the family to overturn management policy.

But Daniel and the dissidents were no longer looking at the privatization in practical terms. Their opposition had become a cause, part of *la lucha*.

With war raging in Nicaragua, the December 1986 meeting of INTRAC in neighboring Costa Rica seemed likely to be sparsely attended. The dissidents, however, turned up in force. When Manuel Jorge told Eddy Nielsen of his exchange with Adolfo and Daniel, Nielsen decided to confront them alone. To stand down would look as if he had been forced out. This was a matter of honor.

Despite the turnout of Daniel's branch, it represented only about 5 percent of Bacardi's overall ownership. Even with the support of Joaquín's children — none of whom were present — they still controlled no more than 15 percent of the empire. Eddy Nielsen, accompanied only by Guillermo Mármol, stressed at the beginning of the meeting that he held proxies for more than 80 percent of the votes. He was making a point about democratic arithmetic. Daniel's group went on the defensive. Here Nielsen was threatening them, brandishing proxies, speaking about majorities when the majority was in the dark.

Nielsen reported on the year's activities, then asked for questions. Jorge Rodríguez Márquez, the husband of Adolfo's sister Marlena Comas Bacardi, asked why Bacardi wanted to go private. Eddy Nielsen patiently explained that having outside shareholders had always presented management with a problem. If the company was private, then there would be no potential conflict between the family and outside shareholders. SEC filings were also a burden. But Eddy Nielsen had misunderstood the question. The dissidents wanted his *real* reasons, his *hidden* reasons. They noted, meanwhile, that Manuel Jorge Cutillas had not assumed the INTRAC presidency, as he had said he would. The reason for Eddy Nielsen's remaining — to meet the dissidents head-on — was considered irrelevant. It was just another "lie." Almost anything Nielsen did was now regarded by the dissidents as bad faith.

Nielsen asked if there was any other business. Daniel rose and pulled a piece of paper from his pocket. He said he wanted a number of new bylaws introduced. Guillermo Mármol read the complex list of "five points," based on those outlined earlier in the year.

Daniel demanded that further diversifications be examined by a broader group. There should be a fixed formula for the distribution of corporate profits: 50 percent as dividends; 25 percent to retained earnings; the use of the remaining 25 percent to be determined by the shareholders. Companies need cash reserves, the dissidents agreed, but these should be specified, and any "excess" should be paid out. The implication was clear: the Devil made work not only for idle hands, but for idle cash balances. Best to remove the temptation. Management couldn't be trusted with the companies' money.

Daniel wanted shareholders to have the right to inspect the reports of auditors and the companies' audit committee. The auditors, he felt, were too chummy with management. He seemed to believe that Arthur Andersen and Coopers & Lybrand had the financial morals of Gerardo Machado and Fulgencio Batista. Daniel also wanted quarterly reports similar to those filed by U.S. public companies. Translation: look how quickly the money disappeared at Bacardi Capital. Leave management unguarded for five minutes and they might piss away another $50 million.

Next, Daniel demanded that a 75-percent majority of shareholders approve any major corporate action, such as an asset sale or merger. Ironically, management often introduced such a requirement to entrench itself. Here, Daniel wanted to make sure that a significant minority had the ability to *block* management.

Daniel wanted each of the five Bacardi companies to distribute to its shareholders all the holdings of other Bacardi companies in its investment portfolio. These cross-holdings, he implied, could be voted in management's interest rather than the interest of the family. He also wanted the Bacardi companies to have first refusal of any shares a family member might want to sell. Finally, he wanted "cumulative voting" for the boards of the major Bacardi companies, thus ensuring the dissidents a directorship on each board.

Daniel's demands represented a challenge as much to management's integrity as to its authority. Mármol suggested that the demands be put to the next meeting of the newly expanded INTRAC board (Nielsen had agreed to increase its numbers from seven to twelve), set for Bermuda on April 21, 1987. When the meeting ended, everybody went off and had lunch together, paid for by Eddy Nielsen. One big happy family.

Most of those at the meeting returned to Miami on the same plane.

Eddy Nielsen and Guillermo Mármol sat beside Adolfo and his wife. Mármol leaned across every now and then to ask Adolfo's help with the minutes. His friendliness reflected Nielsen's desire to defuse the situation. But the dissidents had set their course.

Daniel and the other dissidents, plotting strategy, had already discussed ways to stop the privatization. One route, suggested by Robert O'Brien, an entrepreneur and hotel-owner who lived in Jamaica and was married to Adolfo's sister Amelia Comas Bacardi, was to keep the numbers of shareholders up by creating new ones. Daniel thought it a fine idea, and decided to give out shares of Bacardi Corporation as Christmas presents. The lawyer Sam Butler and his colleague Allen Finkelson at Cravath, Swaine & Moore in New York got one share each; the retired marketing genius and now Bacardi consultant Luis Lasa and his sons were given one each. Dozens of friends and relatives suddenly found themselves the recipients of Daniel's subversive largesse. Adolfo too started to dole out stock: to his wife's grandfather; to his secretary, who was terrified at the prospect of being dragged into the affair; to his secretary's children. Adolfo's mother Ana María also got into the act. The sabotage of the privatization was further complicated by being mixed up with the spirit of Christmas. It all seemed like a big game. Meanwhile, small Puerto Rican shareholders called Adolfo and asked him if they should sell. He said no.

When Bacardi Corporation's tender offer closed on December 15, 1986, one million shares had been tendered. Because of the splitting of shareholdings by Daniel and his group, however, the company now had more shareholders than before. Despite Bacardi Corporation's condition that the shares would be bought only if the number of shareholders were reduced below 300, it bought the tendered shares anyway.

For Eddy Nielsen and the ruling group, the dissidents' actions were the last straw. To disagree with policy was one thing: to frustrate it was another. Daniel's younger followers — Alberto and Jorge Bacardi Bolívar, and Adolfo Comas Bacardi — were no longer seen as troublesome family executives. They were corporate conspirators working against the majority, vipers in the breast of the organization. The dissidents had gone too far. Now they had to pay the price.

On the morning of Thursday, December 18, 1986, Adolfo Comas Bacardi drove to the Cataño plant. He waved to the guard at the gate, as he always did. He drove over the speed bumps, past the palm trees and the well-manicured lawns, past the storage facilities and "the Cathedral of Rum," past the wing-tipped tourist pavilion to the low-rise executive office, with its lily pond at the entrance. He came to work at Cataño as he had for almost twenty years. He was looking forward to a holiday with his family in Jamaica.

Manuel Luis del Valle's wife had been seriously ill, and he had not been in the office for several days. Adolfo saw him that morning. "Hi, Manuel Luis. ¿Cómo estás?" Del Valle looked down in the mouth. It must have been his poor wife. Del Valle told him he had to go out, but he wanted to see him. An hour later, del Valle came by and asked if Adolfo was free. "Certainly," said Adolfo, "Come on in." Del Valle closed the door behind him. Adolfo expected to hear about the last Bacardi Corporation board meeting, where the failure of the tender offer had been discussed. Del Valle would not be pleased with his share-splitting activities, but he expected nothing more than a reprimand.

"Adolfo," said del Valle, "the board has asked me to ask for your resignation."

Adolfo was stunned. He could think of nothing to say. Del Valle said he knew it must have been hard for him recently, with the death of his father. He didn't have to resign at once; he could take a leave of absence. When Adolfo recovered from the initial shock, he said he had no intention of resigning; they would have to fire him. Del Valle said, "Think it over." Adolfo asked del Valle not to say anything until after the Christmas party. Fine, said del Valle, he would not tell anyone.

Adolfo continued to go through the motions of work. Next day he went to the office party, telling nobody what had happened. That weekend, he went to Jamaica. There he received a call from Daniel, who had just heard about his resignation. Del Valle had sent out a memo to that effect.

When he returned to Puerto Rico on January 3, Adolfo went to see del Valle and asked about the memo. Del Valle said resigning looked better than being fired. No, Adolfo said, the memo would have to be corrected; he also wanted the minutes of the board meeting, so he could see why he had been fired.

Adolfo took off for Málaga, Spain, to see his twin brother. He felt about the firing almost as he felt about the loss of his father, except that his father's death had been expected. After the initial period of denial, the enormity of what had happened sunk in. Twenty years with the Bacardi Corporation was down the drain. He felt shell-shocked.

Within days of Adolfo Comas Bacardi's firing, Manuel Jorge Cutillas called Alberto Bacardi Bolívar in Canada. He said that his brother Eduardo was flying up to Toronto. The next day, Eduardo informed Alberto that, by joining Daniel in frustrating the family's wishes, he had forfeited his right to work for the company. He suggested Alberto resign. Alberto, too, refused, and he was fired by the board of the Canadian company early in 1987. Alberto was particularly incensed at being effectively fired by Eduardo — the man who, in the dissidents' eyes, should have borne far more responsibility for the losses at Bacardi Capital.

Next, Alberto's brother Jorge was removed from his job in the Bahamas as a vice-president and director of Bacardi & Company and a director of Bacardi International. Then, in February 1987, after meeting with Manuel Jorge Cutillas to discuss his salary and prospects, Adolfo Comas Bacardi's brother Toten resigned. Toten had been a protégé of Cutillas, who urged him not to do anything rash. But Toten had made up his mind: if his twin had been fired, he must go too.

These dismissals were the most traumatic events in Bacardi since the departure of Pepín Bosch. The ruling group felt it had had no alternative: family was family, but business was business. Disagreement was one thing, but attempting to subvert majority decisions was another. Nielsen and Cutillas believed Daniel was honestly motivated, if misguided. But they felt Alberto and, to a lesser degree, Adolfo, were driven by personal ambition. The dissidents had staged a "them or us" challenge. They had to pay for their failure.

Modern-day corporate wars are sometimes like those novelty pills that, dropped into water, swell and assume unlikely shapes. The convolutions of corporate law — particularly when more than one national jurisdiction is involved — and the lateral thought processes of lawyers almost guarantee escalation. When the combatants are not just shareholders but members of the same family, and when Cuban pride and honor are mixed into the equation, such a fight is destined to take on grotesque proportions.

CHAPTER SEVENTEEN

Enough Is Enough

"Still in modern times the
Spanish-speaking American, like the
Spaniard, is averse from compromise
and concession."
GEORGE PENDLE, *A HISTORY OF LATIN AMERICA*

Miami. April 1987

Amid the sprawling terminals at Miami airport, in a sea of subtropical vegetation and car-rental depots, Latin passion meets American high-tech rationality. At the fringes of that exchange, out on the tarmac, cocaine from Colombia heading north passes cluster bombs being shipped the other way. Miami International is the point where North and South America meet.

In April 1987, two weeks before the Bacardi Corporation annual meeting, Daniel Bacardi Rosell, Alberto Bacardi Bolívar, and Adolfo Comas Bacardi met at the airport. Their mission was a corporate one, but they were nevertheless revolutionaries with a clandestine purpose. They were meeting to discuss the creation of new family trusts. These trusts were not being created for the usual reasons: to avoid taxes, pass along wealth, or conceal ownership. They were being created as financial weapons. They would set off no X-ray surveillance devices, but they represented an investment of $10 million in the good fight, and they would wreak havoc at Bacardi.

The firings had changed everything. The dissidents had regarded themselves as reasonable people with legitimate concerns. Now they were commercial martyrs. Stopping the privatization of Bacardi Corporation had been part of a negotiating strategy they had used to gain more power over management. Giving away Bacardi Corporation shares as Christmas presents had made it all seem like a great game, a family game. Now the thwarting of Bacardi Corporation's privatization scheme had become a signal victory, bought at great price. Keeping the company public became an end in itself.

The dissidents scorned the democratic implications of their minority position. Mere proxy arithmetic ignored their status as the *moral* majority. They were fighting for shareholders who had not joined them only because those shareholders were not aware of the facts.

They were advocating the rights of shareholders being misled by a perfidious management with secret plans. They were representing those who saw only the tip of the iceberg.

Many of the dissidents carried Bacardi as their first surname; they were of the male line. Daniel's branch was that of Emilio, the most eminent of the Bacardis. Alberto and his family might have a slight historical blur at the turn of the century — when their grandfather, José, left the business — and another a little later when their branch had been given its shares as a charitable donation by the rest of the family; but their father, Joaquín "the brewer," had devoted his life to the company. Moreover, the dissident leaders — Daniel, Alberto, Adolfo — were all, or had been, workers, not parasites. This, they felt, gave their votes more weight.

Now there could be no compromise, no going back. Eddy Nielsen and his management had to be "exposed." Bacardi Corporation had to be kept public, under the shining light of SEC surveillance, so that management could not work its unknown but devious purposes. The dissidents were Cubans; they'd been fooled before. Bacardi Corporation had become the public battleground for the family's private dispute, but the real fight was about something deeper than corporate control and power: it was about who the *real* Bacardis were.

Although the dissidents were accusing Eddy Nielsen of being a liar, even implying financial malfeasance in the case of Bacardi Capital, he kept cool. Like his grandfather, Enrique Schueg, he preferred simply to shake his head: Ah, *la familia*. But Eddy Nielsen was half Cuban. He may not have liked fights, but he didn't feel inclined to dodge this one. It was time to get tough.

The family had agreed to take Bacardi Corporation private. That privatization would now have to be attempted more forcefully, via a hardball maneuver known as a 1,000-for-one reverse stock split. Shareholders would receive one new share of Bacardi Corporation for each 1,000 shares of existing stock. The new share would be worth 1,000 times its previous value. Those with fewer than 1,000 shares would be forced to sell, thus reducing the number of shareholders below the magic 300.

On April 1, 1987, Bacardi Corporation issued a proxy statement recommending this reverse split. The statement listed three reasons: to reduce the number of shareholders; to save the "burdens and costs" of regulatory reporting requirements; and to "reduce the diversity of

stockholder interests, thereby simplifying the corporation's management decisions." It was to be voted on at Bacardi Corporation's annual
meeting, due to take place in Jacksonville on April 27. Since the vast
majority of shareholders supported privatization, the vote was a
foregone conclusion.

But the dissidents had no intention of playing dead. Daniel had had
extensive talks with Sam Butler in New York. Butler considered
challenging the legality of the reverse split per se, but eventually they
hit on a more direct strategy. As with the tender offer, the reverse split
would be sabotaged so that Daniel and his group could keep the
number of shareholders above 300. This time, however, the stakes
were a thousand times greater.

At Miami International, the dissidents had discussed the creation
of 238 trusts, each containing 1,000 shares. Since these would be
worth $41,000 each, they would not be doled out to anybody on the
Christmas card list. But they could be kept "in the family" by creating
"round lot" trusts, with family members acting as trustees for their
parents, brothers, or sisters. Daniel, for instance, could be the trustee
in ten 1,000-share trusts in the names of his wife and each of his nine
children; his wife could be the trustee for ten 1,000-share trusts in the
names of Daniel and the children; each of the children could be
trustees in the names of their parents and their siblings.

Daniel met with his son Toten Bacardi Bravo in Nassau, to assemble
documentation. Then they both headed for Puerto Rico and the
offices of Bacardi Corporation's co-transfer agent, Banco de Ponce.
Such visits were not unusual; share transfers were frequently made
within a family, though rarely transfers of this size, and never of this
nature.

Told that they required additional paperwork, Daniel and his son
flew back to Nassau. Toten returned alone to Puerto Rico a few days
later and, on April 23 and 24, he and Adolfo received the new stock
certificates. Of the 238 new trusts, 132 were in the names of Daniel
and his family, 36 in the names of Alberto and his children, 20 in the
names of Alberto's sister Carmen and her family, and 50 in the names
of Adolfo's family. These trusts sat, a ticking bomb, waiting to blow
the reverse split apart.

In the meantime, there were more skirmishes. Alberto's brother
Jorge turned up at a family meeting in Nassau in April with a local
lawyer. When questions were invited from the floor, the lawyer asked
Manuel Jorge Cutillas why he had fired Jorge Bacardi. Cutillas said
that Jorge Bacardi's job as an executive had been to implement

company policy. If he worked actively against that policy, there was a conflict of interest.

But had Jorge Bacardi not done his duty? Had he not carried out his responsibility of defending the trademark? Manuel Jorge cut the lawyer off. "You are an Englishman," he said. "Do you think that Margaret Thatcher would have as a minister a member of the opposition party? Jorge Bacardi crossed over. If you are a Republican, your secretary of state cannot be a Democrat, even if he comes to the department at eight o'clock every morning."

The discussion of Daniel's proposed bylaws was on the original agenda for the April 21 meeting of INTRAC, but relations had deteriorated because of the sabotage of the first tender offer and the firings. Under a new apportionment of INTRAC board seats, only the three "major" family branches — those of Emilio, Facundo, and the Schueg Bacardis — were represented. Emilio's branch — by far the most numerous — had five seats, Facundo's four, and the Schueg Bacardis three. Alberto and the other Bacardi Bolívars were now out in the cold. Although there were five members from Daniel's branch, Daniel too felt out in the cold.

The night before the Jacksonville meeting, Bacardi Corporation's senior executives were given a "friendly" call by Daniel's son Toten. He told them that the privatization could not go ahead: trusts had been created to thwart the plan. Manuel Luis del Valle and Pete O'Hara, Bacardi Corporation's chief executive and chairman respectively, were taken by surprise. They had had no word from Banco de Ponce or from Bank of Boston, their principal transfer agent, about the creation of any trusts.

The Jacksonville meeting convened at the Sheraton Hotel on April 27 at eleven o'clock. When the reverse split came up, the dissident Robert O'Brien took the microphone and asked O'Hara if they planned to go ahead with the privatization, knowing that it would not reduce the number of shareholders below 300.

O'Hara replied that they had heard of some share transfers, but their validity would have to be established. Robert O'Brien asked if Bacardi Corporation planned to merge with another organization if the privatization went through. There had been rumors of merger talks with Coca-Cola, whose chief executive, Roberto Goizueta, was a Cuban exile and a friend of several of the Bacardis. O'Hara said there were no such plans, then adjourned the meeting to examine the alleged trusts.

The trusts came as a shock to Bacardi Corporation's management and the family's ruling group. They felt frustrated and angry. The minority group were playing proxy games. Banco de Ponce had transferred $10 million of shares without telling Bacardi Corporation, the company that paid their fees.

The ruling group became even more annoyed when Daniel, Alberto, Adolfo, and the others decided to follow the time-honored route of fighting Cuban battles in the American press. Daniel retained Hill & Knowlton, the international public relations company, to stir media interest in the case. Daniel saw the strategy as a way of shining light onto the dark secrets — whatever they might be — of the ruling group. Most family members saw it as washing their dirty linen in public.

Adolfo had earlier warned Manuel Luis del Valle that the dissidents might go public. He gave an extensive interview to a staff writer from the *Washington Post,* and the resulting feature was headlined "Bacardi Rum Faces Potent Family Revolt." Adolfo and Toten Comas and Alberto and Jorge Bacardi emerged as wronged heroes, fighting for the "sanctity of the family and loyalty to our forefathers." Manuel Jorge Cutillas and Manuel Luis del Valle emerged as corporate hatchet men. The majority of Bacardi shareholders were portrayed by unnamed dissidents as lotus-eaters. "Most of them have so much money," a dissident was quoted as saying, "they just go from Monaco to Bermuda to Nassau."

"I don't see this as a war or a battle," said Adolfo. "There is a mistake somewhere, or a secret. If there is a secret, let's bring it out in the open. If there is a mistake, let's correct it."

The dissidents planted their suspicions in the *Post* writer, and those suspicions were dutifully recorded: management might want to sell to Hiram Walker; it might want to merge with Coca-Cola. The dissidents didn't mention Nielsen's commitment sixteen months earlier *not* to continue merger negotiations with Hiram Walker. By circulating the story, the *Post* reporter was effectively being used to call Eddy Nielsen and the rest of Bacardi's management liars. Again.

After the Jacksonville meeting there was furious behind-the-scenes legal activity. Bacardi Corporation's lawyers, Kelley Drye & Warren, believed the dissidents' trust creation was an abuse of securities laws; the alleged trusts were a sham, mere dissident manipulations. These were not new shareholders, merely new shareholdings. Kelley Drye maintained there was a difference. Also, the information provided to Banco de Ponce in connection with the trusts had been inadequate. It was because of these alleged inadequacies, the lawyers believed, that

Bacardi Corporation's principal transfer agent, Bank of Boston, had not transferred the trusts to the master file of shareholders.

The Biltmore Hotel, with its 300-foot bell tower, inspired by Seville's Giralda, was built in 1926 as the architectural centerpiece of George Merrick's "City Beautiful" of Coral Gables, Florida, "where castles in Spain come true." The hotel had once had a canal system, complete with gondolas. There had been fox hunts on its grounds. Maidens had swooned on cut-velvet settees to the sound of the Paul ("Pops") Whiteman orchestra playing "Moon Over Miami." A former haunt of the Roosevelts and the Vanderbilts, the hotel had fallen on hard times during and after the Second World War, but it had been refurbished to its former glories by May 14, 1987, when Pete O'Hara brought the Bacardi Capital meeting to order in one of the plush new meeting rooms.

A few small non-family shareholders complained about being squeezed out. They were told they were receiving a fair price. After the meeting, O'Hara filed an SEC Form 15, or notice of termination of registration. The form declared the shareholders of record as being fewer than 200. A note was typed on the bottom: "In determining this figure, Bacardi Corporation . . . has not taken into account approximately 240 alleged 'trusts,' in substantially similar names, which were recently established for the express purpose of attempting to prevent the deregistration of the Company's Common Stock under the Securities Exchange Act of 1934."

In other words, the trusts didn't count. The dissidents' lawyers quickly applied to the SEC for a hearing on Bacardi Corporation's alleged deregistration, on the grounds that "the certification by the Corporation in its Form 15 may be untrue."

The Washington-based SEC was not happy at the prospect of being dragged into the Bacardi battle. The commission saw itself as the guardian of fiscal probity and the champion of the little guy. It didn't relish becoming part of a fight between two segments of a rich family. Besides, the commission had bigger concerns. The ramifications of the Ivan Boesky insider-trading scandal were still unfolding. And the Bacardi case looked messy. In fact, the SEC had never, in its thirty-three-year history, seen anything quite like it. Trying to stay out of the fray, and hoping the family would sort out its problems, the commission responded that it needed additional information on the trusts before it could call a hearing.

The bad blood between the two sides began to infect even the lawyers. The Bacardi management's frustrations became embodied in the tough stance of their principal lawyer from Kelley Drye, Bill Golden. His supposed belligerence in turn rankled the dissidents' lawyer, Sam Butler. In July, after Golden and Butler had had lengthy phone conversations about issuing stock certificates to the dissidents, Butler thought they had an agreement. When Golden sent a letter covering what they'd discussed, however, the letter said Bacardi Corporation would issue *currently dated* certificates. Butler telephoned Golden in a rage. Was Golden taking him for a fool? If he wasn't going to backdate the certificates, what the hell had they been talking about! He called Golden a liar and hung up on him.

As for the allegation that insufficient data had been provided with the trusts, Butler pointed out that it was the fault of Banco de Ponce, not of his clients. And he argued that, since each trust was worth $41,000, it was hardly a "sham," even if its purpose was to stop the privatization. "In view of the dismal record (in activities outside the rum business) of the management of the Bacardi Companies in recent years," Butler wrote in a pleading, "the Minority Shareholders are very concerned about losing the ability to learn what Applicant's management is planning to do . . . If the management of the Applicant is successful in wriggling out from under the 1934 (Securities) Act, perhaps the next step will be a freeze-out of the Minority Shareholders . . . "

Alberto went to a family meeting in Spain to put the dissidents' pitch. But the family wasn't interested. The family wanted the dispute to go away. Instead it spread into new jurisdictions. Kelley Drye brought suit in Nassau to declare most of the Bahamian trusts void. Daniel and Adolfo brought suit in October 1987 in Delaware, where Bacardi Corporation was incorporated, seeking to have the Bahamian trusts declared valid. Kelley Drye challenged the Delaware court action and successfully had it moved to federal court; then they requested that the case be transferred to the federal court in Puerto Rico. The dissidents were keen to thwart that move because Bacardi Corporation was a powerful influence in island affairs.

The legal cast was now reaching operatic proportions. Sam Butler had called in his Washington colleague Alan Levenson. A former head of the SEC's corporate finance division, Levenson now worked for the Houston firm of Fulbright & Jaworski. He signed on to handle the SEC end of the dissidents' case. The dissidents' Delaware suit required the retention of another firm, the Wilmington-based Potter Anderson

& Corroon, also engaged at Sam Butler's suggestion. The Miami partnership of Morgan, Lewis & Bockius was providing advice to Amelia Comas Bacardi's husband Robert O'Brien. And the Nassau firm of Callenders, Sawyer, Klonaris & Smith was handling trust matters in the Bahamas. The dissidents now had six law firms with meters running.

In August 1987, Bacardi repurchased the block of stock bought by Hiram Walker from Pepín Bosch ten years before. Although the sale had little immediate relevance to the battle, it had tremendous significance for the family.

After the acquisition by the British firm Allied-Lyons of Hiram Walker/Gooderham & Worts — and its stake in Bacardi — Eddy Nielsen had traveled to London to meet with Allied's chairman, the affable, aristocratic, and shrewd Sir Derrick Holden-Brown. Nielsen told Holden-Brown that if Allied wished to sell the Bacardi stake, Bacardi would be happy to buy it. Nielsen made clear there was no possibility of a closer relationship, and Allied decided to sell. In August, the 12-percent stake that had been sold in 1977 for $45 million was bought back for $200 million.

The transaction clearly showed how the value of the Bacardi holdings had increased since Pepín Bosch's departure. On the basis of simple arithmetic, the empire was now worth $1.8 billion. The price for the whole operation as a going concern would likely be considerably higher — except, of course, that nobody wanted to sell. The dissidents, rather than acknowledging the growth of the value of the empire, concentrated on Eddy Nielsen's lack of foresight in failing to buy out Pepín Bosch in 1977. Still, Nielsen looked for a peaceful settlement with his detractors. After the December 1987 meeting of INTRAC, held in Nassau rather than Costa Rica to make it easier for the family to attend, the Bacardi lawyer Guillermo Mármol agreed to mediate between Daniel and the ruling group. He and Daniel met on December 23 and December 29. Mármol, who combined a *simpático* nature with a fine legal mind and long experience of dealing with the family's foibles, tried not to pressure Daniel. What exactly, asked Mármol, did Daniel *want*? They spent hours talking, but Mármol found it difficult to pin Daniel down. At their third meeting, on January 2, 1988, Guillermo (Willy) Rodríguez, an INTRAC board member and husband of Manon Grau Bacardi, a granddaughter of

Emilio, offered to help out. He had initially been sympathetic to the dissidents, but after a couple of sessions with Daniel, he, like Mármol, came away frustrated. Daniel didn't seem prepared to compromise. Mármol had been authorized to offer Daniel more information than stipulated by the SEC, but Daniel either did not believe management or wanted victory at the SEC as a personal vindication.

By the spring of 1988, the case had become a legal nightmare. Stacks of claims and counterclaims were building up at the SEC in Washington and in the courts in Nassau and Delaware: were the dissidents' trusts valid? Had they been legally registered? How many shareholders did Bacardi Corporation have? Was it a public company?

Legal fees were in seven figures, and rising. But Daniel was determined to fight on. This was no longer something to be settled through quiet negotiation. No more Ricky Ricardo, the 1950s, pre-Castro model of Cuban fun and fire, throwing up his hands at Lucille Ball's wackiness; this was Al Pacino as a drug lord in the remake of *Scarface*, standing on his balcony blasting away at the invading Colombians, screaming, "Fuck you!"

Eddy Nielsen had five daughters: Gloria, Elena, Lucía, Martha, and Ana. Many executives had joined Bacardi after marrying into the family, the most important being Pepín Bosch. Giving jobs to the husbands of Bacardi women was a way of cementing the larger family, and also — although not necessarily — of bringing talent into the business.

Nielsen's daughter Gloria married Luis Echarte in 1969, the year Echarte graduated in architectural engineering from the University of Florida. He spent the next ten years working in the construction and real estate development business. In 1979, his father-in-law invited him to join Bacardi Imports as an executive assistant to the advertising genius Bill Walker, who had recently been appointed president.

Echarte's first major task was to reorganize Dennis & Huppert, Bacardi Imports' wine subsidiary. His father-in-law was impressed, and in 1981 Echarte was appointed vice-president. A year later, he was elected to the board. In 1984 he became executive vice-president and chief operating officer. In April 1987, he took over from Bill Walker as president. It seemed Eddy Nielsen had even bigger things in mind for Luis Echarte. Perhaps ultimately he might even succeed Manuel Jorge Cutillas as Godfather. But to most of the family and the empire's senior executives, Echarte had come too far, too fast. The prospect of his assuming more power deeply disturbed them, for Luis Echarte had one big problem: he wasn't *simpático*.

Prematurely bald, Echarte had the lean and hungry look of a Mafia hit man, and an executive style to match. He was sometimes less than diplomatic with family shareholders and company executives. He poured scorn on those who had never worked but held board memberships by virtue of shareholdings. He dismissed many of them as Cuban provincials with little understanding of business. The family was sensitive to such slights. Echarte's lavish life also became a topic of family gossip. Who paid for all those big parties he and Gloria threw at their ultra-modern Coral Gables home? What about all that expensive art? What about the Porsche and the other cars? To Luis Echarte's lack of *simpático* was added another of the great Bacardi no-nos: he flaunted his wealth.

Echarte thought himself secure because he was his father-in-law's protégé. "You take care of the business," Eddy Nielsen had said, "and I'll take care of the family." But the forced abandonment of the Hiram Walker mini-merger and the battle over the Bacardi Corporation privatization should have warned Echarte that Nielsen's power was limited. Taking care of the family was no simple matter.

Along with the presidency of Bacardi Imports, Echarte received, in the latter part of 1987, a seat on the executive advisory body (now called the Brand Owner's Coordinating Committee) that oversaw the empire. He was the new guy on the block, but he acted as if he already ran the show. He was critical of his colleagues. He resented the diversion of profits from Miami to Puerto Rico for tax reasons. He regarded the Puerto Rican operation as "a factory" and privately dismissed Manuel Luis del Valle as a "Third World executive," an "islander," with a Puerto Rican's restricted view of the world. He acknowledged that Juan Prado was a good marketer, and that Juan Grau had done a fine job in Mexico, but he regarded them as good old boys from the Santiago Mafia. As for the Cutillas brothers, Manuel Jorge was too much of a consensus man, not hard-hitting enough. And Eduardo — well, Eduardo was nothing more than Manuel Jorge's brother.

Echarte made no secret of the fact that he found the Bacardi management style old-fashioned and cumbersome. Too much deadwood was kept around because they had known the family back in Cuba. Too many family members and senior executives lived in the past. Many had never left Cuba in their minds. The atmosphere of the whole operation was that of a comfortable club; where the executives hunted together and brought back big trophies that made their offices look like something out of an old *New Yorker* cartoon. Echarte wanted to bring in the management consultants and shake the place up, clear the decks and get on with it.

His colleagues on the executive advisory committee thought Echarte had a screw loose. They treasured Bacardi's paternalistic corporate culture; it had produced enviable results. Roots were important; people were important. Who did Echarte think he was? Did he really dare compare himself to Pepín Bosch? Bosch had been tough, sure, but he had earned respect over decades of hard work and inspired leadership. He had led the family and the business out of Cuba.

Ultimately, Luis Echarte ended up resembling Pepín Bosch in at least one way: he inspired a conspiracy against himself. The fellow senior executives he criticized and the family on which he poured scorn knew one another well. It did not take them long to decide that Luis Echarte did not fit. Less than a year after his appointment as president of Bacardi Imports, they quietly agreed that Echarte had to go. Their one big problem: who was going to tell Eddy Nielsen?

Manuel Jorge Cutillas eventually ended up having to break the bad news. Nielsen was understandably upset, not least because he would have to tell Echarte. He approached his son-in-law as tactfully as possible: you, uh, might not be happy at Bacardi in the long term. Echarte was shocked. Didn't the two men have an agreement that Echarte would look after the business and Nielsen would look after the family? Hadn't Nielsen told him he didn't *have* to be a diplomat? Hadn't he told him he was doing a great job?

"Just give me another two years," said Echarte. "Let me do what I want and then take it to the shareholders."

Nielsen said it was out of the question: the family had decided. Luis Echarte resigned, and an announcement was made that he had decided to go into business for himself. Echarte was profoundly upset, as was his wife. Gloria directed her anger at her father. Eddy Nielsen had suffered yet another blow to his prestige.

Nielsen had another son-in-law at Bacardi Imports. Eddy Sardiña, who was married to Ana Nielsen, was regarded as a good deal more personable than Luis Echarte. He had also served his time, having joined the company under Pepín Bosch, whose wife, Enriqueta, had been a great friend of Sardiña's grandmother. Sardiña had worked in Martinique and Spain before coming to Miami. Following Echarte's departure, Sardiña was appointed executive vice-president and chief operating officer at Bacardi Imports. He was also appointed to the Brand Owner's Coordinating Committee, the key group that Manuel Jorge Cutillas consulted on broad strategy. Eddy Nielsen could retire knowing he was leaving a member of his immediate family in the first circle of Bacardi's ruling group.

By the end of 1988, with nothing moving on the Delaware front of the Bacardi court battle, the SEC reluctantly revived its interest in the case. Daniel was now talking to Manuel Jorge Cutillas, and it seemed a solution might be possible. Sam Butler was put in touch with Walter Faulkner, a senior partner of Kelley Drye. Faulkner had a more conciliatory tone than his colleague Bill Golden, but the negotiations fell apart over the question of costs. Daniel and the dissidents wanted the company to pay their seven-figure legal fees. Cutillas and Eddy Nielsen thought this ridiculous: they hadn't started the battle.

In mid-1989, the ruling group again thought they were close to peace. Again negotiations broke down. Now the dissidents wanted more. Daniel's list of demands had grown more complex and now ran to a couple of dozen pages. The dissidents were sustained in their struggle by an SEC decision in September 1989. The SEC denied Bacardi Corporation the right to expand the hearing to include the issue of the trusts' validity and whether they had been formed merely to frustrate the deregistration. This was a severe blow to Bacardi Corporation's management, and a major fillip to the dissidents.

To add to the discord, anonymous letters began to appear in the mailboxes of shareholders. "Dear Bacardi Shareholders," began one, which was received in October 1989. "In these times when the liquor industry is passing through a stage of diminishing consumption . . . and in which writers predict that rum will go out of fashion: times in which the competition expands by acquisitions or economic mergers between firms, our company is led by a group of individuals, late in their years, that have spent their professional careers in countries considered as part of the third world . . . "

The letter dredged up all the old complaints. It claimed the ruling group was "an employment agency" for immediate family members, "some of whom have doubtful professional and educational back-grounds." The group, claimed the letter, "lead by trying to avoid conflict, disagreeable situations, and always looking for consensus." It went on to accuse them of "accumulating our money so that they may feel more comfortable in the management of our Company."

Following some dubious arithmetic about economic performance, the letter concluded: "With this leadership and with the passive attitude of so many of you, what is the future that awaits us?"

Eddy Nielsen's response — in a note to shareholders — was brief and measured. He cited the many achievements of the Cuban "Third Worlders," from Emilio, Facundo, and Enrique through Pepín Bosch to the present. Noting that the anonymous letter had compared the dividend return on Bacardi shares unfavorably with the return from a bank account, Nielsen pointed out that the empire's collective growth in the previous twelve years had been 18 percent per year. "What a great bank we have!" he wrote. "I thank all of the 'Third-Worlders' that have contributed to this fabulous success!

"I am confident that you, my dear relatives, will continue to give the support that this administration so much deserves."

Manuel Jorge Cutillas's executive assistant, Jorge Luis del Rosal (brother of Roberto, who had taken over in Canada when Alberto had been fired), also sent a letter to Bacardi shareholders. His response was more passionate, more like Al Pacino ripping off his jacket and inviting the invisible opposition to go to it. It began: "Not-so-dear Dwarf." Point by point, del Rosal launched a scathing attack on the anonymous writer. In response to the claim that management was "accumulating our money," del Rosal wrote: "I ask you, how is it that these old men, 'third-worlders', failures, bums, air-heads, employment agents that we have as leaders *accumulate* funds? Could it be that they are earning it? Or could it be the work of the Holy Ghost?!"

The letter ended: "Sell, you Dwarf, sell. Let us keep on working and growing in peace. Sell and go with your money and your anonymous letters straight to . . . the bank."

The anonymous writer implied that he wasn't one of the dissidents, but suspicion naturally fell on Daniel and his group. With the breakdown of the midyear negotiations and the adverse SEC decision in Washington, the ruling group decided that enough was enough. They decided to hoist Daniel on his own petard. They would present his package of demands to the family at a meeting in Bermuda. Yea or nay.

When Daniel learned of management's plans, he objected. He knew the vote would be nay. His hefty document was just a basis of negotiation, he said, it wasn't written in stone. But the ruling group was sick of negotiating. It seemed impossible to gain concessions from the dissidents. They had been negotiating for almost three years. They had talked so long only because they wanted Daniel to drop the case before the SEC. At a meeting in Nielsen's Miami office, Nielsen told the dissident leader that even if the dissidents won at the SEC, they would have lost the war. They would have nothing else to bargain with. Daniel was determined to fight on. Knowing they would be voted down, he and the other dissidents refused to appear at the Bermuda meeting on December 6, 1989. Robert O'Brien presented a letter from Daniel claiming he was being "misrepresented" by the suggestion that the document was a list of demands. The dissidents just wanted to talk.

After O'Brien had made his pitch, George Dorion Bacardi, a grandson of Emilio and a Bacardi Corporation board member who worked at the Jacksonville plant, stood up to express the family's sentiment: enough was enough. They couldn't go on pretending they were one big happy family while the opposition continued. This was the end. The dissidents might be family, but they could no longer be friends.

On February 15, 1990, the administrative law judge at the SEC brought down his decision on Bacardi Corporation's deregistration and privatization: the trusts had to be counted as shareholders. Thus the number of shareholders of Bacardi Corporation exceeded 300. The company was, pending an appeal, still public.

Daniel, Adolfo, Alberto, and the other dissidents were elated. Daniel called the decision a "great victory." He told any family member who would listen: "We have embarrassed them. They told the family there was no way they were going to lose this case. We've made them look bad. Maybe now we can get the other shareholders to see things our way."

But Daniel, indeed all the dissidents, missed the point. Through legal maneuvering, they had frustrated the wishes of the majority of the family. Daniel's lawyers had beaten Bacardi Corporation's lawyers, at least in this round. The "victory" didn't establish anything about secret agendas or tips of icebergs. All it did was prolong the struggle.

"These people": That's what the opposite sides now called each other. Alberto claimed: "These people want to sell the company." Adolfo announced: "These people have a secret plan." Eddy Nielsen said: "We're throwing money at these people so they can attack us." Manuel Jorge Cutillas shook his head and sighed: "We just don't know what these people want."

CHAPTER EIGHTEEN

Family Portraits

*"Sometimes you can go quite a long
time before you criticize families,
your own or those by marriage . . .
But even when you have learned not
to look at families nor listen to them
and have learned not to answer
letters, families have many ways of
being dangerous."*

ERNEST HEMINGWAY, *A MOVEABLE FEAST*

Puerto Rico. Christmas 1989

Adolfo Comas Bacardi's Villa Olga, south of San Juan, is approached through wrought-iron gates and a curved drive overhung by luxuriant tropical greenery. The Spanish colonial house has tiled floors, huge rooms, and high ceilings. Bats are a recurrent theme: in a large metal wall-hanging by the front door, in an ornament on a window ledge, on assorted corporate knickknacks. Near the front door is a framed drawing of the Bacardi family tree, onto which a leaf for the Comas Bacardis' latest child has been lovingly grafted. The Comas Bacardis are keen that the tree not die; more precisely, keen to show that the sap is still flowing in their own branch.

At one end of the house is Adolfo's large, shuttered, book-lined study. On one wall is an oil painting of a bespectacled Adolfo, looking benign and businesslike. Below sits the real thing, looking equally benign, but sounding a little hurt and angry, and very combative. He wears an open shirt, slacks, and loafers. With him sits his attentive wife, Olga María Bartes Rodríguez, after whom the house is named. A sleek woman dressed in black, she sports huge diamonds on her fingers and her earlobes.

Adolfo speaks with pride of the branch of his great-grandfather, Emilio, "the most exciting of all the branches." He recalls when he and Olga came to Puerto Rico on their honeymoon and fell in love with the place. He runs through his career with the Bacardi Corporation, and how that career suddenly ended in December 1986. "I never thought they'd fire me," he says. "I thought they might put me aside or send me to Timbuktu to head something there, but to fire me . . . I saw no reason."

Olga breaks in: "After Hurricane Hugo, we went to the plant to get water. When they saw Adolfo, they stopped what they were doing; they ran to hug him and kiss him. It breaks my heart." Olga's eyes moisten. "We really struggled for twenty years." There is a silence, broken only by the tiny tree frogs outside, trilling their Spanish names: *co-qui, co-qui.*

Adolfo launches into his version of the subsequent battle. "They did not believe that we were serious enough to follow all the processes of going legally against them. They never thought we were going to go all the way. Now they are claiming that we are responsible for the expenses of their lawyers, which are huge. And we have found out that we made a mistake by hiring Sam Butler, because *anybody* can defend against their lawyers. They are the worst lawyers in the world.

"We have one right that they cannot take away from us. It is the minority right in a democracy. Fifty-one percent rules, but they cannot rule against the minority, they have to rule for the 100 percent, and that is all we want. We don't want any privilege. We don't want to run the business. We want to protect our rights as a minority, not to overrule. We have to know, and to be able to make a decision, and to be accounted for.

"We always thought the company should be the playground, not the battlefield of the family."

Olga says: "The shareholders know nothing about what's going on. All they know is about dividend cheques. The bigger it is, the better the company's doing. But," she continues, "this is not about money, it's about principles. The company is so different now . . . The love is gone."

Adolfo comes back: "They keep saying, 'What are you asking specifically that you want?' And we say, 'Nothing. Everything is negotiable. All we want is to find a way . . . if it's not through a stockholder agreement, some other way; an amendment to the bylaws. Something. You do whatever you want to. We just want to be sure that we have a safeguard, that the company remains in our hands.' That's the only issue here.

"Everything is negotiable."

The Christmas wreath on the door of Alberto and María Hortensia Bacardí's big, rambling, modern house, on a winding street in a quiet, well-heeled Toronto neighborhood, reads "The Bacardi Family." The house has had several extensions tacked on to accommodate their large family. María Hortensia jokes that her friends call their home, because of its modern style and its size, "Early Holiday Inn." On the wall of a hallway is a big color photograph of Alberto's branch of the family, gathered in his ravine garden, around his father, Joaquín, who died in September 1987. The picture is a crowd scene, but it represents just the smallest branch of the Bacardi family.

María Hortensia is an attractive, vivacious woman who looks remarkable for having borne eight children. Polite, well-scrubbed young Bacardi Bacardis appear at intervals. María Hortensia produces a picture of her father and mother, Daniel and Graziella, and her eight brothers and sisters.

María Hortensia talks of the golden summers of her youth in Santiago, shot through with the frisson of revolution in the nearby mountains. "I remember Batista's men coming into our house with machine guns, and my mother took us into the back of the house and we prayed. There was an old aunt living there. There was shooting going on around us. Actually, it was very exciting.

"When we were in college, a friend of ours from Chicago came back with us, and she couldn't believe it. She said, 'You people don't realize what you have: chauffeurs and big houses.'"

They took it all for granted then — the charmed life. Nobody behind you would blow his horn if you suddenly saw a friend in one of the narrow, one way downtown streets and asked your chauffeur to stop so you could chat. María Hortensia reminisces about how close she and her sisters were to Alberto and his brothers, and also to the Comas Bacardis, and how they all visited at Cayo Smith or Siboney. She speaks fondly of the Fiesta de la Bandera.

As for the dispute, María Hortensia maintains that the dissidents' position is much stronger than mere numbers would suggest: "The majority is more of a minority than we think, because that famous majority is a very arguable majority." She believes the ruling group maintains its position only through control of "voting trusts." María claims that, through these trusts, Nielsen and Cutillas control the "famous majority" that doesn't know what's really going on. "If they had a real democratic election where everybody's allowed to vote what they think," she says, "they wouldn't have a majority. They just have vested interests who are obliged to vote a certain way."

Alberto, handsome and gracious as ever, finally speaks: "There are a lot of people who agree with a lot of what we're saying. Not all of what we're saying, we wouldn't expect that. We've always said we are open to modification. I've always said, if you can convince me that I'm wrong, I will change." But Alberto is heating up, and he sounds like a hard man to convince.

"They are very capable of confusing the shareholders," he says. "These people are expert propagandists. We have never said that we are against individuals in the administration. What we said was that we wanted a structure in the company, a *functioning* board of directors. They've accepted our recommendation for a financial committee, but the committee is not functioning . . . it is a rubber stamp. We are not saying we are better than you. We don't want to get involved in the pettiness at this point. What we are saying is that this Bacardi company does not have a functioning structure for the future."

María, apologizing for the hubbub of the children down the hall, says: "The majority does not have any respect for the minority. You cannot overpower the minority."

"If you are the majority," echoes Alberto, warming to the theme, "you have the right to put your administration in place, but you also have the right to protect the rights of the minority. Inherent in your rights are the rights of the minority. That's government in our system. But we never said that we as a minority are going to put in the administration. They keep saying that we as a minority want to enforce the administration on the company. They are very good at manipulating these things."

"They are arrogant," says María.

"They have been humiliated," says Alberto.

Maria continues: "Fidel managed to bring Cubans from the most easygoing happy people you've ever seen and Fidel managed to bring out from them all this bad blood. The same thing has happened in the company. Who did it? Who brought out all this dirt, all this bad feeling? Never ever was there this problem in this family."

"They lost $70 million [in Bacardi Capital]," says Alberto, "but the explanation that they gave was absolutely ridiculous. We still don't know what happened. We still haven't had a report, and the only report we got from the auditors was that it was incomplete . . . They are hiding and misinforming.

"Maybe," he continues, "we didn't express ourselves as we should have at the beginning. But we don't have secretaries and big lawyers' officers. If there were only twenty shareholders it would be all right, but there are 300 shareholders living all over the world. Manuel Jorge is saying, 'They are trying to limit me.' We say, 'You should be limited.' That's what shareholders do. That's precisely what we've had, an unlimited, irresponsible management, and we continue to have it."

Would the dissidents ever consider selling out?

"We're going through all this because we don't want to sell out," says Alberto. "We're going through all this because we'd like to leave our children the same opportunity that our parents gave us, that these people were given by their parents. What more proof do you want for an injustice than that?"

Would Alberto and María like their children to work in the company?

"Not to work," they say in unison. Alberto expands: "It's the opportunity to be part of it, to be shareholders. To negate that right of any member of the family is to create an injustice."

🦇

Daniel Bacardi Rosell sits in the bar of the Holiday Inn in Coral Gables, Florida. He is a small man now, with swept-back, snow-white hair and a hawk-like nose with slightly flaring nostrils. His brown eyes gaze out through narrow slits beneath drooping, fleshy lids; not in a sinister way, rather in that way of older people for whom it is something of an effort to look out upon the world.

Daniel tells a story about what a small world it is for Cuban exiles. He was in the telegraph office when a customer asked him, "Do you speak Spanish?" He told her she had no need to worry because the clerk spoke Spanish. Then he asked where she came from, and she said Oriente, and he asked which town, and she said Santiago, and he asked her name. She told him and he said, "No, your father's name." So she told him and he said, "Oh yes, he owned the pharmacy." The lady asked, "What is your name?" And he said, "Bacardi," and she said, "Of course, but what is your first name?" He told her and she said, "Yes, you lived at so-and-so. I remember making up prescriptions to be delivered to your house."

There was another lady with the first, and Daniel asked her where she came from. She said Pinar del Río, and mentioned the name of a village. Daniel said, "You must have known Doctor Comas." And she said, "Of course — he had the son who married someone from Santiago." Daniel said, "Yes, my sister!"

Such a small world for Cuban exiles.

Over a Carta Blanca and water, the drink he has taken all his life, Daniel talks happily of his grandfather, Emilio, and of Pepín Bosch and Víctor Schueg. He talks less happily and freely about the Batista dictatorship and his own initial support for Fidel Castro. As for the current war in the Bacardi family — well, Daniel is keen that it be played down. It's not really a major dispute. Everybody wants the same things. He gestures toward his drink. It's more like deciding whether you want ice in your drink or not. The management was young. They didn't have enough experience. They didn't have the talent to diversify. They had diversified without consulting the family. He just wanted some controls on them, that's all. He sounds the theme of the downtrodden minority. "The management should do the will of the majority, but they should look after all the shareholders."

It isn't really a great dispute, he repeats. A few minutes later, however, talking about his health, he says: "They hope that I will die."

Eddy Nielsen has an air of quiet resignation. On the wall beside his desk at Bacardi Imports in Miami is a line drawing of his grandfather, Enrique Schueg, who saw his own share of family problems. On another wall, Nielsen also keeps a smaller drawing of Pepín Bosch. "I left it there on purpose," he says, "because I didn't want it to look as if I was in a vengeful frame of mind, because actually the battle was between him and me. I admired Pepín Bosch very much and I worked with him for many years and I was able to maintain my personality, but he got to a point of no return when it came to bringing in the outsider to run the company."

That all seems long ago. Eddy Nielsen has passed on the mantle of leadership to Manuel Jorge Cutillas, but he remains an important link between the family and the business empire. The great majority of the older members still trust him.

When the dissidents are mentioned, he shakes his head in despair. "Now they not only want directors on boards; they want directors that can't be fired. Perhaps it's my New England background, but why would a group who has no confidence in the management simply not want to sell? We are fueling the dissidents with dividends the way the U.S. fueled Japan with scrap iron.

"What can you do?" he asks wistfully, gazing out over Biscayne Bay. "You have to keep managing and grow the companies."

Manuel Jorge Cutillas's tasteful office at Bacardi & Company in the Bahamas sits at one end of the Nassau headquarters. The entrance to the building is guarded by two restored cannons. The office itself is divided in two. One half has a large board table with leather swivel chairs. On the wall, flanked by the heads of a boar and a game goat, is a large antique map of Cuba.

Manuel Jorge is an affable man with a bustling, no-nonsense style. His problem, in his view, is that he has had to put up with too much nonsense.

"The dilution of ownership is now becoming geometrical," he says. "One of the things we say to the dissidents is that you want to run this like a little family company, but it is not a family any more, and that's what I told Daniel last time. He was saying, 'But you know, the family . . . ' and I said, 'What family? Do you know the children of so-and-so who lives in Spain? Are they family, or are they shareholders?' That's what these people can't get into their heads. This is no longer a family as we knew it in Santiago de Cuba."

Nestor Carbonell, in his book *And the Russians Stayed*, quotes Macaulay on the followers of the Duke of Monmouth in exile: "Delusion becomes almost madness when many exiles who suffer in the same cause herd together in a foreign country." Writing of Cuban exiles in the post-Castro period, Carbonell noted: "This was axiomatic in the case of the Cubans, who clearly preferred consoling illusions to disturbing realities. Craving for upbeat news, they used to accost those who seemed to be on the inside with the lighthearted Cuban saying 'Tell me something good, even if it's not true.'"

As the decade of the 1980s drew to a close, the Bacardi dissidents had gathered in common cause as exiles from the Bacardi company. Just as Cuban exiles fed their hatred of Castro with any story, true or false, so the dissidents were now prepared to persuade themselves of almost any evil on the part of the ruling group. All shades of gray had been eliminated by the shining light of their cause. Their motto now seemed to be: "Tell me something bad, even if it's not true." Their complaints had become woven into a Homeric litany, a story that could not be challenged or changed: the loss of the money at Bacardi Capital had never been explained (even though it had); the ruling group had a "secret agenda," an assertion there was no way of refuting.

The battle had become inextricably tangled with family and loyalty, with the peculiarly Cuban notions of allegiance and conspiracy. To speak with the dissidents was to be involved in a verbal guerrilla war; pinned down on one point, they popped up with another. It was impossible to reason with the dissidents because their cause went beyond reason. Reason was ultimately about two and two equaling four; it couldn't deal with the complexities of carrying the Bacardi name, of owning the company in a way that had nothing to do with equity. What they were arguing about was family feeling, honoring the past, protecting birthrights. There could be no compromise. How could there be when principles were at stake? Being "reasonable" meant mingling what you knew to be true with what you knew to be false. The dissidents wanted only one thing: capitulation.

The dissidents had fallen prey to a peculiarly Cuban trait: they had gone absolutely, utterly over the top. The company's lawyers were now "the worst in the world." The amount lost at Bacardi Capital went up every time the story was told. The anonymous letter said the management was too old; Daniel said they were too young. Even higher dividends became part of management's devious plot to stay in power.

Eddy Nielsen and Manuel Jorge Cutillas considered themselves reasonable people. Their problem was that it took them a long time to realize passion was a black hole into which reason disappeared without trace.

CHAPTER NINETEEN

The Other Bacardi Family

*"It is obvious common sense that
when managerial decisions are
influenced by feelings about and
responsibilities towards relatives in
the business, when nepotism exerts a
negative influence, and when a
company is run more to honor a
family tradition than for its own
needs and purposes, there is likely to
be trouble."*

HARRY LEVINSON

Miami. January 1990

The rack of antlers on the stuffed head behind Juan Grau's desk in Miami marks him as one of the Bacardi old school: a hunter. He is a charismatic and charming man, with a strong jaw and a flashing smile, an executive Ricardo Montalbán. But Juan Grau is no executive facade. He is as good a technician as he is a manager, familiar with putting up distilling columns and with managing people, expert at the analytical techniques of gas chromatography and at dealing with the politics of one-party states. He now sits in the highest-profile job in the Bacardi empire, chief executive at Bacardi Imports.

Bacardi Imports is not the most profitable of the Bacardi companies, but it represents the face of the empire in its most important market. Miami is the hub of the Bacardi empire and the family meeting point, the centre of *el exilio* and the plotting place of *la lucha*. It is the place where the U.S. meets Latin America, often with mutual incomprehension. Biscayne Boulevard also bears the scar of Luis Echarte's excision.

Juan Grau is the perfect man to heal wounds, but he is also important in other respects. He represents what is best about the *other* Bacardi family, the one whose attachments are primarily to the business and the brand. He also symbolizes the fact that Pepín Bosch was, in one critical way, wrong about Bacardi, although in a way that ultimately did him credit. The company was able to survive him and flourish because of the people he had hired but never fully appreciated. Grau is the leading example. He oversaw the most spectacular turn-around of the empire in modern times, that of Bacardi Mexico, which had been teetering on the point of self-destruction at the end of Bosch's reign.

Pepín Bosch had always had a special affection for Bacardi's Mexican operation, having first made his mark there back in 1933. The distillery at La Galarza ranked as one of the most beautiful in the world; the head office complex at Tultitlán was an architectural monument; Mexico had been the first operation to exceed sales of 1 million cases a year. But by the time of Bosch's departure from Bacardi, the Mexican operation was in desperate straits. The problem lay with the man who had made it so successful, Ernesto Robles León, the brilliant but sometimes moody commercial conquistador of the local market.

Robles León had led the Mexican operation to spectacular sales increases in the 1950s and early 1960s. As the years passed, he had come to treat the company as a personal fiefdom. At one time, he had four children working in the operation, including Eduardo, his son and heir apparent. In an uncanny parallel to Bosch, he had eventually fallen out with Eduardo and fired him.

Part of the problem with Robles was his income arrangement: he received 1 percent of Bacardi Mexico's sales. This had started as a modest figure, but, by the mid-1970s, it made Robles León one of the best-paid executives in Mexico. He began to lose interest. He had also made strategic errors. He introduced cheaper products that damaged the brand image; he failed to meet a strong market challenge from the Spanish company Domecq, which developed light, locally produced brandies from a mixture of grape and cane spirits. These brandies were sold on their mixability, traditionally one of Bacardi's great marketing strengths. Domecq began beating Bacardi at its own game. When Robles León's wife died, he stepped up an already active social life, often with the aid of the company plane. But the last straw was his falling-out with the government, which in Mexico could prove fatal.

Mexico, a one-party state, had a tightly controlled economy and an aversion to foreign investment for most of the twentieth century. Laws changed frequently and were applied with considerable ministerial discretion. All this, combined with widespread government ownership and the presence of state-encouraged monopolies in many areas —

such as in advertising, and in the supply of molasses and bottles — meant that business survival depended critically on good government relations.

Robles León had traditionally been on good terms with the government of Luis Echeverría, but in the mid-1970s he made the mistake of getting arrogant with the Mexican Treasury. The dispute was over a tax assessment on spirits the Treasury claimed had been sold, but that had in fact literally disappeared in evaporation as part of the aging process. According to one report, Robles had gone to the Treasury secretary and begun the conversation by saying: "Look, kid, I know your father very well!" The resulting audit lasted four years and led to a tax charge of $160 million, more than the value of the company.

When Pepín Bosch left Bacardi, Robles León felt his own days were numbered. Indeed they were. One of Eddy Nielsen's most challenging tasks in his new role as Godfather was to persuade Robles León to retire. It took six months, and his departure was accompanied by a generous settlement. Juan Grau — who had returned to Bacardi in 1974 to take over the research facility recently built at Jacksonville, named the Schueg Brothers laboratory — was appointed chief executive in Mexico. Manuel Jorge Cutillas became chairman of the board. It was an important test for both of them.

Grau had some outstanding executives to help him turn Bacardi Mexico around. The first was a brilliant young advertising and marketing man named Isaac Chertorivski, whose grandparents had come to Mexico at the time of the Russian revolution. Chertorivski, like Robles and Grau, had tremendous *presencia*. He also had good government connections and limitless ambition. The other was Guillermo Cordera, whom Grau hired from American Express. Cordera was more low-key, a systems man, but he played a crucial role in stanching the losses and setting the company on a growth path.

Bacardi Mexico began tightening financial controls, improving government relations, and reviving the brand image. The cheaper rums were dropped and more emphasis was placed on the higher-margin "quality" products, in particular Añejo and Solera. The sales force — with initial resistance — was made more financially sophisticated. Commissions were skewed toward those products that contributed most to the bottom line. Government relations were greatly improved. In 1982, in the midst of a foreign debt crisis, Echeverría's successor as Mexican president, José López Portillo, demanded that all foreign bank deposits be repatriated. Guillermo Cordera — after much internal corporate soul-searching — dutifully turned up at the bank to deposit a cheque for $2 million. The astonished bank did not know what to do: Bacardi was apparently the only company that had obeyed the injunction. Rather than exploiting loopholes in tax policy, it pointed them out to the Treasury.

This good corporate citizenship paid off. The case over the tax on evaporated spirits was settled with a minimal fine and a specific export commitment. No barriers were placed on the export of dividends, in dollars, to the Bacardi shareholders overseas. The company further burnished its brand name by promoting an important national song festival for young people.

By 1980, a company that had struggled for three years began to look beyond mere survival. There followed a decade of spectacular growth. In 1983, sales hit 2 million cases. In 1985, the year Grau appointed Chertorivski president, they went to 3.3 million. In 1989, they hit 6 million, making Tultitlán the third-largest producer of alcoholic beverages in the world.

With other global markets stagnant, Mexico became responsible for virtually all the Bacardi empire's growth in the latter half of the 1980s, taking the brand through the 20-million-case mark worldwide in 1987, to 21 million cases in 1988, and 22 million in 1989. By then, Bacardi Mexico had also taken over a floundering brandy producer, Vergel, and acquired stakes in a number of sugar mills. Grau, Chertorivski, and Cordera had high profiles in the business community; Chertorivski in particular had close relationships with Carlos Salinas de Gortari, who had become Mexican president in 1988. Bacardi Mexico had become the greatest success of Eddy Nielsen's reign as Godfather.

Juan Grau feels himself very much part of the Bacardi family — not the genetic family, but the family of executives and workers committed to the company, the product, the trademark, and corporate success. This family appears a good deal more united in its purpose and its culture than do the warring relatives who have continued their legal battles into the early 1990s.

Juan Grau does not understand the stance of the dissidents. "In Mexico," he says, "I learned a lot about negotiating from disadvantage. You had a very strong government, which controls many aspects of the economy. We dealt with a number of monopoly suppliers. If you have 15 percent, you are in a position of disadvantage. It is *you* who have to negotiate, not the majority. But if you are not willing to surrender anything, then you can't negotiate. I love all these guys, but we are not strangers who came in and took over the company.

"We feel the Bacardis are like a royal family. There's a family family and a non-family family, and although we have not been shareholders, I think we have enjoyed the company much more than they have."

Juan Grau's sentiments about the "family family" — we love these guys, but — are expressed by other members of the "non-family family." "I really don't understand Daniel and his group," says Juan Prado in Bermuda. "I understand that they are hurt because of the separation of family members from the operation. But if you eliminate that, then I don't understand anything, because this is the most successful company you could think of. The money these guys have made is unreal. Look at the numbers after Bosch. So I have to think it's emotional."

Manuel Luis del Valle in Puerto Rico betrays more frustration than most of the empire's senior executives because he's been in the thick of the privatization battle. "When you deal with family you're dealing with emotions, not facts. But they make you feel part of them. When I lost my wife it was as hard on some of the Bacardis as it was on my own family. They are very considerate. They look after you. They are sentimental, intimate. Even with the dissidents, if there was any effort on their part, the family would get together and forget the whole damn thing.

"Daniel's big problem is that he is emotionally involved. In business you use the head and not the heart. Worst, he appears not to have confidence in management. But if you don't trust management, then sell. But he doesn't want to sell. If the dissidents use their heads rather than their hearts, they would realize that they have nothing to gain from going public. We'll give them anything they want. We have nothing to hide.

"The conditions Daniel demands are ridiculous. One of these days they are going to get tired. They may win legal battles here and there. They may win a hundred court battles, but they will still be the minority."

Many of the "non-family family" are disturbed by the dissidents' attitudes toward the business. Everyone might agree with Adolfo Comas Bacardi that the companies should not be a battleground, but neither do employees want them to be the family's "playground" either. Alberto and María Hortensia want their children to be "involved" with Bacardi but don't want them to *work* there. The implications cause much shaking of heads. Ah, *la familia*.

Family members have always had a rather misty-eyed view about their relationship with the company, but that relationship has changed — in subtle stages, but profoundly — over time. At the beginning, the company and the family were in many ways synonymous. The family gave the company strength and cohesion. But the roles have changed. Particularly after Cuba, the company's achievements have given strength and meaning to the family.

The family may look at the employees as "part of the family," but the employees look at the family in a more equivocal way. They might be called "family," but they can never earn an equity stake. They get salaries for helping make the Bacardis rich.

There has always been a whiff of nepotism. Some companies deal with this problem by insisting that family members be highly qualified. At the rival liquor company Brown-Forman, for example, family members have to have two college degrees. Some family companies require that a relative reach managerial position in an unrelated company, and compete on equal terms, before he or she can be hired. Such a rigid system has never been applied at Bacardi, although in recent years an informal requirement of at least two years' relevant outside experience has been put into effect.

With the dissidents' lawsuit, the "royal" family is in danger of becoming a royal pain. In corporate theory, the prevailing model of the limited-liability company is of shareholders in thrall to professional managers. In family companies it is never like that. At Bacardi, managers have had to keep one eye on the business and one on the horizon, just to make sure some aged relative from Miami or Madrid isn't raising the *grito* of rebellion and leading a posse of shareholders to overturn corporate policy. Managers have had to be not only good at their jobs but gifted students of the subtleties of family power, an exercise that at times makes pre-Gorbachev Kremlinology look simple.

The Bacardi family has always had a unique symbiosis with the business. At times, the family has been a constraint. Now — primarily because of the dissidents' intransigence — it is in danger of becoming a hindrance. Managers are asking themselves what their primary purpose is: growing the business, or catering to the emotional needs of the family. Bacardi originally succeeded because of the family. Now it is succeeding despite it.

Eddy Nielsen once wanted to keep the family involved, to have more consultation; but he has learned the hard way that there are drawbacks to family involvement. As Manuel Luis del Valle perceptively points out: "Eddy Nielsen took a democratic point of view because he came from an American culture, a democratic culture, and that was probably a negative in controlling the family. Pepín Bosch took a hard line. He was tough. He made them feel there was no substitute for himself." Once again, North American values and good intentions have foundered on the shoals of Latin American emotionalism.

The greater closeness of the Latin family is often cited in comparisons between South American and North American values. A charming story is told of an American woman in pre-Castro Havana who developed a toothache. She managed to get an early-morning dental appointment, after which she had to work. When she arrived at the dentist's office, she found, to her dismay, that the waiting room was filled with people. A little boy appeared from the surgery, holding his swollen cheek. An adult got up and took the little boy's hand, and everybody else left as well. The whole family had come along to share the *niño*'s ordeal. The anecdote indicates the extraordinary closeness of the Cuban family. Whether the boy would still want his family in the waiting room once he had grown up and become a senior executive was another matter.

While the internal dispute dragged on at Bacardi, the global liquor industry underwent the most spectacular changes it has seen in half a century. Within a couple of years in the 1980s, three of the four post-Prohibition North American giants — National, Schenley, and Hiram Walker — were swallowed up. So was Heublein, which had thrived through the success of its Smirnoff vodka, the world's number-two brand after Bacardi.

The global action had started in Britain, with the family company Pepín Bosch had once considered a model, Guinness. In 1981, the aristocratic Guinnesses had imported a professional manager, Ernest Saunders, to revitalize their flagging beer empire. Saunders had been a great success. Between 1981 and 1985, he doubled Guinness profits. Then he went on the acquisition trail with the $580-million purchase of Arthur Bell & Sons, producer of Bell's, the largest whiskey brand in the U.K and third-largest in the world. He then joined the battle for the mighty Distillers Co. Ltd., which had come under attack from an aggressive Scot named Jimmy Gulliver. Gulliver claimed that DCL had deteriorated into a group of moribund fiefdoms. DCL replied that Gulliver was "two years too late," pointing out that chairman John Connell had already revitalized the company with a new management philosophy. Saunders emerged as DCL's white knight, buying the company for $4 billion. Then somebody looked under the armor.

In 1986, Ivan Boesky, the man at the heart of the biggest insider-trading scandal in Wall Street history, began — hoping to reduce his own sentence — to name names. That of Ernest Saunders appeared in "Ivan the tenor's" libretto; the Guinness head had used Boesky to manipulate the price of Guinness stock during the takeover of Distillers. Nevertheless, the Distillers acquisition was allowed to go ahead and proved an enormously shrewd one for Guinness.

While the DCL battle was in full swing, the complex and at times acrimonious fight for control of the Canadian giant Hiram Walker/ Gooderham & Worts also broke out. Control eventually passed to Allied-Lyons PLC for a record $2.6 billion (Canadian) — at the time the largest acquisition of any North American company by an outsider. Suddenly, Guinness and Allied-Lyons, charter members of "the beer-age," had become major players on the world liquor stage.

The action did not stop there. Anthony Tennant's International Distillers and Vintners acquired Heublein — and, with it, Smirnoff — for $1.3 billion. After Saunders's disgrace, Tennant was lured over to Guinness and took the company further into U.S. spirits with the acquisition of Lewis Rosenstiel's creation, Schenley, for $480 million.

In the U.S., meanwhile, the liquor arm of American Brands, Jim Beam, swallowed National Distillers for $545 million. Only Seagram, still tightly controlled by the heirs of Sam Bronfman, and Brown-Forman, another highly successful family-controlled company, whose brands included Jack Daniels and Southern Comfort, remained untouched among the major North American players. Along, of course, with Bacardi. Within an astonishingly short time, the face of global liquor had changed beyond recognition.

The new giants also started doing deals among themselves. Allied-Lyons went on to do its own mini-merger with the giant of Japanese whiskey, another family-controlled company, Suntory. Guinness, which had already formed a powerful link with the French giant Louis Vuitton Moët Hennessy (merging their respective U.S. distribution companies to form Schieffelin & Somerset), also engaged in a hefty share swap with LVMH in 1988 and 1989. The strategic link via mini-merger that the Bacardi family had rejected in the case of Hiram Walker had become a model in the industry. Eddy Nielsen, by contrast, because of family pressures, was forced to move the other way, buying back the company's stake from Allied-Lyons.

Now that the dust has settled after all these mergers and acquisitions, the ten largest liquor companies (by case sales) control more than half the free world's spirits volume. The number-one brand is still Bacardi, which has a unique attraction: it controls its spirit category, rum, without offering any direct competition to other brands. It remains, as one Bacardi family member says, "the pretty lady" of the industry. Everybody wants to court it. But the latitude of its new de facto chief executive, Manuel Jorge Cutillas, is severely limited by the family's skittishness about "outsiders."

Bacardi has developed a relationship with Anthony Tennant's Guinness liquor arm, UDG, under which UDG distributes Bacardi products in Asia. In return, Bacardi distributes some Guinness products in Spain and Germany. The Spanish Bacardi subsidiary, Bacardi S.A., has agreed to distill Gordon's gin in Spain and handle a number of major whiskey brands there, including Johnnie Walker. Bacardi Imports has also won the U.S. distribution rights for the products of another big private company, Martini & Rossi.

But even the UDG arrangement, which involves Bacardi taking on UDG's brands rather than the other way around, has caused dark mutterings among some of the dissidents, who suggest this relationship might be the thin end of the wedge whereby the family might lose control. The anonymous letter of October 1989 accused management of "dedicating their efforts towards establishing dangerous commercial relationships with an English group. I say dangerous because are we ready for a 'marriage' after the 'courtship'?"

Older members of the family — the ones who still control the shares and hold great moral sway — have an ideal and simplistic picture of Bacardi that is increasingly out of sync with reality. In the old-timers' view, the various Bacardi companies belong to the family. They sell rum. They look after their employees. They provide jobs for family members who feel inclined to work. Dividends go up. There has to be a family member at the top. It is all very simple.

The business empire has grown farther and farther from what the family members, particularly the older members, think it is. It has also grown much more complex. It has come — quite deliberately — to have little or nothing to do with Cuba. It has found a niche in a global, commercial culture whose symbols are most often associated with the U.S., but whose reality transcends any notion of nationality. In fact, Bacardi has become the ultimate global company. It has no holding company or head office. Its most precious asset, its name, is held in a lawyer's office in Liechtenstein. Its family shareholders live in a dozen different countries. Its image depends on national preference: quality in Mexico; mixability in the U.S.; sun, sand, and sea in Europe. It is somehow appropriate that Cuban exiles — a stateless people — should control this stateless empire.

The continuing controversies surrounding *el exilio* are another reason for divorcing Bacardi from its past. It is partly the old truism that brands and politics don't mix, but it is also part of a desire among Cuban exile businessmen to get on with the future rather than dwelling in the past. But many Cubans are reluctant to let the past die. Older Bacardis in particular have such happy memories. But even those recollections are now bound up with the controversies of *el exilio*.

Each January 1, a group of Cuban exiles, including members of the Bacardi family, gather outside a humble-looking single-story building at 845 Southwest 14th Avenue, not far south of Calle Ocho in Little Havana, Miami. At noon they hoist a Cuban flag, sing the Cuban national anthem, then go inside to eat and reminisce. Emilio Bacardi's Fiesta de la Bandera lives on. The converted suburban bungalow is the headquarters of the Municipio de Santiago de Cuba in Exilio, one of a number of meeting places where exile dreams of Cuban hometowns are kept alive.

The bungalow's internal walls have been knocked out to form a large clubroom. Chairs are of the folding metal variety. The tables are covered with plastic. A piano sits along one wall under a garish cover. Above the fireplace is a collection of pictures and statues of José Martí. Cuban and American flags are on display. Old photographs of Santiago's El Morro and cathedral line the walls. The Municipio's presidents of honor are Felipe Valls, owner of the Versailles restaurant on Calle Ocho, where Cuban exiles come to eat and talk politics; Tony Cuesta, the man who paid such a heavy price for his quixotic speedboat attack on Havana in the 1960s; and Pepín Bosch.

The January/February 1989 edition of *El Cubano Libre*, the official organ of Santiago de Cuba in exile, carries an account of the Fiesta and a full-page editorial calling for "Liberty for Orlando Bosch." A pediatrician, Orlando Bosch (no relation to Pepín) was acquitted of complicity in the bombing of a Cubana airliner in 1976, when all seventy-three passengers were killed, including the Cuban national fencing team. But he was convicted of, among other terrorist

acts, shelling a Polish freighter in the port of Miami. Orlando Bosch —
"You have to fight violence with violence" — is considered a hero by
the Cuban exile community. The Miami City Commission has declared March 25 "Dr. Orlando Bosch Day," but the doctor's approach
to politics causes uneasiness among Miami Anglos and Bacardi's
American customers, as does the sporadic violence elsewhere in the
exile community.

The Bacardi family has not separated itself from the local exile
community — Manuel Jorge Cutillas is a trustee of the Cuban American National Foundation, as is another, Puerto Rico–based member
of the family, José Bacardi González. But the continuing undertone
of violence is one of several reasons why Bacardi does not tout itself
as a "Cuban" company.

Another reason is Mariel. The Mariel exodus in 1980 started with
a small group of Cubans seeking refuge in the Peruvian embassy in
Havana. Peru refused to hand them over. Castro responded by
bulldozing down the embassy gates. Tens of thousands of Cubans
used the opportunity to seek asylum on embassy grounds. Castro
eventually allowed them to leave but attempted to poison the exodus
by emptying prison cells and psychiatric wards into the refugee throng.
Of the 125,000 Cubans who were taken, mostly in small boats, from
the port of Mariel to Florida, 26,000 had prison records and hundreds
more were certifiably insane.

This exodus — coming as it did around the time of the black riots
in the Miami ghetto of Liberty City and the influx of Haitian
refugees — placed a strain on Miami's social services. It also led to a
change in the image of Cuban exiles. Until then it had been Ricky
Ricardo and hard work. (In fact, even Ricky Ricardo had a complex
past. Desi Arnaz's father had worked for Enrique Schueg and become
mayor of Santiago, but he had also been a supporter of the dictator
Machado. When his dictatorship crumbled, in 1933, the teenaged
Desi had been brought as a political exile by his family to Miami.
The Arnaz family continued to hold shares in the original Bacardi
company.) After Mariel the image is tainted by violence and drug
money. In reality, the *marielitos* have been relatively quickly absorbed,
but the controversy remains. Cubans are now easily confused with
Colombians.

The Bacardis remain proud of their heritage and are prepared to
work for the exile cause. Whenever Cubans wash up, on homemade
rafts or old inner tubes, on the beaches of Nassau, local family
members are always there to help. But exile problems are sometimes

messy and often tragic. One of the saddest chapters in the long exile struggle was the suicide in September 1989 of Pepe Pérez San Román, the Cuban commander at the Bay of Pigs invasion. Pérez San Román, who had a history of depression, finally ended his misery with a drug overdose in a Miami trailer park.

The violence, tragedy, and controversy of *el exilio* have further encouraged Bacardi to mold the brand's non-specific and global nature. As Juan Grau puts it, "We have aimed to lower frontiers. We don't want to be seen as having a particular nationality." This approach is very much at odds with the way the older family members view the company, but these older members are now passing on, leaving a middle-aged group whose associations with Bacardi are primarily of the post-Cuban empire. Then comes a generation with little or no direct knowledge of Cuba at all.

Meanwhile, the genetic "family" is now so large that it strains meaningful definition. The outer fronds of the tree are sprouting new members geometrically, in different countries, speaking different languages. There are now more than 200 shareholders, and several hundred more children waiting to inherit stakes in the five main Bacardi companies. In another generation, family shareholders will number in the thousands, presenting an impossibly unwieldy group whose only common interest will be financial. As Manuel Jorge Cutillas says: "We are slowly turning the company into a private enterprise with many shareholders who happen to be family. It's going to be a private company owned by different families."

Within that inevitable transition, the question of the dissidents remains unresolved. In the view of Manuel Jorge Cutillas, and most of the management and family, there is now only one solution: the dissidents should sell out. Cutillas has hired New York–based Morgan Guaranty Trust Co. to draw up a buyout proposal. Whether the dissidents are likely to sell is another matter. Daniel Bacardi has always told his children that Bacardi shares aren't something you sell; they are something you pass on, a patrimony. Putting a price on patrimony is no easy thing.

The Bacardi family, as it enters the 1990s, has turned into a large group of rich people squabbling over emotional and often trivial issues. With the exception of a handful of family executives, the empire could function just as well without them. Indeed, if the entire family disappeared tomorrow, one might argue, the empire would be better off.

Before writing off the vagaries and emotionalism of these private shareholders, and to put the whole affair in perspective, it would perhaps be well to consider the alternative. Rarely is it possible to look at how things might have been. In this case, however, it is possible to travel to a parallel future in which people like the Bacardis have been eradicated or driven out, a place where the wealth of society is determined not by the private efforts of businessmen but by the public good intentions of government: Castro's Cuba, thirty years on.

CHAPTER TWENTY

Cuba Libre?

"Let the cannibal who snarls that the
freedom of man's mind was needed
to create an industrial civilization,
but is not needed to maintain it, be
given an arrowhead and a bearskin,
not a university chair of economics."
AYN RAND, *ATLAS SHRUGGED*

Havana. January 1990

The words "Edificio Bacardi" are still etched above the entrance to the building that stands — like an indictment — on Havana's Avenida Bélgica. Its intricate wrought-iron window-covers still sport a "B" in the middle. At the pinnacle of the building, the glass sphere surmounted by a bat with spread wings remains a defiant symbol of the trademark Castro never got and of the Bacardis' flight from the Cuban revolution. The passage of time and the Castro regime's neglect show in the cracks in the building's elegant, decorated facade, and in the absence of one of the two hefty gilded lanterns that used to flank its imposing, triple-doored entrance.

The Bacardi building's decorative cornucopias seem cruelly ironic in the crisis-ridden Cuba of today. The bat looks over the sad ruin of a once-beautiful city. Havana seems like something out of the Twilight Zone. The most often-remarked symbols of the time warp are the big, round-fendered Chevrolets, Pontiacs, and Fords from the 1950s, the ghosts of capitalism past, which glide along amid increasing numbers of Soviet Ladas.

Havana's hotels are prerevolutionary not merely in structure but in furniture and fittings. The only differences between the Havana Hilton of pre-Castro Cuba and the Havana Libre of today are the name, thirty years of grime, and worse service. The once-magnificent walkway of the Prado — the centerpiece of Old Havana — has cracked paving stones and broken lamps. The buildings flanking it are in disrepair. Amid universal scarcity, the most obviously scarce commodity is paint.

Traces of the Bacardis survive in Havana: not merely the office, but also some Bacardi dwellings. The problem is to find them. In a country without telephone books or street directories, it is hard enough to discover where people live now, let alone where exiles lived thirty years ago. Many of the big, opulent Bacardi homes were taken for "official" purposes, to house military, party, or diplomatic activities, or simply by senior party officials for their own use. As such, they are off limits. The former home of the founder's granddaughter Doña Amalia, whose letter to Eddy Nielsen triggered the family war, is now the Panamanian embassy. The big, rambling bungalow of the founder's grandson Luis J. Bacardi is now the Institute for Tropical Medicine. Hardly anybody in Cuba now remembers Amalia or Luis J. Bacardi. Only in the Cuban rum industry and the city of Santiago, does the aroma of the Bacardi name linger like a well-aged Añejo.

In *Our Man in Havana*, Graham Greene's hero, Wormold, the vacuum-cleaner salesman and part-time spy, sits at one point with the sinister Captain Segura in the Havana Club, a place "owned by Bacardi's rival." Today, the rum brand Havana Club has no Cuban rivals. Having been expropriated from its owners, its brand name — unlike Bacardi's — now belongs to the Castro dictatorship.

The Havana Club plant, at Santa Cruz del Norte, on the coast 25 miles east of Havana, looks badly run down. On one side of the main office building's vestibule, up a flight of stairs, past a huge portrait of Che Guevara, is the compulsory shrine to Cuban–Soviet friendship. In addition to large photographs of Fidel Castro and Mikhail Gorbachev, it features dramatic renditions of Lenin — Lenin holding forth to enthusiastic workers; Lenin posing behind his desk; Lenin framed by red velvet, with a mob in the background; Lenin outdoors, sporting his famous cap and wearing an overcoat; Lenin leaning forward at an improbable angle, like the figurehead on the prow of a ship, looking confidently into the future. Beneath the shrine, dust gathers and paint peels from the walls.

In the company's Protocol Room, with its rummage-sale furnishings, the plant's research director — a wary and harried-looking man — gives a potted history of the plant. Before the "triumph of the revolution" (the phrase by which Cubans and sympathetic Westerners have been taught to designate the events of 1959), this had been a small plant. In 1972, Castro, El Comandante, announced the desirability of expansion, and the plant was extended in several stages. Its capacity had been boosted to 30 million litres of rum a year. The plant was now producing less than a third of that because the major export market, the U.S.S.R., had been sent cold turkey by Mikhail Gorbachev back in 1985. Gorbachev had not only hauled millions of cases of vodka off the shelves, he had also stopped bulk rum imports.

And the Bacardis?

"The Bacardis," says the research director, "lost all knowledge of making good rum when they left Cuba, because they lost the aging facilities and the people, the best rum production men. The people with the experience didn't leave Cuba. Rum production is associated with our nationality. We kept the talent, and we reorganized the rum production under the direction of the people. It was easy to take over rum production after these people left the country. Rum production was not a secret."

Were the Bacardis good employers? "I think," the technical director says carefully, "that the Bacardis had good relations with their workers. I think maybe it was so in Santiago. I have heard nobody speak badly of the Bacardis. Also, the Bacardis have contributed to the propaganda of rum production in the world. But it is not possible for them to produce good rum. They produce too much."

That remark says more about Communism than about the Bacardis. Under the rigidities of central planning, and the laxities of a system in which no individual owns anything — and thus nobody has or wants responsibility — more quantity invariably means less quality.

"We know," he concludes, "that if we were put into the same conditions, had the same facilities, and could afford the same advertising, well, it would be very difficult for Bacardi."

The Bacardi factory in Santiago de Cuba still sits on the old Calle Matadero, opposite the railway tracks. Across the building's cornice, atop red-painted globes, sit a row of bats with spread wings, relatives of the bat that looks out from the Edificio Bacardi in Havana. The factory is virtually as the Bacardis left it in 1960. The storage facilities are full to bursting, further evidence of Gorbachev's 1985 attempt to solve one of Communism's main productivity problems — inebriated or hung-over workers — by treating symptoms rather than causes.

Inside the building, women workers sit chatting in the dim light. The bottling line stands idle. The only significant additions to the vestibule since 1960 are the ubiquitous portraits of Castro and Gorbachev. In an alcove in the vestibule, on a low table, lies the old, leather-bound book that contains the certificates won by Bacardi rum at industrial exhibitions around the turn of the century — Barcelona, Bordeaux, Panama, Buffalo, Seville, and a dozen other places. The book is populated with engraved nymphs and other classical figures, bearing anachronistic gear wheels and hammers, symbols of industrial progress. The book also contains the certificate of Bacardi's appointment as purveyors to the Spanish royal household. On the wall of the alcove are grainy black-and-white pictures of earlier Bacardi buildings on the site and of the now-deceased "faithful palm."

In the building's upstairs lobby, three soldiers, clad in revolutionary olive green, lounge about. The office section contains dusty desks, filing cabinets, and typewriters, all circa 1960. At some of the desks, dour-looking women, cooled by large electric fans, pore over Dickensian ledgers. Along a narrow hallway, through a door with a low beam, and down more stairs is a dimly lit bar. Apart from recent posters of scantily clad Cuban maidens, nothing here seems to have changed in thirty years.

Few workers remember the Bacardis, but Guillermo Dehesa does. An ebullient seventy-year-old, he started with Bacardi as a messenger in 1938. Pepín Bosch made him an executive in 1957, two years before Castro seized power. After the revolution, he became a "statistician." He is still a statistician today. "Anybody who says anything bad about the Bacardis will have to answer to me," he says, with little obvious concern for the official categorization of the Bacardis as "capitalist exploiters."

At the mention of each retired Bacardi executive or family member — Daniel, Joaquín, Luis del Rosal, José Argamasilla — Dehesa's face lights up and he beams: "Un muy amigo mío." Pepín Bosch does not fall into that category. He was more aloof. Dehesa describes him as a man with *mucha presencia*, who didn't take to him at first (most likely because Dehesa had worked under José Espín). But he says that Bosch wrote to him not many years earlier "in a lovely, firm hand."

Dehesa disappears and returns with three crisp black-and-white photographs and a brochure. The first shot is of a company tribute to Pepín Bosch, a group photograph of smiling executives raising glasses around the small, bald, benign-looking Bacardi president. The second picture is of a sales meeting in Varadero in the mid-1950s. Dehesa is presenting a prize to a salesman; Daniel sits in the foreground. The final snap is of another executive gathering — the avuncular-looking Bosch, flanked by Daniel and José Argamasilla, sits behind a table. The clarity of the pictures, the smartness of the executives in their lightweight suits, the smiles of pride and happiness all come from a sunnier time. In the conventional wisdom about Cuban history, of course, this was the "before" than which the present is so much better.

The pamphlet is from the company's 1954 sales meeting. Inside the front cover is a picture of Daniel. On the opposite page is a message about what motivated the Bacardis. It says the Bacardis loved their country, and desired only one title, "él de buenos cubanos" (that of good Cubans). Nobody here argues with that claim. But it raises a question: if the Bacardis were such good Cubans, why did Fidel Castro see fit to expropriate them?

The Castro regime is not sufficiently well organized to have an Orwellian Ministry of Truth to change or obliterate the past. The Bacardis have remained a sore point. A number of magazine articles and at least one slim "history" of the family business have been published in Cuba.

Origins of the Bacardi Rum Company, by Nicolás Torres Hurtado, was published in Santiago de Cuba in 1982. In its introduction, Jorge Aldana, of the University of Oriente's faculty of philosophy and history, declares: "Since the triumph of the revolution . . . articles, essays, and monographs have begun to appear on economic themes, which devote themselves to a fundamental uncovering of economic relations, penetration of monopoly capital, and the indiscriminate robbery of our wealth that North American imperialism has realized with impunity for more than fifty years."

Hurtado's sprint through Bacardi's history — profits are evidence of capitalist guilt — ends with the inevitable accusatory finger pointed at the family: "The most characteristic idea of capitalist exploitation, its anti-patriotic essence, contrary to the genuine interests of the nation, manifests itself in the export of these profits, produced by the sweat of the working class, in the form of investment in other countries; while, on the other hand, with unheard-of indifference, they allow the cancer of unemployment, and moral and cultural backwardness, to grow." Hurtado concludes: "The fundamental objective of this work has served to show the inequality existing in the relations of production between the capitalists and the working class, to establish how the profits obtained by the capitalists at the cost of the proletariat hold back the cultural, economic, and educational progress of the country."

In fact, nothing of the sort is demonstrated, or even attempted.

Cuban history books do not lead via arguments and facts to conclusions: the conclusions come first. There is no need to "prove" the evils of "capitalist exploitation" or show how it has held back the nation's "cultural, economic, and educational progress." In Marxist ideology, these are not assumptions to be examined, they are the "facts" from which the dogma flows.

Some Communist articles on Bacardi reluctantly admit that working conditions at the company were good, but note sourly that it was difficult to get work in the factory. Cubans, it seems, were tripping over themselves to work for the "capitalist exploiters"; but the Bacardis were guilty of giving priority to their own family and to the relatives of Bacardi workers. Tourists at the Bacardi factory in Santiago have been told that the Bacardis were partners in the enterprise with Al Capone. Devoid of real ammunition, the Communists turn to the standby of racism (one of the evils of the old regime that would melt away under Castro's Communism, but never did). One article declares: "It was even said that Negroes weren't allowed to work in the factory because their smell affected the aroma of the rum."

Workers have been quoted in Communist periodicals as praising Pepín Bosch, or at least saying that work was better under him than it had been. But Bosch's success is inevitably given a sinister gloss. "Thus," claims one such piece, "in the hands of Pepín Bosch, Bacardi extended its tentacles to previously unthinkable limits." Such articles always come back to the wicked-capitalists notion, to the claim that "the greatest rum in the world only enriched a privileged clan of a very different kind from those who had worked twelve hours a day and struggled for the independence of Cuba."

The impressive neo-classical building of the Museo Municipal Emilio Bacardi Moreau still sits in a little square in the midst of Santiago's quaint, narrow one-way streets. Its founder's name remains inscribed above the portico's double Corinthian columns. The interior of the building has been subject to a plasterboard "renovation." The entrance leads to a drab foyer with flat, dirty walls and cheap, boxlike benches. In the lobby is a display case with some personal effects of Emilio and his second wife, Elvira Cape: a finely wrought jewelry box, some delicate reading glasses, a gold-embossed fountain pen. The quality of their workmanship mocks the surroundings.

Much of Emilio's original collection remains in the museum.

Display cases are filled with pre-Columbian artifacts, remnants of the Spanish empire and the slave trade, and armaments from the revolutions of the nineteenth century. The second floor is still devoted primarily to the museum's art collection. In a small, dimly lit side gallery, Emilio's Eighteenth Dynasty mummy looks like a camper incinerated in his sleeping bag. Ancient packing material gazes out from the eye sockets of the skull, which still has a few teeth. The gallery also contains two Peruvian mummies, doubled up in the fetal position, jaws open in a permanent death scream.

The art gallery is open to the town's humidity. Many paintings have no frames and are chipped at the edges. The works by local artists include two delicate watercolors by Emilio Bacardí, of a *fusilero* and a *picador*. There are also two sculptures by Emilio's daughter Mimín, one a dramatic, tortured bust of the Indian chief Hatuey, his head pulled to one side; the other a strange, almost surreal, figure of a Negro girl looking down in comic horror at a frog crawling up her body. Female attendants wilt in the heat, their faces blank, their eyes reflexively following visitors, whom they outnumber.

A few miles east of the museum, Vista Alegre remains a neighborhood of large, spacious houses, set amid luxuriant greenery. Once the homes of Santiago's wealthy, they are now state offices or homes for the Communist party elite. The house that Pepín Bosch's father built, the Bosch Palace, stands on a wide boulevard divided by neglected flowerbeds. Behind ornate iron gates, surrounded by bougainvillea and palms, the mansion is still a twin-turreted dream of opulence, painted in pastel blue and white. It is now occupied by Santiago's branch of Cuba's revolutionary youth movement, the Pioneers. Above a sign announcing "Pioneer Palace" is a large, almost psychedelic poster of Che Guevara, an aureole surrounding his head. It features a mystic quote from Fidel: "Che: Un Gigante que se levanta" (Che: a rising giant). To the left of the building, mounted beside a dusty playground, sits a less mystical revolutionary symbol: a MiG-15 jet fighter.

The Pioneers are claimed to be Cuba's equivalent of the Boy Scouts, but a closer look at the building's contents betrays something more militant. Inside the house, on the first floor, is an innocuous enough black-and-white photograph. It shows a smiling Fidel Castro and a group of dignitaries, including Michael Manley, sometime prime minister of Jamaica, facing the mansion. On the second floor, however, there are hand-drawn posters showing how to construct booby traps by placing spiked crosses at the bottom of concealed pits. There are also diagrams of anti-tank devices.

A Cuban Rip Van Winkle who had fallen asleep in 1962 and woken up today might imagine that there had been many other invasions similar to the Bay of Pigs. He would imagine that the tensions of the Cuban Missile Crisis had not abated. It would take him some time to realize that Che Guevara had been dead for more than twenty years. Che's hirsute cult image — Christ in a beret — is everywhere, painted on the sides of buildings, hanging in vestibules, staring down from office walls. Posters exhort the populace to be "ready for defense." Leaflets describe what to do in the event of a poison-gas attack, or a massive surprise air raid.

This state of "continuous revolution" is cited — like the state of continuous war in Orwell's *1984* — as the excuse for economic failure and political repression in Cuba. Apologists for Castro, of whom there is no shortage, particularly in the Western world's academic communities, argue that no judgment should be made of Cuba without due consideration of its history — in particular, the U.S. economic "domination" for the first sixty years of this century that went hand in glove with corrupt dictatorships. Castro's emergence is easier to understand against this historical backdrop, but to understand what happened is not necessarily to condone it.

Goethe once said that the writing of history helps liberate us from the weight of the past. The purpose of what passes for history in Cuba is to do exactly the opposite: to impose a perpetual burden of guilt upon the people and bind them into the straitjacket of Marxism-Leninism. History — the independent inquiry into, and interpretation of, the past — has been dead in Cuba for thirty years.

As you drive down the hill from the airport into the scorching caldron of Santiago de Cuba, there, high on a hill, in huge letters, stand the words SIEMPRE ES 26 (It's always the 26th). Although the heroes of the struggle against Spain in the nineteenth century are feted as the predecessors of Castro's revolutionaries, history for Cubans has been reduced to a handful of events: Moncada in 1953, the *Granma* "invasion" in 1956, and the "triumph of the revolution" in 1959. The attack on Moncada gave its date to the 26 July Movement.

The principal shrine of the Castro revolution, Moncada is now part museum and part school. The museum entrance is set in a wall peppered with reconstructed bullet holes, carefully matched to photographs of those from the 1953 raid. The entrance leads to a chamber of horrors, filled with photographs of martyred revolutionaries, display cases of the torture instruments of the Batista regime, and exhibits of homemade armaments used by Castro and his *barbudos* in the Sierra Maestra. Items of Castro's clothing and blood-stained uniforms of the Moncada revolutionaries are displayed like religious relics. In a courtyard, under a canopy, is the sacred truck in which Castro, following his capture, was brought back to Santiago.

On the road between Santiago and the farm at Siboney, where the young terrorists gathered before the attack, there are monuments named for the Moncada martyrs. These are the revolution's secular Stations of the Cross. Siboney too features "restored" bullet holes. Photographic blow-ups and displays in the farmhouse tell the same grisly story. Some of the "relics" border on the surreal. There is even a blow-up of the bill from the Santiago restaurant where twenty of the revolutionaries ate before the assault. On it, the faithful can see that the martyrs ordered twenty chickens-with-rice, twenty salads, and twenty orders of bread and butter. It is analogous to seeing the tab from the Last Supper.

Pictures of young revolutionaries, lying in pools of blood, are reproduced again and again in Cuban history books and in public museums and displays, including some at the Museo Municipal Emilio Bacardi Moreau. The message is simple: they shed their lifeblood for the revolution; they died for you. To argue with the revolution is to spurn their sacrifice, commit a crime against the dead. Ironically, the majority of those who died at Moncada were staunch opponents of Communism. They wanted free elections and the enactment of the liberal 1940 constitution. But the dead cannot assert their convictions, and their bloodstained images have been recruited to a cause they would have found repugnant.

Screaming headlines, reproduced from pre-revolutionary newspapers, accuse Batista of being an assassin and condemn his regime. The headlines show there was at least a free press before the revolution. Batista kept much of the press tame through bribery; Castro simply shut down all opposition. Criticism of the regime now carries a potentially stiff jail sentence. Dissent in any form has been made almost impossible in Cuba today through a system of Committees for the Defence of the Revolution, or CDRs. The CDRs are Big Brother surrogates on every street in the country. Castro outlined their purpose in 1960. "We're going to set up a system of revolutionary collective vigilence so that everybody will know everybody else on his block, what they do, what relationship they had with the tyranny (i.e. Batista), what they believe in, what people they meet, what activities they participate in . . . When the masses are organized, there isn't a single imperialist, or lackey of the imperialists, or anybody who has sold out to the imperialists, who can operate."

Since a Cuban needs CDR approval to obtain housing, gain admission to university, or land a job, opting out is not a possibility. Enthusiasm for the revolution is the required stance for anyone not wishing to live a marginalized existence. CDR members take turns "patrolling" the local neighborhood looking for "criminal or anti-social" behavior. This includes not merely criticizing the regime but attending church, listening to Radio Martí (the Miami-based Cuban exile station), or having "unexplained wealth" (an offence under the criminal code). Any contact with foreigners is regarded with suspicion. This system forces Cubans to wear two faces: a public face, and one they feel safe wearing only among those they trust with their lives. Foreigners rarely are told what Cubans think. Only older people, such as Guillermo Dehesa, who have little to lose, feel free to speak their minds.

Material standards in Cuba are low, and maintained only with Soviet support, which is estimated to run as high as $7 billion annually. Most of the urban population lives in overcrowded hovels. Food and important consumer goods are rationed. This economic under performance has always been blamed on the fact that Cuba is a Third World nation, or that the costs of its constant defensive awareness are exorbitant. In truth, economic failure and political repression go hand in hand.

After the 1960 takeover of Cuban business, small-scale private enterprise was permitted until 1968. With the help of the CDRs, it was stamped out in a week. A speech Castro made at the time shows his distaste for the profit motive. "Are we going to construct socialism, or are we going to construct vending stands?" he asked. "We did not make a revolution here to establish the right to trade! . . . When will they finally understand that this is a revolution of socialists, that this is a revolution of Communists . . . that nobody shed his blood here fighting against tyranny, against mercenaries, against bandits, in order to establish the right for somebody to make 200 pesos selling rum." All economic activity, then, had to be based on honor, morals, and principles. It also had to be controlled by the state. Cubans, like most people, want material incentives, but material incentives in Cuba are meant to be base, even sacrilegious, beside the blood of the martyrs.

In the mid-1980s, Castro allowed free markets in agricultural produce, but they worked too well. Consumers were able to buy the produce they craved, but farmers began to make money. The markets were closed down. In factories, the charade of working for the revolution rather than for personal gain is kept up by a system of "voluntary" labor. The hidden carrot for volunteering, of course, is that it moves one up the list for rationed items like refrigerators. The not-so-hidden stick lies in the psychological tyranny of the CDRs. Not to volunteer is considered "anti-social behavior."

The source of Cuba's economic problems is not its sugar-based economy. Nor is it the country's Third World status, which has been acquired rather than inherited. Cuba had railways before most of Europe, a steam engine before the U.S., and more televisions in 1958 than Italy. Cuba is an example not of a struggling poor country but of a rich country gone to seed via revolution. The root cause of its abysmal economic performance is the lack of economic freedoms and financial incentives, and the inflexibility and inefficiency of Communist central planning.

The economy has always been subject, like every other aspect of Cuban life, to Castro's whim. Across the lobby of the Edificio Bacardi in Havana hangs a banner: LO MÁS IMPORTANTE ES CUMPLIR LA MISIÓN PLANTEADA POR FIDEL — SIEMPRE LISTOS PARA LA DEFENSA (The most important thing is to fulfill the mission outlined by Fidel — always ready for defense). The economic mission outlined by Fidel seems to change every month. First, he was going to end dependence on sugar; then he decided to place even more emphasis upon it. Giant plants have been built with no raw materials to supply them. The economy has lurched from one crisis to another.

In Castro's Cuba, personal initiative is the least prized of qualities. To seek responsibility is merely to court blame for failure. Devoid of incentives, workers turn to negative satisfactions, to the exercise of their tiny piece of bureaucratic power.

Fidel Castro claimed that he needed absolute power as a countervailing force to the huge power wielded by capitalists and "monopolists." It is perhaps worth comparing the power of Pepín Bosch with that of Fidel Castro, and the achievements of Bacardi with those of its nemesis.

As a businessman, Pepín Bosch had the power to create jobs; as an owner, to create wealth for himself and his fellow family shareholders; as a Cuban and *santiaguero*, to nurture the culture of his country and his city; as a reluctant public servant, to use his skills to straighten out the finances of the country. To be sure, when Bacardi was threatened by expropriation, or when its export markets had erected tariff barriers, he also had the power to build overseas plants. But this geographical diversification was also a response to global opportunities, and by seizing such opportunities Bacardi became Cuba's first multinational, a fact of which Cubans might well be proud. Pepín Bosch's power was rational and ultimately positive. It was never whimsical.

It was said that some people feared Bosch. What they feared was his demands. He expected them to deliver the "Message to García." It was said that he was hard on people, and certainly his demands proved tough on his sons. It was said that he did emotional damage to the Bacardis by ignoring them, or not bothering to listen when they thought they had useful advice. But it is ludicrous to equate the sort of "fear" associated with Pepín Bosch to the sort of dread Cubans feel at the prospect of a knock on the door in the middle of the night.

The men who run the Bacardi plant in Santiago today seem decent enough, but they are no more than creatures on a treadmill under Castro's system. The whole enterprise appears like some industrial *Marie Céleste* that has floated rudderless for thirty years. The technical director at Santa Cruz del Norte, too, seems at heart a decent man. But he mouths the central fallacy of all expropriatory socialist regimes: that entrepreneurs and capitalists are not the most, but the least, essential part of the industrial process; that what they have built can easily be taken over, maintained, and improved by "the people." It is tantamount to the belief that a body could work just as well if the head were cut off. After all, the limbs are what does the work.

Cuban exiles are driven to distraction not merely by what Fidel Castro has done to their country but by the way in which his horrors have been justified, and the past rewritten, by Western liberal writers and academics. Those who rejoice at the literacy of Cuban children under Castro seldom consider what these children have to read. Books from outside the country are rigidly vetted; books produced in Cuba are rigorously censored. Journalism consists primarily of the propaganda of the single daily, *Granma*. Since *glasnost* and *perestroika*, even Soviet publications have been banned.

Sure, Fidel's supporters admit, Cuba has its problems. But it's so much better than it was before. Besides, we shouldn't judge by our "ethnocentric" or, worse, "Eurocentric" standards. Fidel *means* well. He's a moral man. Look at all he's done for medicine and education. And he's so charismatic. He makes tremendous speeches; he's so good with children. Perhaps Cubans aren't free to leave Cuba, but just look at other Third World countries. You might be free to leave Mali, but you can't because you're starving. At least Cubans are fed.

Western journalists and sympathetic academics go on flying visits to Cuba, are squired around by the Communist party, and return to write "balanced" views of Cuba's condition, reproducing these homilies. Typical was a 1986 report in a Canadian magazine, *Maclean's*: "Even the severest critics of Castro's regime acknowledge that the majority of Cubans are now better fed, healthier and better educated than before his takeover." Had the writer, one wondered, seen a Cuban's diet? Had she ever been treated in a Cuban hospital? Did she know the substance of Cuban education? Did she have any idea of what Cuba was really like "before his takeover"?

In a dictatorship, it is easy to place emphasis where it looks good. In fact, the case can be made that Cuba's health system is unbalanced: all brain scans and no Band-Aids. As for the education system, it is more precisely a system of indoctrination. Nor is there reason to think that Cubans eat better now than they did before the revolution. Indeed, to see the average Cuban's diet today, it is hard to imagine that he could *ever* have eaten much worse.

That paragraph from *Maclean's* typifies the easy summation of the excuses that modern liberal thinkers seek for the Castro revolution. It is a revolution with "compassion"; it might have economic problems, but its heart is in the right place. One favorite line chanted by the faithful is: "If only Fidel knew what was going on!" If he knew the daily reality, in other words, he'd set things straight. Exactly the same line could be heard in the Soviet Union in the 1930s and 1940s. "If only Stalin knew."

The door of the dilapidated wooden house on Santiago's Calle 10 Octubre is answered by a frail old woman wearing spectacles. With her gray hair tied back tightly in a bun, she has the quiet and efficient air of a retired librarian. The house consists of one large room, with a curtained sleeping section. Behind the half-open curtain, curled up sideways, lies a nut-brown old man, dressed in baby-blue pajama bottoms. The old lady goes to wake him up, drawing the curtain behind her.

Daylight shows through the planks of the house, but the interior is neat and clean. The walls are painted pink, the sleeping area blue. The furnishings look as if they have known better surroundings. Victorian wicker-backed rocking chairs sit on a scrubbed tile floor. There is a glass-fronted china cabinet. On one wall, above hanging ornaments, is a picture of Christ the Redeemer, rays emerging from behind his head, looking remarkably like the picture of Che outside the Pioneer Palace. Next to it is a painting of an old man with a long gray beard, wearing a black coat and sporting a large medal. An elaborate light fixture hangs from the ceiling. In one corner stands an ancient television; in another, a hand-painted wooden radio.

After a few minutes, the figure in the baby-blue pajama bottoms shuffles out. Santiago Wanton, now in his eighties, is almost blind, but his cataract-covered eyes brighten at the mention of Pepín Bosch. "Pepín!" he exclaims. He has been worried about him; he sent postcards but there was no reply. How was he? Was he well?

Santiago Wanton's affection for Pepín Bosch may seem unusual, for Wanton was once head of the Bacardi labor union. If anyone could tell of "capitalist exploiters," he could. But that is not the story he tells as he leans forward in the rocking chair, his dim eyes looking back to a brighter past. Like Guillermo Dehesa, Santiago Wanton speaks of the long ago as if it were just yesterday. His memories go back to Bacardi's problems with the Machado dictatorship. He recalls the labor troubles when Luis J. and José Espín were in charge, but says that when Bosch took over, things changed greatly. "Pepín got on very well with the workers, and was very kind to them." Asked about Bosch's departure, the old man says sadly: "He left with all the others. I always hoped that one day he would come back."

Santiago Wanton says he still hopes to see Pepín Bosch again. His wife notes softly that, given his eyesight, that would be difficult. They both chuckle. "The world," says Santiago Wanton, "has a great need of men like Pepín Bosch."

Epilogue

Lyford Cay, the Bahamas. July 1988

"Well," says Pepín Bosch, sitting in the big cluttered living room of his house at Lyford Cay, overlooking the pleasure craft in the cerulean waters of the inlet. He has been asked about the war among the Bacardis, and he answers with the careful candor of an old man. "The way that Mr. Schueg operated the company was for the benefit of all the stockholders. We kept them informed of anything they wanted to know or see. I don't know much because, you see, I sold my shares. I wanted to end my life in peace and tranquility, and I didn't want to be bothered with what was happening in Bacardi. But there is a difference now. They operate in a different way. They don't want the stockholders to know. They tell them as little as they possibly can. They have different ideas . . .

"Of course, I am of the opinion that the thing is not to go and buy something you don't know anything about. I wouldn't want to go into electronics. I have been a banker, but I wouldn't consider myself a trader. I know, if I was the head of Bacardi, what I would do. But I will not say. It is not sufficient to know, you have to have the ability and the knowledge.

"The problem they have, in my estimation, is that Edwin Nielsen hates to be questioned. It was different from the way I acted. If anyone asked me a question, I answered. It's a question of political sense. I have political sense. I was born with it. I have gone to conventions of parties in America."

Bosch, although not by reputation given to self-delusion, seems to be imposing a more democratic view of his own leadership than indicated by any of those who ever worked for him. He also obviously still carries considerable bitterness about the events of 1976. And though he may not want to be bothered with Bacardi, he played an important role in the present dispute. Daniel Bacardi, the dissident leader, spent most of his life working with Pepín Bosch and in awe of him. It was to Bosch that he turned for advice in the summer of 1986. It was Bosch who called Romy Martínez to ask about legal advice, and it was Bosch who vetted Sam Butler. He may not be the dissidents' éminence grise, but his moral support is of crucial importance to

Daniel. He is almost certainly not sorry to see Eddy Nielson's discomfort. That is only human nature.

One of Bosch's remarks about the dispute — "This would never have happened in my time" — has been treated, rather as José Martí's statements are cited equally by Fidel Castro and those who oppose him, as providing support for *both* sides in the dispute. Eddy Nielson and Manuel Jorge Cutillas take it to mean that he would have stamped on the dissidents, or ignored them; the dissidents take it to mean that he would never have made the mistakes that they feel justify their rebellion.

Bosch realizes perhaps better than anybody that there is nothing noble about the Bacardis' internal wrangling. Capitalist ownership carries responsibilities. The Bacardis have always realized that. It is now their responsibility to ensure that their internal disputes do not damage the company they are so proud to own. The dissidents claim they are fighting because of the company's failures, but what they are really fighting about is control of the empire's enormous success.

Preoccupied, Pepín Bosch gets slowly to his feet and goes to the kitchen. He has much more important things on his mind than the squabbling Bacardis.

By the spring of 1990, Communist regimes in Hungary, Czechoslovakia, Romania, and Poland were in retreat or had already been defeated at the polls. In the Soviet Union, Mikhail Gorbachev had unleashed an uncontrollable flood of expectations. Lithuania was challenging Soviet authority, and Gorbachev was booed at the May Day parade in Red Square. The Berlin Wall had crumbled, and East and West Germany were heading toward reunification under a democratic system.

In Central America, the ousting of General Manuel Noriega in Panama and the electoral defeat of Daniel Ortega in Nicaragua had put the Castro regime under unprecedented pressure. The critical issue was whether Gorbachev would — or could — continue to subsidize Castro. By March 1990, even the *Moscow News* was describing Cuba as an impoverished police state, whose stability depended only on its degree of repression.

One of the ironies of the startlingly rapid collapse of Communism around the world was that the hammer and sickle was being eclipsed not by the Stars and Stripes but by the golden arches of McDonald's. For the Bacardi bat to fly once more over Cuba would be an even more profound and symbolic victory for Pepín Bosch. The Bacardi empire — with its gleaming plants and well-paid workers — is a monument to capitalist endeavor and pride of ownership.

In 1990, the precariousness of Castro's rule was, ironically, drawing Pepín Bosch back to his Bacardi roots. Despite his own pain from the circumstances of his departure, and the family's shock and dismay at the sale of his stake in the empire, Bosch has never lost contact with the Bacardis. Manuel Jorge Cutillas lives and operates out of Nassau. A gaggle of Bacardis have places at Lyford Cay, including Alberto's brothers Jorge and Joaquín, and Luis Gómez del Campo. A constant stream of family members visit the island. They are always bumping into one another at the airport — where the band plays "Yellow Bird," and the holidaymakers stream through on their way to the glass-bottom boats and the one-armed bandits. Older members of the family — in particular Daniel — have continued to call Pepín for advice, or just to stay in touch. By early 1990, the situation in Cuba promised to reunite Bosch and the family: they might really be going back.

An excited Bosch made more frequent calls to Daniel and José Argamasilla. He told them he already had a plane chartered to whisk them back to Santiago once the Castro regime falls. At ninety-two, he looked forward to the day the Bacardis would regain control of the plant they were forced to hand over thirty years earlier.

Perhaps the Bacardis will never again produce rum on the Calle Matadero. Perhaps Pepín Bosch will never drive the streets of a free Santiago. Perhaps it's all an impossible dream. Perhaps you really can't go home again. But try telling that to Pepín Bosch. Early in 1990, his head was filled with a hundred plans for his beloved Cuba, from reviving the economy to redesigning the kitchen of his house at Punta Gorda.

Pepín Bosch showed his visitor to the door. "I do not believe people enjoy very much to read the stories of retired persons," he said. "But I do have the idea that, if we liberate Cuba, I have an economic plan to make Cuba independent. If the new government accepts this plan and puts it into practice, then I will write a book, because it will be worthwhile to show how a country can go from capitalism to Communism and then back again. That will be a nice story."

CHART A
THE FAMILY OF EMILIO BACARDI MOREAU

☐ Male
○ Female
◼ On board of INTRAC
◼,● Dissidents, male and female

☐ **FACUNDO BACARDI Y MASO**
(*d*. 1886)
m. Amalia Lucía Victoria Moreau ———

☐ **EMILIO BACARDI MOREAU**
(*d*. 1922)
m. 1876 María Lay Berlucheau ———
m. 1887 Elvira Cape ———

☐ **FACUNDO BACARDI MOREAU**
(*d*. 1926)
See chart B for descendants.

☐ **JOSÉ BACARDI MOREAU**
(*d*. 1907)
See chart B for descendants.

○ **AMALIA BACARDI MOREAU**
See chart B for descendants.

☐ **EMILIO "EMILITO" BACARDI LAY**
m. Zoila Luyando

☐ **JOSÉ BACARDI LAY**
m. Zenaida Rosell Franco ———

☐ **FACUNDO BACARDI LAY**
Twin of José Bacardi Lay (above)
m. Caridad Rosell Fernández ———

○ **MARÍA BACARDI LAY** ———
m. Pedro Lay

○ **CARMEN BACARDI LAY** ———
m. Gustavo Rodríguez

☐ **DANIEL BACARDI LAY**

○ **MARINA BACARDI CAPE** ———
m. Radames Covani

○ **LUCÍA BACARDI CAPE** ———
m. Pedro Grau Triana

○ **ADELAIDA BACARDI CAPE** ———
m. William Julius Dorion

○ **AMALIA BACARDI CAPE** ———
m. Eusebio Delfin

These family trees were prepared by the
author with the kind assistance of several
members of the Bacardi family. Because
the family is so widely dispersed and the
space for the charts was limited, they are
necessarily incomplete.

O Zenaida Bacardi Rosell *6 children incl.*
m. José Argamasilla Grimany
- ☐ LEÓN ARGAMASILLA BACARDI *m.* ———— *3 children*
- ☐ JOSÉ ARGAMASILLA BACARDI *m.* ———— *4 children*
- ▯ AMARO ARGAMASILLA BACARDI *m.* ———— *3 children*

■ EMILIO BACARDI ROSELL
m. Josefina González Vega *4 children incl.* ——— ■ JOSÉ BACARDI GONZÁLEZ *m.* ———— *3 children*

● ANA MARÍA BACARDI ROSELL
m. Adolfo Comas
- ■ ADOLFO COMAS BACARDI
  m. Olga María Bartes Rodríguez ———— *4 children*
- ■ TOTEN COMAS BACARDI *m.* ———— *2 children*
  Twin of Adolfo Comas Bacardi (above)
- ● LUCÍA COMAS BACARDI
- ● MARLENA COMAS BACARDI ———— *4 children*
  m. Jorge Rodríguez Márquez
- ● AMELIA COMAS BACARDI ———— *3 children*
  m. Robert O'Brien

■ DANIEL BACARDI ROSELL
m. Graziella Bravo Viñas *9 children incl.*
- ● MARÍA HORTENSIA BACARDI BRAVO ——— *8 children*
  m. ALBERTO BACARDI BOLÍVAR *See chart B*
- ■ TOTEN BACARDI BRAVO *m.* ———— *No children*
- ■ FACUNDO BACARDI BRAVO *m.* ———— *2 children*

O MARÍA LAY BACARDI
m. Robert Williams ———— *3 children*

☐ ERNESTO LAY BACARDI
m. María Sole Segura ———— *2 children*

☐ EDUARDO LAY BACARDI
m. Marta Rosell ———— *No children*

☐ PEDRO EMILIO LAY BACARDI
m. Loretta Monohan ———— *2 children*

O CLARA RODRÍGUEZ BACARDI *3 children incl.*
m. Ignacio Carrera Justiz
- ▯ FRANCISCO "FRANKIE" CARRERO JUSTIZ
  RODRÍGUEZ *m.* ———— *Children*

O CARMINIA RODRÍGUEZ BACARDI
m. Rolando de León ——— O ANA MARÍA DE LEÓN RODRÍGUEZ *m.* ——— *Children*
m. Andrés Peon García

☐ GUSTAVO RODRÍGUEZ BACARDI
m. Clotilde Gispert ———— *2 children*

☐ GUILLERMO RODRÍGUEZ BACARDI
m. Ruby Myers *(div.)* ———— *4 children*
m. Carmen Rey Santiago ———— *2 children*

O OLGA COVANI BACARDI
m. Manuel Cutillas
- ▯ MANUEL JORGE CUTILLAS COVANI
  m. Rosa María Dubois ———— *1 child*
- ☐ EDUARDO CUTILLAS COVANI
  m. Ana María Fernández ———— *2 children*

O MARINA LYDIA COVANI BACARDI
m. Luis del Rosal Rosende
- ☐ JORGE LUIS DEL ROSAL
  m. Zoila Cabrero ———— *3 children*

O ELVIRA COVANI BACARDI
m. Eloy de Castroverde
- ☐ ROBERTO DEL ROSAL
  m. Flora María Fanjul ———— *5 children*
- ———— *2 children*

O MANON GRAU TRIANA BACARDI
m. ▯ Guillermo "Willy" Rodríguez Salazar
- ☐ GUILLERMO RODRÍGUEZ GRAU *No info*

☐ GEORGE DORION BACARDI
m. Dorothy Simpson ———— *4 children*

☐ ROBERT DORION BACARDI
m. Anna María Ferber ———— *5 children*

☐ WILLIAM DORION BACARDI
m. Elaine Hart ———— *2 children*

▯ EUSEBIO "CUCHI" DELFIN JR.
m. Sally Noyes *(div.)*
m. Hilda Fuentes
- O AMALIA DELFIN *m.* ———— *1 child*
- ☐ JORGE DELFIN *No info*
- O ALICIA DELFIN *m.* ———— *2 children*

CHART B
THE FAMILIES OF FACUNDO BACARDI MOREAU,
JOSÉ BACARDI MOREAU, AND AMALIA BACARDI MOREAU

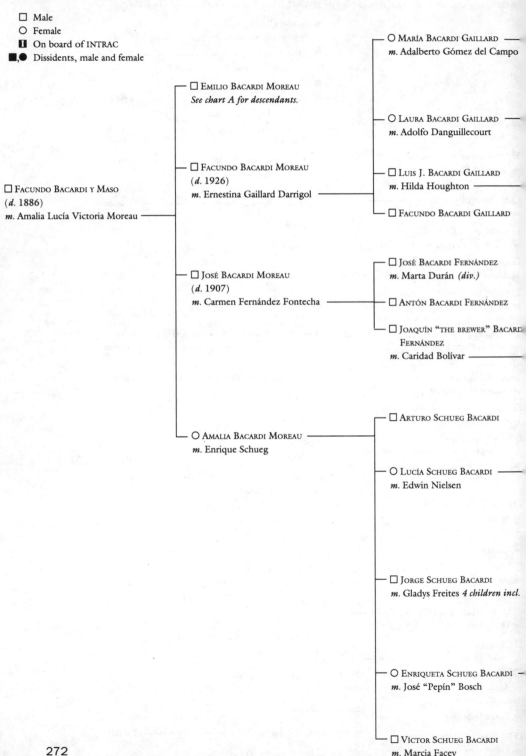

□ Male
○ Female
■ On board of INTRAC
■,● Dissidents, male and female

□ FACUNDO BACARDI Y MASO
(*d.* 1886)
m. Amalia Lucía Victoria Moreau

□ EMILIO BACARDI MOREAU
See chart A for descendants.

□ FACUNDO BACARDI MOREAU
(*d.* 1926)
m. Ernestina Gaillard Darrigol

□ JOSÉ BACARDI MOREAU
(*d.* 1907)
m. Carmen Fernández Fontecha

○ AMALIA BACARDI MOREAU
m. Enrique Schueg

○ MARÍA BACARDI GAILLARD
m. Adalberto Gómez del Campo

○ LAURA BACARDI GAILLARD
m. Adolfo Danguillecourt

□ LUIS J. BACARDI GAILLARD
m. Hilda Houghton

□ FACUNDO BACARDI GAILLARD

□ JOSÉ BACARDI FERNÁNDEZ
m. Marta Durán (*div.*)

□ ANTÓN BACARDI FERNÁNDEZ

□ JOAQUÍN "THE BREWER" BACARDI
FERNÁNDEZ
m. Caridad Bolívar

□ ARTURO SCHUEG BACARDI

○ LUCÍA SCHUEG BACARDI
m. Edwin Nielsen

□ JORGE SCHUEG BACARDI
m. Gladys Freites *4 children incl.*

○ ENRIQUETA SCHUEG BACARDI
m. José "Pepín" Bosch

□ VÍCTOR SCHUEG BACARDI
m. Marcia Facey

■ Luis Gómez del Campo Bacardi *m.*

○ Elena Gómez del Campo Bacardi
m. Armando Pessino *(div.)* ——————— *3 children*
m. ■ Jerry Lindzon

○ Laura Danguillecourt Bacardi
m. ■ Juan Alvarez Guerra

■ Adolfo Danguillecourt Bacardi
m. Christina Maduro ——————— *3 children*

☐ Luis Bacardi Houghton
m. Ruby Morales ——————— *3 children*

■ Alberto Bacardi Bolívar
m. María Hortensia Bacardi Bravo ——————— *8 children*
See chart A

■ Jorge Enrique Bacardi Bolívar
m. Barbara Stivers

● Carmen Bacardi Bolívar ——————— *4 children*
m. Orlando Rivas Melo

■ Joaquín Bacardi Bolívar
m. Joyce George ——————— *2 children*

■ Edwin "Eddy" Nielsen
m. Marta Ariosa ——————— ○ Gloria Nielsen
m. Marcia De Lourdes   *m.* Luis Echarte
                              ○ Ana Nielsen
                                m. Eddy Sardiña
                              ○ Lucía Nielsen
                              ○ Martha Nielsen
                              ○ Elena Nielsen

■ Henry "Jimmy" Nielsen
m. Patricia Jenny ——————— *4 children*

○ Joan Nielsen ——————— *4 children*
m. Luis de Hechavarría

○ Yvonne Marie Schueg ——————— *4 children*
m. ■ Víctor Arellano

○ Vilma Schueg ——————— *4 children*
m. Fernando Arellano

☐ Jorge Bosch
m. ○ Yvelise Molina ——————— *2 children*

☐ Carlos "Lindy" Bosch
m. Hortensia Esteva ——————— *4 children*
m. Ermina Eguilior

273

Top 25 Spirit Brands Worldwide in 1989

Rank	Brand	Company	Type	1986	1987	1988	1989E	Percent change 1988–1989E
				(Millions of 9-litre cases)				
1	Bacardi	Bacardi & Co. Ltd.	Rum	19.1	20.7	21.2	22.0	3.8%
2	Smirnoff	Heublein Inc. (IDV/GrandMet)	Vodka	13.9	14.0	14.1	14.8	5.0
3	Ricard	Groupe Pernod Ricard	Anis/Pastis	7.2	7.4	7.4	7.4	–
4	Gordon's Gin	United Distillers (Guinness)	Gin	6.7	6.9	6.8	7.3	6.4
5	Johnnie Walker Red	United Distillers (Guinness)	Scotch Whiskey	6.7	6.3	6.3	6.8	8.0
	Total Top 5			53.6	55.3	55.8	58.2	4.4
6	J&B Rare	IDV (GrandMet)	Scotch Whiskey	4.6	4.7	5.0	5.3	6.0
7	Ballantine's	HWAV (Allied-Lyons)	Scotch Whiskey	4.3	4.4	4.8	5.0	4.2
8	Jim Beam	Jim Beam Brands Co. (American Brands)	Bourbon	4.5	4.5	4.7	4.8	2.8
9	Suntory Old	Suntory Ltd.	Japanese Whiskey	5.5	4.5	4.3	4.4	2.3
10	Seagram's 7 Crown	The Seagram Co. Ltd.	American Blended Whiskey	4.8	4.6	4.5	4.4	–2.2
	Total Top 10			77.3	78.0	79.1	82.2	3.9
11	Jack Daniel's Black	Brown-Forman Corp.	Tennessee Whiskey	3.8	4.0	4.2	4.4	3.9
12	Presidente	Pedro Domecq SA	Brandy	4.0	4.2	4.2	4.3	2.4
13	Bell's	United Distillers (Guinness)	Scotch Whiskey	3.9	4.0	4.1	4.1	–
14	Suntory Reserve	Suntory Ltd.	Japanese Whiskey	3.3	3.3	4.0	4.0	–
15	Popov	Heublein Inc. (IDV/GrandMet)	Vodka	4.0	4.0	4.0	4.0	–
	Total Top 15			96.3	97.5	99.6	102.9	3.3
16	Jose Cuervo	Tequila Cuervo SA (Groupo Cuervo)	Tequila	2.4	2.9	3.5	3.8	10.3
17	Seagram's Gin	The Seagram Co. Ltd.	Gin	3.4	3.4	3.6	3.8	5.6
18	Dekuyper	Johs De Kuyper & Zoon BV	Liqueur	4.3	4.1	3.9	3.7	–5.1
19	Larios	Larios SA	Gin	4.1	4.1	3.6	3.7	2.8
20	Dewar's	United Distillers (Guinness)	Scotch Whiskey	3.5	3.5	3.5	3.7	4.3
	Total Top 20			114.1	115.6	117.7	121.6	3.3
21	Canadian Mist	Brown-Forman Corp.	Canadian Whiskey	4.0	3.8	3.7	3.6	–2.3
22	Absolut	V&S Vin & Spirit	Vodka	2.1	2.2	2.9	3.6	24.0
23	Baileys	IDV (GrandMet)	Liqueur	2.5	2.6	2.9	3.3	13.8
24	Chivas Regal	The Seagram Co. Ltd.	Scotch Whiskey	2.6	2.9	3.0	3.2	6.7
25	Canadian Club	HWAV (Allied-Lyons)	Canadian Whiskey	3.2	3.0	3.1	3.1	–
	Total Top 25			128.4	130.1	133.2	138.4	3.9%

Source: *Impact International*, January 1 and 15, 1990

TOP 100 BRANDS LEADING COMPANY PERFORMANCE ANALYSIS

Company	Number of brands in top 100	(Millions of 9-litre cases)				Percent change 1988– 1989E
		1986	1987	1988	1989E	
International Distillers & Vintners Ltd. (Grand Met)	11	36.6	36.7	37.8	40.4	6.8%
United Distillers (Guinness)	8	29.3	29.2	29.2	30.7	5.1
Bacardi & Co. Ltd.	2	20.2	21.8	22.4	23.2	3.6
The Seagram Co. Ltd.	10	21.8	22.1	22.4	22.9	2.1
Suntory Ltd.	8	20.3	19.3	19.8	19.9	0.5
Total Top 5	39	128.1	129.1	131.6	137.0	4.1
HWAV (Allied-Lyons)	8	18.9	19.2	19.3	19.8	2.8
Groupe Pernod Ricard	4	12.1	12.5	12.5	12.6	0.7
Brown-Forman Corp.	4	11.4	11.4	11.6	11.9	2.4
Jim Beam Brands Co. (American Brands)	3	8.0	8.0	8.1	8.0	-1.2
Pedro Domecq SA	3	7.5	7.7	7.7	7.9	2.6
Total Top 10	61	186.0	187.9	190.9	197.4	3.4
Other	39	63.0	67.7	68.7	70.9	3.3
Total Top 100 Brands	100	250.9	255.6	259.6	268.4	3.4%

Source: *Impact International,* January 1 and 15, 1990

Notes

For full references to the books cited below, see the Select Bibliography, page 287.

PROLOGUE

PAGE

1. For E.P. Taylor and Lyford Cay, see Newman, *The Canadian Establishment*.

2. "Great Family Fortunes": *Forbes*, October 24, 1988.

CHAPTER ONE

7. For an overall history of rum, see Barty-King and Massel.

8. The "bats in the distillery" version of the birth of the trademark is the one reproduced in most current company pamphlets. The "bats in the trees" version comes from Woon, the "bats on the jars" version from Alegría. El Coco details from Alegría.

12. For Catalonians and Bourbons, see Hooper.

CHAPTER TWO

14 ff. For the Spanish-American War, see particularly Foner, Hagedorn, and Thomas. Foner's writing is deeply colored by his enthusiasm for the Castro revolution, as was the original version of Thomas's work. Most of the material on Emilio Bacardi and Wood comes from Hagedorn.

CHAPTER THREE

21. For the Fiesta de la Bandera, see Alegría.

24. Commission on Cuban Affairs, particularly Chapter IV, "Family Organization and Standards of Living."

PAGE

27. "Dance of the millions" details from Thomas (*Cuba*).

31. *New York Times*, August 30, 1922, "Emile [*sic*] Bacardi Dead." *Diario de Cuba* quote reproduced in *Luz de Oriente*, September 1922.

32. Emilio's will from Alegría.

33. *New York Times*, November 24, 1926, "Facundo Bacardi, Rum Distiller, Dies."

CHAPTER FOUR

34. For Prohibition, see Kobler. For Canadians and Prohibition, and also Prohibition in general, see Gervais, Hunt, and Newman (*Bronfman Dynasty*).

37. On moonshine and fake Bacardi, see "Whiskey" (and related articles), *Fortune*, November 1933. For the origins of rum-and-lime cocktails, see Barty-King.

38. Descriptions of Santiago from Alegría, Clark, Fergusson, and Woon. For Bacardi's Prohibition popularity, see "Daiquiri, Martini, Planter's Punch . . . ," *Fortune*, November 1933, and "Speakeasies of New York," *Fortune*, June 1933.

40 ff. Historical details mainly from Thomas (*Cuba*).

41. On Cuban rum taxes: *New York Times*, January 18, 1931: "Bacardi Escapes New Tax." Details of aborted Gibara coup from Thomas (*Cuba*).

44. On Machado's flight, see Thomas (*Cuba*). The story of the razorback hog is from "Behind the Cuban Revolt," by Hudson Strode, *The New Republic*, October 4, 1933.

46. "Bacardi Dies of Accidental Pistol Wound," *Havana Post*, July 24, 1932. The anecdote about Facundo in the speakeasy is from Woon.

47. "Bacardi Near Death in Pistol Accident," *New York Times*, July 19, 1932.

CHAPTER FIVE

48 ff. For the "Barons of Booze," see Newman (*Bronfman Dynasty*); Gervais; Hunt; "Whiskey," *Fortune*, November 1933; "Seagram in the Chips," *Fortune*, September 1948; "Cheerio, Hiram Walker," *Saturday Night*, April 1989.

53. For the Kennedy family's involvement in liquor, see Collier and Horowitz; Goodwin.

54. On Dorion, see "President Herrera's Nephew to Wed," *New York Times*, November 24, 1921.

55. Details of Bosch's early career are from transcripts of the District Court of Puerto Rico, 1937, in the trademark-use dispute. Schenley bar details from Alegría. The tale of the mythical goat and details of post-Prohibition shipments are from Alegría.

58 ff. For Puerto Rican history, see Carr and Pendle.

CHAPTER SIX

68. Early beer details and postwar statistics from Alegría.

71. On the "whiskey king," Sam Bronfman, see "Seagram in the Chips," *Fortune*, September 1948.

73. On Hemingway's Papa Doble, see Lynn.

74. For Grau and Prío, see Thomas (*Cuba*). For the "suitcases" anecdote and details of Bosch's period as finance minister, see "Cuba: An Honest Man," *Time*, March 19, 1951.

75 ff. Schueg details from Alegría. Also: "Head of Bacardi Co. Dies," *New York Times*, August 11, 1950.

76. *Alerta* quoted in "Cuba: An Honest Man," *Time*, March 19, 1951.

CHAPTER SEVEN

77 ff. For kidnapping, see "Cuban Boy Is Safe After Kidnapping," *New York Times*, February 20, 1954. Also: "Bacardi Kidnapper Sentenced," *New York Times*, March 10, 1954.

279

PAGE

87. Hearst details from Thomas (*Cuba*).

92. For Pawley testimony, see the hearings of a sub-committee of the U.S. Senate Judiciary Committee, published as *The Communist Threat to the U.S. Through the Caribbean*. Also: Earl E.T. Smith.

CHAPTER EIGHT

94 ff. For details of the Castro takeover, see Dubois (both titles), Hart Phillips, Monahan and Gilmore, and Thomas (*Cuba*).

96. Dubois quotes Joaquín Bacardi in *Fidel Castro*.

102. Dumont quote from Thomas (*Cuba*). Rino Puig's story from Carbonell.

105. Luis Aguilar's columns in *Prensa Libre* – particularly those of March 21, June 12, June 27, November 1, and November 24, 1959, and that of May 13, and December 1, 1960 – provide a poignant record of the passing of free speech in Cuba.

106. Castro on nationalization: *Coronet* magazine.

107. "What Has Happened to Cuban Business?" *Fortune*, September 1959.

CHAPTER NINE

109. For Bosch's petroleum problems, see "Personality: From Sugar to Banking to Rum," *New York Times*, June 9, 1963. Quotations from Law 890 are taken from the Department of State translation.

115. The Castro official was quoted in "What Has Happened to Cuban Business?" *Fortune*, September 1959.

117. "Operation Bootstrap" and other Puerto Rican development details from Carr.

118 ff. On Mies van der Rohe, see Schulze.

121. Lobo anecdote from Thomas (*Cuba*).

CHAPTER TEN

123 ff. For anybody wishing to gain some idea of the intensity of the pro- and anti-Castro debate at the time, the following articles might prove useful: "Castro's Cuba" by Robert Taber, *The Nation*, January 23, 1960. In the same publication, on May 23, "Dialogues in Cuba," by Barbara Deming. *The New Republic* contained a lengthy and intriguing exchange, starting with a resolutely pro-Castro article, "Cuba: A Dissenting Report," by Samuel Shapiro, on September 12, 1960. It was followed by "History Will Not Absolve Castro," by Daniel Friedenberg, October 10, 1960; "Replying to Castro's Admirers," by George Sherman, October 24, 1960; a letter, "Our Men in Havana," November 14, 1960, from John C. Carrington; a reply from Shapiro on December 5, 1960, entitled "Castro and His Critics"; and finally a letter, January 2, 1961, from Rodolfo J. Walsh, headed "Cuba Sí, Yanqui No."

126 ff. For the Bay of Pigs invasion, see Carbonell, Johnson, and Thomas (*Cuba*).

128. Girón beach sign from *Maclean's*, April 21, 1986: "The New Cuba." For the Cuban Missile Crisis and its aftermath, see Allman, Didion, Thomas (*Cuba*), and "Class Reunion: Kennedy's Men Relive the Cuban Missile Crisis," *New York Times Magazine*, August 30, 1987.

130. Milton Eisenhower is roundly criticized in Lazo.

132. For exile groups in Miami, see Carbonell. For the Cuban American National Foundation, RECE, and Tony Cuesta's attack, see "Leader's Zeal Powers Exile Lobby" and "Cuban Exile Lobby Builds High-Profile Capitol Hill Base," in *Miami Herald*, April 10 and 11, 1988.

133. For Miami and Cuban exiles, see Allman, Didion, and Carbonell. Also: "A Reporter at Large: the Second Havana," by David Rieff, *The New Yorker*, May 18, 1987; "Can Miami Save Itself: A City Beset by Drugs and Violence," *New York Times*, July 19, 1987.

PAGE

CHAPTER ELEVEN

136 ff. On Bacardi's post-Cuban board meetings and expropriation fight, see "Guide to Trademark Usage," a booklet produced by Bacardi & Company Limited.

143. Coca-Cola history from Cleary.

146. Alegría contains the "unexpurgated" version of the Cuba Libre story.

CHAPTER TWELVE

156. For Rockefellers dropping names, see "The Rockefellers: End of a Dynasty?" *Fortune*, August 4, 1986.

158. "Retired?" Not Chief of Bacardi," *New York Times*, March 8, 1970.

161. "Bacardi Threat to Move Sparks Inquiry," *New York Times*, August 28, 1975.

162. "Conflicts That Plague Family Businesses," by Harry Levinson, *Harvard Business Review*, March/April 1971. "Transferring Power in the Family Business," by Louis B. Barnes and Simon A. Hershon, *Harvard Business Review*, July/August 1976.

167. "Complex Bacardi Empire Tries Collective Leadership," *New York Times*, August 16, 1976.

170. "Make Mine Bacardi," *Forbes*, February 20, 1978. "Hiram Walker: A Move into Rum Fills a Major Product Gap," *Business Week*, April 24, 1978.

CHAPTER THIRTEEN

177. For Bronfman ads see Newman (*Bronfman Dynasty*). Liquor expenditure figures from *Jobson's Liquor Handbook* (1985). Market trends from a speech by Marvin Schanken at the 45th Annual Convention of the Wine and Spirits Wholesalers of America, Inc., in Boston, April 19, 1988.

PAGE

178 ff. U.S. market figures from *Impact*, May 15, 1983. For rise in anti-alcohol sentiment, see F.A. Meister's speech, "An International Partnership," to the International Federation for Wines and Spirits, on May 26, 1987. Also, William A. Walker's speech to the 45th Annual Convention of the Wines and Spirits Wholesalers of America, Inc., in Boston, April 20, 1988.

179. *Impact*, March 1984.

CHAPTER FOURTEEN

181 ff. Nielsen and Cutillas speeches are from a family booklet produced to commemorate the Acapulco meeting (author's translation).

183. My translation of poem.

186. For globalization and Levitt, see Fallon. Anthony Tennant's speech was made before an *Impact* seminar, London, April 3, 1985. For the "British invasion" of North America, see also "UK Brewers and US Liquor," a research report by Kevin Feeny and Philip Augur of Warburg Securities, April 1988.

188 ff. For Hiram Walker's diversifications, the Reichmanns, and the battle with Allied-Lyons, see Foster.

191. My translation of letters.

CHAPTER FIFTEEN

195 ff. Much of this chapter is based on the internal Arthur Andersen report on Bacardi Capital, prepared by Joel Miller.

CHAPTER SEVENTEEN

221. "Bacardi Rum Faces Potent Family Revolt," *Washington Post*, May 10, 1987.

222. For Biltmore Hotel, see Muir. "Vote on Reverse Stock Split Fails to End Bacardi Battle," *Washington Post*, May 15, 1987.

PAGE

CHAPTER NINETEEN

245 ff. For the Guinnesses, Saunders, and Tennant, see Pugh. Also: "Bright Young People," *Fortune*, December 1933; interviews in *Impact International*, February 1, 1986, with James Gulliver, William Spengler, and David Connell; "The New Guinness after the Distillers Acquisition," *Impact International*, December 1 and 15, 1986; "Britain's Own Boesky Case," by Richard I. Kirkland Jr., *Fortune*, February 16, 1987.

248. For Orlando Bosch, see Didion. For Mariel, see Didion and Allman.

CHAPTER TWENTY

260 ff. For the CDRs, see Puddington. Also Foster, "Forever Fidel," *Saturday Night*, January 1989; also the main report of the Third Congress of the Communist Party of Cuba (Editora Politica, Havana, 1986).

261. For subsidy figure, see "Is Fidel Losing It?" *Newsweek*, February 12, 1990. Castro speech from Szulc.

264. "The New Cuba," *Maclean's*, April 21, 1986.

Sources

Cuban history is an ideological battleground. The British historian Hugh (now Lord) Thomas's enormous *Cuba or The Pursuit of Freedom* is regarded by many as the definitive work on the subject. Yet there is at least one book devoted to the *errors* in Thomas's work (see Angel Aparicio Laurencio below). Thomas's is undoubtedly the most encyclopedic treatment of Cuban history up to the early Castro period, but it is also sloppy in parts, the obvious result of collective research. Emilio Bacardi Moreau and the Bacardi company are briefly mentioned in Thomas. Pepín Bosch also appears, sometimes as José M., once as "Pepe," but the author does not appear to be aware that they are the same person.

Perhaps the most arresting fact about Thomas's book, as with most Cuban histories, is how little is written of those, like the Bacardis, who built the island's wealth. Cuban history books, like those of many other countries in the twentieth century, are filled with the deeds not of those who created assets but of those who seized them at the point of a gun.

There are a number of areas in which I disagree with Thomas's assumptions and interpretations, which are typical of the anti-capitalist bias of much modern history. Nevertheless, Thomas's work is the one against which others are measured. Tad Szulc's *Fidel: A Critical Portrait* also contains a huge amount of useful material, although its overall tone is somewhat adulatory.

Apart from Thomas and Szulc, I have mainly relied for pre-Castro Cuban history on the works of Clark, Fergusson, Foner, Hagedorn, Pendle, and Strode listed below. Entries on Cuba, Santiago de Cuba, and the Spanish-American War in *The Encyclopedia Americana (International Edition)* and *The New Encyclopaedia Britannica* were also useful.

There are a number of devastating accounts of the course — and betrayals — of the Castro revolution. These include the works of Dubois, Hart Phillips, Lazo, Monahan and Gilmore, Suárez, and Valladares. The force of these accounts, however, appears to have been much diluted by a liberal desire to present a more "balanced," i.e., pro-Castro, account. Many of those who teach Cuban history today made huge psychic investments in Fidel and Che in the 1960s. For them the dream is dying hard.

A conference called "Thirty Years of the Cuban Revolution: An Assessment" was held in Halifax, Nova Scotia, November 1-4, 1989. These three papers were especially interesting: Carlos Alberto Montaner, "Cuba: A Model for Assembling Post-Socialism"; Adolfo Rivero and Dr. Emilio Adolfo Rivero, "The Failed Revolution"; and Philip S. Foner, "The Role of the United States in the Evaluation of the Historical Roots of the Cuban Revolution." The conference proceedings are being prepared for publication.

As for the ongoing condition of Cuban exile, three books were particularly useful: Joan Didion's brilliantly incisive *Miami*; T. D. Allman's *Miami: City of the Future;* and Nestor Carbonell's *And the Russians Stayed: The Sovietization of Cuba: A Personal Portrait.* If one wanted to point to a weakness in the works of both Didion and Allman — particularly the latter, since he seems to have fallen prey to the notion that the golden images of pre-Castro Cuba held by exiles are a pure fiction — it is that neither of them appears to have visited Cuba.

A number of the Bacardi companies have produced historical pamphlets. One was published to celebrate the hundredth anniversary of the company in 1962; Bacardi Corporation put out a fiftieth-anniversary brochure in 1986; and Bacardi & Company has also produced a brief pamphlet. The dates in these pamphlets are not always consistent. I have also used a corporate history commissioned by Pepín Bosch in the 1950s: *La Compañía Bacardi en su cien años de vida.* Written by a Peruvian, Ciro Alegría, and dated December 10, 1959, the work was never published. Its main shortcoming is that Alegría obviously knew little of business. It also suffers from the objectivity problems found in every commissioned history. Nevertheless, it contains much interesting material. I have used my own translation. Parts of Alegría's work subsequently appeared in *Emilio Bacardi en su tiempo*, compiled by Amalia Bacardi Cape and published in Spain in 1986. This work also contains various monographs about Emilio Bacardi.

The September 1922 edition of a Santiago magazine, *Luz de Oriente* (available in the Richter Library, University of Miami), is devoted almost entirely to homages to the life and achievements of Emilio Bacardi. Again, I have relied on my own translation. The Richter Library also has a copy of "A Message to García" and the dispatches from the *Virginius* incident that were presented to Elvira Cape.

Professor Luis Aguilar wrote a brief outline of Emilio Bacardi's life in a two-part article, *Emilio Bacardi, en su tiempo y para el tiempo*, in *Diario Las Américas*, on March 25 and 26, 1988.

As well as giving me their time, Andrew Duany in Miami and Silvia Zimmerman in Washington also let me see unpublished manuscripts, both of which proved valuable.

For the Prohibition and post-Prohibition periods, Kobler's *Ardent Spirits* and articles in *Fortune* magazine were very useful. By far the most comprehensive sources of information about the liquor industry in the past decade are the New York-based magazines *Impact* and *Impact International*. Among many other periodicals I found *Business Week, The New Republic*, and the *New York Times* especially informative.

Select Bibliography

Alegría, Ciro. "La Compañía Bacardi en su cien años de vida." Unpublished corporate history, dated December 10, 1959.

Allman, T.D. *Miami: City of the Future*. The Atlantic Monthly Press. New York. 1987.

Aparicio Laurencio, Angel. *¿Es Historia el Libro que Hugh Thomas Escribió Sobre Cuba?* Editorial Catoblepas. Madrid. 1985.

Bacardi Cape, Amalia. *Emilio Bacardi en su tiempo*. Spain. 1986.

Barty-King, Hugh, and Anton Massel. *Rum: Yesterday and Today*. Heidelberg Publishers Ltd. London. 1983.

Blasier, Cole, and Carmelo Mesa-Lago (editors). *Cuba in the World*. University of Pittsburgh Press. 1979. (In particular the chapter "The Economics of U.S.-Cuban Rapprochement.")

Carbonell, Nestor. *And the Russians Stayed: The Sovietization of Cuba: A Personal Portrait*. William Morrow and Company. New York. 1989.

Carr, Raymond. *Puerto Rico: A Colonial Experiment*. Vintage Books. New York. 1984.

Casuso, Teresa. *Cuba and Castro*. Random House. New York. 1961.

Clark, Sydney A. *Cuban Tapestry*. Robert M. McBride and Company. New York. 1936.

Cleary, David Powers. *Great American Brands: the Success Formulas That Made Them Famous*. Fairchild Publications. New York. 1981.

Collier, Peter, and David Horowitz. *The Kennedys: An American Drama*. Summit Books. New York. 1984.

Collis, Maurice. *Cortés and Montezuma*. Faber and Faber Limited. London. 1972.

Commission on Cuban Affairs. *Problems of the New Cuba*. Foreign Policy Association. Washington. 1935.

Didion, Joan. *Miami*. Pocket Books. New York. 1987.

Dubois, Jules. *Fidel Castro: Rebel Liberator or Dictator?* Bobbs-Merrill. New York. 1959.

Dubois, Jules. *Operation America: The Communist Conspiracy in Latin America*. Walker and Company. New York. 1963.

Fallon, Ivan. *The Brothers: The Rise and Rise of Saatchi & Saatchi*. Hutchinson. London. 1988.

Fergusson, Erna. *Cuba*. Alfred A. Knopf. New York. 1946.

Foner, Philip S. *The Spanish-Cuban-American War and the Birth of American Imperialism 1895-1902*. Volume II: 1898-1902. Monthly Review Press. New York and London. 1972.

Foster, Peter. *The Master Builders*. Key Porter. Toronto. 1986.

Franqui, Carlos. *Diary of the Cuban Revolution*. The Viking Press. New York. 1980.

Gervais, C.H. *The Rumrunners: A Prohibition Scrapbook*. Firefly Books. Thornhill, Ontario. 1980.

Gitlin, Todd. *The Sixties: Years of Hope, Days of Rage*. Bantam Books. Toronto/New York. 1987.

Goodwin, Doris Kearns. *The Fitzgeralds and the Kennedys: An American Saga*. Simon and Schuster. New York. 1987.

Hagedorn, Hermann. *Leonard Wood: A Biography*. Harper and Brothers Publishers. New York and London. 1931.

Hart Phillips, Ruby. *The Cuban Dilemma*. George McLeod Ltd. Toronto. 1962.

Hooper, John. *The Spaniards: A Portrait of the New Spain*. Penguin Books. London. 1987.

Hubbard, Elbert. "A Message to García." The Roycrofters. East Aurora. 1899.

Hunt, C.W. *Booze, Boats and Billions*. McClelland and Stewart. Toronto. 1988.

Jenks, Leland Hamilton. *Our Cuban Colony: A Study in Sugar*. Vanguard Press. New York. 1928.

Johnson, Haynes. *The Bay of Pigs: The Leaders' Story of Brigade 2506*. Norton. New York. 1964.

Johnson, Paul. *Modern Times: The World from the Twenties to the Eighties*. Harper and Row. New York. 1983.

Kobler, John. *Ardent Spirits: The Rise and Fall of Prohibition*. G.P. Putnam's Sons. New York. 1973.

Lazo, Mario. *Dagger in the Heart: American Policy Failures in Cuba*. Funk and Wagnalls. New York. 1968.

Lynn, Kenneth S. *Hemingway*. Fawcett Columbine/Ballantine. New York. 1987.

Matthews, Herbert. *The Cuban Story*. George Braziller. New York. 1961.

Monahan, James, and Kenneth Gilmore. *The Great Deception*. New York. 1963.

Muir, Helen. *The Biltmore: Beacon for Miami*. The Pickering Press. Miami. 1987.

Newman, Peter C. *Bronfman Dynasty. The Rothschilds of the New World*. McClelland and Stewart. Toronto. 1978.

Newman, Peter C. *The Canadian Establishment*. McClelland and Stewart. Toronto. 1975.

Pastor, Robert A., and Jorge C. Castañeda. *Limits to Friendship. The United States and Mexico*. Vintage Books. New York. 1989.

Pendle, George. *A History of Latin America*. Penguin Books. London. Revised edition. 1976.

Puddington, Arch. "The Eyes and Ears of the Revolution" (pamphlet). Freedom House. New York. 1990.

Pugh, Peter. *Is Guinness Good for You? The Bid for Distillers – The Inside Story.* Financial Training Publications Limited. London. 1987.

Ripoll, Carlos. *Cubans in the United States.* Eliseo Torres and Sons – Las Américas Publishing Co. New York. 1987.

Schulze, Franz. *Mies van der Rohe: A Critical Biography.* University of Chicago Press. Chicago. 1985.

Shevchenko, Arkady N. *Breaking with Moscow.* Ballantine Books. New York. 1985.

Smith, Earl E.T. *The Fourth Floor: An Account of the Castro Communist Revolution.* Random House. New York. 1962.

Smith, Robert S. *The U.S. and Cuba: Business and Diplomacy 1917-1960.* Bookman Association. New York. 1960.

Strode, Hudson. *The Pageant of Cuba.* Harrison Smith and Robert Haas. New York. 1934.

Suárez, Andrés. *Cuba: Castroism and Communism, 1959-1966.* The MIT Press. Cambridge, Massachusetts. 1967.

Szulc, Tad. *Fidel: A Critical Portrait.* Avon Books. New York. 1987.

Thomas, Hugh. *Cuba or The Pursuit of Freedom.* Eyre and Spottiswoode. London. 1971.

Thomas, Hugh. *An Unfinished History of the World.* Pan Books. London and Sydney. 1981.

Torres Hurtado, Nicolás. *Orígines de la Compañia Ron Bacardi.* Editorial Oriente. Santiago de Cuba. 1982.

Valladares, Armando. *Against All Hope: The Prison Memoirs of Armando Valladares.* Translated by Andrew Hurley. Alfred A. Knopf Inc. New York. 1986.

Woon, Basil. *When It's Cocktail Time in Cuba.* Horace Liveright. New York. 1928.

Index

Absolut (vodka), **187**
Acapulco Princess (hotel), **181**
Aguilar, Luis, **105**
Alcoholic Beverages Law (1936, Puerto Rico), **59**
Aldana, Jorge, **256**
Alemán, Senator José, **73**
Alerta (newspaper), **76**
Alfonso XII, **12**
Alfonso XIII, **12**
Allied-Lyons PLC, **193, 224, 246**
Allman, T.D., **129, 134**
Ambrosio Bacardi, Pedro, **56**
American Bacardi Rum Corporation, **56**
American Bar (Havana), **146**
American Brands, **246**
American Society of Newspaper Editors, **99**
And the Russians Stayed (Carbonell), **237**
Añejo (rum), **182, 241, 253**
Ansonia Hotel, **54**
Antilles, **58**
Anti-Saloon League, **35-36**
Arellano, Victor, **174**
Argamasilla Bacardi, León, **151, 161-162**
Argamasilla Bacardi, Amaro, **151**
Argamasilla Bacardi, José (Tito), **151**
Argamasilla Grimany, José, **66, 151, 269**
Arnaz, Desi, **249**
Arquitectónica, **142**
Arthur Andersen (accounting firm), **195, 201, 205, 213**
Arthur Bell & Sons, **245**
Artisans Fair (Puerto Rico), **204**

Asa, Bonifacio, **99**
Atlas Shrugged (Rand), **122**
Australia, **2**
Auténtico party, **74, 80**
Avenida Bélgica, **38, 252**

B&B (liqueur), **187**
B&G (wines), **54**
B-13 (customs document), **49-50**
Bacardi Bolívar, Alberto, **150, 174, 189-190, 193-194, 214, 217-218, 219, 230, 232-233**
Bacardi Bolívar, Jorge, **216, 219-220**
Bacardi Bravo, Facundo, **77**
Bacardi Bravo, María Hortensia, **77, 78**
Bacardi Bravo, Toten, **219, 220**
Bacardi Cape, Adelaida (Lalita), **15, 54, 136**
Bacardi Cape, Amalia, **31, 190-192**
Bacardi Cape, Lucía (Mimín), **79-80**
Bacardi Cape, Marina, **136**
Bacardi Fernández, Antón, **45, 67, 68**
Bacardi Fernández, Joaquín ("the brewer"), **45, 64, 68, 69, 96, 149, 165**
Bacardi Fernández, José, **42-43, 45, 68**
Bacardi Gaillard, Ernestina, **32**
Bacardi Gaillard, Facundo, **32, 45-47**
Bacardi Gaillard, Laura, **32, 47**
Bacardi Gaillard, Luis J., **32, 47, 56, 61, 62, 63, 136, 165, 166**
Bacardi Gaillard, María, **32, 47**

Bacardi Gonzáles, José, 249
Bacardi Lay, Daniel, 45
Bacardi Lay, Emilio (Emilito), 15, 44-45
Bacardi Lay, José, 32, 33
Bacardi y Maso, Facundo, 5, 7, 10, 11, 25, 182
Bacardi Moreau, Amalia, 7, 13
Bacardi Moreau, Emilio, 7, 28-29
  as businessman, 12, 23, 24, 31-32
  early political involvement, 9, 10, 11, 15, 17
  in exile, 11, 15, 23, 85
  as mayor of Santiago, 18, 19, 21, 22
  place in Cuban history, 29-31
  private life and personality, 30, 31, 32, 45
  as writer, 9, 30
Bacardi Moreau, Facundo, 7-8, 9, 12, 23, 24, 32, 33, 45-46, 110
Bacardi Moreau, José, 7, 8, 11, 12, 23, 24, 45
Bacardi Rosell, Ana María, 112, 203, 214
Bacardi Rosell, Daniel, 31, 66-68, 82, 110, 149, 211, 228, 235-236
  and Bacardi Capital, 204, 206, 213
  and Bacardi Corporation, 183, 193, 204, 209, 210, 212-213, 214, 217-218, 219, 228, 229-230, 250
  and Bacardi Imports, 136
  and Cuban politics, 88, 91, 98, 111, 112
  kidnapping of son of, 77, 78
Bacardi Bar (New York), 55
Bacardi breweries
  in El Cotorro (Cuba), 71-72, 73, 80, 96, 116
  in Manacas (Cuba), 72, 116
  in San Pedrito (Cuba), 68, 71
Bacardi business empire (see also

individual Bacardi companies
and brand names)
  advertising, 43, 72-73, 142-143, 144-148, 150, 174, 204
  beer operations, 68, 71-72, 73, 96, 116, 148, 183
  expands into Brazil, 120, 137, 157
  as family business, 25, 32-33, 45, 47, 156, 164-165, 166, 173-174, 190, 191-192, 216, 235, 237-238, 243-245, 247
  as global business, 247-248, 249, 250
  growth of, 2, 23-24, 33, 71, 72, 117-118, 137, 152, 176-177, 179, 181-182, 224, 242
  management succession, 152-153, 155, 156-157, 162, 163-166
  trademarks, 8, 56-60, 90, 136, 137, 138-140, 182
Bacardi cocktail, 37, 38, 39, 54, 55, 56-57
Bacardi-and-Coke (drink), 145-146, 150, 155. See also Cuba Libre; rum-and-Coke
Bacardi Capital Ltd., 182-183, 196-197, 198-203, 204, 206, 238
Bacardi & Company Limited (Nassau), 148, 170, 175, 190, 236
Bacardi Corporation (Puerto Rico), 57, 58-60, 69, 72, 141, 154-155, 158, 159, 160-161, 166-167, 204
  growth of, 155, 169-170, 176-177, 179, 184-185
  privatization and ensuing dispute: see Bacardi family, dissidents
  ownership, 25, 155, 159, 164-165, 170, 173, 174-176,

190; *see also* Bacardi family, dissidents
Bacardi Corporation museum (San Juan), **13**
Bacardi Corporation of America (Pennsylvania), **57**
Bacardi distilleries
  in Brazil, **120-121, 137**
  in Canada, **150**
  in Mexico, **116-117, 118-120, 137, 181, 183**
  in Nassau, **137, 148**
  in Puerto Rico, **59, 118, 137**
  in Santiago, **24**
Bacardi family, **25, 45, 77-78, 155, 203-204, 250**
  and business, **25, 32-33, 45, 47, 156, 164-165, 166, 173-174, 190, 191-192, 216, 235, 237-238, 243-245, 247**
  dissidents, **184, 189, 191, 193, 203-225, 228-230, 232, 233-235, 236, 237-238, 242-244, 247, 250, 267-268**
  and Santiago/Cuba, **6, 24-25, 39, 79-80, 101, 112-115**
  women in, **25, 43, 79-80, 225**
Bacardi Imports, Inc., **70, 72, 136, 137, 141-143, 144-148, 152, 158, 170, 174-175, 178, 225-226, 239-240**
Bacardi International Limited (Nassau/Bermuda), **119, 148-150, 151-152, 158, 159, 164, 170, 195**
Bacardi Mexico, **41, 42-43, 68, 70, 72, 116-117, 118, 119-120, 137, 170, 240-242**
Bacardi rum, **8, 37, 43, 177, 179;** *see also* individual brand names
  awards for, **11, 12, 13, 23**
  bat symbol, **8**
Bacardi Rum Company/Compañía Ron Bacardi S.A. (Cuba), **41, 54-56, 62-63, 64, 71-72, 82, 103-104, 116, 136-137**
  development of, **23, 33, 68**
  expropriation of, **106, 108-115, 122, 138-139, 256, 257**
  hundredth anniversary, **137**
Bacardi S.A. (Spain), **247**
Bailey's Irish Cream, **187**
Ballantine (whiskey), **52, 169**
Ball, Lucille, **225**
Bamboo (nightclub), **203**
Banco de Ponce, **219, 220, 221, 223**
Bank of Boston, **220**
Bank of Nova Scotia, **138**
Barnes, Louis B., **162, 163**
Barrio (proprietor of American Bar), **146, 147**
Bartes Rodríguez, Olga María, **231**
Bat, origin as Bacardi trademark, **8**
Batista, Fulgencio, **44, 61, 62, 74, 81-82, 85, 86, 88-90, 91, 92-94**
Bay of Pigs invasion, **127-128, 129, 137, 149, 150, 205, 250, 259**
Beer, in Bacardi business, **68, 71, 72, 73, 96, 116, 182, 187**
Belén Jesuit College, **84, 116**
Bellas Artes (school), **30**
Bell's (whiskey), **245**
Berlin National Gallery, **119**
Bermuda, **2, 37, 49**
Biltmore Hotel (Coral Gables, Fla.), **222**
Birán (Cuba), **83**
Black & White (whiskey), **52**
Blas Roca, Francisco Calderio, **81**
Boesky, Ivan, **246**
Bogotá (Colombia), **84**
Bolívar, Simon, **174**
Bollinger (champagne), **187**
Boniato (Cuba), **19**
Bootlegging, **37, 48**
Bootstrap, Operation, **117**
Bosch, José M. (Pepín)
  birth and early life, **26-27**

boating accident, **64-65, 69**
and Castro, **1-3, 84, 86, 87,
88, 92, 95-96, 99-101, 110,
123-126, 140, 269**
and Cuban exiles, **2-3,
123-126, 130, 132-133, 140,
269**
leaves Cuba, **108-109**
marriage to Enriqueta Schueg
Bacardi, **27**
and oil business, **109**
personality, **27-28, 64, 65,
140, 195, 263**
political activity (before Castro),
**1, 41-42, 73, 74-75, 76,
80-81**
CAREER AT BACARDI:
and Bacardi Corporation
(Puerto Rico), **54-55, 57,
59-60, 61-62, 69-70,
117-118, 154, 157, 159,
160-161, 166**
and Bacardi family, **11, 47,
63-64, 65-69, 71, 72, 141,
161-162, 163, 164-167, 173,
209, 236, 263, 267-268, 269**
and Bacardi Imports, **69-71,
141-142, 143**
and Bacardi International, **119,
148, 149, 150, 151-152, 159**
and Bacardi Mexico, **43, 61,
62, 90, 116-117, 118-120,
240**
and Bacardi Rum
Company/Compañía Ron
Bacardi S.A. (Cuba), **62-66,
71-72, 76, 103-104, 116,
136-139, 255, 257, 263, 265**
expanding Bacardi, **47, 61,
116-121, 135, 137, 140-141,
148, 156-157, 240, 263**
retires (1969), **155**
retires (1976) and sells interest,
166, 167, 168-171
search for successor to,
152-153, 155, 156-157, 162,
163-167, 173
Bosch, José (Pepín's father), **25-26**
Bosch, Orlando, **248-249**
Bosch Palace (Santiago), **26, 258**
Bosch Schueg, Carlos (Lindy), **90,
149, 157, 158, 159**
Bosch Schueg, Jorge, **157-159**
Bourbons, the (royal family), **12**
Bourbon (whiskey), **48, 51**
Boutellier (French wine merchant),
8
Brand Owner's Coordinating
Committee, **226, 228**
Bravo Viñas, Graziella, **67, 77, 78,
79, 82**
Brazil, **120, 137, 157**
Brennand, Francisco, **141**
Brigade 2506, **126, 129**
Bronfman, Edgar, **186**
Bronfman, Phyllis, **119**
Bronfman, Sam, **49, 50, 51, 52,
119, 160, 161, 169, 177, 246**
Brook, Smith, French & Dorens,
142
Brooke, General John, **19**
Brooklyn (battleship), **21**
Brown-Forman (liquor company),
244, 246
"Brown" spirits, **177-178**
Buchanan-Dewar, Ltd., **52**
Buckingham Corporation, **187**
Burnett (gin), **52**
Butler, Sam, **209-210, 214, 219,
223, 224, 228, 232**

Café Rialto (Santiago), **46**
Café Venus (Santiago), **18**
Calle Aguilera Baja (Santiago), **18,
23, 64, 67**
Calle Cedro (Mexico City), **157**
Calle Matadero (Santiago), **8, 9,
10, 23, 254, 269**
Callenders, Sawyer, Klonaris &
Smith, **224**
Calle Neptune (Havana), **146**
Calvert Reserve (whiskey), **71**

Camaguey (Cuba), **68**

Camp Columbia, **97**

Canada
Bacardi involvement in,
150-151, 174, 189
and Prohibition, **36, 37**

Canadian Club (whiskey), **50,
142, 169, 171, 177**

Cancio y Martín, Saenz, **120**

Candela, Felix, **119-120**

Candler, Asa, **144**

Capablanca, José Raúl, **72**

Cape, Elvira, **15, 25, 30**

Capone, Al, **50, 257**

Carbonell, Nestor, **133, 237**

"Caribbean initiative," 179

Carillon, **187**

Carta Blanca/White Label (rum),
46, 73, 182

Carta de Oro (rum), **46, 182**

Casa Granda (Santiago), **66**

Casero, Luis, **76, 79, 85**

Castillo Duany, Demetrio, **19**

Castro, Angel, **83-84**

Castro, Fidel (*see also* Cuba, under
Castro)
comes to power, **94-99**
and Communism, **92, 97, 100,
102, 104, 106-107, 121,
124-126**
media image, **86-87, 88, 92,
95, 97, 99, 100, 104, 123, 124**
and Pepín Bosch, **99-101**
political program, **95, 97, 100,
101, 102-107, 109**
as revolutionary, **82-83, 84-88,
90, 91-92, 103**
in youth, **74, 116**

Castro, Raúl, **47, 95, 99, 103, 114**

Casuso, Teresa, **100**

Catalonia (Spain), **5, 12**

Cataño (Puerto Rico), **118, 176,
204, 215**

"Cathedral of Rum," **118**

Cayo Smith (island), **80**

CBS Television, **95, 97, 104**

CDR (Committee for the Defence
of the Revolution), **260-261,
262**

Centennial Philadelphia
Exposition, **10-11**

Central Intelligence Agency (CIA),
92, 132, 134

Central Santa María (sugar mill),
41

Céspedes, Carlos Manuel de, **9-10,
39, 72-73, 95**

Céspedes Park, **76, 94**

Chabebe, Father José, **88, 97, 98,
99**

Charles Hosie (German liquor
company), **150**

Chertorivski, Isaac, **241, 242**

Chibas, Eduardo, **74, 80**

Chicago Tribune, **88, 129**

Chrysler Building, **54**

Churchill, Winston, **72**

CIA (Central Intelligence Agency),
92, 132, 134

Cienfuegos (Cuba), **91**

Ciudad Mar (Cuba), **80**

Civil War, U.S., **34**

Club San Carlos (Santiago), **18,
66, 94, 98**

Club 300 (Santiago), **66**

Coca-Cola, **43, 80, 112,
143-147, 150, 220, 221**

Columbus, Christopher, **5, 18, 58**

Comas, Adolfo (Adolfo Comas
Bacardi's father), **112, 203**

Comas Bacardi, Adolfo, **96, 185,
203, 204, 210, 211, 214-216,
217-218, 219, 230, 231-234**

Comas Bacardi, Amelia, **214**

Comas Bacardi, Toten, **204, 206,
216**

Committee for the Defence of the
Revolution (CDR), **260-261,
262**

Communism in Cuba, **61, 81,
100, 102, 106-107, 124-125,
129, 131, 254, 257**

Compañía Ron Bacardi
  Nacionalizada (Cuba), **139**
Compañía Ron Bacardi S.A.
  (Cuba), **23, 124.** *See also*
  Bacardi Rum Company (Cuba)
Connell, John, **245-246**
Consumers Gas, **188**
Coolidge, Calvin, **40**
Coopers & Lybrand, **197, 199,**
  213
Cordera, Guillermo, **241-242**
Cortés, Hernán, **6, 43, 97**
Costa, Daniel, **9**
Coubre (freighter), **104**
Country Club (Havana), **73**
Country Club Park (Havana), **28,**
  75
Courvoisier (liquor), **169**
Covani, Radames, **136**
Cox, Jennings, **38, 147**
Cravath, Swaine & Moore, **209,**
  214
Cream of Kentucky (whiskey), **54**
Cristina, María, **12**
Crónicas de Santiago de Cuba
  (Emilio Bacardi Moreau), **30**
Crowder, Enoch, **40**
Cuba, before Castro
  Bacardis' role in history of,
    28-31
  under Batista, **44, 61-62, 76,**
    81, 85, 88-94
  Castro's rise to power, **90-97**
  colonial history of, **5-6, 9-10,**
    39
  corrupt governments in, **28,**
    40, 73-74, 76, 92
  economic crisis in, **41, 74, 104**
  independent republic, **21-22**
  Prohibition image of, **37-40**
  and Spanish-American War,
    16-17, 38
  Ten Years' War in, **10, 64**
  and U.S. government, **16-22,**
    24, 28, 40-41, 44, 91-93
Cuba, under Castro (*see also*

Castro, Fidel): **97-115, 121,**
  124-126
  American public support for,
    99, 100, 104, 123-126,
    130-131
  expropriation of industry, **106,**
    108-115, 122, 138-139, 256,
    257
  INRA, **101, 102, 106, 109,**
    111
  present-day, **252-265**
  revolutionary justice, **98-99,**
    103, 105
  and Soviets, **104, 125**
  and U. S. government, **92,**
    100, 104, 106, 134 (*see also*
    Bay of Pigs; Cuban Missile
    Crisis)
Cuba Betrayed (Batista), **89**
Cuba Libre (drink), **143, 146,**
  150. *See also*
  Bacardi-and-Coke;
  rum-and-Coke
Cubana Airlines, **92**
Cuban American National
  Foundation, **2, 132, 249**
Cuban Central Railway, **22**
Cuban Chamber of Commerce in
  the United States, **55**
Cuban Communist party, **61, 81.**
  See also Communism in Cuba
Cuban Dilemma, The (Phillips), **96**
Cuban Electric Company, **106**
Cuban exiles, **123-135, 156,**
  248-250, 263
Cuban Missile Crisis, **128, 134,**
  137, 259
Cuban Refugee Centre, **143**
Cuban Revolutionary Council, **132**
Cuban Telephone Company, **106**
Cuentos de Amalia (Emilio Bacardi
  Cape), **31**
Cuesta, Tony, **133, 248**
Cutillas, Eduardo, **149, 176, 196,**
  197-198, 199, 202, 203, 206,
  216

Cutillas, Manuel Jorge, **99,**
112-114, 116, 167, 182, 196,
226, 236-237, 241, 249, 250,
269
and Bacardi Capital, **196**
and Bacardi & Company,
236-237
and Bacardi Corporation, **211,**
228, 230
and Bacardi International, **148**
and Bacardi Mexico, **120**
and Bacardi Rum Company, **98,**
111
and Hiram Walker/Gooderham
& Worts, **187-188**
and INTRAC, **173, 212**
Cutty Sark (scotch), **187**

Daiquiri (beach), **16**
Dance of the Millions, **27**
Danguillecourt Bacardi, Adolfo
(Adolfito), **63, 116, 136, 166,**
173
Danguillecourt Bacardi, Laura,
190-191
DCL. *See* Distillers Co. Ltd.
de Beauvoir, Simone, **105**
Dehesa, Guillermo, **255, 261, 265**
Delfin, Eusebio (Cuchi), **173-174**
del Rosal, Jorge Luis, **229**
del Rosal, Roberto, **86, 151**
del Rosal Rosende, Luis, **151**
del Valle, Manuel Luis, **176, 185,**
210-211, 215, 220, 221, 226,
243
Dennis & Huppert, **225**
Detroit (Michigan), **50, 168**
Detroit River, **50**
Dewar (whiskey), **52, 53**
Diario de la Marina (newspaper),
105
Díaz-Balart, Mirta, **82**
Dickson, Fred, **145**
Didion, Joan, **142, 205**
Dill, Nicholas, Jr., **196**
Directorio Estudiantil, **41**

Directorio Revolucionario, **88**
Distilled Spirits Council of the
United States (DISCUS), **179**
Distillers Co. Ltd. (DCL), **48, 49,**
51-52, 187, 245-246
Distillers Corp.-Seagrams Ltd., **49.**
See also Seagram (liquor
company)
Distilling Co. of America, **51**
Dolores (school in Santiago), **84**
Domecq (brandies), **240**
Don Emilio (tequila), **182**
Dorcasbarro, Miguel, **42**
Dorion Bacardi, George, **230**
Dorion, William Julius, **54**
Dórticos, Osvaldo, **133**
Downing, Bud, **170, 188, 192,**
206
Doyle, Jack, **55**
Drake, Sir Francis, **58**
Dry Sack (sherry), **187**
Duany, Andrés, **26**
Duany, Andrew, **83, 97, 114**
Dubois, Colonel Jules, **88, 95, 96,**
98-99, 129-130
Dubois, Rosa María, **99**
Dubonnet (vermouth), **54**
Duchesneau, Luc, **199**
Dumont, René, **101-102**
Du Pont (chemical company), **186**
Durán, Marta, **43**

Echarte, Luis, **225-227**
Echevarría, Luis, **241**
Echevarría, Manuel, **78**
Edificio Bacardi (Havana), **38, 39,**
55, 89, 108, 110, 115, 252
Eguilior, Ermina, **195**
Eguilior, Ricardo, **151-152**
1873 (rum), **182**
Eisenhower, Dwight, **95, 106, 108**
Eisenhower, Milton, **130**
El Caney (Cuba), **88**
El Coco (tree), **8-9, 10, 23, 93**
El Cotorro (Cuba), **71, 72, 73,**
80, 96

El Cubano Libre (newspaper), **248**
El Encanto (department store), **79**
El Morro (prison; Puerto Rico), **58**
El Morro (prison; Santiago), **6, 11, 21, 38, 39, 80, 248**
El Mundo (newspaper), **26, 60**
Emilio Bacardi en su tiempo (Amalia Bacardi Moreau), **190**
Empire State Building, **55**
Espín, José, **47, 61, 62, 63**
Espín, Vilma, **47, 86**
Esso, **106**
Estrada, Bartolo, **56, 70, 148, 165**
Estrada Palma, Tomás, **22, 26, 28, 30, 38**
Exiles, Cuban, **123-135, 156, 248-250, 263**
Expropriation of Cuban industry, **106, 108-115, 122, 138-139, 256, 257**

Fair Play for Cuba Committee, **105**
Family businesses, **45, 47, 156, 162-163**
Faulkner, Walter, **228**
FBM Distillery Co. Ltd., **150-151, 174, 189**
Fernández Fontecha, Carmen, **23**
Fidel: A Critical Portrait (Szulc), **84**
Fidel Castro: Rebel Liberator or Dictator (Dubois), **129-130**
Fiesta de la Bandera (Festival of the Flag), **21, 76, 94, 233, 248**
Financial Options Group Inc., **197**
Finkelson, Allen, **214**
First National City Bank (Havana), **27, 143**
Fitzgeralds, the, **53**
Five Crown (whiskey), **53**
Fonst, Ramón, **72**
Forbes (magazine), **2, 171**
Fortune (magazine), **37, 43, 46, 49, 50, 52, 102-103, 106-107**
Founders Plaza (Tultitlán), **120**
Four Roses (whiskey), **71**

Frente Revolucionario Democrático (FRD), **132**
Fulbright & Jaworski, **223**

Galbraith, John Kenneth, **163**
García, Calixto, **20, 87**
García Menocal, General Mario, **28, 41**
Gardner, Richard, **148**
Gattorno (artist), **55, 142**
Gibara (Cuba), **42**
Gin, **48.** *See also* individual brand names
Gitlin, Todd, **131**
Goizueta, Roberto, **220**
Golden, Bill, **223**
Golden Wedding (whiskey), **52, 71**
Gold Reserve (rum), **182**
Gómez, Máximo, **14-15, 21, 39**
Gómez del Campo Bacardi, Elena, **110**
Gómez del Campo Bacardi, Luis, **63, 136, 173, 190, 269**
Gooderham & Worts, **50.** *See also* Hiram Walker/Gooderham & Worts
Gorbachev, Mikhail, **253, 254, 268**
Gordon's (gin), **2, 52**
Grand Marnier (liqueur), **187**
Grand Metropolitan Hotels, **186**
Granma (yacht), **85, 86, 259**
Grant, General Ulysses, **34**
Grau, Juan, **116, 117, 118, 120, 148, 157, 176, 226, 239-240, 241-243, 250**
Grau Bacardi, Manon, **224**
Grau San Martín, Ramón, **74**
Greene, Graham, **126, 253**
Gropper, William, **55**
Guantanamo (Cuba), **44, 102**
Guerra Chicita, **11**
Guevara, Che, **1, 2, 85, 101, 102, 105, 106, 121-122, 123, 253, 258, 259**
Guinness (company and family),

63-64, 245, 246
Gulliver, Jimmy, 245

Hagedorn, Hermann, 18
Haig & Co. Ltd., John, 52
Haig & Haig (whiskey), 53
Halifax (Nova Scotia), 49
Hamilton (Bermuda), 151
Hanahan, Timothy, 198
Hannoteaux, Gabriel, 15
Harvard Business Review, 162
Hatch, Cliff, Jr., 150, 188, 192
Hatch, Cliff, Sr., 168-169, 170
Hatchetation (play), 35
Hatch, Harry, 50, 51, 52
Hatuey (beer), 68, 71, 72, 73,
  96, 116, 148, 183
Havana, 6, 16, 19, 37, 38, 61,
  73, 85, 252
Havana Biltmore, 73
Havana Club (rum), 253, 254
Havana Hilton, 85, 252
Havana Post, 29, 46, 85
Hawley-Smoot Tariff, 41
Hearst, William Randolph, 16, 23,
  87, 97
Hedges & Butler, 149, 159
Hemingway, Ernest, 71, 73
Hershon, Simon, 162, 163
Herter, Christian, 100
Heublein (liquor company), 169,
  178, 245, 246
Hevia, Carlos, 80-81
Hill & Knowlton, 221
Hiram Walker/Gooderham &
  Worts, 36, 48, 50, 51, 52, 71,
  160, 168, 169-171, 177, 178,
  186, 187-188, 193, 204, 221,
  224, 245, 246
Hiram Walker Resources Ltd.,
  188, 193
History Will Absolve Me (Castro),
  84
Hobson, Captain R.P., 17
Holden-Brown, Sir Derrick, 224
Holguín (Cuba), 42

Home Oil, 188
Hotel Nacional (Havana), 85
Hubbard, Elbert, 20, 28

Illinois Institute of Technology,
  119
Impact (magazine), 179
Institute for Agrarian Reform
  (INRA), 101, 102, 106, 109,
  111
Institute for Tropical Medicine,
  253
Internal Revenue Service (IRS),
  U.S., 174
International Distillers and
  Vintners (IDV), 186-187, 246
Interprovincial Pipeline (IPL),
  188, 193
INTRAC S.A., 172, 173-174, 176,
  189, 190, 193-194, 211, 212,
  213, 220, 224
Isabella, Queen (of Spain), 9
Isle of Pines, 85
ITT, 196

J&B (scotch), 142, 187
Jack and Charlie's 21 (speakeasy),
  39
Jack Daniels (whiskey), 142, 246
Jacksonville (Florida), 160, 161
Jacobi, Harold, 55
Jim Beam (liquor company), 246
John Haig & Co. Ltd., 52
John Haig (whiskey), 52
Johnnie Walker (scotch), 2, 52,
  187
John Walker & Sons Ltd., 52
Joseph E. Seagram & Sons
  Limited, 49. *See also* Seagram
  (liquor company)
Journal (Hearst newspaper), 87

Kahlúa (liqueur), 169
Kelley Drye & Warren, 210,
  221-222, 223, 228
Kennedy, Jacqueline, 128

Kennedy, John Fitzgerald, **54,
123, 128, 129, 133, 134**
Kennedy, Joseph, **53**
Kennedy, P.J., **53**
Kid Chocolate (boxer), **72**
King, W.L. Mackenzie, **36**
Klee, Paul, **152**
Kobler, John, **35**
Kuhn, Loeb, **168**

La Floridita (Havana bar), **37, 39,
73**
La Galarza (distillery), **117, 140**
La Libertad (newspaper), **29**
Lamont, Corliss, **124, 125-126**
Lasa, Luis, **142-143, 144-145,
149, 214**
Laurent, Emilio, **42**
Law 890, **109, 111**. *See also* Cuba
under Castro, expropriation of
industry
Lay, María, **15**
Lay Bacardi, Pedro, **59**
Levenson, Alan, **223**
Levinson, Harry, **162**
Levitt, Theodore, **186**
Licensed Beverage Information
Council (LBIC), **179**
Liechtenstein, **2, 139, 248**
Life (magazine), **145**
Lincoln, Abraham, **34**
Liquor business, **2, 52, 186**
during Prohibition, **34-37,
48-53**
as global business, **186-187,
245-248, 250**
growth of, **48, 52-54, 56,
177-178, 247**
and neo-prohibitionism,
177-179
See also individual brand names
and companies
Lloyd's Electronics, **184, 185**
Lobo, Julio, **121-122**
López Portillo, José, **241**
Louis Vuitton Moët Hennessy

(LVMH), **246**
Luyando de Bacardi, Zoila, **45**
Lyford Cay (Bahamas), **1, 168,
267**

McCallum, Archie, **206**
McCann-Erickson, **144**
McCarthy, Joseph, **131**
Macdonald, David, **202**
Macdonald, Ian, **197, 199-202**
Maceo, Antonio, **14, 15, 45**
Maceo, José, **15**
Machado, Gerardo, **40-41, 42,
43-44, 115**
Mackay, Charles, **198**
McKinley, William, **16, 18, 19**
Maclean's (magazine), **264**
Maine (battleship), **16, 104**
Manacas (Cuba), **96, 116**
Manas, Arturo, Jr., **160, 167**
Manley, Michael, **258**
Manufacturers Trust, **109**
Mariel exodus, **249**
Mármol, Guillermo, **65, 75, 86,
90, 108, 115, 163-164, 172,
194, 213, 224, 225**
Martí, José, **10, 14-15, 16, 39,
84, 95, 248**
Martínez, Román (Romy) IV,
168, 169, 170, 209
Mas Canosa, Jorge, **132, 133**
Masferrer, Rolando, **74, 80**
Matanzas (Cuba), **95**
Matos, Huber, **103**
Matthews, Herbert, **87, 95, 123,
125-126, 129**
Maurice, Stewart, **57**
*Memoirs of Extraordinary Popular
Delusions and the Madness of
Crowds* (Mackay), **198**
Merrick, George, **222**
Merrimac, **17, 39**
"Message to García, A"
(Hubbard), **20, 28, 156, 263**
Mexico, **2, 41, 42-43, 70,
240-241**

Miami (Allman), **129**
Miami (Didion), **142, 205**
Miami (Florida), **2, 133-135**
Mies van der Rohe, Ludwig,
   118-119, 152, 195
Miguel Gómez, José, **28**
Mikoyan, Anastas, **104**
Miller, Joel, **201-202, 205**
Miramar Yacht Club (Havana), **73**
Modelo (brewery), **71-72, 73, 96,
   116**
*Modern Corporation and Private
   Property, The* (Berle and
   Means), **163**
Moët Hennessy, **187**
Moncada, **82-83, 259-260**
Moreau, Amalia Lucía Victoria, **7,
   8, 25**
Morgan, Harry, **71, 134**
Morgan, Henry, **6, 7**
Morgan, Lewis & Bockius, **224**
Morgan Guaranty Trust Co., **250**
Moscow News, **268**
Mujer, Eusebio, **89**
Municipio de Santiago de Cuba in
   Exilio, **248**
Muñoz Marín, Luis, **117, 118,
   161**
Museo Municipal Emilio Bacardi
   Moreau (Santiago), **30, 39, 40,
   114, 257-258, 260**

Nassau, **37, 148**
Nassau Royale (liqueur), **182**
National Distillers Products
   Corp., **48, 51, 52, 53, 71,
   245, 246**
Nation, Carry, **35**
Neo-prohibitionism, **178, 179**
Ness, Eliot, **49-50**
New Providence (Bahamas), **137,
   148**
New York Club, **55**
New York Times, **78, 86, 87, 95,
   97, 123, 124, 129, 147, 167**
Nicaro (nickel company), **138**

Nielsen, Ana, **225, 227**
Nielsen, Edwin (Eddy), **159, 167,
   175, 181, 218, 228, 229,
   236, 244-245**
   and Allied-Lyons, **224, 246**
   and Bacardi Capital, **196, 206**
   and Bacardi Imports, **148,
   165-166, 225, 227**
   and Hiram Walker/Gooderham
   & Worts, **187, 188-190**
   and INTRAC, **172, 174, 176,
   211, 212**
   and Pepín Bosch, **165, 166,
   170**
Nielsen, Edwin (Eddy's father),
   165
Nielsen, Elena, **225**
Nielsen, Gloria, **225, 227**
Nielsen, Lucía, **170, 225**
Nielsen, Martha, **225**
Nixon, Richard, **100**
Noilly Prat (liquor), **54**
Nunes, John, **7, 8, 23**

O'Brien, Robert, **214, 224, 230**
O'Darby's Irish Cream, **182**
O'Hara, Alfred (Pete), **138,
   139-140, 166-167, 174, 175,
   176, 196, 201, 205, 207,
   220, 222**
Ojeda, Fernando, **88**
Old Havana, **38, 252**
Old Man and the Sea, The
   (Hemingway), **73**
Old Quaker (whiskey), **54**
Oliva González, Erneido, **132**
*Operation America: The
   Communist Conspiracy in Latin
   America* (Dubois), **130**
Operation Bootstrap, **117**
Orange Bowl, **128**
Organic Act of Puerto Rico, **60**
*Origins of the Bacardi Rum
   Company* (Hurtado), **256**
Ortodoxo party, **74**
Oswald, Lee Harvey, **134**

Our Man in Havana (Greene), 126, 253

Paddington, 187
País, Frank, 91
Palma Soriano (Cuba), 83
Papa Doble (drink), 73
Parrish, Maxfield, 38
Pawley, William, 92
Pazos, Felipe, 86, 102
Pazos, Javier, 86
Peláez, Orfilio, 148, 149
Pemberton, John, 143-144
Peoria (Illinois), 50
"Pepín's Folly", 118
Pérez San Román, José (Pepe), 127, 132, 250
Pérez Serantes, Archbishop Monseñor, 76, 82, 95
Pessino, Armando, 110
Philadelphia, Centennial Exposition, 10-11
Phillips, Ruby Hart, 86, 96, 129, 130
Pinar del Río (Cuba), 203
Pioneers, Cuban, 258-259
Platt Amendment, 21-22, 40, 44
Playitas (Cuba), 14
Plaza Reina (Santiago), 17, 18
PLP (Progressive Liberal Party, Bahamas), 139
Ponce de León, Juan, 58
Popocatepetl, 117
Popov (vodka), 178
Porter, Seton, 51, 52
Potter Anderson & Corroon, 223-224
Prado, José, 115
Prado, Juan, 83-84, 89, 110, 111, 112, 137, 148, 149, 159, 176, 226, 243
Prensa Libre, 105
Primo de Rivera, General Miguel, 12
Prío Socarras, Carlos, 65, 73, 74, 75, 80-81, 86, 88

Progressive Liberal Party (PLP, Bahamas), 139
Prohibition, 34-37, 48, 51, 52-53, 71
Puerta de Tierra (building), 118
Puerto Rico, 2, 57, 58, 59, 60, 117-118
Puig, Ñongo, 115
Puig, Rino, 102, 110, 115
Pujals, Roberto, 138
Pulitzer newspapers, 97
Punta Gorda (Cuba), 64, 80, 114, 195

Radio Martí, 261
Radio Rebelde, 90
Ramos, Angel, 60
Ramos, Félix, 152
Rand, Ayn, 122
Reagan, Ronald, 179
Recife (Brazil), 120-121
Reichmann brothers, 189, 193
Representación Cubana de Exilio (RECE), 132-133
Revolución (newspaper), 109
Ricardo, Ricky, 225, 249
Righter, Brewster, 196-197, 199, 200-202
Robinson, Edward G., 72
Robles León, Ernesto, 116-117, 118, 240, 241
Rodríguez (chauffeur to Daniel Bacardi Rosell), 77
Rodríguez, Fausto, 145-147
Rodríguez, Guillermo (Willy), 224
Rodríguez Bacardi, Guillermo, 59
Rodríguez Márquez, Jorge, 212
Rogers, Hoge & Hills, 136, 138
Ronrico (rum), 160
Ron Samba (rum), 57
Roosevelt, Franklin D., 48, 117
Roosevelt, Jimmy, 53
Roosevelt, Teddy, 16, 17, 19
Rosell, Guillermo, 184
Rosell, Zenaida, 33
Rosell Fernández, Caridad, 67

Rosenstiel, Lewis, **49, 51, 52, 70**
Ross Roy (advertising agency), **142**
Ross, William Henry, **52**
Rough Riders, **16, 17**
"Round lot" trusts, **219**
Rowan, U.S. Army Lieutenant, **20**
Rum, manufacture of, **7.** *See also*
    individual brand names
Rum-and-Coke (drink), **143, 146,
    147.** *See also*
    Bacardi-and-Coke; Cuba Libre
Rumrill-Hoyt (advertising agency),
    142
Rye (whiskey), **48, 51**

Saatchi & Saatchi, **142**
St. Pierre and Miquelon, **37, 49**
Sánchez Arango, Aureliano, **80, 86**
San Feliu de Llobregat
    (Barcelona), **118**
San Juan Hill (Cuba), **16, 17, 26,
    39, 99**
San Juan (Puerto Rico), **58**
San Pedrito (Cuba), **71**
Santiago Brewing Co., **68**
Santiago Chamber of Commerce,
    88
Santiago (Santiago de Cuba), **5-6,
    9, 16-19, 38-39, 61, 68, 79,
    82, 84, 86, 91, 94-95, 98, 119**
Santo Domingo, **6, 58**
Sardiña, Eddy, **227, 228**
Sartre, Jean Paul, **105**
Saunders, Ernest, **245, 246**
Schenley Distillers Corp., **48, 49,
    53, 54-55, 70, 71, 178, 245,
    246**
Schenley Reserve (whiskey), **71**
Schieffelin (distribution company),
    187
Schieffelin & Somerset
    (distribution company), **246**
Schlesinger, Arthur D., Jr., **129**
Schueg, Enrique, **13, 33, 45, 64,
    75**
    as Bacardis' partner, **23, 24, 31,**

41, 47, 54, 56-57, 61, 68
    and Prohibition, **36-37, 43**
Schueg Bacardi, Arturo, **42, 45**
Schueg Bacardi, Enriqueta, **24, 27,
    72, 80, 161, 164, 165**
Schueg Bacardi, Jorge, **45, 59**
Schueg Bacardi, Lucía, **165**
Schueg Bacardi, Víctor, **45, 56,
    63, 66, 90, 111**
Schueg Brothers laboratory, **241**
Scotch (whiskey), **51, 53, 54**
Seagram Building, **119**
Seagram (liquor company), **36,
    48, 49, 51, 53, 71, 160, 169,
    177, 178, 186, 204, 246**
Seagram & Sons Limited, Joseph
    E., **49**
Second World War, **61**
Securities and Exchange
    Commission (SEC), U.S., **155,
    174, 210, 211, 218, 222,
    228, 230**
Seton & Porter (engineering
    consultants), **51**
Seven Crown (whiskey), **53, 71,
    169, 177**
*Seventeen Hundred Cocktails by the
    Man Behind the Bar*, **56**
Shafter, Brigadier General, **16**
Shane, Chris, **198, 199-200**
Shanghai, China, **37**
Shell (oil company), **106**
Sibelius, Jean, **72**
Siboney (Cuba), **80, 260**
Sierra Maestra, **15, 85, 86**
Singer, Thomas E., **164**
Sir Robert Burnett & Co. Ltd, **52**
Sloppy Joe's, **12, 37, 55**
Smasher's Mail, The (newspaper),
    35
Smirnoff (vodka), **2, 142, 169,
    177, 178, 245, 246**
Smith, Al, **55**
Smith, Earl, **91**
Solera (rum), **182, 241**
Somerset Company, **54**

Somerset Importers, 187
Southern Comfort (liquor), 246
Spain, 2, 5, 12, 118, 247
Spanish-American War, 16-17, 38, 58, 87, 97, 146
Spanish Civil War, 12
State Department, U.S., 92
Sugar business, Cuban, 7, 26-27, 40, 41, 44, 106, 122, 123
Sullivan, Ed, 95
Sullivan, John L., 35
Suntory (liquor company), 246
Szulc, Tad, 84

Tanqueray (gin), 187
Tavenot (head of Hedges & Butler), 149, 150
Telebauta, América, 91
Television, 97
Temperance movement, 35-36, 50. See also Prohibition
Tennant, Anthony, 186, 246, 247
Ten Years' War, 10, 64
Tequila, 42
Texaco, 106, 138
Thomas, Benjamin Franklin, 144
Thomas, Hugh, 14, 62, 74, 80, 81, 89, 95
Thousand Days, A (Schlesinger), 129
Three Feathers Reserve (whiskey), 71
Tía María (liqueur), 169
Time magazine, 1
To Have and Have Not (Hemingway), 71
Torres Hurtado, Nicolás, 256
Trademarks. See Bacardi business empire, trademarks
Tultitlán (Mexico), 118-120, 183, 242
26 July Movement, 9, 86, 90-91, 94, 259

UDG (distributor), 247
United States

Bacardi involvements in, 54-56. See also Bay of Pigs, Bacardi Imports, Inc.
"Caribbean initiative," 179
relations with Cuba/Castro, 16-17, 19-20, 21-22, 23, 24, 28, 40-41, 44, 91-93, 108, 123. See also Cuban Missile Crisis
United States Brewers Association, 35
United States Commission on Cuban Affairs, 24
Universal Exposition (Chicago), 13
University of Havana, 41, 74, 76, 84, 86, 106
University of Miami, 31, 70
University of Oriente, 88, 98, 111, 116
Urrutia, Manuel, 88, 98, 101
U.S. Food Products Corp. (formerly Distilling Co. of America), 51

Valdez Miranda, Augusto (Polo), 96, 110, 135
Valls, Felipe, 248
Vedado district (Havana), 85
Vedado Tennis Club (Havana), 73
Velázquez, Diego, 5, 68
Vernon, Admiral Edward, 37
Vietnam, 134-135
Villa Elvira, 28-29, 30, 79, 99, 114
Villa Olga, 231
Virginius, 10
Vista Alegre (Santiago), 26, 79, 80, 82, 90, 99, 114, 258
Vodka, 177. See also individual brand names
Volstead, Andrew Joseph, 36
Volstead Act, 36, 49
V.O. (whiskey), 177

Walker, Bill, 142, 145, 147, 225
Walker & Sons Ltd., John, 52

Walkerville (Ontario), **50, 168**
Wanton, Santiago, **265**
Washington Post, **221**
WCTU (Women's Christian
    Temperance Union), **35**
Wheeler, Wayne Bidwell, **36**
Whiskey, **48, 49, 51-53, 71.** *See
    also* Bourbon; Rye; Scotch; and
individual brand names
Whiskey Trust, **51**
Whitbread (beer company), **187**
Whitehead, Joseph B., **144**
White Horse (whiskey), **52**
Whiteman, Paul ("Pops"), **222**
White Label/Carta Blanca (rum),
    46, 73, 182
"White" spirits, **177-178**
Wile, Julius, **187**

Wilken Family (whiskey), **54**
Wilson, Woodrow, **36**
Windsor (Ontario), **50**
Women's Christian Temperance
    Union (WCTU), **35, 178**
Wood Gundy, **202**
Wood, Leonard, **16, 17-20, 21,
    29, 30, 38, 146**
Woodruff, Ernest, **144**
Woodruff, Robert Winship, **144**
Woolavington, Lord, **52**
World Telegram, **55**

Xalisco (tequila), **182**

Zanjón, Treaty of, **10**
Zayas, Alfredo, **29, 40**
Zayas Park, **44**

The typeface in this book is Galliard, designed in 1978 by Matthew Carter. It is based on the old style typeface of the French punch cutter Robert Granjon (1513–80). Carter's Galliard is a more dashing interpretation of the Granjon letter and is better suited to film composition, the italics being drawn with particular verve. Carter is currently a partner with Mike Parker in Bitstream, a design agency in Cambridge, Massachusetts, concentrating on the digitization of type-faces for laser printers and other new ways of generating print.

BOOK DESIGN
Derek Ungless and Noël Claro

Type set by Tony Gordon Limited